Palgrave Studies in the Enlightenment, Romanticism and Cultures of Print
General Editors: **Professor Anne K. Mellor** and **Professor Clifford Siskin**

Editorial Board: **Isobel Armstrong**, Birkbeck & IES; **John Bender**, Stanford; **Alan Bewell**, Toronto; **Peter de Bolla**, Cambridge; **Robert Miles**, Victoria; **Claudia L. Johnson**, Princeton; **Saree Makdisi**, UCLA; **Felicity Nussbaum**, UCLA; **Mary Poovey**, NYU; **Janet Todd**, Cambridge

Palgrave Studies in the Enlightenment, Romanticism and Cultures of Print will feature work that does not fit comfortably within established boundaries—whether between periods or between disciplines. Uniquely, it will combine efforts to engage the power and materiality of print with explorations of gender, race, and class. By attending as well to intersections of literature with the visual arts, medicine, law, and science, the series will enable a large-scale rethinking of the origins of modernity.

Titles include:

Melanie Bigold
WOMEN OF LETTERS, MANUSCRIPT CIRCULATION, AND PRINT AFTERLIVES IN THE EIGHTEENTH CENTURY
Elizabeth Rowe, Catharine Cockburn, and Elizabeth Carter

Ildiko Csengei
SYMPATHY, SENSIBILITY AND THE LITERATURE OF FEELING IN THE EIGHTEENTH CENTURY

Elizabeth Eger
BLUESTOCKINGS
Women of Reason from Enlightenment to Romanticism

Ina Ferris and Paul Keen (*editors*)
BOOKISH HISTORIES
Books, Literature, and Commercial Modernity, 1700–1900

John Gardner
POETRY AND POPULAR PROTEST
Peterloo, Cato Street and the Queen Caroline Controversy

George C. Grinnell
THE AGE OF HYPOCHONDRIA
Interpreting Romantic Health and Illness

Anthony S. Jarrells
BRITAIN'S BLOODLESS REVOLUTIONS
1688 and the Romantic Reform of Literature

Jacqueline M. Labbe
WRITING ROMANTICISM
Charlotte Smith and William Wordsworth, 1784–1807

Michelle Levy
FAMILY AUTHORSHIP AND ROMANTIC PRINT CULTURE

April London
LITERARY HISTORY WRITING, 1770–1820

Robert Miles
ROMANTIC MISFITS

Tom Mole
BYRON'S ROMANTIC CELEBRITY
Industrial Culture and the Hermeneutic of Intimacy

Robert Morrison and Daniel Sanjiv Roberts (*editors*)
ROMANTICISM AND *BLACKWOOD'S MAGAZINE*
'An Unprecedented Phenomenon'

Catherine Packham
EIGHTEENTH-CENTURY VITALISM
Bodies, Culture, Politics

Nicola Parsons
READING GOSSIP IN EARLY EIGHTEENTH-CENTURY ENGLAND

Jessica Richard
THE ROMANCE OF GAMBLING IN THE EIGHTEENTH-CENTURY BRITISH NOVEL

Andrew Rudd
SYMPATHY AND INDIA IN BRITISH LITERATURE, 1770–1830

Erik Simpson
LITERARY MINSTRELSY, 1770–1830
Minstrels and Improvisers in British, Irish and American Literature

Anne H. Stevens
BRITISH HISTORICAL FICTION BEFORE SCOTT

David Stewart
ROMANTIC MAGAZINES AND METROPOLITAN LITERARY CULTURE

Rebecca Tierney-Hynes
NOVEL MINDS
Philosophers and Romance Readers, 1680–1740

P. Westover
NECROMANTICISM
Travelling to Meet the Dead, 1750–1860

Esther Wohlgemut
ROMANTIC COSMOPOLITANISM

David Worrall
THE POLITICS OF ROMANTIC THEATRICALITY, 1787–1832
The Road to the Stage

Palgrave Studies in the Enlightenment, Romanticism and Cultures of Print
Series Standing Order ISBN 978–1–403–93408–6 hardback
978–1–403–93409–3 paperback
(*outside North America only*)

You can receive future titles in this series as they are published by placing a standing order. Please contact your bookseller or, in case of difficulty, write to us at the address below with your name and address, the title of the series and the ISBN quoted above.

Customer Services Department, Macmillan Distribution Ltd, Houndmills, Basingstoke, Hampshire RG21 6XS, England

Women of Letters, Manuscript Circulation, and Print Afterlives in the Eighteenth Century

Elizabeth Rowe, Catharine Cockburn, and Elizabeth Carter

Melanie Bigold

© Melanie Bigold 2013

Softcover reprint of the hardcover 1st edition 2013 978-1-137-03356-7

All rights reserved. No reproduction, copy or transmission of this publication may be made without written permission.

No portion of this publication may be reproduced, copied or transmitted save with written permission or in accordance with the provisions of the Copyright, Designs and Patents Act 1988, or under the terms of any licence permitting limited copying issued by the Copyright Licensing Agency, Saffron House, 6–10 Kirby Street, London EC1N 8TS.

Any person who does any unauthorized act in relation to this publication may be liable to criminal prosecution and civil claims for damages.

The author has asserted her right to be identified as the author of this work in accordance with the Copyright, Designs and Patents Act 1988.

First published 2013 by
PALGRAVE MACMILLAN

Palgrave Macmillan in the UK is an imprint of Macmillan Publishers Limited, registered in England, company number 785998, of Houndmills, Basingstoke, Hampshire RG21 6XS.

Palgrave Macmillan in the US is a division of St Martin's Press LLC, 175 Fifth Avenue, New York, NY 10010.

Palgrave Macmillan is the global academic imprint of the above companies and has companies and representatives throughout the world.

Palgrave® and Macmillan® are registered trademarks in the United States, the United Kingdom, Europe and other countries.

ISBN 978-1-349-44154-9   ISBN 978-1-137-03357-4 (eBook)
DOI 10.1057/9781137033574

This book is printed on paper suitable for recycling and made from fully managed and sustained forest sources. Logging, pulping and manufacturing processes are expected to conform to the environmental regulations of the country of origin.

A catalogue record for this book is available from the British Library.

A catalog record for this book is available from the Library of Congress.

10 9 8 7 6 5 4 3 2 1
22 21 20 19 18 17 16 15 14 13

Transferred to Digital Printing in 2014

For my parents,
Carol and Mike Bigold

In many ways we find in the past what we look for: by and large, we only come up with answers to questions we think to ask.

Elaine Hobby *Virtue of Necessity*

Contents

List of Abbreviations	viii
A Note on Transcriptions	x
Preface	xi
Acknowledgements	xvi
Introduction	1
1 Letter-writing, Community, and Virtuous Exemplarity: Elizabeth Rowe's Theatre of Happiness	18
2 A Saint Everlasting: Elizabeth Rowe and Biographical Exemplarity	62
3 'The new and untrodden path': Catharine Cockburn, Philosophy, and the Republic of Letters	92
4 '[H]ow Obscure her Lot': Catharine Cockburn's Double Afterlife	142
5 Elizabeth Carter: 'a very extraordinary Phaenomenon in the Republick of Letters'	169
6 Elizabeth Carter and the *Theatrum Mundi*	213
Notes	239
Bibliography	269
Index	284

List of Abbreviations

BF	*Bluestocking Feminism: Writings of the Bluestocking Circle, 1738–1785.* Gen. Ed. Gary Kelly. Volume II: *Elizabeth Carter.* Ed. Judith Hawley. London: Pickering and Chatto, 1999
Friendship and LME	*Friendship in Death: in Twenty Letters from the Dead to the Living. To which are added, Letters Moral and Entertaining, in Prose and Verse. In Three Parts. By the same Author.* 3rd edn (1733)
GM	*Gentleman's Magazine*
Letters (1809)	*A Series of Letters between Mrs. Elizabeth Carter and Miss Catherine Talbot, from the Year 1741 to 1770. To which are added, Letters from Mrs. Elizabeth Carter to Mrs. Vesey, between the Years 1763 and 1787; published from the original manuscripts in the possession of the Rev. Montagu Pennington, M.A.*, 4 vols, 2nd edn (1809)
Letters (1817)	*Letters From Mrs Elizabeth Carter to Mrs Montagu, between the Years 1755 and 1800. Chiefly upon Literary and Moral Subjects. Published from the Originals in the Possession of the Rev. Montagu Pennington*, 3 vols (1817)
Memoirs	*Memoirs of the Life of Mrs. Elizabeth Carter with A New Edition of her Poems, some of which have never appeared Before; to which are added, some Miscellaneous Essays in Prose, together with her Notes on the Bible and Answers to objections concerning the Christian Religion* (1807)
MW	*The Miscellaneous Works in Prose and Verse of Mrs Elizabeth Rowe. The Greater Part now first Published, by her Order, from her Original Manuscripts, By Theophilus Rowe. To which are added, Poems on Several Occasions, By Mr. Thomas Rowe. And to the whole is prefix'd, An Account of the Lives and Writings of the Authors.* 2 vols (1739)

ODNB   *Oxford Dictionary of National*, edited by H. C. G. Matthew and Brian Harrison. Oxford: Oxford University Press, 2004. Online edn, ed. Lawrence Goldman, May 2009.
PMLA   *Proceedings of the Modern Languages Association*
TLS   *Times Literary Supplement*
Works *The Works of Mrs. Catherine Cockburn, Theological, Moral, Dramatic, and Poetical. Several of them now first printed. Revised and published, with an account of the Life of the Author, by Thomas Birch.* 2 vols, 1751.

A Note on Transcriptions

I have tried as far as possible to produce diplomatic transcriptions of the manuscripts included in this work. This means I have retained contractions, superscriptions, strikethroughs, etc. Uncertain readings or blotted text are indicated by small braces: { }. Any additions are included in square brackets: [ ].

Preface

> *Some have felt that these blundering lives are due to the inconvenient indefiniteness with which the Supreme Power has fashioned the natures of women: if there were one level of feminine incompetence as strict as the ability to count three and no more, the social lot of women might be treated with scientific certitude. Meanwhile the indefiniteness remains, and the limits of variation are really much wider than any one would imagine from the sameness of women's coiffure and the favorite love-stories in prose and verse.*
>
> George Eliot, *Middlemarch*

History of the book studies have reached an exciting and critical juncture. Monographs and reference texts devoted to the histories of print culture, authorship, and the book trade regularly appear in the catalogues of academic as well as popular presses; many of these studies have enhanced our understanding of the complexity of the literary marketplace and intellectual thought in the period. However, in the general rush to hail the 'rise' of print, the related fields of manuscript studies and textual criticism have, with significant exceptions, been neglected. *Women of Letters, Manuscript Circulation, and Print Afterlives in the Eighteenth Century* addresses this gap in the current literature and features a timely exploration of the ways in which eighteenth-century manuscript culture continued to function as an efficacious mode of engagement with the republic of letters in England. Excellent work has been done on manuscript circulation and publication in sixteenth- and seventeenth-century studies, but, during the so-called print revolution in the eighteenth century, the emphasis has remained on the finished product: the printed text and its variant editions. While work has multiplied on the impact and importance of manuscript culture in an age of print, few scholars have considered the status of manuscripts when considering the careers of women writers in the long eighteenth century.

For many scholars, the seventeenth and eighteenth centuries represent the most significant watersheds in the history of women's writing and the studies, critical and biographical, which have appeared with steady regularity since the last decades of the twentieth century confirm the rich scope of material produced by British women writers and their continental counterparts.¹ There is still, however, a perceptible bias in the degree of scrutiny accorded women who published political or sexually subversive poetry, drama, and fiction, in comparison to those whose works circulated largely in manuscript. Amongst this latter group, women with scholarly preoccupations or who wrote from a religious or philosophical perspective are even less likely to garner attention.² Access to manuscript archives is obviously a significant deterrent, but it is more likely that the miscellaneous nature of the writings of many religious and philosophically minded female authors discourages easy categorisation and therefore narrativisation in the form of the institutional monograph. The predominance of familiar letters in manuscripts by women especially tends to encourage biographical speculation at the expense of textual criticism. Therefore, despite the fact that the lives of many women of letters have been compassed in a number of broad historical or biographical surveys, these catalogues of notable females have only just begun to counteract what George Eliot called the 'inconvenient indefiniteness' of the virtuous (read bland) historical female.³

The aim of *Women of Letters, Manuscript Circulation, and Print Afterlives in the Eighteenth Century* is to tackle Eliot's 'inconvenient indefiniteness' by considering more particularly the similarities, differences, and successive innovations in the manuscript and print careers of three 'exemplary' female writers from the long eighteenth century: namely Elizabeth Singer Rowe (1674–1737), Catharine Trotter Cockburn (1674?–1749), and Elizabeth Carter (1717–1806).⁴ This book tells the stories of these women's writing lives: the social and literary contexts which shaped their allegiance to manuscript circulation, the histories of their successful as well as failed forays into print, and their agency and/or diffidence in regards to their public careers. At the same time, my study broaches larger thematic issues: the degree and significance of women's involvement in the English republic of letters – particularly in relation to their relevance and engagement in contemporary debates within Christianity; the evidence for a more robust climate of manuscript circulation in the long eighteenth century; and reception history – specifically the notion of print afterlives and the critical tradition.

The primary focus of the monograph is the reinterpretation of the material, social, literary, philosophical, and religious contexts of women's letter-writing in the long eighteenth century. Drawing upon a significant amount of original research on unpublished writings, and developed through the connected but contained tales of the three case studies, it shows how letter-writing functioned as a form of literary manuscript exchange. In contrast to current emphases on the importance of the print revolution in the period, my book argues for the productive status of manuscript circulation as an accepted method of engaging with the republic of letters throughout the long eighteenth century. However, this study does not exclude print and actively explores the interface of the two mediums. In the case of the three authors included as case studies, both manuscript copies and print editions of their familiar, fictional, and polemical letters have survived, and individual chapters discuss their compositional genetics in detail. In the process of exploring the print publications the book also addresses issues of influence and adaptation in reference to writers such as Anthony Ashley Cooper, third Earl of Shaftesbury, Blaise Pascal, John Locke, Samuel Johnson, Samuel Richardson, and Frances Burney.

The book consists of an Introduction and six chapters. The Introduction provides a summary survey of previous work on women's literary history. It also sketches out an expanded history of manuscript circulation – the current works in the field are largely concerned with male and/or aristocratic writers and end at the start of the eighteenth century. Finally, it offers a fresh and innovative account of women's involvement in the English republic of letters which focuses on the importance of understanding the distinctive material as well as intellectual contexts of the English scene.

Chapter 1, on Elizabeth Rowe, provides a detailed comparison of her manuscript familiar letters and her printed fictional correspondences. A study of the editorial emendations to which she subjected her original letters in order to effect their transformation into fictional missives reveals the degree to which she knowingly constructed an enthusiastic literary persona. Enthusiasm is an important term in relation to Rowe's life and works; whilst historically it was most often deployed as a pejorative label for Protestant dissenters of the seventeenth and eighteenth centuries who entertained, in Samuel Johnsons's terms, 'I. A vain belief of private revelation; a vain confidence of Divine favour or communication', recent critics have recognised the significant aesthetic and moral contributions of the movement.[5] Shaun Irlam, in particular, argues that the figurative language and 'otherworldliness' of enthusiastic discourse was assimilated by poets of sensibility who 'worked to mitigate the mechanic and rationalistic proclivities of the Enlightenment program in order to make it [...] more accommodating to [...] other modes and forms of knowledge (religious, affective, literary, artistic, psychological, romantic)'.[6] Rowe is one of the best examples of a writer who not only dramatised her enthusiasm and otherworldly impulses in her letters and poetry, but also maintained her status as a 'figure of knowledge, virtue, truth, and moral authority'.[7] No doubt this was in large part due to her concerted effort to engage in a wide range of philosophical and literary debates in her letters. Rowe's decision to use letters as her public mode confirms the wide-ranging acceptance of letters as meritorious literary products, and showcases women's crucial role in shaping the aesthetics of religious devotion and the discourses of ethical philosophy in the republic of letters in the eighteenth century.

Chapter 2 assesses the impact biographical exemplarity had on the posthumous literary valuation of Rowe's works and particularises the range of historical contexts in which Rowe the author and the saint were deployed. Specifically, I differentiate between the uses and reception of her works and the representations of her life. Rowe was one of the most reprinted authors in the eighteenth and early nineteenth centuries, and, as a result, exerted considerable literary influence on subsequent writers. Rowe's posthumous pre-eminence was not without contention, however, and part of the reason she 'disappears' from later literary accounts of the era is the confusion associated with the discourse of enthusiasm in her life and works. Nevertheless, this attention to the particulars of her biography demonstrates the importance of her legacy and the seriousness with which it was treated.

Chapter 3 turns to Catharine Cockburn. I contend that the current picture of her literary and critical output is severely constrained by an undue focus on print publications. To this end I detail the social contexts and editorial decisions which shaped the suppression or presentation of Cockburn's works, as well as her role in that process. Cockburn entertained a fraught relationship with print culture, but her public and private letters reveal a consistent and effective polemicist on religious and philosophical ideas associated with enlightenment modes of thought. Despite her iteration of the reciprocity of intellectual exchange and Christian affections, Cockburn's most prominent mode was that of a directing didacticist and her letters reveal the degree to which she controlled the terms of discussion and, therefore, her own exemplary image.

Chapter 4 supplements Cockburn's brief afterlife by revisiting the subscribers and the subscription process of her collected works. I also discuss how the complicated nature of Enlightenment discourse in England, particularly the disjunctive nature of internal debates within the clerical and university communities, has meant that Cockburn's rapid descent into obscurity is more a symptom of her subjects than her critical merit.

Chapter 5, on Elizabeth Carter, reiterates the model of authorship so far explored. However, unlike the previous chapters, I combine the discussion of Carter's manuscript and print career with that of her print 'afterlife'. The primary reason for this is that it is almost impossible to discuss Carter's letters without first taking into consideration the editing process they went through. Montagu Pennington, Carter's executor, heir, and editor, is the most intrusive of all the editors I look at in this book, but I argue that his construction of Carter and presentation of her letters reveals his commitment to showcasing the scribal, classical humanism, and moral nature of her life and works. Finally, Chapter 6 returns to the issue of literary contexts and explores the discourses of theatre and happiness in relation to Carter's letters.

The stories of why and how the letter collections of these women made it into print are riddled with holes, literal and figurative, but they are nevertheless tales worth telling. Textual criticism, bibliographical research, the history of the book – whichever title one favours – has long been practiced on the works of the great canonical authors, but has only recently begun to be applied to the works of less-canonical women writers. Katherine Philips has been a popular subject and, more recently, Alexander Pettit has considered the case of Eliza Haywood, and Kathryn Sutherland that of Jane Austen. Most women writers are still waiting for scholarly editions let alone the sort of textual analysis that relies so heavily on the archive resources of the major national or university libraries. However, my interest in the connections and disjunctions in our understanding of the circulation of ideas, the history of the book, and the manuscript heritage are particularly important at the moment given the emphasis upon online juggernauts such as *Early English Books Online* (*EEBO*) and *Eighteenth Century Collections Online* (*ECCO*). As the creators of the Perdita Project and database argue, the focus on print alone 'has produced a strange picture of women's literary history'.[8] In contrast to print-based tools, the present study seeks to maintain and advance an approach to scholarship that appreciates the diverse and palimpsestic nature of literary production.

My book places primary importance on women's writing rather than discourses about women, or directed readings of feminist content. The work makes a quieter ideological statement and practices a more particularised methodological pattern; however, I hope that this enables texts, in all their layers and lacunae, to come to the forefront, opening up possibilities for new approaches and new prisms through which to view women's letter-writing in the eighteenth century.

Acknowledgements

It is a pleasure, at the end of a long process, to record my thanks to the people who have made this work possible. My first debt of gratitude must be to Ros Ballaster. The present book began life as my Oxford D.Phil. thesis and Ros's expert supervision, professional guidance, and long-term support have been instrumental in the completion of the project. Grateful thanks are also due to Kathryn Sutherland, who has been the best of mentors and a kind friend.

For help along the way, I would like to thank Isabel Rivers, my examiners, Abigail Williams and Harriet Guest, and the anonymous readers who have provided such helpful and constructive criticism. In particular, the invaluable erudition of Paula Backscheider has greatly enriched the final work. Many thanks to Clifford Siskin and Anne Mellor for including me in their excellent series, to Paula Kennedy and Ben Doyle for their unfailing professionalism, and to Nick Brock and Linda Auld for shepherding the work through the final stages. Hopefully the final work merits all of these people's generous time and effort.

My research would not have progressed without the support of numerous institutions. I was extremely fortunate in receiving a doctoral fellowship from the Social Sciences and Humanities Research Council of Canada (SSHRC), without which my studies at the University of Oxford would have been impossible. St Anne's College and the University of Manitoba were also very generous with scholarships. A SSHRC postdoctoral fellowship at the University of Toronto provided the welcome respite of a new and engrossing project, whilst Research Leave from Cardiff University and a Visiting Fellowship at Chawton House Library finally provided the time and congenial surroundings to polish the manuscript. I would like to express my thanks to all of these institutions for their generous support. Thanks are also due to the wonderful librarians at the Bodleian Library, British Library, Chawton House Library, St Anne's College, and Trinity College, Cambridge, for access to and assistance with their incredible treasures.

An early version of Chapter 1 appeared as 'Elizabeth Rowe's Fictional and Familiar Letters: Exemplarity, Enthusiasm and the Production of Posthumous Meaning,' in the *British Journal for Eighteenth-Century Studies* 29/1 (2006): 1–14. My thanks to John Wiley and Sons for permission to reproduce this material. I drew on research undertaken for this book for my new chapter on 'Letters and Learning' in *A History of British Women's Writing*, ed. Ros Ballaster (Palgrave Macmillan, 2010). My thanks to Ros and Palgrave Macmillan for providing an opportunity to contribute to this excellent series. Elaine Hobby has kindly given me permission to reproduce, as my epigraph, a quotation from her groundbreaking work, *Virtue of Necessity*. I would also like to thank His Grace the Duke of Northumberland and his staff for their hospitality during a visit to Alnwick Castle and for permission to quote from manuscripts in the Duke's private collection.

Since 2008, members of the School of English, Communication and Philosophy at Cardiff University have been a model of collegiality. In particular, I would like to thank members of the 'Book Club' for their feedback on an early version of the introduction. I owe a massive debt to Irene Morra, who not only read and commented on large portions of the manuscript, but has also provided so much moral support. I would also like to acknowledge those scholars of the modern republic of letters who have shared their knowledge and enthusiasm over the years: Jacqui Grainger, Isobel Grundy, Paulina Kewes, Thomas Keymer, Judi Loach, Victor Nuovo, Anne Birgitte Rønning, and Betty Schellenberg. I am still, over a decade on, thankful to John Rempel for his inspiring classes. His memory is everywhere alive in the subjects I study and write about.

On a more personal note, I have been very fortunate in my friendships and take great pleasure in expressing my gratitude to Sid and Kerry Bailey, Jeff Bibbee, Johanna Brierley, Michael Caruana, Imogen Goold, Rich and Jamie Jones, Emily, Maria, and Wayne Mar, Ruth McElroy, Martin Willis, and Adrian Viens. My greatest indebtedness, however, belongs to my lovely family. Belinda, Jeremy, Brodie, and Michelle Bigold have been a constant source of intellectual and creative inspiration over the years. Ava and Ralph Stemmer are a fantastic addition. Richard Hawking has been quite wonderful in so many ways, and, of course, I owe my parents everything. This book is dedicated to them.

Introduction

In November 1753, the writer and later Bluestocking Catherine Talbot documented a rather disappointing, if typical, encounter with textual history. While visiting the Duchess of Somerset, she had been given the opportunity to read one of the Duchess's manuscript copies of Elizabeth Singer Rowe's writings. In a journal addressed to Julia Berkeley, Talbot notes, 'since I came up to go to Bed (I could not resist the temptation for one half hour)' of reading 'in a MS [manuscript] Book of Mrs Rowes.' She adds, however, 'There is very little however in this MS [sic] but what has since been printed.'[9] Talbot's desire to find something unprinted, 'new', and presumably revelatory by Rowe is a familiar impulse to most literary historians. She was eventually rewarded with just such an item when, a couple of weeks later, 'The good Duchess had given me a Treasure – a Manuscript Letter of Mrs Rowes that was never printed.'[10]

Talbot's interest in Rowe's literary 'remains' was more than just a passing interest in a favourite author. As A.S. Byatt romanticised so well in her novel *Possession*, the search for lost letters, manuscript writings, and literary careers can be an absorbing historical exercise, one that seeks to recover a lost inheritance, particularly the lost female literary inheritance. However, it is also a complicated conceptual engagement with the notion of textual presence and possession; Talbot's treasured because possessed (in both senses of the word) scrap of paper speaks to her sense of the numinousness of Rowe's writings and life. It also reflects her desire to perpetuate that literary inheritance in her own social circles.[11] Talbot was a keen champion of women writers, and she played a significant role in inspiring and promoting contemporaries. She encouraged Elizabeth Carter to complete her magnum opus, *All the Works of Epictetus* (1758); she helped various subscription efforts, including Catharine Cockburn's; and routinely discussed and circulated the works of such women writers as Katherine Philips, Madame de Sévigné, Madame de Maintenon, Mary Jones, Sarah Fielding, Lady Mary Wortley Montagu, and Mary Leapor.

Talbot's interest in Rowe's textual history and her wider sense of women's literary history were not unusual in the seventeenth or eighteenth centuries. Eighteenth-century scholars, many of whom were clergymen, were particularly interested in learned ladies. Susan Staves has pointed out the large proportion of well-placed Church of England clergy who personally educated their daughters, wards, or friends, who participated in intellectual exchanges with women writers, and who facilitated the publication of women's writing.[12] In their calls for more female education, in their own constructive relationships with learned women, and in their celebration (in sermons and printed histories) of learned women's abilities these scholars were not alone. The popular press and women writers themselves were increasingly championing a history of exemplary learned women. Students of the eighteenth century are familiar with Mary Astell's and Daniel Defoe's proposals for female academies, but these tracts were only a small proportion of the print and manuscript debate about the female right to education. A large part of the argument for education was promulgated in the histories of learned women that appeared in print throughout this period. Of these, George Ballard's 1752 *Memoirs of Several Ladies of Great Britain who have been celebrated for their writings or skill in the learned languages, arts and sciences* is perhaps the most well-known, but there were many more before him.[13] Ballard's criteria for including the various women was that they had to be learned, but more importantly that they, or someone else, had to have produced something in print based upon their learning. For Ballard, the survival, possession, documentation, repetition, and dissemination of these texts is a central concern.

The history of women's literary history has made significant advances since the state of historical yearning and scholarly dismay expressed in my prefatory epigraph from Eliot, and in Ballard's antiquarian quest to recover England's lost female intellectuals. However, as the following quotations from Margaret Ezell and Susan Staves suggest, the current scene continues to be vexed and challenged by complex critical and historical tensions. Ezell writes:

> Writing women's literary history has been compared to doing archaeology, to receiving an inheritance, and to replanting a mother's garden. In writing this book, I am obviously starting with the belief in the value of this activity, however it is characterized. What concerns

me in my reading of contemporary feminist theory is that the structures used to shape our narrative of women's literary history may have unconsciously continued the existence of the restrictive ideologies that initially erased the vast majority of women's writings from literary history and teaching texts. That is, there appear to be several underlying assumptions about gender, genre, and historical progress which link together even the well-recognized divisions within feminist criticism. Such historiographical structures, although they have in fact enabled the serious study of women's texts in the university, privilege certain genres and periods; the effect has been that those of us interested in earlier women's writings find ourselves continually explaining the existence and significance of the texts we work with in much the same way as the pioneers of women's studies did.[14]

And Staves contests:

I agree that new aesthetic values can be found in some previously devalued women's writing, but I do not agree with those who contend that we cannot make aesthetic evaluations of literary works that have any use or objectivity. Aesthetic or literary merit is an important principle of selection in my literary history.[15]

Ezell likens the recovery and celebration of this tradition of women writers to an archaeological dig. Even more apt perhaps, given the textual nature of the exercise, is the idea of the palimpsest. Editorial and textual criticism have provided invaluable resources towards the evaluation, celebration, and perpetuation of canonical authors. By providing the bibliographical analysis so crucial to notions of textual authority, this book attempts to make present the critical assumptions about the value of women's writing which Staves and others have so usefully outlined in their larger histories. By focusing on the manuscript and print heritage of these significant women writers, this book will expose some of the many critical assumptions that have informed such processes. In so doing, it will highlight the exciting possibilities presented by manuscript heritage itself.

Revisiting women's literary history

In her ground-breaking and influential works, *The Patriarch's Wife: Literary Evidence and the History of the Family* (1987) and *Writing Women's*

Literary History (1993), Ezell explores the many difficulties with which the literary historian of seventeenth- and eighteenth-century women writers has to contend. In the earlier work, Ezell questioned critical perceptions of an 'absence of literary evidence' for the existence of the outgoing, intellectual seventeenth-century woman. Crucially, *The Patriarch's Wife* was one of the first works to highlight the continuing importance of manuscript circulation as a form of 'publication' for women writers.[16] Her later revisionist work, *Writing Women's Literary History*, not only helps to illuminate the repetitive nature of the historical reclamation project – showing how successive generations of feminist scholars have had to reaffirm the generic variety and intellectual range of women's writing for a new audience – but also focused attention on the ways in which those reaffirmations have been undermined by untested assumptions about the past. In particular, she questions the many studies of individual female authors that attempt to establish teleological theories about women's writing. Ezell deconstructs the critical discourses that surround twentieth-century anthologies and studies of women writers, arguing that critics such as Elaine Showalter, and Sandra Gilbert and Susan Gubar, 'base their analyses of a particular period or group of texts on assumptions about the circumstances of writers in preceding periods and on assumptions concerning the connections between generations of women writers'.[17] Such practices uncritically use the more distant past of the seventeenth and eighteenth centuries to affirm their own arguments about a later, usually Victorian, period.

The problem, as Ezell sees it, is that this retrospective process has led to a rather limited set of assumptions about women's literary history: first, 'that there is a "tradition" of women's writing to be recovered'; second, and more problematically, 'that this tradition reveals an evolutionary model of feminism'.[18] Any attempt to contain the many histories of women's writing within a single, feminist trajectory risks ignoring the extent to which that narrative is resisted or problematised by diverse historical and individual realities.

> [T]hese texts lament the oppressive effects of society on early women writers, using the potent myth of Judith Shakespeare to represent the tragic fate of talented women. Society, this theory maintains, silenced women, and where it could not, it drove them mad and characteristically infused their writings with bitterness and anger... In this model of women's literary history, anger is an identifying characteristic of the "female" (biological) reacting to the "feminine"

(socio-cultural). It also is a linking mechanism in the chain of female literary ancestors.[19]

This model has often ensured the marginalisation of those pre-1700 and pre-1800 authors who do not appear to conform to a tradition of anger and proto-feminism. Ezell argues that the search for 'angry' forebears who are 'good feminists' has occluded our sense of the differences within the female literary tradition, particularly among the conservative element.[20] Thus numerous 'seventeenth-century women writers, such as Margaret Cavendish and Mary Astell, have extensive apologies offered up on their behalf for their "conservatism" or are dissected as not being sufficiently feminist.'[21] She adds that '[o]ther early women writers suffer harsher criticism for not being ideologically sound or being too acceptable to the male establishment': a particular fault of Katherine Philips.[22]

Susan Staves similarly argues that: '[t]he modern canon has especially valued the transgressive writers like Aphra Behn and Delarivier Manley, whose willingness to treat female sexuality and to attack male oppression of women made them appear to be our most usable foremothers.'[23] She attempts to redress this trend in a chapter specifically devoted to 'Partisans of virtue and religion, 1689–1702'. Rowe, Cockburn, and Carter offer a particularly fruitful example of the greater complexity that can be added to narratives about eighteenth-century women writers. Although they were celebrated in their lifetimes and after as religious exemplars and highly accomplished learned ladies, these women nevertheless failed to provide the anger or proto-feminist elements sought by twentieth-century scholars. Yet all of these writers identified themselves with a contemporary female tradition. This tradition privileged piety, virtue, and learning, and found its roots in the expression of the Royalist poet, Katherine Philips. Rowe, Cockburn, and Carter were not only frequently compared to their forebear, Philips, but they also – consciously or not – implicitly established a distinct tradition for themselves. This tradition was reinforced in a publishing practice of manuscript circulation with select print publication. It was also articulated in their clear dialogue with each other in poetics, in religious/philosophical discourses, and in their conscientious attempt to lead exemplarily virtuous lives.

When considering female traditions and the importance of Philips to subsequent female writers, it is important to recognise that the debt of Rowe, Cockburn, and Carter both to Philips and each other needs to be balanced against their own artistic agency and changing historical contexts. To build chains of similarities can lead to the 'erasure of particular differences'.[24] At the same time, however, acknowledging points of convergence can help us to understand the extent to which these women were also forging independent paths. By referencing this so-called counter-tradition of virtuous female authors, I do not mean to set up an oppositional spectrum of the 'good versus the bad girls' in literary history; rather I aim to foreground the continuity of the mode and method of these women's interventions within literary culture. It also pointedly contradicts Virginia Woolf's assertion in *A Room of One's Own* that there was no intellectual, independent tradition of women writers for a writer such as Woolf to draw upon.[25] This study charts the careers of three women who were not only cognisant of a choice of female traditions, but were actively concerned to perpetuate the influence of one of those traditions to later generations. Moreover, contrary to claims that the basis for such emulation was founded on social prescription (for example, the virtuous image) rather than literary influence, my work with their manuscripts and printed texts has produced unique evidence of imitation and adaptation over the years.[26]

Since Ezell's twentieth-century re-evaluation of early modern women's writing, the twenty-first-century critical fortunes of 'virtuous' writers such as Rowe, Cockburn, and Carter have risen dramatically. New editions and revised critical opinions of their work have been appearing in increasing volume. A number of these works emphasise the proto-feminist, professional/publishing model which these women represent. Still more have begun to explore the discursive domains in which these women participated and for which they functioned as exemplars.

Elizabeth Rowe is on the threshold of becoming one of the most significant of the 'new' women writers of the eighteenth century.[27] The contrast between her early and late careers has presented difficulties for scholars, but, as Kathryn King has persuasively argued, she is both a manuscript poet and a publishing phenomenon.[28] Catharine Cockburn has had a more fragmented critical reception. She has been noticed by a number of literary critics interested in late Restoration drama, but quite separately by philosophers. This disciplinary duality stems from Cockburn's sharply divided textual history: the majority of her play texts were not published with her posthumous volume of collected works. It also derives from a critical bias towards women writers whose print history appears to align them with a teleological feminist literary tradition. The young Trotter was keen to publish and promote herself and seems to have had few problems obtaining patrons and encomiasts for her plays and poems. The older and married Cockburn, however, entertained a more fraught history with print culture, and her large body of philosophical letters (in manuscript and print) are not easy to contain. Perhaps as a result, she does not as yet occupy the same critical position as Rowe.[29] Elizabeth Carter has been more consistently well served by critics, the beneficiary of a growing interest in the Bluestocking circle.[30] She is arguably the most famous learned woman of the mid-eighteenth century and one of the most fascinating for her long and varied career.

The study of these women provides a multifaceted perspective on early modern literary and intellectual endeavour. As a result, their works and lives illuminate a much more complex and varied female literary tradition than that assumed by reductive scholarly celebrations of angry or proto-feminist women writers.

Manuscript culture and letters

One of the most significant similarities between the careers of Rowe, Cockburn, and Carter is their allegiance to manuscript circulation or 'publication'. Their letters in particular act as a primary medium for intellectual and literary exchange. Letter-writing could and did function as a form of literary manuscript circulation in the eighteenth century and, though much has been made of the print revolution in the period, a revised awareness of the continuation and importance of manuscript circulation as an accepted method of engaging with the wider republic of letters is crucial to a re-evaluation of women's writing in the period.

The silences or marginalisation critics have attributed to many women writers is an error founded on an incomplete picture of authorship in the period. For the most part scholars have been content to assess a writer's engagement and importance based on their productions in print. However, approaching the period from a more holistic point of view – one that recognises that there was a form of social authorship wider than the print market – enables us to see that not only were women not silent, but that they were much more prolific and involved than is generally assumed. Letters, in so many instances, were a version of literary manuscript performance. These manuscripts could effectively advance careers or friendships as much as the occasional commendatory verse. Despite representing a less emphatic gesture of authorial ambition, these letters nevertheless paved the way for future forays into the literary marketplace.

Aside from Ezell's works, *The Patriarch's Wife* and *Social Authorship and the Advent of Print*, most critical works in the field of manuscript circulation and scribal publication tend to focus on a much earlier period and are primarily concerned with male writers and aristocrats.[31] Indeed, it is widely recognised that many male writers chose this form of 'publication' over that of print. John Wilmot, the Earl of Rochester and Jonathan Swift (and his fellow Scriblerians) are well-known examples, but scores of middling writers also pursued this mode (particularly in antiquarian, academic, and clerical circles).[32] Except for *Women's Writing and the Circulation of Ideas: Manuscript Publication in England, 1550–1800* (2002), a compilation edited by George L. Justice and Nathan Tinker, there has been very little focus on women writers and even less on the eighteenth century proper.[33]

A number of the issues which these works raise are, however, pertinent to the present study and take on especial significance when applied to women's writing. First and foremost of these is the notion of the 'stigma of print'; second is their encouragement for the need to problematise and reimagine the traditional binary of the 'public' print career versus the 'private' manuscript one; and, third, the importance of the ways that the materiality of the text impacts on the traditional history of the book triad of authorship, publication, and reading. In all of these respects, letters and letter-writing have been undervalued and underexplored.

i. 'The stigma of print'

Stories about women writers' embarrassment, anger, dismay, helplessness, and, according to some, false modesty at appearing in print are inescapable in texts from the early modern period. Perhaps one of the most famous protestations from the period, Katherine Philips's oft-quoted disclaimer, '[I] never writ any line in my life with an intention to have it printed', has perpetuated the myth of the horror of print shared by Philips and many of her female contemporaries.[34] Numerous critics now question whether Philips was being disingenuous about the 'unauthorised' publication of her poems in 1664: Philips had in fact published numerous individual poems (with and without her name) in other poetry miscellanies, as well as her play *Pompey* (1663). Nevertheless, as an antidote to this perceived modesty, feminist literary history has celebrated those women who actively eschewed the distinction. Behn's claim to 'value Fame as much if I had been born a Hero' has been noted for its appropriation of militaristic male valour.[35] Similarly, Margaret Cavendish's confident and synecdochal projection of her works as an everlasting paper embodiment of herself has resonated with feminist scholars.[36] What was it, then, about the printed text that impelled so many writers to disclaim the act of publication? More importantly, why has the 'stigma of print' been given such prominence in discussions about women writers?

Philips's vocal affinity for manuscript circulation and 'private' poetry conforms to what Ezell has argued was the normal practice of poets who sought recognition through conservative means. For Philips, this meant showcasing her poems through aristocratic connections and court circles, as well as a wide array of literary, intellectual, and spiritual mentors. If her manuscript volume did not go through these avenues first, it would not garner the patronage and protection she so obviously craved. Geographical and historical circumstances also likely factored in Philips's choice of mode. As a Royalist poet living in rural Wales, Philips's deployment of the themes of retirement, friendship, and platonic courtly love in tandem with manuscript circulation was a way of highlighting her withdrawal from public affairs during the Interregnum years. Enacting the rituals of a banished court was, Carol Barash explains, a 'way of demonstrating loyalty to a temporarily discredited system of values'.[37] Because she did not live to see her volume of poems properly presented, we will never know what was her final intention regarding print. Based on her ideal of coterie exchange, however, we do know that she saw her poems as functioning in a limited sphere, if only because most people would be in 'ignorance of what occasion'd them'.[38]

According to H.R. Woudhuysen, this notion of disavowing print was first put forward by J.W. Saunders in his article, 'The Stigma of Print: A Note on the Social Bases of Tudor Poetry'.[39] Saunders introduced the now-familiar construct that, for amateur court poets, it was '*socially* desirable' to avoid print, whereas for the professional poets outside or on the edges of the court 'print became an *economic* necessity'.[40] Saunders likewise observed that whilst the stigma of print was widespread in the sixteenth century, there were numerous 'strict and elaborate' conventions 'for bypassing it'.[41] Woudhuysen elaborates:

> When popular or professional poets descended into print they liked to cover their fall through all those deceptions, disclaimers, and evasions which make the modern editor's task of unravelling the true circumstances surrounding a book's publication so hard. The motives for this coyness revolve around the rank of the poet and the perceived status of poetry at this time. Many professional poets found that getting their works into print was a powerful weapon for self-advancement, not least through the use of dedications to win patronage; but the paradox of the stigma of print was that all this had

to be done with a certain lofty distaste, genuine or assumed, for the business of self-promotion through the grubby medium of print.[42]

Woudhuysen's language is telling for two reasons: first, it encapsulates the way in which discussions about manuscript and print have been shaped by their association with class and political economy; and, second, it identifies, along with Saunders, a contemporary awareness of the conventional nature of authorial 'coyness' towards print. Both of these issues can be seen in Philips's response to the pirated edition of her poetry.

In direct contrast to Elizabeth Eisenstein's or Ian Watt's rise of the printing press/novel/capitalist individual, therefore, Woudhuysen's language presents us with the story of the fall or decline of aristocratic status and culture (for example, 'lofty distaste', 'deceptions', 'descended', 'fall', and 'grubby medium'). Ezell notes in *Social Authorship and the Advent of Print* that 'histories of print and of bookselling have framed their narratives as histories of a type of civil strife, with the new (young, democratic) technology overthrowing the established (old, aristocratic) one to usher in a new, better world'.[43] She cautions that this political and class-oriented formulation of the 'rise' of print unduly constructs manuscript circulation as an aristocratic and amateur pastime, and the eighteenth-century writers who still adhered to it as outdated, if not regressive. Instead, she claims 'that even after 1710 and the institution of the Act of Queen Anne, script was still competitive, if not the dominant, mode of transmitting and reading what we term "literary" and "academic" materials'.[44] The careers of Rowe, Cockburn, and Carter – all of whom were middle-class, all of whom wrote and circulated manuscripts after the death of Queen Anne – are examples of the vitality of manuscript circulation in the eighteenth century.

While Woudhuysen draws attention to the often-disingenuous nature of the authors' protestations against appearing in print, he also notes the problem of creating opposing constructs between the publicising aims of print and the relative privacy of manuscript. As the example of Philips's response to just *one* print publication attests, the literary trope of authorial modesty can too often be extrapolated into a historical distinction that is no more reflective of contemporary practice than the problematic and now contentious construction of public and private spheres.

Many women writers did, of course, publish fictional and non-fictional works, including those in this study, and acquired public reputations as a result. As Ezell has shown in *The Patriarch's Wife*, however, in the overlapping worlds of manuscript and print publication in the early modern period, sticking to manuscript circulation did not necessarily prevent a public reputation as a poet or philosopher.[45] In fact, the notion of women's 'modesty' as the inhibiting factor in their desire to get into print is a false construction of the seventeenth-century context of print versus manuscript culture. For Ezell, 'women's participation in... [manuscript] practices is not so much a mark of "modesty" as conservatism, the preference for the older form of literary transmission which left control of the text in the author's hands rather than signing it over to the bookseller.'[46] Ezell's study ends with the 1720s, but her contentions can be stretched to provide the histories of 'authorship' which she calls for, rather than just those of printers and booksellers.

The writing lives of Rowe, Cockburn, and Carter show, in Kathryn King's terms, a 'tactical' perspicacity in their relations with print culture.[47] Whether that meant establishing poetic reputations in early periodicals such as the *Athenian Mercury* or *The Gentleman's Magazine*, or negotiating patrons and commendations for printed dramatic quartos, they show an acute awareness of the demands of the medium and willingly engage within those parameters. Indeed, though they sometimes distance themselves from youthful publications, they never disown their print ambitions. At the same time, they clearly privilege an older form of literary exchange that is limited, sometimes personal, but always carefully constructed for literary effect or intellectual improvement. The circulation of their manuscript letters, treatises, devotions, poems, and essays reveals their concerted efforts to perpetuate classical constructs of civic friendship and, particularly, humanistic ideals of intellectual reciprocity.

ii. Letters

This study, therefore, is concerned with the ways epistolarity and the eighteenth-century republic of letters interface with authorship, print production, and reading practices in the period. Two recent works have contributed significantly to my understanding of the constituent elements of the letter's cycle of text production and the literary possibilities, or 'cultural poetics', of the form: Eve Tavor Bannet's study of the transatlantic *Empire of Letters* and Clare Brant's monograph on *Eighteenth-Century Letters and British Culture*.[48] Bannet illuminates the scope and specificity of letter-writing forms and the functions of eighteenth-century letters and letter manuals, recovering 'what people knew then about letters that we have forgotten'.[49] Bannet's collational and comparative approach reveals that contemporary readers were able to adduce very subtle shifts in emphasis amongst the various letter types in a given manual – from affection to hostility to quite subtle codes of deference.[50] The interpretive and critical skills thus acquired could then be brought to bear not just on a wide range of social form letters, but also on the printed letters to be found in periodicals (the letter-essay), published correspondences, and even epistolary novels. This evidence provides the most comprehensive basis yet for establishing an evaluative difference between ordinary practitioners and those who wrote what we generally recognise as 'literary' familiar letters.

Indeed, the eighteenth-century print market was inundated with books that sought to reference, recreate, and revision the material life of the letter. Brant calculates that 'Between 1700 and 1800, more than twenty-one thousand items were published that used the word "Letter" or "Letters" in their title', a sum that excludes any epistolary texts which did not advertise letters in the title.[51] What this plenitude suggests is a widespread engagement with the letter as text, whether manuscript, print, or textual metaphor.[52]

Nevertheless, this obvious market significance has not translated to sustained (sustainable?) attributions of literary value beyond the work of the most acclaimed epistolary writers (for example, Pope, Montagu, Richardson, Johnson, and Walpole). The most significant problem with so many authors whose writings fall under miscellaneous branches of literature is the perceived lack of value attached to such output. As Brant notes in an earlier article on 'Varieties of women's writing', '[ma]ny women writers in eighteenth-century Britain were not novelists, poets, or dramatists. They were writers of letters, diaries, memoirs, essays – genres of sometimes uncertain status then and certainly liminal status now.'[53] The diversity evident in the Perdita catalogue of women's manuscript writings between 1500 and 1700 confirms this generic variety. Importantly, Staves sees new possibilities in these marginal forms, and claims that 'new aesthetic values can be found in some previously devalued women's writing'.[54] Scholars of the novel who once overlooked Eliza Haywood's amatory fictions, for example, now devote considerable space to her in important surveys of the form. Similarly, Lady Mary Wortley Montagu's epistolary brilliance (and with it the fortunes of the familiar letter in general) benefited from the editorial work of Robert Halsband and Isobel Grundy, and the critical perspicacity of Bruce Redford and Cynthia Lowenthal.[55] Whilst this study makes aesthetic claims for the epistolary art of Rowe, Cockburn, and Carter, its broader aim is to understand their literary careers in relation to their historical culture. Just as more detailed studies of the writings and careers of a William Walsh or even the more well-known Isaac Watts would help to enrich our understanding of coteries, manuscript circulation, religious writing, patronage, publication, and reception history in the late seventeenth and early to mid-eighteenth century, so too do the case studies that follow.

This study aims not only to recover the manuscript 'careers' of these authors, but also to offer a fresh appraisal of the textual and contextual complexity of their letters. Though Rowe, Cockburn, and Carter wrote many incidental and conversational missives, their correspondences are only partly examples of the metonymic recreation of polite sociability so celebrated as the hallmark of the eighteenth-century epistle.[56] The majority of their letters are concerned with literary, philosophical and religious topics, and function as a type of intellectual correspondence course for their respective participants. These women read, re-imagined, defended, opposed or celebrated the works of the classical humanist tradition – from Greek and Latin authors to Enlightenment thinkers – and their writings reflect the range of their interests.

They were also committed moral philosophers in their own right and it was the moral imperative which often compelled them into print. Learning, virtue, and piety were only as useful or meaningful as the number of souls they could redeem. Thus, all three women actively sought to understand the parameters by which one could personally understand and ground moral obligation and virtue and, therefore, earthly happiness. These aims are best captured in the phrase 'a theatre of happiness': by which I mean the construction of a rhetorical framework capable of encapsulating the practice of moral virtue that will result in the most ethically and religiously acceptable grounds for happiness in this so-called probationary state. An important term in contextualising these constructions is 'affection'. 'Affection' in the early part of the century was often identified as the Christian ideal of benevolence and devotion directed towards, and received back from, God. At the same time, affection could also signify the sociable ideal that privileged interpersonal feelings as the most effective means of encouraging a sense of community and a shared recognition of the worth of moral virtue. However, whilst most commentators could agree on these positive aspects of affection, there was considerable disagreement regarding the obligating impetus underlying them. The study of the human affections – how they function, how they can be aroused and directed in the service of God – therefore becomes of central importance.

In line with this eudaemonic theatre I argue that the familiar letters of these women function as epistolary performances, that they perform – are an '"act" in the theatrical sense as well as a "speech-act" in the linguistic'.[57] I use this theatrical metaphor in the sense that Bruce Redford and David Marshall use it in *Converse of the Pen* and *The Figure of Theater* respectively.[58] That is, as a constructive and imaginative trope about the letter's ability to make absence presence and as a way of articulating the paradox at the heart of authorial agency: the experience of both creating and viewing textual representations of oneself. All of the women in this study were aware of their roles as exemplary women, poetesses, learned ladies, and their acute sense of a watching world, of the spectatorial nature of writing and being written about, manifested itself in highly self-referential prose. As might be expected given their religious preoccupations, they also created elaborate set pieces featuring supporting casts of ghosts, angels and assorted literary characters. Most importantly, these women dwelt on the delights of another world – the hereafter.

Print afterlives

Their preoccupation with futurity and everlasting happiness in heaven meant that Rowe, Cockburn, and Carter were often diffident about acquiring the rewards of success in the here and now, but it also meant that they were particularly concerned about the effect of their works over the long term. Thus my book explores the scope of these writers' literary afterlives. As I have noted, these women identified themselves and each other as the virtuous opposition; however, their exemplarity also meant that beginning with the 'Lives' written by their editors, and continuing with their appearances in catalogues of 'female worthies' and various encomiums, their literary and polemical accomplishments were largely subsumed by their exemplary images. Much of the blame for this has rested on their male eighteenth- and nineteenth-century biographers and editors. In contrast, I argue that by dismissing or ignoring the editorial ethos of these men we lose a crucial ally in our quest to reconstruct the lives and writings of these women of letters.

Compositional genetics are a crucial consideration in the production of a printed volume of letters, likewise the ideological concerns of the (often) male editors, and finally the intellectual interests and relative virtue of the respective authors of the letters. These textual and contextual concerns are all predicated on the perceived integrity of the 'primary utterance' of the author, as evident in surviving manuscript autographs.[59] However, our literary quests after these holy grails of authorial intention and biographical enlightenment have often blinded us, or rather prejudiced us, to the merits of the very editorial process we seek to deconstruct and discredit. In our desire to possess/own our literary inheritance it has become a critical commonplace to disparage eighteenth- and nineteenth-century editors such as Theophilus Rowe, Thomas Birch, and Montagu Pennington (the final editors of Rowe, Cockburn, and Carter respectively). However, I believe that it is possible to find in their editions a recreation of the, admittedly, nebulous textual realities of these women's epistolary careers.

Republic of letters

Finally, it is precisely these editors who helped to recreate and perpetuate these women's status in the republic of letters. Jane Stevenson recently posed the problem: 'When we ask what intellectual women – women writers – could and did achieve in the early modern world, one dimension which has not as yet received much attention is women in the international *Respublica litteratum*.'[60] She likewise points out that '[e]arly modern culture was aware of the existence of a female international republic of letters', and notes the need for more comparative work on European women of letters and their English counterparts in the late sixteenth and seventeenth centuries.[61] Her essay documents a transnational intellectual sphere full of underexplored networks, connections, and collections, and offers tantalising glimpses of the narratives which might be developed regarding women writers in the period. While the present study does not answer Stevenson's call for archival research on sixteenth- and seventeenth-century continental writers and their intellectual correspondence networks, it does seek to illuminate the continuing presence of this epistolary public sphere in Britain in the eighteenth century.[62]

In a volume which does answer, in fact predates, Stevenson's call – the large, interdisciplinary, *Women, Gender and Enlightenment* – it is made clear that the republic of letters is also the crucial discursive space, the network, and 'the media of Enlightenment'. That is, in the words of editors Barbara Taylor and Sarah Knott, the notion that the 'Enlightenment was a living world where ideas were conveyed not only through "high" philosophical works but also through novels, poetry, advice literature, popular theology, journalism, pornography, and that most fluid of eighteenth-century genres, the "miscellaneous essay"'.[63] In this new historicist formulation, the miscellaneous genres of both high and low culture become the cotextual matrix which constitutes an enlightened discursive sphere. Hence,

> to imagine a unitary Enlightenment seems fatuous [...]. Indeed, a focus on the gender element in Enlightenment – where ideas were not just disparate but often directly opposed – underlines the point. Yet when we examine these ideas, their spokespeople and media, on a wide, comparative basis, as this book does, we find not a babel of contending voices but a world of interlocking influences and intellectual exchanges, an international network of advanced minds... Not a monolithic Enlightenment, then, but a powerful movement of innovatory thought and practice whose tributaries and counter-currents demand, and here receive, no less attention than its would-be orthodoxies.[64]

Enlightenment here becomes the continuous negotiation and/or repetition of other voices in a dialogic universe: 'a world of interlocking influences'; 'international networks'; 'tributaries'; 'counter-currents'. More importantly, it is the textual space where the intellectual woman/woman writer/woman of letters comes together with her male counterparts in something resembling the coffee house public sphere.[65]

The republic of letters I refer to in this book is, therefore, an attempt to frame a textual landscape which is more inclusive, and hence less divisive, than the traditional set of binaries with which we tend to frame the material practices of authorship in the period: public/private, manuscript/print, 'real' letter/fictional letter. It is an alternative way of mapping and interpreting the role of epistolary communication and manuscript production in a climate of technological advance and expanding intellectual and literary skills. As Clifford Siskin has shown, the 'new' technology of writing, or the 'work of writing', fundamentally changed those who used it.[66] New forms of mediation make new areas of literary production possible; the republic of letters, as a network or media for a non-unitary Enlightenment, seems to have been a particularly fruitful area for women writers.

Eighteenth-century writers seem to recognise a similar construct. Thomas Birch, when describing Elizabeth Carter, refers to her as 'a very extraordinary Phaenomenon in the Republick of Letters, and justly to be rank'd with the Cornelia's, Sulpicia's, and Hypatia's of the Ancients, and the Schurmans and Daciers of the Moderns'.[67] For Birch, the republic of letters is an intellectual sphere which has a sense of its own tradition (not just the sixteenth- and seventeenth-century heritage to which

Stevenson alludes, but also an ancient one) and membership (here we see him specifically delineate a female, 'lettered' tradition). It is not, in Birch's context, an attempt to capture a political landscape constructed out of particular discursive practices, but a discursive practice which in itself constitutes literary and intellectual endeavour.[68] Birch's quotation also draws attention to the function of the *femme savante* as 'visible totems of national cultural aspirations'.[69] Both Stevenson and, more recently, Karen O'Brien, have noted that, as exemplars and symbolic sites of national pride, women became the litmus test for progressive ideas about the civilising process and, indeed, civilisation.[70] The three women in this study were clearly such totems in their own time; however, in the case studies which follow, I hope it will become even clearer why their exemplarity and literary productions justify a more sustained presence in eighteenth-century studies.

1
Letter-writing, Community, and Virtuous Exemplarity: Elizabeth Rowe's Theatre of Happiness

Elizabeth Singer Rowe (1674–1737) was one of the most lauded and idealised woman writers to appear on the literary scene in the late seventeenth and early eighteenth centuries. Extolled well into the nineteenth century for her piety, virtue, and reclusiveness, Rowe's biographical exemplarity has been the primary legacy of her literary career. Often identified as one of the significant links in a chain of female exemplars, Rowe's role as part of the virtuous opposition – held up in antithesis to the scandalous female writer who wrote for profit and fame – has buried her works under the potentially uninteresting image of the pious and enthusiastic recluse.

Margaret Ezell's work has helped to explain why Rowe and others like her failed to ignite the critical imaginations of twentieth-century feminist literary historians. Recent studies of Rowe have sought to resuscitate her image by distinguishing her as a writer replete with romantic, feminist, and politicised possibilities. Sarah Prescott has argued that Rowe's use of the seduction narrative in her prose works marks her out as a follower of the popular amatory novelist, Eliza Haywood.[71] Sharon Achinstein has found evidence of a latent feminism in Rowe's spiritual expressions, arguing that she used it as a powerful register of female sexuality.[72] More recently, Prescott has noted that 'the accepted image of Rowe obscures the aspects of her authorial persona for which she was initially applauded and brought to public attention: her political and religious affiliations'.[73] She particularly focuses on Rowe's 'whiggish poetic agenda' in her poems published in John Dunton's periodical, *The Athenian Mercury* (1691–1697), and her *Poems on Several Occasions by Philomela* (1696).[74]

The purpose of this chapter is to supplement such work with an account of Rowe's identifiable literary practices and goals as they appear in the manuscript evidence still available to us. A comparison of contemporary transcriptions taken from Rowe's manuscript letters and versions of those letters published in *Friendship in Death, Letters Moral and Entertaining*, and the *Miscellaneous Works* foregrounds the importance of letter-writing and the formative impact it had on her fictional compositions.[75] The comparison also reveals the relative continuity of her moral, religious, and literary concerns across her literary career. Central to my argument is the notion of Rowe as a key figure in the creation of a community of writers dedicated to the reinvigoration of the language of religious devotion and ethical philosophy. Hopefully this approach will help to clarify Rowe's own agency in the construction of her authorial image and her literary works.

Elizabeth Singer

Elizabeth Singer was born on 11 September 1674 in Ilchester, Somerset, to Walter and Elizabeth Singer, née Portnell. Her father was a dissenting minister who had been imprisoned during the reign of Charles II, but later prospered in the wool trade and who, at the time of his death in 1719, could afford to leave Elizabeth substantial property in Frome.[76] From the last decade of the seventeenth century until her death at 62, in 1737, Rowe spent the majority of her time at her father's house in Frome and many of her literary productions were composed and then sent to London from this residence. She lived in London from 1710 to 1715, the years of her brief marriage to Thomas Rowe, but there is almost no record of letters or fictional writings from this period.

The standard description of Rowe's *public*, that is print, productions consists of poetry, published for the most part before 1710, and prose fiction and devotional literature published from 1728 onwards.[77] The major sources for Rowe's poetry and prose are: *Poems on Several Occasions, by Philomela* (1696), published anonymously by John Dunton and compiled by him from poems she submitted to the *Athenian Mercury* from 1693 to 1696; *Divine Hymns and Poems on Several Occasions* (1704); a number of miscellanies, notably Tonson's *Poetical Miscellanies* (5th and 6th parts, 1704, 1709), Matthew Prior's *Poems on Several Occasions* (1709), Pope's edited miscellany for Bernard Lintot, *Poems on Several Occasions*[...] (1717), and Alexander Pope's *Eloisa to Abelard*, 2nd edition (1720); *Friendship in Death, in Twenty Letters from the Dead to the Living* (1728); *Letters on Various Occasions* (1729);[78] *Letters Moral and Entertaining, in Prose and Verse*, in two more parts (1731 and 1733); *The History of Joseph in Eight Books* (1736); *The History of Joseph in Ten*

Books (1737);[79] *Devout Exercises of the Heart* (1738); and, finally, *The Miscellaneous Works in Prose and Verse of Mrs Elizabeth Rowe* (1739). Of these works, the combined volumes of *Friendship in Death* and *Letters Moral and Entertaining* would be reprinted the most over the course of the next century, appearing in over forty editions.[80]

The two most complete biographical studies of Rowe are the 'Life' that prefaces the *Miscellaneous Works*, which was partly written by her old friend, the dissenting minister and academy tutor, Henry Grove, and completed at his death by her brother-in-law, Theophilus Rowe, and Henry F. Stecher's *Elizabeth Singer Rowe, The Poetess of Frome: A Study in Eighteenth-Century Pietism*. There are considerable problems with both accounts. Despite Theophilus Rowe's contention that, 'when you have the history of one week, you have the history of the whole' (*MW*, I: liii), Elizabeth Rowe's life and works are much more idiosyncratic than either study suggests. Theophilus Rowe, to his credit, realised his inadequacies as her biographer and relied almost entirely on a pseudo-biographical construction of her through her familiar letters; many of his quotations about her character are her own protestations and self-deflecting asides written to the Countess of Hertford. Stecher provides an admirably thorough biography, but does not consider some of the manuscript evidence. In particular, he fails to draw attention to the discrepancies between the Alnwick manuscripts (amongst which are manuscript transcriptions of Elizabeth Rowe's letters and poems to the Countess of Hertford) and the letters that appeared in *Letters Moral and Entertaining* and the *Miscellaneous Works*.[81]

Neither biography confronts the confusion that crops up amongst contemporaries regarding Rowe's religious biases or the exact degree of devotional enthusiasm evident in her works. She is alternately labelled an evangelical, a mystic, a prophetess, an enthusiast, and a lover of 'Cant & Nonsense'; appellations she sometimes perpetuates and at other times repudiates, but all of which hail from members of her (mostly Anglican) coterie. Are these just friendly accusations or do they speak to the difficulties contemporaries had with Rowe's ardent style? The documentary evidence is contradictory and inconclusive, and seems to support Jeremy Gregory's observation that, 'it may be misleading to draw too hard and fast a line between nonconformity and conformity in this period, given that it was not unusual to attend both the nonconformist meeting-house and the parish church'.[82]

In 1945 H. Bunker Wright discovered and printed a series of manuscript letters which Matthew Prior sent to the young and single Elizabeth Singer. Bunker Wright characterises the exchange as both gallant flirtation and professional networking, but the letters also contain some hints about her nonconformity and enthusiastic leanings.[83] In one letter from 1703 Prior writes to Singer that, 'You want a quarrel mightily when you tell me I am a high Churchman, & I never knew before that you could like Cant & Nonsense in a Barn, rather than Harmony & reason in a Cathedral, but I have nothing to do with your Religion.'[84] Susan Staves interprets Prior's letter as playful teasing at the expense of Rowe's dissenting affiliations.[85] Rowe's father was, of course, a dissenter, she was a close friend of the 'most prominent representative of Georgian Nonconformity', Isaac Watts, and she was active herself in the Congregationalist church in Frome.[86] Unfortunately, we do not have Rowe's replies, but in other letters Rowe is more generous to writers of various denominations. In a letter to the Countess of Hertford written around 1727 Rowe disavows any bias in favour of the writings of dissenters and praises instead the writings of William Law, the nonjuror.[87] She champions the deist James Thomson against the pious rectitude of her companion, enthuses, albeit ironically, about the writings of Shaftesbury, but also finds great comfort in the corrective works of Bishop Berkeley.[88] She repeatedly denies enthusiastic tendencies and never writes anything that would suggest that she was anything but an orthodox Christian (as dissenters believed themselves to be).

Nevertheless, we can identify Rowe as an 'enthusiast' in many respects. As R.A. Knox identifies it, the term 'Enthusiasm' was used to describe a group who attempted to cultivate a life less worldly and a heart more attuned to the Holy Spirit.[89] In the eyes of many contemporaries (whether Anglican or nonconformist), this is something Rowe epitomised in a very positive sense. It is, however, harder to judge the degree of her enthusiasm when even admirers like Watts accuse her of exhibiting the 'language of the mystical writers' and having an 'evangelical turn' in later life.[90] According to Prior and Watts, and despite the 35 years separating their remarks, Rowe's religious tendencies could verge towards the extreme. However, in her letters to the countess throughout this period, her interest in and acceptance of writers of various religious persuasions suggests that she read authors of different creeds with a catholic acceptance, though with an eye for sentimental affect and persuasive reasoning. Given her wide circle of friends and the popularity of her works, it seems reasonable to assume that many of her contemporary readers approached the issues in a similar matter. Indeed, Watts makes clear in his preface to *Devout Exercises* that the affective nature of Rowe's expressions is precisely what makes them of use to those who find that their own devotions fall short of the inspired ideal.

A point in favour of the Grove/Rowe biography is its distinct unwillingness to categorise Rowe, but the contested nature of the terms they use to describe her religious expressions and habits causes more problems than it solves. A close reading of the contemporary or immediately posthumous records of how Rowe's religion was characterised only affords insights into the elaborate construction of her exemplary image. Stecher, presumably not interested in perpetuating Rowe's image, nor caught up in eighteenth-century poetical-religious language wars, never adequately explores Rowe's remarks on Dissenters, Deists, non-jurors, and Anglicans, or what Dissenters, Deists, non-jurors, and Anglicans had to say in turn about her. Interestingly, he places her within a tradition of German Pietism, finding the Pietist interest in nature and concern for the inner emotional life as a means to religious knowledge perfectly aligned with her personal theology.[91] However, he admits that he is wary of attributing emotional evangelicalism to her and agrees with H.N. Fairchild's assessment that Rowe was much too sentimental to be a mystic.[92]

Stecher is excellent on the subject of Rowe's extensive social and intellectual connections, including those with John Dunton, the Thynne family, Matthew Prior, Bishop Ken, Isaac Watts, and many others. It is this community of writers and public figures which crucially influences Rowe's specific religious, aesthetic, and philosophical reasons for publishing her manuscript works.

Coteries and letters

My discussion of Rowe's works focuses on what I consider the most important aspect of her literary output: her familiar and fictional letters.[93] Rowe's prose works, that is her letters and many of the devotional pieces, far outnumber her poetic appearances in print. She often embedded the poetry she did write within her fictional and familiar letters, which suggests that poetry was an integral part of the composition and exchange of literary letters and not necessarily a separate exercise. Rowe's letters, beginning with *Friendship in Death* (1728), the three parts of *Letters Moral and Entertaining in Prose and Verse* (1729, 1731, 1733), and her familiar letters published in the second volume of her posthumous *Miscellaneous Works* (1739), make up the most voluminous portion of her literary compositions. Her epistolary prolixity has, however, been overlooked as part of a general lack of interest in women's letters as representative of anything other than biographical appendages to the private lives of women.[94] All of the women in this study were prolific letter-writers, and a crucial tool in the construction of their posthumous images was the evidence for virtuous exemplarity found in their familiar letters. In contrast to this retrospective exemplification of their lives through epistolary biography is the contemporary manuscript evidence for their letters as a type of social, literary, and intellectual performance. These performances were then transformed into various published texts, suggesting that the writing of certain kinds of coterie letters was a gesture towards authorial ambition in the wider realm of the republic of letters. Specifically, they were the genre in which Rowe chose to actively and repeatedly publish, whilst her poetic pieces only appear in a few select miscellanies after the early Dunton publication. Thus Rowe's 'agenda', if we can describe it as such, is most likely to be found in the epistolary works which she took such care and interest in submitting to public censure.

A number of critics have surveyed Rowe's epistolary fictions as part of the miscellaneous genres that pre-date the rise of the novel, but they have little to say about her besides the fact that she wrote didactic prose fiction in epistolary form.[95] Likewise, evidence attesting to the popularity of her epistolary works in Britain, Europe, and America throughout the eighteenth and nineteenth centuries has yielded no detailed assessments of the eighteenth-century editing of either her private or fictional letters.[96] The explicit connection between Rowe's autograph missives, addressed to a coterie audience, and her epistolary productions for a wider public escape all but passing comment.[97]

Composition

My research on Alnwick MS 110, a letter book belonging to Frances Thynne Seymour (1699–1754), the last Countess of Hertford, later Duchess of Somerset (1750–4), and one of Rowe's primary correspondents, has yielded new material in relation to the editorial processes underpinning Rowe's works. MS 110 is currently in the private collection of the 12th Duke of Northumberland at Alnwick Castle. Algernon Seymour (1684–1750), Frances Seymour's husband, inherited the Barony of Percy from his mother in 1722, and was afterwards made Earl of Northumberland (1749). The Seymour's only surviving child, Elizabeth, inherited the Barony and her husband became Earl of Northumberland. He was made the first Duke of Northumberland in 1766. In 1754 Elizabeth inherited her mother's library and brought it to Alnwick Castle. MS 110 is one of a number of letter books kept by the countess, though it is the only one dedicated to a single writer, and is bound in handsome green leather with marbled endplates. There is a red-ruled side margin and perfectly aligned writing throughout. There are 373 pages with 159 letters and an index. Helen Sard Hughes, the countess's biographer, identifies the handwriting as Frances Seymour's.

This pre-bound volume consists of letters and verses that the Countess of Hertford transcribed over a number of decades and facilitates a comparison of Hertford's contemporary transcriptions (the closest we have to Rowe's 'original' letters) with those used in Rowe's 'fictional' *Letters* (1729) and the 'biographical' *Miscellaneous Works* (1739). Despite my nominal division of these works as 'fictional' and 'biographical', I hope to show that the categories are not so easily delineated in Rowe's letters. For Rowe, letter-writing was a fundamentally formative literary activity that reinforced her sense of a literary vocation in the republic of letters, and the constant shaping of her material for religious and morally persuasive ends, as well as for fanciful entertainment, prevents any straightforward access to a biographical history of exemplarity in the letters. Nevertheless, Rowe's biography has been the focal point of her literary legacy. The memoir of Rowe included in the *Miscellaneous Works* constructs her in overtly saintly terms and calls on the evidence of her familiar letters as proof of her manifestly exemplary life. However, her brother-in-law was probably closer to the truth than he realised when he noted that 'She could hardly write a familiar letter but it bore the stamp of a poet' (*MW*, I: xv). That is, the ornamental and editorial hand of the poet, for Rowe's letters to the countess and others reveal that she constructed distinct epistolary roles for herself and that these roles changed as her literary interests and aims evolved.

Evidence of this evolution in style can be found in the Alnwick letter book. It appears to have been planned as a posthumous document to Frances Seymour's family's long friendship with Rowe, though it also became a crucial tool in the genesis of *Letters Moral and Entertaining* during both their lifetimes. It begins with letters from Rowe to Hertford's mother, the Honourable Mrs Thynne (née Grace Strode and the 'Cleone' addressed in a number of Anne Finch's poems), in 1697. There are 16 letters to Grace Thynne in the book, four letters to Arabella Marrow, a friend and correspondent of the Thynne family, one to Mrs Nevinson, a dependant of the Thynne family, and the rest to the countess, for a total of 159 letters. Throughout the book, letters are interspersed with Rowe's own poetry, verses she was passing along from others, and latterly the countess's own literary attempts.

What becomes immediately clear when studying the letter book is the presence of the Countess of Hertford (the original recipient of most of the letters) and her editorial principles in the composition of the book. There are numerous notes from Hertford scattered throughout the letters, and around 1725 she begins to edit out names, primarily in cases of gossip or criticism. She also prefaces certain sections of the letter book with an account of what prompted the letters, as, for example, those written after an extended visit between the two in 1725 after the countess's mother had died. The letter book also contains an index to the letters and verses. We know that it became a showpiece for visitors to the countess, including Catherine Talbot in 1753.[98] What is perhaps most interesting is that Rowe herself saw the letter book filled with her letters: Rowe refers to having re-read her letters in the 'Green book', the colour of the leather on the letter book.[99] That the content and arrangement of letters and poetry in Rowe's fictional *Letters Moral and Entertaining* largely follow the pattern of this letter book suggests that Rowe was not only trying to mimic coterie exchange, or even this particular letter book in a print publication, but that she was partly allowing the countess's selection of letters to dictate the tone of the new book (it is clear from the discontinuity between some of the letters that not all her letters to the countess were transcribed into the letter book).

The countess's involvement is important given the frequent charges of enthusiasm levelled at Rowe. With coterie manuscript exchange Rowe was provided with controlled parameters for her fervent religious expressions and romantic fancies. Through the Thynne family at Longleat she enjoyed a receptive and sympathetic audience who, for the most part, shared her religious preoccupations, but also forced her to recognise the necessity of social virtues versus reclusive ones. Thus, the correspondence with the Countess of Hertford is one of the most fascinating examples of the female exemplar negotiating poetic licence and public virtue. Rowe's evocative writings about the moral worth of retreat and the evils of public life are balanced by exhortations to the countess to provide an example of active virtue in the court. Similarly, her awareness of the class and social demands placed upon her worldly reader – the countess – led her to moderate her valorisation of solitary life and her numinous philosophising. In one revealing letter she writes to the countess: 'in the view of the world and a public life, 'tis hardly possible to persuade one's self to be singular; and perhaps it might have an ill effect, and would dress up virtue in too rigid a figure' (*MW*, II: 67, Letter XXVII). And while she would continue to perform a 'singular' role herself, she seems to have been aware that her license for doing so was her adherence to an aristocratic legacy of private coterie exchange.[100]

'Private' coterie exchange was anything but private and sticking to manuscript circulation did not necessarily preclude a public reputation.[101] Rowe's works were already in wide circulation before her marriage in 1710 and writers such as Matthew Prior and Isaac Watts were praising her unpublished poetry in their own publications. Later Alexander Pope must have seen a manuscript version of her 'Death of Thomas Rowe': he included it in his 1717 *Miscellany* and in the second edition of his *Eloisa to Abelard* (1720), constituting, in Germaine Greer's mind, the 'sincerest compliment he ever paid to a woman.'[102] But poetry was not the only writing being transcribed and passed around. Rowe's letters were equally popular literary specimens of her romantic but pious style, and the letter book charts the gradual emergence of her dominant themes of friendship, learning, retreat, and apparently enthusiastic piety.

While the three-part *Letters Moral and Entertaining* and the *Miscellaneous Works* portray an author preoccupied to the extreme with virtuous renunciation in life, the horrors of death, and the rewards of heaven, the Alnwick letter book reveals this obsession as an aspect of a carefully constructed persona. This is not meant to discount the personal experience of her young husband's death in 1715; rather, the letters clearly show a conscious literary transformation and not an enthusiastic outpouring. Her early letters (those not included in the *Miscellaneous Works*) reveal the traditional epistolary tropes of the letter as a stop-gap enterprise in friendly conversation, 'written to the moment' and highly reminiscent of Madame de Sévigné's anecdotal brilliance.[103] Her later letters become the stuff of fiction, because by the 1720s it is clear that Rowe has found a new voice, and it is distinctly otherworldly.

In her earlier letters, especially those addressed to Grace Thynne, we read gossipy entertainment in the form of judgements passed on aristocratic women visiting Longleat, or, as Richardson's Pamela does, she often recites what she was doing just before writing the letter, what she looks like while writing the letter, and what she is going to do as soon as she seals the letter. As an example of her earlier style, this letter, from 1697, is representative. Addressed to Grace Thynne, it has never appeared in print.

> tis 9 of the clock now [...] but I shall be so Impertinent as to goe on wth my Story whether you'll hear me or not. and to be Short here was yesterday the old lady How[104] and the young Lady who made a Shift to pass away the afternoon in no less pleasant then profitable remarks on fanns & gloves & the indispensable nessisity

of Tags & tyeing hoods close to ones chin this hot weather (wch by the way your Ld^{shp} may observe is the fashion) but my Lady H[ow] was So troublesome & serious in her trifling formalitys, y^t were all conversation burthen'd with so much ceremony I'de leave the Impertinent world and pass my Days in a cell – what a reflection tis on the conduct of Humane life that the greatest part of the world should conspire to make such adoe about nothing [...] I must goe to prayers for I was not there yesterday. now enter Mrs Judy bcause [sic] I have nothing else to tell ye (madam) this morning you shall have her caracter[105] – she's servilely officious & careful to please, fond of fine shows & fine Ladys, has a world of intimate particular friends and loves them all to the height of extasie and having a mind conscious of no real worth values her self upon the smiles & little favours of the great on whom (with her fellow fools she fawns most slavishly while with

> A heart that's nobly true
> At all those little arts I laugh
> That doe the world subdue

I left off just here yesterday, & am as good as my word to vissit y^r Ld^{shp} every morning tho I can't stay now for I am just a going into the garden which is the most ravishing place in the world & where I undisturbed shall injoy the most friendly & pleasing thoughts of you

> And thus we shall no absence know
> nor shall we be confin'd
> our active souls will daily goe
> to learn each others mind

madam it is now 12 o'clock at night & I am just come to my chamber but so sick I can hardly hold my pen therefore can't as I design'd enlarge and to morrow morning I have ordered to be sent for home I am loath to conclude so abruptly but could your Ld^{shp} see how dismall & like a lover I look you'd excuse

> y^r obliged humble servant
> Philomela (MS 110, Letter 3, ff. 8–11)

Three key features of this letter are the performance of breathless social conversation, the promotion of platonic ideals of friendship, and the importance of her early poetic persona 'Philomela' to her early epistolary self-construction. There is also little evidence of the religious fervour that characterises her later writings, though contempt of worldliness is certainly there. The two poetic excerpts she includes are both from Katherine Philips: 'A Country Life' and 'To Mrs. Mary Awbrey at parting'.[106] The inclusion of these extracts is revealing, given that nowhere in any of her published writings is there any mention of her admiration for Philips, though there is clear evidence of borrowing by Rowe in poems that appeared in *Poems on Several Occasions by Philomela*. 'Platonick Love', which originally appeared in the *Athenian Mercury* on 24 December 1695, touches on a number of Philips's favourite themes and images, but also shows significant similarities with Philips's poem, 'Friendship'. In stark contrast is this next letter written in 1717, after the death of her husband, and again addressed to Grace Thynne.

> My letters ought to be call'd Epistles from the Dead to the Living for I know nothing relating to this world to entertain my surviving Freinds with nor are People very fond of keeping Correspondences with Ghosts and Phantoms, or receiving Intelligencys from another world, and as there are no Shades in these Desolate Regions, of greater Consequence than my self nothing happens remarkable enough to bear a recital; when I was alive I never was very fond of talking of my self But being the greatest novelty in this place I am now forc'd upon the Subject for want of som'thing more considerable, if I had liv'd among mortals I shou'd certainly have known how to direct to L^{dy} Brooke[107] but being in a state but [sic] being in a state of seperate Existence this ignorance is excusable & whether I am Dead or alive I am always y^r most faithful. (MS 110, Letter 13, f. 64)

The insistent self-styling of the second letter reappears in various guises throughout Rowe's letters for the next twenty years and represents the bulk of what Theophilus Rowe quotes from in the 'Life' as biographical evidence of her enthusiastic and pious mind. This ghostly persona that the older Rowe adopted and then performed for her admiring circle of friends is an intentional literary act. Though there is sincere religious conviction behind her work, Rowe frequently reassures the countess that she is only trying to elicit sentimental reactions from her reader, rather than convey expressions of her own heart and mind. For the most part these revelations are left out of the letters in the *Miscellaneous Works*. One clear example of this is in the following letter, written some time after 1729, and addressed to the Countess of Hertford.

> [Y]ou will pardon me Madam for copying the following Petition, Since 'tis by no means to Impose a form of prayer on you, or out of an affectation of being thought better than I realy am. To keep you from that mistak, I assure you 'tis rather a flight of Fancy than Sincere Devotion; tis more the Language of my Imagination than of my Heart. (MS 110, Letter 117, f. 262, mispaginated as 261)

There are numerous other examples of this sort where Rowe specifically notes the fact that she is imitating a sentiment or style that she thinks will evoke an emotional response, and this aim is important when considering the apparent religious enthusiasm conveyed in her familiar letters.

Comments about the revision of her poetry, awareness of her own elevated style, and of others' construction of her retreat are plentiful in MS 110. Letter 33, addressed to the countess, reveals Rowe's authorial self-doubt.

> I wish the Pope wou'd conffer some of his infallibility upon me that I might make an unerring judg'ment of my self tho' I believe such a judg'ment wou'd not raise my vanity for on cool and reasonable reflection I condemn one hour what I admir'd just before I write about six lines to his Holiness and think them the most bright the most Surprising & Harmonious Verses that ever were writt that they are worthy of Apollo himself and never to be excell'd, I read them with Approbation and Rapture And do my self the highest justice; till on a more deliberate view I sink from the Height of my Elevation and grow exceeding humble to find every line Dull and impertinent, and how many Essays I shall make before I am satisfy'd is yet uncertain. (MS 110, Letter 33, ff. 111–12)

On the theme of her elevated style she mockingly writes, 'you know my penetration is always on the extreme, either it falls Short, or goes beyond the reason and nature of things and was perhaps ungrounded whimsy' (MS 110, Letter 118, f. 264). Likewise, after a particularly melancholy passage and poem Rowe acknowledges, 'This may perhaps be all the Effect of the Spleen and a gloomy turn of Thought, I wish it may, but I am so Capable of every Sort of folly & inadvertency, that I have just reason to suspect my Self' (MS 110, Letter 78, f. 191).

Letter 23 reveals her acute consciousness of how idiosyncratic her ways may appear to the world:

> Y^r Sentiments are certainly just that tis more glorious to Despise the World in the midst of all its gay Temptations than to gain the Victory by a Cowardly flight, but as {Wolf} says I am only a meer Mortall & can't pretend to those Celestial Heights of Vertue however if I had happen'd to have been a Roman Catholick I might have got Perhaps the Reputation of a Saint by this Retreat but being of a more reasonable Religion People will sooner Impute my Retirement to Distraction than Devotion. (MS 110, f. 85)[108]

Rowe was well aware of the extremes of her style, but she continued to utilise those excessive elements precisely because they did provoke a strong response from the countess. Her knowledge of her reader's responses then helped her shape the letters she would use in her fictional works to maximise the sentimental impact.

Editing

Letters (1729) was the sequel to *Friendship in Death* (1728) and appeared with the full title, *Letters on Various Occasions, in Prose and Verse, from the author of Friendship in Death. To which is added Ten Letters by another hand*. Those ten letters were by the Countess of Hertford under the pen name Cleora. Two subsequent volumes came out in 1731 and 1733, now entitled *Letters Moral and Entertaining*, and Hertford had unattributed contributions in both.[109] The most interesting exchange, however, is in the eight letters addressed to Cleora in the 1729 volume, as these letters are all culled directly from the letter book and give us a rare opportunity to see the editorial emendations Rowe made to her own letters.

As we might expect, Rowe edits out names, or, in some cases of scandal, changes the sex. The printed edition also contains numerous changes to accidentals that were probably made by the compositor at the printing house. However, her most significant change to the countess's copy of the letters is her selective transcription of almost all her letters, and her rearrangement of them into more coherent and consistent narratives. What these relatively minor adaptations signal is how little Rowe actually needed to expunge from the letters, and how fluid a transition it was to the printed page.

This next letter (made up of two letters), written to the countess some time between 1725 and 1728, is one Rowe edited and included in the

Letters (1729). Here is part of the edited version: "'Tis certainly better for your self, and more the Security of Mankind, that you should live in some rural Abode, than appear in the World; such Persons as you are fatal to the Publick Tranquillity, and do Mischief without ever designing it.'[110] In the original letter what follows this opening is more personal information in which Rowe discusses the real reason Hertford is in the country: she is recovering from an illness. So the opening flourish about the virtue of her retirement is thinly disguised flattery and consolation for the countess. The manuscript version then discusses a letter that she is transcribing from one of the countess's friends (Miss St. John), one of the countess's translation attempts, and the love affairs of an unnamed man.

This is very different from the published version which continues through many more paragraphs on the virtues of removing oneself from ambitious mankind. In the published version, Rowe fuses part of another letter written in the late 1720s as well, so that it continues in the same vein: 'But I must own when Belles and Beaux retire to Country Shades for the sake of heavenly Contemplation, the World will be well reformed.' She goes on to contrast the 'fantastick' and fleeting amusements Cleora would enjoy at Hyde Park and the Opera with that of 'sweet solitude' and retirement. She also quotes an excerpt from Thomas Tickell's poem, 'On the Prospect of Peace' – incidentally a poem which supported the Tory policy of peace and features an encomium to Queen Anne in almost every stanza, but in which Rowe manages to find the one passage dedicated to theology: one about the hereafter promised to the virtuous who have taken the time to contemplate heaven in solitude.[111]

Both versions of the letter end in the same way, with Rowe declaring that, 'Without any Apology, I am going to talk to myself', and continues with the acknowledgement that 'what follows may properly be called a Digression'. The digression begins with an apostrophe: 'Let me lose the Remembrance of this busy world, and hear no more of it's distracting tumults! Ye vain Grandeurs of the Earth! Ye perishing riches and fantastick pleasures, what are your deluding boasts?' (*Letters* (1729), Letter I, 141). The address continues for another page, finally ending with the observation that, 'In the height of this romantick insult, I am, Madam, Your most obliged Humble Servant.' Surely this is the 'aside' of an author aware of her performance persona.

In comparing the two versions of the letter(s), the only significant changes are the excised personal details about the countess's illness, Miss St. John's letter, and the unknown Mr ---'s love life. In place of such private details the inserted passage from the second letter expands on her usual reclusive ideals, and exhorts the reader to consider the usefulness of retirement in preparing one's mind for death. Thus the published letter appears to be a sustained discourse on the virtue of retirement, rather than the discontinuous narrative of the original. Which is not to say that the version which contains the information about the Countess of Hertford's ill-health lacks coherence, in some respects it is more engaging; rather the message is less emphatic than in the published version. What this suggests is that Rowe tuned her public works to a higher pitch, and thus the pietistic repetitiveness that we find so often in the *Letters* (1729) was probably a conscious editorial and literary choice.

The comparison of the manuscript and printed works reveal that the surface impression conveyed by Rowe's public 'fictions' of a high-note operatic diva, straining to achieve the ecstatic aria with every performance, is close to Rowe's aesthetic aim. Knowledge of her audience's susceptibilities through her coterie responses meant that Rowe knew her target and, in her professional literary guise, she never varied the performance. As a result, she appears less artful or rhetorically sophisticated when trying to appeal to a general readership than when she wrote to her coterie correspondents. This is not to imply that she was less in control artistically in her published works; on the contrary she was never more so, but the unvaried tune of the printed works hides the intellectual subtleties that are nevertheless present. For Rowe did not confine herself purely to the sublime and the beautiful in her published works, and her manuscripts demonstrate that she was continually transposing the ideas culled from her extensive reading onto the pages of her familiar and fictional letters. Her appropriation of contemporary as well as ancient philosophical and religious arguments transforms her letters into creative vehicles of intellectual exchange and represents her attempt to engage with the wider republic of letters. In order to gauge her success at combining learning with sentimental fantasy, however, I want to look at her contextual links with the writers who dealt with the philosophical and spiritual problems she explored. These contexts help to reveal the extent of the intellectual investments behind her epistolary productions.

Contemporary contexts

In 1726 Rowe sent a letter to the Countess of Hertford which claimed that 'at this rate my letters will deserve to be call'd memoirs of Literature and save you the trouble of reading the works of the learned'.[112] *Memoirs of Literature* was the title of a contemporary literary journal that reported in English on the activities of continental scholars.[113] Rowe clearly, if somewhat mockingly, saw her epistolary writings as part of 'the works of the learned' and not just polite missives between absent friends. Indeed, the familiar letters reveal that Rowe was an avid reader and her critical and literary responses to the texts she read and shared among her friends is part of the enduring interest of her letters. They highlight Rowe's influences, appropriations, misreadings, and simplifications of contemporary philosophical and literary debates, but also her iconoclasm within the conventional genres of religious writing.

Many of the themes Rowe explored in her familiar and fictional letters were dominant topics of intellectual discourse in the seventeenth and eighteenth centuries. Discussions of the degeneracy of modern times and the efficacy of friendship and retirement are to be found in the works of prominent male writers of the period, but Rowe's interest in these popular literary discourses has tended to deflect attention away from her forays into the more weighty polemical fields of theology and philosophy. Her emphasis on the former topics only partly explains why the more interesting elements of her spiritual philosophy and religious convictions have been neglected. The unsystematic nature of Rowe's epistemological attempts often obscures the fact that she deploys a philosophical understanding richly informed by continental and English philosophers, and one which contemporary learned readers could readily identify.[114]

Rowe had access to books, tutorials, and discussions unavailable to many of her female contemporaries. Henry Thynne, her patron's son, taught her French and Italian; the ousted Bishop Ken proposed poetic projects, possibly lent her books, and seems to have sparked her interest in theological subjects. She had access to the library at Longleat in her youth and borrowed many books from the countess in later years. Thomas Rowe, her husband, had an impressive library which Elizabeth inherited at his death, and the 'Life' of Rowe prefacing the *Miscellaneous Works* tells of the many late night study sessions she shared with her scientifically minded sister. The weight of all this reading is evident on a number of levels in her productions and Rowe's relish for the philosophical, theological, poetic, dramatic, and historical works of others provided the all-important context in which her compositions could appear to best advantage.

In the letters of the Alnwick letter book and the *Miscellaneous Works* she frequently mentions the books she is reading, what the 'world' is reading (often in contrast to herself), and, every once in a while, her opinions of or responses to those texts. Many of the usual suspects are there: Addison, Baxter, Blackmore, Burnet, Cowley, Hervey, Law, Milton, Norris, Pope, Prior, Shakespeare, the *Spectator*, Thomson, Watts, and Young. There are also less well-known poets, such as Tickell, Pitt, Lansdowne, Grove, and even a youthful attempt by Thomas Birch (the eighteenth-century scholar who figures prominently in later chapters). She singles out various sermon collections: Charnock's, Watts's, and the French sermons of Saurin, and, like many eighteenth-century readers, she was interested in lives and read, among others, those of the Countess of Warwick and André Rivet.[115]

There are also a few surprises, most noticeably in the number of plays she read despite her professed aversion to public performances of them. Rowe's *Jane Grey* is frequently cited as a favourite, but she also records having read Molière's *Misanthrope*, some 'Italian tragedies', Shakespeare's *Henry V*, Vanbrugh-Cibber's *The Provok'd Husband*, Gay's *Beggar's Opera*, Addison's *Cato*, Thomson's *Sophonisba* (which she prefers to *Cato*), and Fielding's *The Modern Husband*. Perhaps as a possible corrective she also extols William Law's treatise against plays for its 'witt and piety.'[116]

She is, unsurprisingly, interested in religious and philosophical texts, amongst which are a number of obscure titles as well as famous names. Berkeley's *Alciphron*, Burnet, Fénelon, the Greek Fathers, Pascal, Rapin, Seneca, Shaftesbury's *The Moralists*, and Sylvester's translations of Du Bartas are all mentioned with approval. One of the few women writers extolled in her letters is the French moralist, Madame de Lambert. On the other hand she is very disparaging about Swift's *Gulliver's Travels* (which she claims only to have read an excerpt from, though she seems to know a lot of key points in it).

In most instances, the mention of a writer or book sparks no more than a brief note of recommendation, or a lengthy quotation from the text in question, but the works of these male philosophers, poets, and divines also inspired Rowe to compose verses or letters based upon the ideas she had drawn from their writings. Attributing Rowe's poetry and prose to innate or 'natural' poetic genius, as Theophilus does, diminishes her studied engagement with and investment in contemporary intellectual concerns.[117] Rowe was a conscientious reader who interpreted and deployed the texts she read in a historically unique way; therefore, despite lacking wholly original ideas, Rowe's works intersect with the ideas of their parent texts in imaginative ways.

Rowe's reading and poetic interpretation of Shaftesbury's *The Moralists* provides an informative case study for the way she used contemporary philosophy to bolster her own spiritual polemics. Anthony Ashley Cooper, third Earl of Shaftesbury (1671–1713), was a moral and aesthetic philosopher whose works, particularly those comprising *Characteristicks of Men, Manners, Opinions, Times* (1711, revised 1714), attracted vigorous critique, ridicule, and imitation throughout the eighteenth century. Polemicists as varied as Mary Astell, Bernard Mandeville, George Berkeley, and Joseph Butler mounted spirited attacks against Shaftesbury; at the same time, poets such as Rowe, Alexander Pope, James Thomson, and Mark Akenside imitated his influential style. According to Isabel Rivers, Shaftesbury's popular 'moral vocabulary' was a 'very carefully calculated' 'mixture of philosophy and rhapsody, reason and enthusiasm, the scholastic and the polite, the didactic and the poetic'.[118] Such a vocabulary can be seen at work in Rowe's letters where she often shows a conscious awareness of philosophical versus numinous language. A comparison of the diction deployed in poems written before she read *The Moralists* with that in poems and letters written after her encounter with his language and ideas, reveals a definite change in Rowe's poetic arsenal.

For example, 'An Epistle to a Friend. Written in the Spring, 1710', displays the political bias which made the young Elizabeth Singer so popular as a Whig poet.[119] The 181-line poem begins with a paean to Anne, whose 'conqu'ring arms/ Fill pow'rful guilt with just alarms' and will 'bless the jarring world with peace' (*MW*, II: 266, ll.1–2, 4). It then segues into an unrequited love poem, with the male poet-speaker lamenting his state to his friend Daphnis. Daphnis, it transpires, has the love of Strephon, but he in turn is loved by Delia, the poet-speaker's object of affection. In the course of praising his friendship with Daphnis and proposing what poetic feats his muse could reach if he enjoyed Delia's love, the poet-speaker comes full circle back to eulogising the Queen as well as the Duke of Marlborough. As the characters' names suggest, the diction comprises pastoral delights – rural retreats, young love, and invocations to the classical muse – but as with earlier cavalier poetry there is a strong undercurrent of political instability. The speaker hopes that 'when the black storms blow o'er' (l. 167), 'And wars and tumults are no more' (l. 169), he 'With new-born strength shall dare to rise' (l. 174) 'And sing the Hero and the Queen' (l. 177).

In contrast to the early political poetry, Rowe's later works clearly evince her interest in Shaftesburyan moral philosophy. However, despite her extensive reading, Rowe significantly narrows her intellectual compass when she attempts to confine philosophy, or, perhaps more accurately, ethics and aesthetics, to rhyming couplets. In the

'Poem ocasion'd [sic] by reading a Discourse of Lord Shaftsbury's Call'd the Moralist', Rowe extracts Shaftesbury's descriptive phrases that aid lyrical rhapsody, but fails to engage at all with issues of religion and virtue, ethics and aesthetics, and certainly not his controversial freethinking. Instead she spends 38 lines wandering in 'Ye Groves and Woods', tracing the sacred connections between God and the natural world. Her pastoral description of 'The Silent Vall'y, and the Lonely Grove' is evocative language for impressing the divinity of created nature, but its status as a real work of Shaftesburyan soliloquy is tenuous. Shaftesbury's all important 'return ticket' is noticeably missing from the end of her poem:[120]

> Ador'd artificer! What skill divine!
> What wonders in the wide creation shine!
> Order and majesty adorn the whole,
> Beauty and life, and thou th'inspiring soul.
> Whatever grace or harmony's express'd
> On all thy works, the God is there confess'd.
> But oh! from all thy works how small a part,
> To human minds is known of what thou art!
> Fancy gives o'er its flight in search of thee;
> Our thoughts are lost in thy immensity. (*Letters* (1729), 62-3)

Though Rowe ostensibly sets up a scene of enthusiastic soliloquy, she confines it to a pastoral and revelatory version of divine communion and her narrator never comes down from his/her apostrophising heights. A comparison of her poem with Theocles' rhapsody in part three, section one of *The Moralists* further levels Rowe's poem to the status of uninspired poetic imitation, as the poetic phrasing is lifted directly from Shaftesbury's numbered prose.[121] Rivers confirms that most contemporary readers who were 'friendly' to Shaftesbury's writings 'seem either to have read selectively or not to have been disturbed by the complexities of Shaftesbury's method and the tensions in his argument', and that they 'took from him what they wanted, whether ideas, language or style, without allowing this to come into conflict with their own religious views'.[122] It would appear that Rowe chose to focus almost exclusively on the providential aspect of Shaftesbury's natural description rather than issues of morality and virtue despite her own interest in precisely these aspects of philosophy.[123]

However, this poem had two incarnations, and the contextual apparatus Rowe provides with each one significantly alters potential readings.

In the Alnwick letter book the poem is identified as 'A Poem ocasion'd [sic] by reading a Discourse of Lord Shaftsbury's Call'd the Moralist', and is transcribed along with two other poetic pieces independent from any letters.[124] In the letter to the countess that follows the three pieces, Rowe refers, in a somewhat self-mocking vein, to her delight in Shaftesbury's work and her intention of turning 'enthusiast'. Here the poem suggests the derivative tendencies noted above, and Rowe's equivocal/conciliatory remarks to the countess do nothing to enhance the philosophical purport of the verse. Rowe writes:

> My thoughts are not at present entirely consistent. _ I have been reading my Lord *Shaftsbury's Moralist*, which has fill'd my head with beauties, and love, and harmony, but all of a divine and mysterious nature. However superior his notions may be to my capacity, I have been agreeably led on thro' I know not what enchanting scenes of happiness. I wish you would read it, for it would make you the most charming and agreeable enthusiast in the world. (*MW*, II: 41)

While this quotation suggests Rowe's propensity for culling affecting language and themes from the texts she read, there is no suggestion that she is in any way alert to the inconsistencies and ironies in Shaftesbury's work.

In *Letters* (1729) the poem appears without the identifying title and is inserted near the end of Letter XI, ostensibly a missive from a retired statesman to another Lord. His letter descants on the merits of retirement from public life and the poem is presented just before the end of the letter as one of his poetic exercises in soliloquizing the 'great Spirit of Nature' (98). The letter begins, however, with the statesman describing how retirement has led to his romantic and dramatic rediscovery of selfhood. The statesman writes:

> 'Tis well I have your gracious Indulgence to talk of my self, and be the Hero of my own Romance; for without Vanity I meet nothing here more considerable, nor is it without Justice, that I claim the Privilege of personating the superior Part in the Dramma [sic].
>
> Indeed I was never more sensible of my own Dignity; abstract from Business or Diversion, my Mind retires within it self, where it finds Treasures till now undiscover'd. (91–2)

Here Rowe recycles lines from another one of her own letters, but the crux of the passage is the statesman's acknowledgement of his role as both spectator and actor in the assessment and performance of the inner self.[125] David Marshall has discussed a similar 'figure of theater' in Shaftesbury where:

> the play of characters created by a view of the self as a persona, a role, or a representation... can display or conceal or counterfeit the signs of inner feeling. Theater... represents, creates, and responds to uncertainties about how to constitute, maintain, and represent a stable and authentic self; fears about exposing one's character before the world; and epistemological dilemmas about knowing or being known by other people.[126]

Marshall's imaginative thesis about the theatrical trope's ability to conceal and reveal the writing subject squares perfectly with Rowe's performative techniques in her epistolary fictions and familiar letters. The confusion of public and private, intention and performance are manifested in the statesman's remark that he knows he is 'the Hero of [his] own romance', and Rowe's private acknowledgement that 'I perceive I am the Heroine of this Epistle' (MS 110, Letter 33, f. 112).

In Letter XI and her private letters, Rowe's acute awareness of being read and put on display and therefore being judged enables a construction of a performing other. Thus, whether in a private or public epistle, the author/subject/actor of each letter is forced to vacillate between apparent self-revelation and a pessimistic distrust of their addressee's constructions of such revelations. For example, the statesman, after expressing his new-found delight in thoughts of immortality, acknowledges his addressee with:

> You smile, I know, and take this for an imaginary Triumph... You will tell me, this Contempt of Grandeur appears with an ill Grace, in one that has the Possession of a splendid Post in the Government: But this, my Lord, is what has given me a just Opinion of the World, and of my self. (93)

After this acknowledgement of his reader's potential scepticism he pauses and asks, 'Why am I not at Rest?' The rhetorical question is a preface to a narrative of his past selves (we know that he is, at the time of writing this letter, at rest), and it forces the reader to witness the subject's various transformations, from disgust with the human condition: 'Had I these reflecting Powers to make me thus nicely miserable?'; to satiated apathy: 'The yielding Beauty, by granting my Desires, lost my Esteem.... This put a Period to my Gallantries'; to recycled hopes and desires: 'Distinction and Power, Titles and Equipage, now employ'd my Thoughts: Ambition took full Possession of my Soul'; and back again to despair: 'I reach'd the envy'd Height, and made my self gloriously miserable' (94–6).

Rowe takes the narrative of the self one step further and makes the statesman re-enact his epiphanic moment. He writes that he retired to his apartment to try and contemplate the joys of his titles and grandeur. The font style then switches to italics and the statesman delivers a rousing monologue.

> *The most Noble! --- The Right Honourable! --- Ye potent Words!* I cry'd, *Where is your Energy! --- Ye mighty Sounds! that once fir'd my Soul, where is your accustomed Force? Have ye no pleasing Magick to still the Tempest within?*[...] *While I am surrounded with the Pageantries of State, and see so many Badges of my own Dignity, why does not my Mind elate it self, and brighten into Extasy?* (96–7)

The statesman's inability to find solace in the dignities of state then leads him to a 'romantick Retreat, surrounded with a charming Variety of Woods [...]. Here I rove unattended and free, with no Circumstance of Grandeur, but the Consciousness of a reasonable and immortal Being' (98). Rowe, on the last two pages of the letter, pits male grandeur and language – the 'potent words' that he delivers in his self-involved performance of subjective angst – against a non-gendered world of pastoral beauty, conscientious politeness, and enthusiasm directed outside of the self. Here at last she lets loose a Shaftesburyan soliloquy and its outwardly focused language offers a welcome contrast to the tortured monologue that came before. Verse that seemed heavily derivative on its own suddenly appears light, even elegant, after the loaded language of the letter. 'From mortals flying', the poet fleetingly searches out the divinity immanent in grove, valley, stream, flower, birdsong, stars, and sun, and though the poem is riddled with exclamations and apostrophes to God, the speed at which the images overtake one another prevents the verse from getting weighed down at each ejaculation.

Rowe even manages to bring her poet out of his reverie and closes the letter in a composed manner. Concluding the letter in rational prose suggests that she understood Shaftesbury's view of enthusiasm as one where the 'actual apprehension of the Divine' is achieved through imagination *controlled by reason*. After all, the statesman's prefatory note to the soliloquy avers:

> I have try'd what Delights were to be found in Madness and Folly, and am now in pursuit of what Wisdom and Philosophy can yield. In the fair Creation I trace an Almighty Power, and see the immense Divinity impress'd on all his Works. Inspir'd with a charming Enthusiasm, I address the great Spirit of Nature in these soliloquies. (98)

Rowe's well-crafted performance of a modern statesman torn between worldliness and otherworldliness successively grasps Shaftesbury's 'divided' language of philosophy and polite culture, and, though there is still a hint of uncontrolled revelatory imagination, Rowe's various comments on enthusiasm and religious controversy almost always disclaim her total susceptibility to their charms.[127]

Shaftesbury was not the only philosopher whose works Rowe mined. One of her favourite authors and an important influence on her writings was the polymath, Blaise Pascal (1623–62). In detailing the various ways Rowe deployed Pascal's language and ideas in her works, I intend to show how she used Pascal as a convenient textual link with current philosophical and religious debates. Moreover, the claim Pascal made for the subjective self as realised through religion has significant repercussions in Rowe's epistolary styling. Rowe's affinity for Pascal is indicative of her belief that the self-reflexive nature of personal thoughts/*pensées* was a valid mode for literary and philosophical expression. Or, simply, that meditating on religious themes was a way of being intellectually perspicacious.

John Barker, in his 1975 monograph tracing Pascal's influence on English writers during the seventeenth and eighteenth centuries, calls attention to Rowe's appropriation of Pascalian language and ideas. He notes her use of Pascal to '[give] focus and an improved literary form to her rather pedestrian sentiments', going on to remark that many of her shorter pieces are simply extended quotations from the *Pensées*.[128] Though he is correct to note Rowe's habit of including long passages lifted from other writers, Barker's overall dismissal of her writings as unliterary and pedestrian is peremptory and overly biased against works of 'popular piety'. Understandably, he is more interested in the serious polemical discourses in Pascal's controversial Port Royal treatises and this necessitates sidelining a popular fiction writer from the list of earnest intellectuals engaging with Pascal's works. However, he fails to consider that Rowe may have been trying to engage in just such discourses through her pointed use of quotations from Pascal. Despite describing the *Pensées* as Pascal's apology for the Christian religion – written as a specific challenge to free-thinkers – he fails to recognise that Rowe's epistolary fictions had exactly the same aim.[129] Rowe lived in constant fear of the decline of religion and spirituality in the polite world, and her envisioned readers were clearly the educated, and, as she believed free-thinking, members of the upper classes, familiar with modern languages (she quotes Pascal in the original French) and a wide range of literature. Barker even notes that, '[a]lthough for several years the *Pensées* were available only in French, the reader able to comprehend the originality of the work and the precise method of reasoning employed by the author was likely to recognise in it, for all its unfinished state, a discussion of matters of intellectual and religious belief carried through in a peculiarly congenial and forceful manner.'[130] Instead of relegating her works to the lesser circles of 'popular' devotional literature on the periphery of intellectual debate, her participation in this discourse should be seen as an attempt to disseminate Pascalian ideas to an educated and polite English readership.

The passages from the *Pensées* Rowe quotes are generally the same ones Barker highlights as the popular choices of polemical, male seventeenth- and eighteenth-century writers, and it was possibly early male mentors who introduced Rowe to the writings of Pascal. Barker notes that among many Church of England men, including Bishop Ken, there was an interest in works stemming from the Port Royal controversy. Ken's library at Longleat held a number of Pascal's and other Port Royal writers' works. Of Pascal's works Barker claims that, in particular, the *Lettres Provinciales* contributed substantially to the 'vigour' of seventeenth-century Protestantism.[131] Ken had considerable influence on Rowe's early education and choice of poetic topics: he is credited with recommending that Rowe turn her attention to Biblical paraphrases. Barker also records Matthew Prior as possessing copies of the *Pensées* and *Lettres Provinciales* and states that Pascal's influence is evident in *Solomon on the Vanity of the World* (1708), a poem Rowe responded to with commendatory verses.[132] During the first part of the eighteenth century Rowe's exact contemporary, Basil Kennet (1674–1715), produced his English translation of Pascal's *Pensées*, entitled *Thoughts on Religion, and other Curious Subjects. Written Originally in French By Monsieur Pascal* (1704, second edition 1727).[133] Kennet's elevation of Pascal's merits over those of the ancients is carried on by Rowe (she often refers to Stoic maxims, but always prefers Christian ones), and the combination of 'the philosophical mind joined to a Christian disposition' foregrounded by Kennet is very similar to Rowe's use of Pascal.[134] Rowe even attached a translation of Port Royal writings to her first prose publication: *Friendship in Death...To which are added, Thoughts on Death, Translated from the Moral Essays of the Messieurs du Port Royal* (1728).

Quotations from Pascal crop up throughout Rowe's letters: in *Letters* (1729), in the *Miscellaneous Works* (1739), and in the Alnwick letter book. One popular passage which Rowe utilises is that of the wager, in which Pascal argues that it is better to believe in immortality on the chance that you can win eternal happiness, as opposed to not believing and risking eternal damnation. In the second volume of the *Miscellaneous Works*, the 'real' letters are prefaced by two 'Letters under fictitious names'. Letter I, addressed to an unknown man-about-town from his pious friend, Carlos, reproduces Pascal's gaming table wager. Carlos writes:

> WHAT advantage can you men of pleasure propose, in divesting yourselves and the rest of mankind of this privilege of immortality? The prospect perhaps of a future hell may molest your tranquillity: But after all, will confidence and raillery lessen its certainty? Are you arriv'd at a demonstration that there are no burning lakes to punish the vitious, nor celestial crowns to reward the virtuous? Are your principles grounded on unquestionable evidence? Or do you pretend to no more than an equal *hazard* that things may, or may not be as you wish them? Grant but this, and there is no excuse for your extravagance. Were a future state but a mere possibility, 'twere madness to *stake* infinite ages of bliss against the *pleasures* of a day: Even that short time is more than you can *secure*; you are altogether uncertain of the next moment's fruition of these trifles you value so much for being what you call visible and present; and of this you are as uncertain, as you think the pious man is of all his visionary hopes and fancy'd paradise. [...] And if religion is a delusion, 'tis the most lasting and fortunate one in the world. But if there are indeed fields of bliss and shades of love, infinite pleasures and immortal day, you men of the world will find you have made a *fatal bargain*. (*MW*, II: 17–18. Italics mine)

He goes on to address the 'gambler' in French, adumbrating his charms in the eyes of women, and ends the letter with a quotation, again in French, 'from one of the greatest men in the world' (*MW*, II: 18–19). Rowe here makes use of a passage from chapter one of the Port Royal

Pensées, 'Contre l'indifference des Athées,' in order to reinforce the inevitability of death:

> C'est en vain qu'ils détournent leur pensée de cette éternité qui les attend, comme s'ils la pouvoient anéantir en n'y pensant point. Elle subsiste malgré eux, elle s'avance, & la mort qui la doit ouvrir, les mettra [infailliblement] dans peu les tem[p]s dans l'horrible nécessité d'e[s]tre eternellement ou anéantis, ou malheureux. (*MW*, II: 20)[135]

> ['Tis in vain for Men to turn aside their Thoughts from this Eternity which awaits them, as if they were able to destroy it by denying it a Place in their Imagination: It subsists in spight of *Them*, it advanceth unobserved; and Death, which is to draw the Curtain from it, will in a short Time infallibly reduce them to the dreadful Necessity of being for ever Nothing, or for ever Miserable.][136]

This particular passage is underscored in one of the Bodleian copies of the *Pensées*.

The wager passage is identified by Barker as one of the most recognisable seventeenth-century appropriations from the *Pensées*, but his assertion that 'it is chiefly among literary men of the late Restoration period that the most conspicuous instances of English appreciation of the *Pensées* occur,' excludes Rowe from their ranks.[137] While many writers from the period utilised the same passage – John Locke in his *Essay Concerning Human Understanding* (Bk II, Ch. XXI, para. 70) and Pope in the fourth epistle of his *Essay on Man* (ll. 315–16) – Rowe's letter device allows her to combine 'ornaments of romance' (the trifling world of social gambling) and contemporary intellectual/religious polemics (Pascal's wager) in a manner calculated to appeal to male and female readers of both profane romances and philosophical treatises.[138] The fact that this fictional letter was still unprinted at Rowe's death suggests that she continued to rehearse this type of moral essay as an effective means of proselytising, and, perhaps, was preparing more letters for publication when she died.

The one excerpt Barker uses to exemplify Rowe's unrefined appropriation of Pascal comes from *Letters* (1729). He observes that she uses a quotation from another one of the popular chapters for English writers, in this case chapter twenty-six of the Port Royal edition, but he avers, 'the overall impression is of a short composition built around one of Pascal's reflections rather than of an incidental quotation in the context of her own remarks.'[139] He is right, but not for the reasons he thinks. The letter he is referring to is one of the eight letters addressed to Cleora, and thus one of the letters Rowe substantially extracted and then revised from the Alnwick letter book. Letter V in *Letters* (1729) opens with material lifted from Letter 68 in the letter book. The Pascal quotation does not exist in the original letter. Instead, Rowe discusses an example from William Law's *Christian Perfection*. The manuscript runs thus:

> Mad^m
> your reflections on Sir Isaac Newton's Death has something in them so charming and agreeable that I am recompenc'd for his loss whatever Damage the rest of the world Suffers by it: but while I see you dispos'd to think so Justly of this world and the next, I must confess the manner of Life to which you seem Condemn'd excites my compassion, indeed you may dispence with me for practising this height of charity while you are the object of almost everybody's envy, but be as happy as the world can make you tis all but sleeping and dreaming, and being amused with a vain succession of Shadows and as Mr Laws says the utmost that the greatest monarch of the East Cou'd give his highest favourite was only to be dress'd in royal apparel and led on Horse back thro' the city, and if a nurse was to please her child she must talk the same Language {an} please it with the same fine things [...]
> (MS 110, Letter 68, ff. 173–4)[140]

The printed version of 1729 is substantially different:

> YOUR Reflections on ***'s Death have something in them so just and agreeable, that I am recompenc'd for his Loss, whatever Damage the rest of the World suffers by it.
> It pleases me to find you so often returning to a Subject, that most People take so much pains to avoid. If Immortality is the Pride and Happiness of human Nature, why should it not be mention'd with the same Gaiety, with which we talk of other agreeable Things? The other World is at least a greater Novelty than this; nor is it such a glorious Round of Action, to eat, to drink, and sleep, that People should have an aversion to think, if not to try what variety of Enjoyments a future Life will give them. But to forget this, is the Design of all the thoughtless Amusements the Wit of Man can invent. What Monsieur *Pascal* says, is perfectly just.
>
> *L'Origine de toutas* [sic] *les Occupations tumultuares des Hommes, & de tout ce qu'on appelle Divertisement ou Passe-tems, & en effet que d'y*

laisser passer le tems sans le sentir, ou le plûtôt sans le sentir soy-même, & d'eviter en perdant cette Partie de la Vie le Dégoût in térieur. L'Ame est jétte dans le Corps pour y faire un Séjour de peu de Durée. Elle sçait que ce n'est qu'un Passage à un Voyage éternel, & qu'elle n'a que le peu de Tems que dure la Vie pour s'y preparer. Mais ce peu le commode si fort, & t'embarasse si étrangement qu'elle ne songe qu' á le perdre. Celuy est une Peine insupportable a voire & de penser á soy. Ainsi tout son soui est de s'oublier soy même, & de laisser couler le Tems si court & si prétieux sans Reflection, en s'occupant des Choces qui l'empechent d'y penser.

[THIS is the Ground of all the tumultuary Business, of all the trifling Diversion amongst Men; in which our general Aim is to make the Time pass off our Hands without feeling it, or rather without feeling ourselves; and, by getting rid of this small Portion of Life, to avoid that inward Disgust and Bitterness, which we should not fail to meet with, if we found Leisure to descend into our own Breasts. For 'tis undeniable certain, that the Soul of Man is here incapable of Rest and Satisfaction. And this obliges her to expand her self every Way, and to seek how she may lose the Thoughts of her own proper Being in a settled Application to the Things about her. Her very Happiness consists in this Forgetfulness: And to make her exquisitely miserable, nothing more is required but the engaging her to look into her self, and to dwell at Home.][141]

I'll stop here, or you will certainly think I am going to transcribe the whole Book, to save the trouble of throwing away your Money on a Moral Essay. (*Letters* (1729), 151–3)

As Barker contends, the quotation from Pascal dominates the composition of the fictional missive, but it also makes Rowe's moral point much clearer. Instead of utilising Law's expression of a 'vain succession of Shadows' and his example of the trifling rewards offered in foreign courts, Rowe finds a quotation from Pascal that not only reinforces her theological point, immortality, but also contains aesthetically and philosophically appealing images connected to feelings and interiority.

In the above quotation Pascal critiques the confusion and perpetual hurry in which people waste their allotted time on earth, and, more importantly, their concerted efforts to divorce themselves from thought and feeling. Also, because Rowe blanks out Newton's name (on odd choice given his fame), the passage becomes a purely generalised essay on the lack of self-reflection in contemporary society. Moreover, in the chapter from which Rowe takes her excerpt, chapter twenty-six, or 'Misere de l'homme,' Pascal claims that the primary cause of people's temporal misery is their innate inability to sustain a retired and contemplative life without the assistance of devotion. Pascal argues that whenever human beings look within, they confront only disgust and bitterness with their condition, and to allay such feelings they must seek constant diversions to drive away thoughts of themselves. If, however, they considered their relation to God while they meditated, Pascal contends, they would be able to live in complete harmony:

> Je ne parle que de ceux qui se regardent sans aucune veiie de Religion. Car il est vray que c'est une des merveilles de la Religion Chrestienne, de reconcilier l'homme avec soy-mesme, en le reconciliant avec Dieu; de luy rendre la veüe de soy-mesme supportable; & de faire que la solitude & le repos soient plus agreables à plusieurs, que l'agitation & le commerce des hommes. Aussi n'est-ce pas en arrestant l'homme dans luy-mesme qu'elle produit tous ces effets merveilleux. Ce n'est qu'en le portent [sic] jusqu'à Dieu, & en le soutenant dans le sentiment de ses miseres, par l'esperance d'une autre vie, qui l'en doit entierement délivrer.[142]

[I speak of those alone who survey their own Nature, without the Views of Faith and Religion. 'Tis indeed one of the Miracles of Christianity, that by reconciling Man to God, it restores him to his own good Opinion; that it makes him able to bear the Sight of himself; and in some Cases, renders Solitude and Silence more agreeable, than all the Intercourse and Action of Mankind. Nor is it by fixing Man in his own Person, that it produceth these wonderful Effects; 'tis by carrying him to GOD, and by supporting him under the Sense of Miseries, with the Hopes of an assured and complete Deliverance in a better Life.][143]

Thus, with the assurance of a better life through belief in God, spiritually informed philosophical contemplation can now help in the attainment of happiness. The similarity between Pascal's argument and the way Rowe presents her Shaftesburyan statesman is striking: both use the argument of man's inevitable disgust with himself and supply numerous examples of the way people seek to occupy their time and thoughts with pointless pursuits.

In this chapter, and in the *Pensées* in general, the particular emphasis Pascal places on meditation, thought, self-reflection, and solitude as the keys to happiness in this life and rewards in the next, is echoed throughout Rowe's letters. Whilst these thematic similarities may seem facile at first (these themes are common enough in most religious literature of the period and intelligent letter-writers of all ages tend to convey some sense of meditative self-consciousness in their letters), they are nevertheless suggestive of more interesting parallels. Pascal's informal notes, presented to seventeenth- and eighteenth-century readers as polished essays, mirror the formal and aesthetic transformations Rowe's own work underwent. Pascal's movement away from the external world of nature to the internal world of self-consciousness is echoed in Rowe's letters from the dead to the living and many of her devotional pieces. The internal moral dilemmas her epistolary characters confront are dramatised through the external agency of the letter from the dead friend. Similarly, the devotional pieces that she circulates among her coterie dramatise her self-conscious subjection to higher powers. The affinity the two writers share on thematic issues, despite their different religious persuasions, showcases the integrative approach Rowe took in her literary compositions. Readers of Rowe's fictional letters did not encounter overt controversy or theological dispute, but they were treated to a sort of hidden polemical agenda through the inclusive inculcation of the related religious, philosophic, and literary ideas of writers from various creeds. Her efforts appear to be based on a desire to present the most exemplary devotional, literary, and philosophical ideals available within a form that could accommodate the variety necessary to appeal to the greatest number of readers.

The letters: familiar and fictional

The implications of Pascal's interiorised world and Shaftesbury's ambivalent performative one are evident across a range of Rowe's publications, including the fictional letters in *Friendship in Death* and the familiar letters in the *Miscellaneous Works*. This has led me to question whether habits of meditation, self-reflection, and solitude as presented in the familiar versus the fictional letters reveal differing levels of subjectivity in the letter-writer. In Rowe's familiar letters, the form of the letter acts as a unifying agent between the subjective and objective worlds of the letter-writer. As I noted in the sections on composition and editing, Rowe often presents an inset character of herself within her own letters: delivering a poem, a devout exercise, or a prose monologue, which she then comments on as the objective first-person narrator of the letter. In the fictional letters, especially those from 'the dead', Rowe presents a less complex narrator, one less likely to perform roles than to narrate a scene. Nevertheless, this narrator is sometimes more prescient than Rowe could ever hope to be in her own letters. Writing from an omniscient vantage point in heaven these narrators have unlimited access to the inner motivations of their correspondents and are therefore able to predict their future actions. In these instances Rowe's affective method of describing the moral predicaments of the characters in *Friendship in Death* shares similarities with Nancy Sherman's explication of Aristotle's notes on good character in the *Nicomachean Ethics*.[144] Sherman notes Aristotle's emphasis on the importance of emotions as well as reason in a virtuous character's moral response, and suggestively notes that, 'he [Aristotle] will argue that... our judgement of particular cases and our knowledge of how to "compose the scene" is itself part of the moral response. Discerning the morally salient features of a situation is part of expressing virtue and part of the morally appropriate response.'[145] Rowe's ability to discern and direct a 'morally appropriate' and therefore virtuous response through each of her dead letter-writers, and later in her *Letters Moral and Entertaining*, was probably one of the aspects of her work that attracted the approbation of moral arbiters like Edward Young and Samuel Johnson. It is also, perhaps, one of the reasons she was so closely identified with the moral content of the work. Her exploration of virtue, or good character, albeit through the indirect method of fictional characters, was a way of displaying her own moral perspicacity. By extension, imbuing her works with the integrity of her own character led to the perpetuation of an image of exemplarity as long as her works were in print. This is a crucial factor in the longevity of her posthumous image and it is worth noting her own hand in its production.

Up to this point, I have primarily used examples from the first part of *Letters Moral and Entertaining*, but this text was not Rowe's first foray into epistolary publication. In 1728 she anonymously published *Friendship in Death, in Twenty Letters from the Dead to the Living*. The epistolary genesis of this text is less certain, but it would appear from her 1717 letter to Grace Thynne, quoted above, that she had early formed an idea of 'Epistles from the Dead to the Living' and 'keeping Correspondences with Ghosts and Phantoms'.[146] Despite the fact that none of the letters printed in *Friendship in Death* are in the Alnwick letter book, this work can still be tied to Rowe's private letters through her explicit references to real characters inspiring certain letters, and her evident thematic interest in letters as a form of conversation with the dead.[147] More importantly, *Friendship in Death* shows the impact Rowe's private letters had in shaping her wider spiritual aims. It seems a shame, in fact, that the work is often classified as purely didactic literature today, something that carries a mildly pejorative ring, when we know that in the eighteenth century the lack of distinction between genres such as the essay, devotional treatise, moral tale, and real or fictional letters meant that Rowe's letters were capable of being read and appreciated on many different levels.[148] The letters were meant to be uplifting, forceful expressions of Rowe's strong religious beliefs, and revelation, rather than overt instruction, would better characterise the nature of Rowe's message in this text. Moreover, the work rewards sustained analysis with its unique romantic presentation of a future system of rewards, its inventive construction of a rational afterlife, its exploration of subjecthood, and its serious engagement with the subject's internal and external performances of ethical dilemmas and religious belief.

Friendship in Death is a series of letters written from departed spirits to mortal friends or relations informing them about the nature of the afterlife, or, in some cases, warning them against potentially impious or unvirtuous acts. While this aspect suggests it is a didactic handbook about the afterlife and how to get there, the text's affinity with what Ros Ballaster has called 'seductive forms' of language shows that Rowe was more inventive with her material than one might expect.[149] The letters are populated by libertines, pining nuns, harsh fathers, lecherous brothers-in-law, potentially incestuous siblings, and, of course, besotted lovers. With such a cast, comparisons with amatory novelists cannot be far behind; yet Rowe managed to avoid such direct comparisons in a number of ways. First, the work was not a novel. It is, as the title indicates, just twenty letters, and, though some letters have sequels, most are meant to stand alone in the text, acting as discrete moral fables. Second, the work came out anonymously, with a dedication specifically noting the author's lack of interest in monetary gain. This is in stark contrast to the prefaces of Aphra Behn, Eliza Haywood, and Delarivier Manley which often note their need for money. Also, the dedicatee was the very respectable Edward Young, who Rowe did not personally know, but to whom she sent the manuscript anonymously, asking him to get it printed. He did and added a commendatory preface extolling the letters' ability to '*impress the Notion of the Soul's Immortality*' (*Friendship*, sig. A3r). And it is in the realm of the 'Soul's Immortality' that Rowe staked her literary claim. Reiterated throughout *Friendship in Death* and the three volumes of *Letters Moral and Entertaining* are the undeniable fact of heaven and the almost indescribable intellectual and romantic bliss that lay in wait as a reward to the virtuous.

Aligning such fictional fantasy with Rowe's coterie letters may seem forced; however, the fact that Rowe chose to carefully shepherd the work to the press anonymously, and then subsequently denied her authorship of it to friends, suggests that she knew there were enough identifying characteristics to mark the work as her own. These identifiable hallmarks were precisely those aspects of her letters that her coterie correspondents always commented on: her numinous and romantic language on nature and the afterlife, her subjective and highly performative approach to philosophic contemplation, her enthusiasm, and her interest in morally perspicuous narratives.

In a letter which predates *Friendship in Death*, and which has already been cited above, Rowe describes her letters to Grace Thynne as 'Epistles from the Dead to the Living'.[150] Her construction of her own letters as a form of conversation between one dead to the world but in a state of sanctity, and those still susceptible to the trifling pastimes of the *grande monde*, was an early one. She sends similar statements to Arabella Marrow, advising her that 'you have more Mementos of mortality than my letters' (MS 110, Letter 18, f. 80), and in another letter to her writes:

> tis a hard matter for people that are quite out of the World to converse with those that are in it, as I am cut off from the ways of the living & seem to Exist in the state of departed Spirits I know not how to entertain my surviving Freinds, news from the Dead I fancy would not be very aggreable to many of them especially to those that are very well at ease in a state of Mortality & have all the Gay part of life before them but Ah Madam how soon will the Soft deluding Vision fly, how swiftly will the Circling years convince you of the vanity of all y^r Expectations from this false world, you'll think I am very well at leisure to utter these wise Maxims, I don't expect y^u to believe me but upon y^r own experience. (MS 110, Letter 20, f. 82)

The similarity of Rowe's argument in this passage with the precepts set forth in Edward Young's preface to *Friendship in Death* confirms the stylistic and thematic continuities between the familiar and fictional letters. Young's preface states:

> *Some who pretend to have no Scruples about the Being of a God, have yet their Doubts about their own Eternal Existence,*[...and] *since no Means should be left unattempted in a Point of such Importance, I hope endeavouring to make the Mind familiar, with the Thoughts of our Future*

Existence, and contract, as it were, unawares, an Habitual Persuasion of it, by Writings built on that Foundation, and addressed to the Affections and Imagination, will not be thought improper, either as a Doctrine, or Amusement; Amusement, for which the World makes by far the largest Demand, and which generally speaking, is nothing but an Art of forgetting that Immortality, the firm Belief, and advantageous Contemplation of which, this Amusement would recommend. (*Friendship*, sig. A3r–v)

In an even more revealing letter to the Countess of Hertford, circa 1716, Rowe makes the imaginative leap to the fictive possibilities of her epistles from the dead:

My concern for you is Perhaps the stamp of Heaven on my Soul, since it Chiefly regards y^r future felicity whatever other Change Death May make on my Mind this disposition must rise to a more generous Height in the regions of perfect amity & bliss; I often please my self with the thoughts that departed Spirits supply the place of Guardian Angels to their Friends, that they delight themselves to follow them in their Solitary walks, & watch their nightly Slumbers, & make impressions on their Sleeping fancys, to warn them of approaching ^Dangers Its not unlik'ly that the tempest of humane Passions are som'times compos'd by the Soft inspiring whispers of those propitious Beings while the Seats of joy have open'd their Glorys in visionary Scenes to the Sleeping imagination: One wou'd think I were got in to some golden Dream, & fancy'd my self in Paradice , I find Some occasion to ask my self whether I am awake or asleep, Dead or alive, among the number of Mortals or departed Spirits. (MS 110, Letter No. 72, ff. 180–1)

For Rowe, carrying this visionary scene and its supposed salutary effects into the public domain was a way of indulging her descriptive imaginings in a more concrete form, but it was also a proactive measure in the fight against worldliness and religious apathy. In her brief but polemical dedication to Young she writes that, 'THE Author of these Letters is above any View of Interest, and can have no Prospect of Reputation, resolving to be concealed: But if they prove a serious Entertainment to Persons whose leisure Hours are not always innocently employed, the End is fully answered' (*Friendship*, sig. A2r–v). She continues with the caveat, 'THE greatest Infidel must own, there is at least as much Probability in this Scheme, as in that of the FAIRY TALES, which however Visionary, are some of them Moral, and Entertaining' (*Friendship*, sig. A2v). She explicitly renounces any contentions for fame, 'interest', or even fictional realism, but does claim her work is serious literature that can also provide entertainment, something she likewise claimed of her private letters.[151]

Young and Rowe clearly believed that the amusements of contemporary society were having a pernicious effect on people's devotional practices and agreed with William Law's assessment in *A Serious Call to a Devout and Holy Life* (1729):

> W]e are exhorted to work out our salvation with *fear* and *trembling*; because unless our *heart* and *passions* are eagerly bent upon the works of our salvation; unless *holy fears* animate our endeavours, and keep our consciences strict and tender about every part of our duty, constantly examining how we live, and how fit we are to die, we shall in all probability fall into a state of negligence, and sit down in such a course of life, as will never carry us to the rewards of heaven.[152]

Rowe's aim, like Law's, was to reinvigorate people's private spiritual and philosophical speculations. This meant retiring from the world in order to better prepare oneself for death, while still actively practising the theological virtues (hope, charity, and, most importantly, faith). Unsurprisingly, therefore, Rowe's primary method of argument in her fictional works is to passionately affirm rather than philosophically demonstrate the existence of heaven and the ineffable beauty and love of God. She frequently couches descriptions of heaven in revelatory language and, although such uninhibited language led to many of the critical charges of enthusiasm against her, Rowe nevertheless let this aspect of her writing stand in later works. In fact, she saw it as something of a personal trademark and frequently points out when she is about to embark on a sublime rant. Letter 56 in the Alnwick letter book, which appears in a highly altered state as Letter VII in *Letters* (1729), segues from a polite compliment to Lord Hertford and Lady Betty, the countess's husband and daughter respectively, into an encomium on the countess's son. Rowe declares:

> at present my Lord Beauchamp is my Hero. I am told he is the most beautyfull thing under the Sun, above it I suppose he has some rivals
>
> > Where Smiling Seraphs touch the golden String
> > And rosie cherubs soft responses sing

a propos, now I am in the Sublime I'll let you know how m^{ch} I wish'd to Converse with you while I was looking at the lights in the Skies. (MS 110, Letter 56, f. 153. Italics mine)[153]

She essentially uses a social compliment as an introduction to celestial themes.

In another letter, after briefly discussing the death of George I (1727) and the state of the nation, she notes:

> What a Dialect am I got into! I am entirely out of my own character and wandering from my rural simplicity: the Sylvan Scenes are much more suited to my taste and Language; where amidst all the tumults of the world, I find repose in the reflection of the immutability of the Supream mind and tho your Ladyship has not much leisure I hope you'll find some to listen when I (tho unskilfully) touch the Lyre on so great a subject as "The Divine Veracity". (MS 110, Letter 71, f. 178)

The transition from epistolary prose to devotional verse is never jarring in Rowe's letters, and Rowe is just as skilful at integrating her various poems into the narratives of her prose works as she was in introducing them in letters to the countess.[154] Again, the Alnwick letter book is crucial in revealing this aspect of Rowe's compositional style, as she will often set up a poem by introducing a feigned enthusiastic strain into the letter which then 'prompts' a piece of ecstatic verse. She introduces 'A Degression' with the quip: 'Without any Apology I am a going to talk to my Self and what follows may properly be call'd a Degression' (MS 110, Letter 58, ff. 156–7). Following this is the prose piece that begins: 'Let me lose the Remembrance of this basir world and hear no more of it's distracting tumults,' but ends with the observation that, 'this is talking in Buskins you'll think' (ff. 157–8). In another letter she brings herself out of a verse description of the 'Ever blooming Fields of Paradice' with the remark, 'This Description fell into Rhime without the least labour or design this gay scheme is I believe suited to your taste tho I am afraid it would not be at all agreeable to the Reverend Mr Claverings Sagacity to whom I beg you will give my Service' (MS 110, Letter 128, f. 310 , *c.*1732 to Mrs Nevinson). Such concessions to the variable literary tastes amongst her coterie letter recipients show that Rowe knew how to deflect criticism of her enthusiastic style, often attributing it to her wish to entertain her reader in a suitably fanciful and pious manner.

When she wrote for a general reader, though, Rowe chose unabated rapturous language. Hence, in *Friendship in Death*, the use of verse is almost never deflated by self-reflexive authorial asides. In her most ecstatic letter about the afterlife, Letter VII, Rowe avers that there are a 'thousand Beauties un-reveal'd, and a thousand Delights un-nam'd' (*Friendship*, Letter VII, 23), but nevertheless goes on to describe many of those beauties and delights that constitute her image of heaven. The departed spirit, Delia, writes:

> the Paradise of God open'd before me [...] the happy Groves stood crown'd with unfading Verdure; the lucid Currents danc'd along o'er Sands of Gold; the charming Bowers display'd their everblooming Pride, and breath'd *Ambrosia*; the Palaces of the Heavenly Powers ascended with exquisite Magnificence. (*Friendship*, 23–4)

She then goes on to recount her reunion with her lover, noting that, in heaven, 'Hope and languishing Expectation are no more, and all Desire is lost in full and compleat Fruition. Love reigns in eternal Triumph, here it governs every Heart, and dwells on every Tongue' (*Friendship*, 24–5). Following this are eight lines of verse echoing the exact themes Delia has just expressed in prose. After this revelatory rapture, Delia ends her letter with the apostrophe: 'Ye sacred Mysteries un-reveal'd to Men, Ye Glories unprophan'd by mortal Eyes, forgive the bold Attempt that would describe you! --- The only Description that Mortals can receive of you is, that you are not to be describ'd' (25).[155] Rowe's combination of a scene of romantic fulfilment with the unveiling of God is quite suggestive, but in fusing the fantasy and sensuality of an amatory plot with numinous language, Rowe offers her readers an easily identifiable script with which they can embark on their own religious epiphany. Her choice of the letter form perfectly serves the function she requires in *Friendship in Death*, for the epistolary genre excels in performing an imaginative bringing forth of presence in absence, of remembering one person to another, and there is no being whose presence Rowe wants her readers to feel more than God's.

Maintaining a proper balance between ecstatic language and pious prescription was fraught with problems, however, and Rowe's works were, as has been noted, liable to charges of religious enthusiasm. Samuel Johnson's definition of enthusiasm warns against the type of personal revelations Rowe frequently employs. For him, enthusiasm is: '1. A vain belief of private revelation... 2. Heat or imagination; violence of passion, confidence of opinion... [or] 3. Elevation of fancy; exaltation of ideas.'[156]

It is surprising that Johnson found no fault in Rowe's fictional letters, commending their 'copiousness and luxuriance', as well as their ability to 'use the ornaments of romance in the decoration of religion.'[157] Even Boswell found something to his taste in Rowe's letters, though the one that he singles out as his own personal favourite is notable for its lack of overt enthusiasm.[158] Instead the sentimental mixture of consolatory pathos and philosophical reasoning provides an interesting counterpoint to the many letters involving romantic scenarios that are more regularly cited.

Boswell's choice was Letter III, 'To the Countess of ***, from her only Son, who died when he was two Years old', an affecting account of a baby spirit, Narcissus, observing his still-grieving mother and trying to reconcile her to his new and improved state. The letter opens:

> YOUR Grief is an Allay to my Happiness. The only Sentiment my Infant State was conscious of, was a Fondness for you, which was then pure Instinct and natural Sympathy, but is now Gratitude and filial Affection. As soon as my Spirit was releas'd from its uneasy Confinement, I found myself an active and reasonable Being. I was transported at the Advantage and superior manner of my Existence. The first Reflection I made was on my lovely Benefactor, for I knew you in that Relation in my infant State: But I was surprised to see you weeping over the little breathless Form from which I thought myself so happily deliver'd, as if you lamented my Escape. The fair Proportion, the Agility, the Splendor of the new Vehicle, that my Spirit now inform'd, was so blest an Exchange, that I wonder'd at your Grief. (*Friendship*, 9)

Before his metamorphosis from a 'little breathless form' into a superior vehicle he is only capable of 'pure Instinct and natural Sympathy' for the mother, but this animal state is transformed at death into 'Gratitude and filial Affection'. The transformation, or rather loss, that makes this Shaftesburyan attainment of politeness and reason possible is the loss of the body and the ascendance of the mind/soul. Rowe here presents immortal souls as beings that still engage in interpersonal affections, but who acquire ever more refined notions, and she contrasts these rational and cultivated spirits with the irrational worldly beings who take pride in public significance and material possessions, or carry their grief too far. In effect, Rowe partly secularises her version of the afterlife in this letter so that philosophically attained social affection between parted family members takes precedence over the presentation of devotional affection towards God.

Narcissus's letter is undoubtedly the most interesting missive in the collection, and this stems from its emphasis on philosophical rather than theological reasons for consolation. Rowe may have had Seneca's formal *Epistulae Morales* in mind when writing this letter, but she gives it an effective eighteenth-century 'spin' in her entertaining tirade against the baseness of worldly materialism. Narcissus not only demeans the family estate as good for nothing but 'four-footed Animals', and the family coat of arms as 'such a Toy, that if Burlesque had not been beneath the Dignity of an Angel, I should have thought the mentioning it a Ridicule on mortal Men', but also characterises 'the whole earthly Globe' as 'the Dregs of Creation' (*Friendship*, 11). Rowe's wit here is quite sharp and seems at odds with a consolation letter to a grieving mother, but her curt treatment of earthly existence is a purposefully Stoic response to socially sanctioned passions and desires. The mother does not lament the son so much as the son's lost social prestige, and the heavenly sprite seeks to show his mother that, had she inured herself to these hopes, she would have found solace rather than grief in his altered state. Rowe reminds her readers of the ephemeral nature of bodily existence compared to the everlasting joys of the immortal world. Fittingly, Narcissus concludes his letter, 'I am now in the Perfection of my Being, in the Elevation of Reason' (12).

The other 19 letters of the collection are significantly different from Narcissus's *consolatio* and tend, like Delia's Letter VII, to mine the language and plots of contemporary amatory fiction rather than ancient Stoic doctrines. However, the theological and philosophical underpinnings of the work are still evident in the iterated representations of immortality and the tentative steps toward the exploration of subjecthood which we have already seen manifested in the later letters dealing with Shaftesbury and Pascal.

Rowe's theologically minded fictions may lack any overt doctrine or argumentation, but it is nevertheless apparent that she had a polemical purpose in writing them. 'Impressing the notion of the soul's immortality' was not work to be undertaken lightly, and the motivating factors for Rowe were her sincere religious convictions and her belief that contemporary morality was at an all-time low in the upper classes. (Rowe is, in fact, quite class-biased in her representation of characters. Rural swains and lasses are only rusticating gentry or aristocracy while the true labouring classes are nowhere to be seen.) According to Rowe, 'People are not Sent into the world as Idle Spectators to wake, & Sleep, to Stare at the vain Show for a few years & then make their Exit' (MS 110, Letter 113, f. 255). Rather, with Pauline 'fear and trembling', human beings are expected to meditate on their eventual end, as well as actively practise Christian and civic virtues. In the same passage as the above quotation Rowe states, 'I have not the vanity to pretend to a devout retirement, nor affect any recluse notions of Religion my Thoughts of that are Just the reverse & all easie & Sociable' (MS 110, Letter 113, ff. 255–6).[159] However, for Rowe, such contemplation could only take place in an idealised realm of subjective experience. Her cast of exemplary characters in *Friendship in Death* are not just there to affirm life after death, but also provide examples of morally concerned readers/writers (of letters) who learn to question themselves and, in the process, find the rationale to act virtuously. The spiritual and ethical programme behind Rowe's letters is one that, spiritually, seeks to instill an idealised and aesthetically pleasing notion of the afterlife and heaven, and, ethically, questions individual morality through the narrator's inquiries into the subjectivity of the characters. The queries each letter-writer raises about moral and religious standards are directed as much at the general reader as the subject of the letter, asking them to look both inward and upwards to heaven in the process.

An example of Rowe's tendentious, but visually rich, amatory styling is Letter II from *Friendship in Death*, in which a gentleman who has died on his travels writes to reassure a friend in England of his improved state. After explaining how he had been in a declining way ever since his love, Almeria, had died, he describes the moment of his death as the prelude to a romantic rendezvous. Wandering along the shores of the Bosphorus he throws himself down on a flowery bank and falls into a slumber in which he imagines he hears Almeria's voice. It turns out her voice is the call of death, and thus:

> the Curtain fell, and the invisible World appear'd. The first gentle Spirit that welcom'd me to these new Regions, was the lovely *Almeria*; but how Dazling! how divinely Fair! Extasy was in her Eyes, and inexpressible Pleasure in every Smile! her Mien and Aspect more soft and propitious than ever was feign'd by Poets of their Goddess of Beauty and Love: What was airy Fiction *there*, was *here* all transporting Reality. (*Friendship*, 7)

Instead of Almeria's nightgown billowing open at this point, however, she welcomes him into a celestial chariot which carries them off to the Morning Star. This letter is a fairly straightforward narrative encomium on the merits of love in the afterlife, and is characteristic of the languid scenic descriptions and ecstatic language employed in the praise of heavenly love in almost all the letters – language and scenes similar to those deployed in many amorous escapades in the novels of the period.[160] Rowe's appropriation of amatory discourse – she modestly compares them to fairy tales in her dedication – appears to be a calculated appeal to the fashionable taste for novels such as Eliza Haywood's, which dominated the market in the 1720s. The romantic topos is certainly uppermost in Rowe's letters, but, as I have suggested, there are other, weightier issues at play given her interest in philosophical and theological matters.

Letter IV, addressed to Lord *** from a young nun named Ethelinda, complicates the unambiguous style of the preceding amatory letter in its posthumous celebration of a forbidden love, providing the reader with a clear depiction of a hierarchy of acceptable desires. In this letter, the heroine explains that she had to force herself to turn away from earthly desires because, though she was in love with Lord ***, she had already taken her vows to the church when she met him, as hers 'was a Heart devoted to superior Ardours, and sacred to Heaven alone' (*Friendship*, 14). Her anguished resolution not to listen to her lover's protestations against confinement is rewarded by a Clarissa-like death, which is described as a sacrifice to 'Chastity and Truth' and a release from 'Misery and Mortality'(14).[161] Once the heroine dies she describes how:

> Here are no Vows that tear us from our Wishes, no Conflict betwixt Passion and Virtue; what we like we admire, what we admire we enjoy.... That unhappy Passion which was my Torment and Crime is now my Glory and my Boast. Nothing selfish or irregular, nothing that needs Restraint or Disguise mingles with the noble Ardour [...]. The Substance of Love, my Lord, dwells in Heaven, its Shadow only is to be found upon Earth. (*Friendship*, 15)

Through her renunciation and virtuous death, the passion that could have contributed to an irreligious act is instead rewarded in heaven, promising readers a similar fulfillment of their own illicit desires in the afterlife if they restrain themselves in the present.

Multiple readings are possible here, as Rowe's unabashed expressions of spiritual love hint at physical sexual fulfillment. It is possible to see phrases such as 'what we admire we enjoy', 'nothing needs restraint', and 'the Substance of Love' as indicative of the nun's acceptance of her sexual nature. But Rowe is at pains throughout the letters to stress the transformation at death as one of physical alteration, leaving one with a purely rational mind and new 'vehicle' in which to reside. The representation of desire as an experience rooted in the material body is jettisoned in favour of the representation of desire in an imaginative and more fulfilling spiritual love. The method for achieving this idealised version of love is explicitly subjective. Rowe's usual descriptions of a superior divinity imprinting the natural world with meaning are replaced by a claustrophobic depiction of the enclosed world of the convent and the nun's anguished internal battle with desire and virtue. We find out that she tells no one at the convent about her forbidden passions and confides only in 'the compassionate and forgiving Powers above'. However, the real power in operation is Ethelinda's own mind as she grapples with her moral dilemma: whether to adhere to her precipitous vow of chastity or give in to her avowed love for Lord ****. Instead of having the nun relate a third party's ethical and spiritual crisis, Rowe lets her tell her own tale, and, in so doing, personalises the letter-writer's quandary. As Ethelinda relives her climactic moment of internal questioning, the passage abounds in first person pronouns. Crucially they appear when Ethelinda remarks that the higher guidance she invoked only 'confirmed *my* resolution' (*Friendship*, 13, emphasis mine). The debate, like the private choice, was always hers to make.

Rowe's tactics of articulating the greater fulfillment of desire in heaven may not be as transgressive or feminist as contemporary criticism might like, but the unique licence she gained for the expression of such desire is nevertheless of great interest. Here was a writer, identified almost from the outset of her career as a virtuous exemplar, who managed to deploy enthusiastic poetics and amatory narratives in the name of virtue and religion. Rowe's language of desire need not be read only as a form of 'sacred eroticism',[162] therefore, but as an effective appropriation of sentiment and enthusiasm in the name of religion.

Rowe also offers her readers the example of retirement as a means to spiritual awakening and knowledge, presenting a number of characters who retire from the world in the search of the 'wisdom and philosophy' that religion offers, but her most consistent, and most effective, point is the perpetual imminence of death. In two letters to Leonora, the departed spirit, Clerimont, is waiting for the imminent death of his love, but when it fails to take place he is consoled by his acceptance of the unknown nature of the moment of death. Seeming to come and recede at will, life's 'tempestuous ocean' is contrasted with the 'harbour' of heaven, and mortals are clearly better off getting beyond the waves and dying young. Rowe had similar thoughts around 1725, during a severe illness, and set about writing one of her 'private' letters from the dead. Due to the fact that she was premature in her presentiments, she was able to oblige the countess with a copy of the epistle. As the letter so succinctly summarises her literary aims in *Friendship in Death*, I include it in its entirety:

> Madam
> I have weeks or days or but a few hours to live tis Heaven only can determine but as I think my time very Short I find A great deal of Pleasure in taking my leave in this Solemn manner of my Friends you may be satisfy'd I am now sincere in the Esteem I express for you I am past the Ceremonys of the Living and therefore cannot treat you with the least formality: my thoughts have often visited the mansions of the Dead and the part I am now to perform has been so often acted over in my immagination that I am not discompos'd to think that in a few days the circumstances will be reall People have generally a curiosity to know to know the thoughts of their friends when they are just on the Borders of those Strange and unknown regions from whence there is no return – tis indeed – a Serious thing to face the approaches of Death but Vertue disarms the Gloomy King of all his Terrors and Brightens the Prospect of Futurity: I have read the Spectators on this Subject with constant pleasure and have been charm'd with with his instances of the Roman Fortitude but the Christian Religion must arm the Mind with a resolution More just and Noble as it assures us with the Clearest Evidence that Immortality and Pleasure are the reward of Pious Actions A long Adieu on Earth but I am perswaded we Shall meet in the Regions of unmolested Peace and Happiness. (MS 110, Letter 33, f. 110)

Rowe's decision to shift these sentiments out of the private world of conversational circles and manuscript into the public world of print and social responsibility was a way of providing an example of the active virtue she so often preached. With the aid of a fictional arsenal of departed spirits standing in for herself, Rowe was able to translate her own letters into a work which could forward the cause of virtue beyond the scope of her immediate coterie. Rowe's first-hand experience of the sentimental and pious efficacy of her letters to the countess clearly inspired her to extend her letter-writing to a wider public and highlights the truly formative impact private letters had on Rowe's public literary performances.

What, then, were the public to make of those private letters when they too were published?

The main problem with the fanciful flights of Rowe's fictional letters was that the general reader, belatedly introduced to her familiar letters in 1739, discovered the elevated language of the fictional works in the private writings. The familiar letters revealed not just an exemplary character, as was clearly Henry Grove and Theophilus Rowe's aim, but also a writer who, in the midst of a private letter, indulged in poetic transports of a rather uninhibited nature. As my work with Alnwick MS 110 has shown, the reverse is actually the case and Rowe cultivated her pious and enthusiastic language as a conscious literary mode and, more likely than not, added her poetic and religious apostrophes as entertaining set pieces in her letters. What is apparent to readers of both the manuscript and published versions of the letters is that Rowe is actually more in control of her argument in her private letters than she is when she tries to rhapsodise and elevate the tone. Her numinous language, as popular as it was, deflects attention away from the philosophical and ethical issues she often cites as her guiding principles, burying the witty and considered responses she makes beneath predictable religious fantasy.

Nevertheless, Rowe's enthusiasm was problematic for her admirers and even favourably inclined readers such as Theophilus Rowe, Henry Grove, Isaac Watts, and Elizabeth Carter felt the need to posthumously censor her unrestrained use of revelatory religious language. The reservations these writers express provide instructive clues about the posthumous conflation of Rowe's writings and lifestyle as interchangeable mediums of artistic and religious expression. And, though her familiar letters were not the first casualties to her exemplary image, they soon acquired a biographical importance that has overshadowed their literary merits.

2
A Saint Everlasting: Elizabeth Rowe and Biographical Exemplarity

This chapter assesses the impact biographical exemplarity had on the posthumous literary value of Elizabeth Rowe's works. In so doing it seeks to particularise the range of historical contexts in which images of Rowe the author and the saint were deployed. Rowe's works became almost inseparable from her 'Life'; however, without straying too much into revisionist biography, I try to differentiate between the uses and reception of her works and the representations of her life. Delineating the variations betwixt reception and reputation should also help us to gauge Rowe's literary influence on subsequent writers, which will have important implications in later chapters.

In the mid- to late eighteenth century Rowe's name, allied to her works, was a frequent point of reference for those seeking to exemplify virtuous female literary achievement. This is unsurprising when we consider her publication history: a general survey of Rowe's appearances in print, carried out on the *Eighteenth Century Short Title Catalogue* and *Eighteenth Century Collections Online*, reveals the astonishing fact that, between the years 1737 and 1820, something by or about Rowe was published almost every year. Whilst a number of these appearances may be attributed to the numerous letter manuals and lives of eminent women she appeared in, the vast majority are editions of her own works – usually the combined *Friendship in Death* and *Letters Moral and Entertaining*, or her *Devout Exercises* – and, though there are a few gaps of one or two years, it is a remarkable print run by any standard. Even some of the century's finest writers cannot boast such longevity or evident popularity.

Given her seeming ubiquity, a close study of Rowe's afterlife should reveal interesting details about habits of reading and conceptions of literary value that are rarely broached in studies concerned with the major figures of the period. For instance, in the three centuries since her death, Rowe's diminishing literary esteem mirrors the changing models of value attached to women's (and men's) miscellaneous works. As I argue below, Frances Burney's critical conflation of Rowe's life and letters (both familiar and fictional) shows how quickly elisions and misreadings developed. She therefore provides a useful case for reassessing genre-based reasons for women's customary exclusion from the literary canon. Her extraordinary print presence, however, provides an interesting counterpoint to our still evolving understanding of women's fraught relationship with the world of print. Allied to these widely discussed scholarly issues is the consignment of Rowe's works to the periphery of the 'rise of the novel' tradition. Relegated to the realm of didactic and religious writing, Rowe's works have been de-polemicised, de-fictionalised, and, as a result, their multifarious literary alliances have been left largely unexplored. The previous chapter detailed Rowe's investment in a wide range of philosophical and literary debates. The continuation of those concerns in later writers is important evidence for a more wide-ranging, if still fraught, acceptance of letters as meritorious literary products and of women's crucial role in the republic of letters tradition.

Rowe's posthumous pre-eminence was not without controversy, however, and while she was continually revered for her virtue and piety, her enthusiastic and sometimes melancholic productions could cause uneasiness during a period when the rise of Methodism was putting rational religion on the defensive. Both camps – Methodists and traditionalist Church of England supporters – found Rowe's life and works useful in the battle for people's spiritual hearts and increasingly secular minds. Her appearance in texts such as John Wilford's *Memorials and Characters* (1741), a stoutly Anglican account of mostly loyal Church of England aristocrats, gentry, and clergy, did not preclude her inclusion in the evangelical, if still Anglican, collections of John Wesley.[163] Rowe appeared in Wesley's *Collection of Moral and Sacred Poems* (1744), and though this collection was not one of his most popular ones, it does suggest that Rowe's biography and poems were reaching a wide, if sometimes divided, audience.[164] It did, however, mean that proponents of rational religion had to account for her dual appeal by acknowledging the efficacy of her enthusiasm in reinvigorating the language of religion; something they were, unsurprisingly, not always willing to do. What is surprising is the fact that Rowe's biographers and editors chose to represent her in such a way as to make her a contentious figure. Isaac Watts, Henry Grove, and Theophilus Rowe all broach the topic of her enthusiasm, but their lack of distinction between Enthusiasm (with a capital 'E'), like the ranting associated with the civil war Puritans and the contemporary Methodist movement, and enthusiasm (with a lower case 'e'), ostensibly referring to literary style, complicates rather than clarifies our picture of Rowe.[165] The ambivalence inherent in their assessments foregrounds the problems writers of the eighteenth century had with the discourse of enthusiasm and these difficulties make their way into later representations of Rowe. Part of the reason she 'disappears' from later literary accounts of the period, and is relegated to the edificatory realms of exemplary biography and religious handbook, is the conflation of these two very different aspects of enthusiastic discourse in her life and works. Nevertheless, what this attention to the particulars of her biography hints at is the importance of her legacy and the seriousness with which it was treated.

Despite the fraught issue of Rowe's enthusiasm, her 'Life' still became an exemplary specimen for literary, religious, educational, and social purposes. Moreover, as a *female* exemplar Rowe cast a long shadow over future women writers, and their appropriations of the Rowe legacy never fail to take into account her biographical exemplarity. Elizabeth Carter, Catherine Talbot, Anna Barbauld, Frances Burney, and numerous other female writers substantially contributed to prolonging Rowe's afterlife, but their purposes in so doing varied considerably. Each of these authors' rehearsals of female exemplarity contributed new intellectual achievements to the list of feminine accomplishments, but a significant step in all of their careers was a tribute to the life of Elizabeth Rowe. What is frequently missed in these appropriations, however, is that, despite the ubiquity of biographical details in all works that referred to Rowe, her literary legacy was likewise a stimulating influence on the later writers. Her fictional letters, *Devout Exercises*, and *History of Joseph* were still being reprinted around the world almost a century after her death, and each of the above-listed female writers specifically refers to Rowe's writings while in fact distancing themselves from contentious aspects or representations of Rowe's life.[166]

Women writers were not the only ones availing themselves of Rowe's exemplarity, and a wide range of religious texts, educational anthologies, histories, and poetry made use of her life as the necessary adjunct to her literary worth. What these various posthumous appearances tell us about the Rowe legacy may seem fairly straightforward, but her inclusion alongside male writers and her ability to transcend religious differences suggests that there was more to her popularity than is generally assumed. In the following sections I consider some of the reasons for this popularity and also explore the reasons for its eventual disappearance. The chapter sets out the immediate contemporary reactions to her death and then documents her belated but widespread fame once the reading public knew the full extent of her literary endeavours. In addition to others' efforts to popularise Rowe's writings I delineate her own role in the memorialisation of her life and work. Following this general survey of Rowe's burgeoning afterlife, the succeeding sections seek to identify and particularise the various ideologically motivated portrayals of Rowe's life and the impact these had on her publication history and long-term literary appreciation. Within these sections I also explore Rowe's literary influence on subsequent writers, as well as the intertextual afterlife of her brand of enthusiastic religious writing in fiction as well as familiar letters.

The posthumous career

My analysis of Rowe's transformation from private coterie correspondent and poet to public moralist and woman of letters stresses the posthumous nature of her fame simply because it is very difficult to assess the degree to which the general reading public were acquainted with her authorship of various works during her own lifetime. She was certainly not unknown, her name had often been appended to her poetic pieces in the miscellanies and she was a pivotal figure in the Countess of Hertford's coterie. However, her most famous works, the letters, were all released anonymously and there is little indication that those outside the immediate circle were aware of either her own or the countess's surreptitious productions. At her death, Rowe's name unequivocally became the marketable commodity Sarah Prescott has suggested was a factor in her earlier career. Prescott notes that Rowe was known primarily as a poet, but this needs to be qualified with the caveat that this was only during her own lifetime. For instance, just months before her death, Edmund Curll, that *bête noire* of all respectable writers in the eighteenth century, sought to capitalise on Rowe's poetic ties by reprinting her earliest work and dedicating it to Alexander Pope. Though he named her as 'Mrs Elizabeth Singer, now Rowe' in the title, even he did not identify her as the author of the various letter collections. The posthumous publication history clearly indicates, however, that Rowe was latterly identified primarily with her letters and devotions.

Rowe died on 21 February 1737, and the notice of her death followed quickly in the March 1737 issue of the *Gentleman's Magazine*, where, after describing her as an 'Ornament of her Sex, and the Honour of the County of *Somerset'*, it immediately identifies her to the public as the author of *Friendship in Death, Letters Moral and Entertaining*, 'besides several excellent Poems in the Miscellanies'.[167] It then directs the reader to page 183, on which is the poetic encomium, 'On the DEATH of the celebrated Mrs ROWE, (formerly Mrs SINGER) by a young Lady, her Intimate', and signed by one AMATA. The 36 lines focus on the ties of friendship the author shared with Rowe, and Rowe's poetic and biographical exemplarity. It avers, 'No vulgar themes, no starts of amorous fire, / Stain'd her chaste Muse, her thoughts still center'd higher.'[168]

In the next issue, April 1737, Elizabeth Carter's first of numerous versions of 'On the Death of Mrs Rowe', identified 'Philomela' as Rowe's early poetic pseudonym.[169] After these repeated advertisements of Rowe's various aliases all subsequent editions of her works included her name on the title page. The publication of the *Miscellaneous Works* two years after Rowe's death further raised public awareness of her character, and, after its appearance, many other publications began to include abridged versions of the Grove/Rowe 'Life'. In addition, to advertise the works, the *Gentleman's Magazine* spent the first half of 1739 whetting the public's appetite with the republication of her popular poem, 'On the Anniversary of her husband's death' (February 1739), followed in March by Elizabeth Carter's second attempt at 'On the Death of Mrs Rowe', along with 'Verses to the Memory of Mrs Rowe. By a Friend' (this time the Countess of Hertford), and 'On the present publication of Mrs Rowe's Poems after her death'. And finally, from May to June, Edward Cave offered an incomplete serialisation of the 'Life', prefaced with the observation: 'Having found that the Lives, which we have inserted of eminent Persons, were favourably received by the Public, we believe it will oblige our Readers to give them some Account of the Life of the Excellent Mrs Rowe, that Ornament of her Sex, on whom we daily receive Encomiums in Verse, and who herself was pleased sometimes to honour us with her Correspondence.'[170]

What cannot be discounted in this picture of Rowe's spreading literary fame is her own agency in the perpetuation of her image and works. She may have published anonymously during her lifetime, but the large collection of miscellaneous pieces still unprinted at her death suggests that she was saving some works specifically for posthumous publication. In none of the cases was anonymity requested or, it seems, assumed. She left her *Devout Exercises* for Isaac Watts to edit and publish and he included her name in the title. And, as I have already suggested, the familiar letters being transcribed by the Countess of Hertford were clearly seen as potentially publishable, and those not already edited and included in *Letters Moral and Entertaining* were cobbled together and added to the *Miscellaneous Works*. Rowe even wrote personal 'letters from the dead' for her friends to receive once she died, likely aware that her relations would print them. Theophilus included these letters in the *Miscellaneous Works* with the exception of those written to him.[171] Further, the full title of the *Miscellaneous Works* notes Rowe's desire to publish her papers posthumously: *The Miscellaneous Works in Prose and Verse of Mrs Elizabeth Rowe. The Greater Part now first Published, by her Order, from her Original Manuscripts*. Another, longer version of the *History of Joseph* was also ready for print when she died.

The primary reason behind Rowe's quest for anonymity during her own lifetime was her apparent wish not to acquire popularity or profit from her creations. Ascribing this desire to social strictures against women appearing in print is inapplicable in her case; indeed, the anxiety towards print attributed to many female authors of the period is not evident in the careers of Rowe, Cockburn, or Carter (which is not to say that they were not ambivalent about the medium). The fluid relationship between manuscript and print publication evidenced in Rowe's literary career effectively complicates current discussions about the manuscript and print divide in the seventeenth and eighteenth centuries. She printed books she felt would be profitable to the public in a moral sense, but declined payment based on her own desire not to profit from work based on religious foundations. The one time she did accept payment from a publisher was when she wanted money for a family in need. Otherwise, she seemed to have no qualms about releasing pieces that might have been susceptible to biographical constructions (for example, the letters to Cleora), and the only time she expressed outright displeasure over the appearance of her name in print is when it was associated with that of Edmund Curll. More tellingly, Rowe's attachment to a creed of immortality suggests that an exemplary posthumous record was probably more important to her than contemporary fame.

Ezell has usefully characterised posthumous publication as 'part of a complex system of authorship practices and manuscript coterie dynamics' in the seventeenth and eighteenth centuries.[172] She notes, 'It is not unlikely, however, that when encountering posthumous editions of women's writings… we may be still predisposed to view them as manifestations of the restrictive power of the hegemony of "feminine modesty" and to see their authors as cultural victims who lacked the nerve, will, or means,… "to value themselves" and "to write for publication".'[173] Ezell discredits this view, arguing that posthumous publication was not an indication of lack of self-worth; rather it was contingent on whether print was the medium in which the female writer defined herself as an author during her own lifetime. Often, it was the older, more established mode of manuscript transmission with which she chose to ally herself. The evidence from Rowe's career confirms Ezell's argument, proving that, during the early eighteenth century at least, the choice could vary based on the author's goals for their work.

The personal manuscript and print remains are not the only factors that contributed to the enduring presence of Rowe's afterlife. The representations, both biographical and imaginative, the intertextual uses made of her works and her life, and the ideological importance of biographical exemplarity all played significant parts in her influence on later writers and her lasting place on the list of female worthies of literary England. Questions remain, however: how much did Rowe contribute to these mutually implicated aspects of her afterlife? To what extent did she encourage or discourage 'fictionalised' versions of herself in her familiar letters, and, in turn, to what degree are her fictional works invested with elements characteristic of her private writings?

There are a number of different avenues to explore when discussing the posthumous representations of Elizabeth Rowe's life. The most familiar and well-trodden path is the biographical one, which, in the case of Rowe, requires considerable revision. Negotiating the various accounts of her life quickly reveals the acute importance which image, especially the social construction of the feminine image, played in the subsequent success of Rowe's productions. Her biographers' attempts to appeal to as many different spiritual persuasions and literary tastes as they could tends to muddle our understanding of Rowe's religious affiliations and private character. Moreover, there is much dissension amongst Rowe's admirers as to her 'enthusiastic' tendencies, and the religious and literary worth of this aspect of her compositions. Reading the *Miscellaneous Works* and *Devout Exercises* in the context of eighteenth-century enthusiasm illuminates many of the discrepancies in the various accounts. Of significant interest as well are Rowe's last letters from the dead, the ones she left for her friends and relations to receive after she had died. These letters combine all that is best in Rowe's epistolary style, but also many of those elements that eventually made her works too didactic for a reading public eager for less overtly zealous entertainment.

Another trail worth exploring is the discourse surrounding female exemplarity. In order to understand the reverential approach writers like Elizabeth Carter and Anna Barbauld took to the Rowe legacy, we need to have an appreciation of the importance placed on women who could be considered part of a tradition of female worthies. The concept of 'female moral authority' was being advanced through the creation of catalogues (such as Ballard's) and biographies (such as Rowe's) of female exemplars. These exemplars could then be cast as angelic forebears to later women writers, licensing in turn those writers' authority to propound intellectually sophisticated ideas about philosophy and religion. The most significant cases of influence and intertextual appropriation, therefore, are those instances when later women writers rehearse female exemplarity as a necessary accessory to literary achievement. Conversely, some women found the Rowe legacy inhibiting, and struggled with ways to incorporate as well as reject her influential works.

The fact remains, Rowe was, despite all the adulation and encomiastic tributes, a problematic figure for any writer who chose to admire, emulate, or perpetuate her life and literary style. Aligning oneself with Rowe's seemingly exemplary history could, therefore, be a subtle means of advertising one's own iconoclasm and willingness to distance oneself from the status quo. If they agreed on nothing else, Rowe's critics could all agree that she was unquestionably a true original in life and literature.

An original contribution: letters from the dead to the living

Rowe's most 'original' contributions to literature were her letters from the dead to the living. *Friendship in Death* and *Letters Moral and Entertaining* were appreciated by contemporaries and later generations as unique affirmations of the life to come and were seen to offer a 'fresh vision' and 'hope to the reader'.[174] The afterlife of these writings is a long one, filled with accolades and imitations. Most importantly, Rowe's letters from the dead were ineluctably identified with the writer and seen as personalised calls to holiness from the saintly author precisely because she actually did send customised letters from the dead to her friends and relations. Amongst her papers after her death were found letters to the Countess of Hertford, the Earl of Orrery, Arabella Marrow, James Theobald, Isaac Watts, Mrs Sarah Rowe (her mother-in-law), and Theophilus Rowe. These letters were printed in the *Miscellaneous Works* with the exception of Arabella Marrow's, Watts's (printed in *Devout Exercises*), and Theophilus's, which he chose to withhold because of its personal nature. These 'real' letters from the dead were reprinted in many letter collections throughout the century, and reveal the particular interest publishers and the public took in Rowe's private writings.

One of the obvious reasons for the popularity of these last letters is their superior compositional style. Rowe plainly crafted the letters with particular care and an eye to posthumous publication and it shows in their careful structure and elevated tone.[175] They are also, despite their obvious similarities in theme, individualised works, and show Rowe's ability to subtly differentiate the message for each recipient. For the Countess of Hertford, special attention is paid to their future reunion in the blissful regions but also to Rowe's assessment of her earthly 'works', by which she clearly means her writings. Since the countess was one of the few people aware of Rowe's authorship of the popular epistolary fictions she was in a position to understand and validate Rowe's statement: 'How poor were my hopes, if I depended on those works which my own vanity, or the partiality of men, have called good; and which, examined by divine purity, would prove, perhaps, but specious sins!' (MW, xliii). The letter also reiterates Rowe's Calvinistic belief in justification by faith alone and ends with an apostrophe to Christ stressing that he 'is all my salvation, and all my hope' (MW, xliii). The letter to the Earl of Orrery, on the other hand, shows off Rowe's literary knowledge and includes a number of quotations from Pope. For instance, she quotes stanza three from one of her favourite poems of Pope's, 'The Dying Christian to His Soul', which was also the poem she purportedly recited when she thought she was dying about a year before her actual decease.[176] Samuel Richardson has Clarissa Harlowe quote from the same stanza in her dying moments.[177] It seems probable that Richardson used the exemplary Rowe as a basis for elements of Clarissa's character and for incidental plot elements; for example, Clarissa favours her friends and relations with eerily cheerful letters from the dead.

James Theobald's letter is uncommon given the short acquaintance he had with Rowe, but she uses the opportunity to promote the idea that 'It would not be worth the while to cherish the impressions of a virtuous friendship, if the generous engagement was to be dissolv'd with mortal life' (MW, xlvi). Thus, friendship can begin at any stage of life because, if genuine, it will be renewed in heaven. She likewise notes that:

> while my affection for my surviving friends was never more warm, my concern for their happiness was never more ardent and sincere.
> This makes me employ some of the last part of my time in writing to three or four persons, whose merit requires my esteem, in hopes this solemn farwel [sic] will leave a serious impression on their minds. (MW, xlvii)

But it is the letter to Sarah Rowe, her mother-in-law, that is the most distinct, because it manages to combine easy familiarity and a frank discussion of the practicalities of death with the most elevated religious language. The letter begins prosaically enough: 'I am now taking my final adieu of this world, in certain hopes of meeting you in the next. I carry to my grave my affection and gratitude to your family' (*MW*, xlviii). Then the tone rises: 'I would collect the powers of my soul, and ask blessings for you with all the holy violence of prayer' (*MW*, xlviii–xlvix). After a brief respite – '"Tis but a short space I have to measure, the shadows are lengthening, and my sun declining' – it rises again with an apostrophe about being justified before the 'supreme tribunal' (*MW*, xlix). In spite of these extremes this letter is one of Rowe's most frequently reprinted pieces. Perhaps it was the familial and female connection that appealed to later readers (Sarah Rowe is often identified in the later collections as Elizabeth's actual mother), but it is equally likely that the stylistic range caught the eye of those compilers intent on presenting letters that could teach readers how to deploy grand sentiments when the occasion demanded.[178] What is even more compelling about their interest in these letters is that Rowe's enthusiasm never enters the equation. Though heightened religious fervour and explicit Calvinism is expressed, no one seems to have accused her of excessive enthusiasm in relation to them. Perhaps her deathbed scenes of piety were exempt precisely because she did confess perfectly orthodox Calvinistic tenets in these particular letters, and did not stray into any of the obscure strains of evangelicalism which many associated with her work, especially her devotions.

Problems with enthusiasm in the *Miscellaneous Works* and *Devout Exercises*

I briefly raised questions about the Henry Grove/Theophilus Rowe biography at the outset of Chapter 1, and the following discussion will try to flesh out my concerns with the accuracy, agenda, and failures of their account. It also considers the galvanising influence the combined publication of the 'Life', the letters, and the poetry had on all subsequent representations of Rowe. In tandem with the Grove/Rowe account, I explore Isaac Watts's problematic preface to *Devout Exercises of the Heart* (1738), which I argue planted many of the seeds of dissension that affected future interpretations of Rowe's life and works, including the Grove/Rowe biography. The discourse of enthusiasm Watts introduced is the spectre that plays the most significant role in any discussion of Rowe's afterlife because the instability associated with it haunts so many of her subsequent representations.

As Jon Mee has argued in his study of the complexity of responses that enthusiasm engendered throughout the eighteenth and nineteenth centuries, the policing of enthusiastic language was an ongoing cultural exercise. Mee's contention that, 'throughout the eighteenth century and beyond, enthusiasm remained as suspect as it had always been, if not properly regulated', suggests that Rowe somehow breached a regulatory threshold given the number of defensive or admonitory comments made about her writings after her death.[179] Before the appearance of her life and familiar letters in 1739 Isaac Watts took issue with Rowe's expressions and practices in his preface to her *Devout Exercises* (1738). However, many of his strictures stem from a critical misrepresentation of her text that has had a long-term effect on literary appreciations of Rowe.

Devout Exercises of the Heart in Meditation and Soliloquy, Prayer and Praise, as the title indicates, is a miscellaneous collection of reflections written, Rowe claims, 'for my improvement' (*Devout*, xxvii). In manuscript and print, these pieces were meant to play a role in private devotional rituals: the hortatory language and effusive sentiments effectively reorienting the writer's (and reader's) focus on spiritual rather than earthly things.[180] However, in his dedication, addressed to the unidentified Countess of Hertford, Watts frames Rowe's pieces in problematic terms:[181]

> I know, Madam, your tenderness and indulgence to every thing Mrs. ROWE has written, cannot with-hold your judgment from suspecting some of her expressions to be a little too rapturous, and too near a-kin to the language of the mystical writers; yet your piety and candor will take no such offence as to prevent your best improvement by them in all that is divine and holy. (*Devout*, sig. A3)

In accusing Rowe of mysticism and rapturous language it appears that Watts is trying to distance himself from the work; however, he goes on to claim that her devotional pieces will nevertheless improve the reader 'in all that is divine and holy'. Indeed, the idea of Watts trying to discredit expressions of affectionate religion is unlikely, as both he and Philip Doddridge were accused of just such expressions themselves.[182] In fact, Watts's uneasy vacillations between defensively reverential statements about Rowe's 'bright and sparkling' genius and 'sublime' virtues, and admonishing strictures against her old fashioned 'fervours of devout love [...] in the style of the *Song of Solomon*' (*Devout*, ix), are indicative of his own problems in accommodating enthusiastic language. He continues:

> I must confess that several of my composures in verse, written in younger life, were led by those examples [i.e. the Song of Solomon] unwarily into this track. But if I may be permitted to speak the sense of mature age, I can hardly think this the happiest language in which Christians should generally discover their warm sentiments of religion, since the clearer and more spiritual revelations of the New Testament. Yet still it must be own'd, there are some Souls favour'd with such beautifying Visits from Heaven, and raptur'd with such a Flame of divine Affection, as more powerfully engages all animal Nature in their Devotions, and constrains them to speak their purest and most spiritual Exercises in such pathetick and tender Expressions as may be perversely profaned by an unholy Construction. (*Devout*, xiii–vi [sic], xix is mispaginated as vi)

In his own *Reliquiae Juveniles* (1734) we see a similar defence of 'tender Expressions':

> Nor is it within the Power of any Man who writes, to escape the Censure of those whose Minds are so full of vile and uncleanly Images, that they will impose their own dishonest and impure Ideas upon Words of the most distant and innocent Sound. Every low and malicious Wit may turn even sacred Language to wicked and abominable Purposes, and clap a Set of perverse Ideas on the purest Diction [...]. But the Crime is in him that construes, and not in him that writes.[183]

Here again the blame is placed on readers who intentionally misconstrue the language of true devotion.

It seems that the fault in Rowe's works was that they were supposedly private devotions: Watts refers to the 'secret' nature of the '*Devotions of her Heart*' (*Devout*, ix–x). Didactic fiction such as *Friendship in Death* could be excused for displaying affecting language because 'to transform enthusiasm into art was to make it relatively safe', but evidence of Rowe using ecstatic language in her private devotions had the potential to destabilise the image of a virtuous exemplar and politely 'safe' writer into that of a ranting versifier.[184] At stake for Watts was the image of a powerfully effective religious writer who, to contemporary tastes, might appear worryingly evangelical in her enthusiasm. Despite his no doubt contrary intentions, Watts misrepresents the writings as strictly private devotions, written in the heat of religious meditation, when in fact they are described by Rowe as imaginative recreations for others' devotional reading and were circulated in manuscript amongst her coterie. In an undated letter to the Countess of Hertford which contained a selection of the pieces from *Devout Exercises*, Rowe claimed that, 'it is writt in imitation of Something of this kind which I read in manuscript wrote by one that Dyed very young and with great joy and Satisfaction which probably was from the Sense of having in this Solemn manner renewd her Sacred engagements made for her in Baptism' (MS 110, Letter 97, f. 234). Rowe's description of the work goes on to note her use of the devotional piece to aid her own prayers. The composition of her own piece, therefore, is shown to be either derivative of the earlier manuscript, or, more likely, a mixture of the original with her own fanciful additions. Watts's suggestion that it was the product of a poetic and religious delirium is almost certainly false. By presenting *Devout Exercises* as poetic excess, Watts blurred the line between Rowe's life and her writings, a problem that has persisted in Rowe scholarship to this date.

Theophilus Rowe's publication of the *Miscellaneous Works* one year later, in 1739, further exacerbated the conflation of her life and works. The nominal purpose of the *Miscellaneous Works* was to fulfil Rowe's request that all her remaining works should be published after her death, a common practice amongst practitioners of manuscript circulation in an age of burgeoning print publication. In addition to the author's bequest, Ezell notes that posthumous publication could function as a type of monumental tribute from surviving family members, where the physical memorials often stressed 'the fidelity of the printed text to the departed author's living voice, that those who knew the author in life will "recognize" the... characteristic "voice"'.[185] Rowe's 'voice' in the *Miscellaneous Works* was at the mercy of many who could not 'recognise' the coterie performer as distinct from the private individual. Theophilus's edition, which, in the hands of Grove, may have originally been intended as a tribute of the monumental kind, became a work primarily directed outwards to the buying public. It is not dedicated to any surviving family member or friend, and is advertised instead as the final text for those wishing to possess the complete works of Elizabeth Rowe. It even directs readers to a select list of her oeuvre, though attention is drawn to the fact that the 1696 publication of her poems should not be considered part of her mature works.

Theophilus's edition of the *Miscellaneous Works* emphasises and, in effect, consolidates the notion that Rowe's literary compositions are exemplary specimens of morality, as well as useful spiritual aids *because* of the way she lived. Chantal Lavoie argues that it conveys a sense of 'completion, of life and *opus'*, but in reality the text is constructed in such a way as to bookend the miscellaneous pieces with the 'Life' at one end and the familiar letters at the other.[186] Clare Brant, in her study of women's miscellaneous collections, points out that biography often works as the thread that holds together the pieces in a miscellany because, 'if writings are generically diverse, the figure of the author can stabilize them'.[187] Given that the variety of compositions still in manuscript at Rowe's death ranged generically from fictional letters, paraphrases, translations, hymns, original poetry to or about her coterie, and, of course, her familiar letters, the need for a stabilising figure is clearly necessary in Rowe's case. The problem with subsequent eighteenth-century biographical interpretations of Rowe's poetry is that it is often based on an inaccurate understanding of her life. Rowe's reclusive nature, combined with a dearth of people familiar with her early history, meant that a consistent account of the author was not actually possible from those still alive. The figure used to 'prop up' the heterogeneous collection is, in many respects, quite as fictional as the characters in *Friendship in Death*. This partly fictional 'Life' quickly took on an expansive literary life of its own.

First and foremost, though, the 'Life' was designed as an exemplary record for the benefit of public edification. Henry Grove began the 'Life' as such; however, he died shortly after beginning it and Theophilus Rowe was left to complete the task. In order to fill out his scanty account Theophilus appended a 'life' of her late husband and his brother, Thomas Rowe, which tells us infinitely more about Thomas's education and scholarly writings than it does about Elizabeth's. Surviving friends of Elizabeth found several faults with portions of the 'Life' and, though Theophilus readily admitted his own inadequacies as her biographer, he and Grove made no attempts to canvas Rowe's early acquaintances for more information on or even confirmation of certain aspects of her youthful career.[188] His version of Elizabeth's 'Life' is largely her own and the countess's performative renditions of it available to him through the familiar letters of the Alnwick letter book and the letters collected from the surviving members of the Rowe family, including her mother-in-law. Unfortunately, there appear to be no extant manuscript letters between Rowe and her famous literary acquaintances, or between herself and the male divines such as Watts, Grove, and Benjamin Colman who wrote so much about her after her death.[189] Even though the accounts these men circulated about Rowe appear to offer intimate knowledge about Rowe's history and personality, they are often scanty on specifics and heavily influenced by ideological factors. What we are left with are a number of male interpretations of Rowe's character that are rife with inaccuracies and extraneous polemics.

For example, the Grove/Rowe biography, like Watts's preface, tries to tackle the issue of Rowe's 'fire and elevation' (*MW*, xv). In contrast to Watts's clear hierarchy of acceptable expression, however, the overlapping terms used to describe the undesirable language of enthusiasm and the acceptable expressions of religious fervour in the 'Life' make it difficult to construct a clear picture of what Theophilus Rowe and Henry Grove thought of Rowe's works. They certainly do not seem as concerned about the appearance of dangerously rapturous language as Watts does in his 'defence'. This may partly be explained by Theophilus Rowe's familiarity with her manuscript letters and the stylistic genesis of her enthusiasm in the fictional works (he was entrusted with seeing *Letters Moral and Entertaining I–III* through the press).[190] Nevertheless, the 'Life' vacillates between presenting Rowe as an inspired poet/prophet and a reasonable exemplar of religion and sociability.

Grove opens the discussion of Rowe's poetic style with the encomium: 'Poetry indeed was her favourite employment [...] So prevalent was her genius this way, that her very *prose* hath all the *charms* of *verse* without the *fetters*, the same fire and elevation, the same bright images, bold figures, rich and flowing diction' (*MW*, xv). However, when dismissing the early publication of her youthful poems by Dunton in the *Athenian Mercury* and *Poems on Several Occasions by Philomela*, Grove paints a tamer picture of Rowe's poetic inspiration.

> Tho' many of these poems are of the religious kind, and all of them consistent with the strictest regard to the rules of virtue; yet some things in them gave her no little uneasiness in advanced life. To a mind that had so entirely subdued its passions, or devoted them to the honour of its maker, and endued with the tenderest *moral sense*, what she could not absolutely approve, appear'd unpardonable; and, not satisfied to have done nothing that injur'd the sacred cause of virtue, she was displeas'd with her self for having writ any thing that did not directly promote it. (*MW*, xvi–xvii)

Grove's depiction of Rowe is notable for its sentimental construction of her wounded 'moral sense', but his highly subjective account of her reasons for repudiating passion in her later life is at odds with the image he actually invokes of a writer who was 'not satisfied to have done nothing' and believed in actively promoting 'the sacred cause of virtue'. Alternating between images of respectable subjection and strident purposefulness, Grove seems as much at a loss concerning Rowe as was Watts. Neither writer manages to reconcile the literary and polemical aspirations Rowe evinced with their own conceptions of her social role.

Theophilus Rowe takes up the issue of enthusiasm more directly, perhaps in response to Watts's preface in the *Devout Exercises*, and though he agrees that some of her expressions may seem 'a little too rapturous', he continues:

> a just regard to the sex, and particular genius of the author, will, I hope, prevail for a gentle censure. It could scarce be expected that a lady should be vers'd in the arts of strict reasoning; and it ought to be easily forgiven, if she wrote on religious subjects, even in prose, rather with the fire and bold license of a poet, than the accuracy of a divine and a philosopher. (*MW*, 1)

Not bothering to hide behind equivocations, Theophilus acknowledges her weak points but blames the lapse on biology rather than enthusiasm. While Grove admires the results of the 'fire' in Rowe's prose, Theophilus censures the same aspect for its tendency to exhibit theological and philosophical inaccuracy, specifically attributing such deficiencies in general to her sex. He does, however, footnote this passage with a quotation from Rowe acknowledging her excessive enthusiasm to the countess. What gets lost in Theophilus's otherwise faithful account of Rowe's objective awareness of her enthusiasm is the sheer number of times Rowe does account for its appearances in her letters and poetry. As I noted above, many of the passages Theophilus expunges from the familiar letters in the *Miscellaneous Works* are the frequent references Rowe makes regarding her sources of inspiration and stylistic reasons for writing in an enthusiastic vein. Instead of identifying Rowe's enthusiasm for what it was, a literary device, he accounts for its presence by acknowledging it as a feminine weakness she could not control.

Later female writers also perceived Rowe's enthusiasm as a 'weakness' and hence a potential problem for their own increasingly professional authorial image. Elizabeth Carter's father warned her against adopting too many of Rowe's fervent expressions, and Carter in turn warned her friend, Catherine Talbot, about the pitfalls of self-imposed solitude and excessive religious meditation. Nevertheless, Carter still found reasons to persevere in her emulation of Rowe, and continued to recommend her works to younger acolytes. Talbot also formed a late friendship with the Countess of Hertford (by then the Duchess of Somerset), which provided her with the opportunity of viewing Rowe's letters in manuscript. Similarly, Frances Burney's first impression of the enthusiasm in Rowe's works was decidedly unfavourable, but her later concessions to the possible merits of religious enthusiasm suggest that she too found this aspect of Rowe's works a marker of strength rather than weakness. Ultimately, what prevails in all the posthumous assessments of Rowe is her biographical exemplarity. The following sections, therefore, explore two very different rehearsals of female exemplarity specifically attributable to the Rowe legacy.[191]

Elizabeth Carter and Rowe

Elizabeth Carter's association with the *Gentleman's Magazine* and admiration for Rowe is an interesting example of a later female exemplar's interaction with Rowe's life and works. Rowe was the subject of Carter's poem, 'On the Death of Mrs Rowe', which first appeared in the April 1737 issue of the *Gentleman's Magazine*. It was then revised for the March 1739 issue, and, at the request of Theophilus Rowe, she sent the 1739 version of the poem to him for inclusion in Rowe's *Miscellaneous Works* (1739), and included yet another revision of the poem in her own *Poems on Several Occasions* (1762). The transformations from one text of the poem to the next reveal Carter's growing awareness of her own place in relation to Rowe and the female tradition, and clearly outline what the young poet drew inspiration from in the example of Elizabeth Rowe.

In the 1737 version Carter opens with the simple declaration: 'Accept, much honour'd shade! the artless lays,/ The muse a tribute to thy mem'ry pays', and continues to address Rowe's departed being throughout the poem.[192] There is no mention of linking herself with Rowe at this point, but, in couching her praises for Rowe in terms of learning and piety, she was obviously identifying very strongly with those aspects of Rowe's writings. She declares:

> Farewell, our sex's ornament and pride!
> Born with a genius fitted to excell,
> And, blest with sense t'apply that genius well.

She likewise notes that Rowe chose to 'withdraw the mind,/ to relish pleasures of a nobler kind'. She then contrasts Rowe with the female wits who write 'Th'intriguing novel, and the wanton tale', and uses the occasion to extol, 'What diff'rent subjects in thy pages shine!' The poem thus sets up Rowe as a type of virtuous exemplar in the choice of genre and content she chose to print.

The version for the 1739 issue begins with the same opening stanza, but by the second stanza has introduced a new observation:

> Oft did Intrigue its guilty arts unite,
> To blacken the records of female wit;
> The tuneful song lost ev'ry modest grace,
> And lawless freedoms triumph'd in their place.[193]

Her allusion to the female wits as fallen angels is a much more powerful statement than the previous version of the poem made, and echoes Elizabeth Johnson's preface in *Poems* (1696), where she too laments fallen women like Aphra Behn. Carter follows these lines with her own view of the moral purpose of art:

> The Muse, for vices not her own accus'd,
> With blushes view'd her sacred gifts abus'd:
> Those gifts for nobler purposes design'd,
> To raise the thoughts, and moralize the mind,
> The chaste delights of virtue to inspire,
> And warm the bosom with seraphic fire,
> Sublime the passions, lend devotion wings,
> And celebrate the *first great cause* of things.

Her position now clear, she goes on to describe how, 'These glorious Tasks were *Philomela's* Part', and in language that echoes the pious Rowe at her most enthusiastic, declares:

> When to the vocal grove, or winding stream,
> She hymn'd th'almighty author of its frame,
> Transported echoes bore the sounds along,
> And all creation listen'd to the song.
> Bold as when raptur'd seraphs strike the lyre,
> Chaste as the vestal's consecrated fire,
> ...
> Where rapt in joys to vulgar minds unknown,
> She felt a flame ecstatic as their own.

The most significant change in this version of the poem comes in the last eight lines, where Carter specifically aligns herself with Rowe on moral and literary grounds in her own 'attempt for fame'.[194]

> Fix'd on my soul shall thy example grow,
> And be my genius and my guide below:
> To this I'll point my first, my noblest views,
> Thy spotless verse shall regulate my Muse.
> And oh! forgive (tho' faint the transcript be,
> That copies an Original like thee)
> My highest pride, my best attempt for fame,
> That joins my own to *Philomela's* name.

Carter draws a dividing line between poets like herself and Rowe, and the fallen female wits who produce romances, intrigues, and wanton tales. Through her admiration and imitation of Philomela, she attains a role and a reason to publish works that will counteract the blackened records of female wit.

Carter's enthusiasm for Rowe caused some disquiet for her father, though, and his cautionary advice seems to have influenced her against the excesses of Rowe's passionate religion.[195] In the *Poems on Several Occasions* (1762) version, Carter makes a concerted effort to lessen the enthusiastic element while heightening the tone. For example, in the line: 'In her was ev'ry bright perfection join'd', 'perfection' is changed to 'Distinction' in the 1762 copy; likewise, 'passions' is changed to 'Motions'; 'Bold' to 'Full'; 'blissful seats' to 'blest Abode'; and, 'Where rapt in joys to vulgar minds unknown' is changed to 'Where, rapt in Joys to mortal Sense unknown'. The older, more confident artist still retains the closing lines, however, manifestly linking herself with Rowe and her exemplary record. Montagu Pennington, Carter's nephew and editor, notes with pride that Carter worked hard at the 'polish of her compositions', and specifically cites the many versions of the Rowe poem as evidence of her diligence.[196]

It is also worth noting that Carter's poem on Rowe avails itself of a far more important eighteenth-century writer, Alexander Pope. Claudia Thomas lists a number of phrases and images that Carter transposes from Pope's works, and notes that Carter's 'creative' misreading of Pope's passive depictions of women's virtue, in 'The Rape of the Lock' and 'To a Lady', leads her to assert the active virtue of a woman like Rowe.[197] Creating an intertextual mosaic with the fusion of Rowe's life and Pope's poetry allows Carter to critique Pope in the process of extolling Rowe, and highlights the ways in which women writers reacted to and rewrote the male tradition whilst advancing a female one of their own.

Carter also recommended Rowe's works to younger women writers like Hester Chapone (1727–1801). In 1761, Chapone sent Carter the following analysis of Rowe's style:

> I have just been reading Mrs. Rowe's letters from the Dead to the Living, and those called Moral and Entertaining.
> [...] I am extremely charmed with the first, where her luxuriant imagination has so fine a field to display itself in. But the other set of letters, which treat of matters we are more acquainted with, seem to me much too romantic and unnatural. [...]
> [H]er devotion is too poetical for me, and savours too much of the extravagancies of the mystics. When I hear persons addressing the Supreme Being in the language of the most sensual and extravagant love, I cannot help fancying they went mad on a disappointment of that passion. This, however, was not Mrs. Rowe's case, for I think she was remarkably happy in marriage. [...] I know she is a great favourite of yours, and, perhaps, you will hardly forgive this censure.[198]

For Chapone, *Friendship in Death* showcases the fictive luxuriance of Rowe's imagination, yet very similar scenarios in the later work are problematic. Suddenly Rowe's language is too ardent to be art and too romantic to be useful for practical devotions. Interestingly, Chapone's comments on Rowe's luxuriance echo a Johnson review (discussed below), and her recourse to Rowe's biography (it is her knowledge of Rowe's happy marriage that redeems Rowe from sensuous enthusiasm) suggest that Rowe's legacy was still generating a mixed response.

Carter's admiration for Rowe never faded, though, and at the age of 62 she visited Rowe's house in Frome, Somerset.[199] Carter's love of landscape and scenes of majestic natural beauty undoubtedly led her to view the rural retreat of one of her favourite authors, but it also betrays the importance she laid on Rowe's life as an extension of her works. Pennington likewise tried to conflate his aunt's life and works. His editorial preface in the edition of letters to Elizabeth Montagu declared, 'Those who sit down to the perusal of these letters, with no view to moral, literary or religious improvement, will certainly derive from them neither advantage nor pleasure' (*Letters* (1817), xviii–xix). Finding evidence in her letters analogous to the moral seriousness expressed in her *Rambler* essays and introduction to *Epictetus*, Pennington helped to perpetuate the image of the female exemplar as one in whom 'piety, virtue, and genius were the foundation; and learning and accomplishments [...] the ornamental parts of the superstructure' (*Memoirs*, 86). He was, however, at pains to note that, 'Her piety was never varying; constant, fervent, but not enthusiastic' (*Memoirs*, 12). The example of Rowe, as enabling and inspiring as it was, could still cause problems for the female writer who believed in rational religion and sought to foster an image of professional competence.

Frances Burney 'displays the author' in *Camilla*

Sixty-eight years after Rowe first released *Friendship in Death*, Frances Burney (1752–1840) published her third novel, *Camilla*. Burney's successes with *Evelina* (1778) and *Cecilia* (1782) meant that the 1796 appearance of *Camilla, or a Picture of Youth* was the work of a practised and a respected novelist. Burney was free of her servitude at court, happily married to Alexandre d'Arblay, the mother of a new baby boy, but short of money, and thus a return to print seemed in order.[200] The story was one she had intermittently worked on during her court years, but by the time she began writing in earnest late in 1794, the plot had changed considerably. Some original notes suggest that the work was going to stress the 'disjunction between the generations', but eventually the focal point shifted to the vicissitudes of youth and the inscrutableness of 'the Heart of man', or human mind.[201] Margaret Anne Doody notes too that the novel is nominally about female education, but disagrees with the notion that the book is conservative or didactic.[202] Instead, she sees an element of scepticism running through the novel which repeatedly highlights 'the difficulty not only of making choices but of seeing the truth'.[203] Thus, one of the crucial concerns of the novel is our ability to accurately judge others, a question I believe Burney struggled with in the case of one of her female characters and the historical figure it was based upon.

Similar to Jane Austen's *Pride and Prejudice* or *Emma*, the novel deals with the social and moral education of the heroine, Camilla Tyrold, in her quest for a companionate marriage. As in *Pride and Prejudice*, the heroine has a number of sisters and cousins who need marrying off, and the question of inheritance and fortune is a central concern throughout. Camilla's suitor, Edgar Mandelbert, is likewise a prototype of Emma's Mr Knightley in his mentorship of Camilla. Unfortunately, he is as young and inexperienced as her, and, rather like Watts, Grove, and Theophilus Rowe, frequently misreads feminine performance through an unimaginative and morally prosaic prism. Edgar is particularly anxious about Camilla's choice of close female friends, and the novel superficially validates Edgar's censorious impressions of many of the women Camilla befriends. However, during the course of the novel, Burney offers two wonderfully enigmatic women for Camilla to learn from and, though Edgar immediately distrusts both, Burney's complicated presentation of them suggests that she was more open to their idiosyncrasies than conservative assessments of her writing might suggest.

The women in question are the wonderfully sardonic Mrs Arlbery and the ingenuous Mrs Berlinton. They are, without a doubt, flawed human beings, but they nevertheless manage to avoid complete consignment to female caricature. This does not mean that Burney lets them escape their narrative functions; rather, their interactions with and influence over with the heroine of the novel are much more complex than their minor supporting status signifies. Despite the disreputable insinuations cast on each of them, the novel finds room to validate aspects of their opinions and lifestyles. Mrs Arlbery is undoubtedly the more experienced and appealing character, as well as the one contemporaries identified with the author, Mrs D'Arblay.[204] What concerns me here, however, is the use Burney makes of Elizabeth Rowe and her works in the story of the mercurial Mrs Berlinton, and, through this character, Burney's 'unholy construction,' to use Watts's phrase, of the Rowe image.

In her Journal of 1768, the 16-year-old Burney records:

> I have Just finish'd Mrs Rowe's Letters from the Dead to the Living— & moral & Entertaining.—I had heard a great deal of them before I saw them, & am sorry to tell you I was much disappointed with them: they are so very enthusiastick, that the religion she preaches rather disgusts & cloys than charms & elevates—& so romantick, that every word betrays improbability, instead of disguising fiction, & displays the Author, instead of human nature.[205]

A fascinating commentary on Rowe's style, but, unfortunately, like Watts's defence, quite misleading. The key phrase of course is that she thinks the work 'displays the Author', and the character of Mrs Berlinton, in *Camilla*, appears to do the same duty. The 44-year-old Burney better understood the gulf between fiction and reality, however, and her depiction of Rowe and Rowe's work, *Friendship in Death*, consciously plays with ideas of misreading and misrepresenting, as does the novel as a whole. In *Camilla* there is an interesting dialectic forged between the rational tradition that finds Rowe too enthusiastic and religious to be of use, and the exemplary tradition that credits Rowe with the rehabilitation of religion and religious language.

Mrs Berlinton is introduced in Volume III, Book VI in a chapter titled, 'A Walk by Moonlight', a common setting for many of Rowe's letters from the dead to the living.[206] Camilla, out for a moonlight stroll with an acquaintance, catches 'a glimpse of a figure in white' talking to herself (387). While they debate whether it could be a ghost, they realise that the figure is actually reading a letter from a 'lovely friend' (who will later turn out to be the duplicitous Alphonso Bellamy – that is, 'Belle ami'). There are a number of subsequent meetings with the unknown beautiful lady until Camilla finally discovers her name, but the most telling is when the former is interrupted reading Rowe's *Friendship in Death*. She is also described reading other so-called enthusiastic writers, such as Akenside and Collins, but the Rowe reference appears to be the most explicit clue to the romantic, enthusiastic, and irrational nature of Mrs Berlinton given Burney's own youthful critique of the work. Mrs Berlinton's brother, Melmond, is likewise a romantic figure, but his exhibitions of extreme manly sensibility have their basis in his university education and an acceptable understanding of literary affections, unlike the uneducated solitude of his sister. Edgar too shows signs of sensibility when he hears Melmond read from Thomson's *Seasons* (101), and yet Mrs Berlinton's displays of these affections are somehow *de trop*. Evidently it is only acceptable to lose oneself in the 'pleasures of the imagination' if one has been schooled in the classics. Nevertheless, in Camilla's eyes, Mrs Berlinton is an inestimable paragon and their mutual love for poetry and enthusiastic prose helps to cement their friendship. Furthermore, Burney's mockery of classical learning in the figure of Dr Orkborne, and even latterly Dr Marchmont, proves that even the classics cannot save one from imbecility or erroneous impressions.

Unregulated whimsy is more pernicious, however, and whatever concessions are allowed Mrs Berlinton based on her beauty, sensitivity, and affections fall away when Burney reveals the evils to which her irresponsibility can lead. This side of Mrs Berlinton has nothing to do with the Rowe persona, but the gaming, debts, and illicit affairs which come into play may very well have been an unconscious allusion on Burney's part to scenarios drawn from Rowe's works, especially *Friendship in Death*. In fact, the didactic message behind the downfall of Mrs Berlinton is exactly the same one used by Rowe in many of her tales about vapid town beauties. Mrs Berlinton's established status as a star in the social firmament would have condemned her in Rowe's eyes as much as Edgar's, and we need only read Rowe's many remonstrative letters to the countess while she was at court to remind us that Rowe saw 'the world' as a corrupting and desolate place for an immortal soul to sojourn in. In this respect Burney and Rowe agree, and both paint retired domesticity as the social ideal for men and women.

Perhaps some of the most damning criticisms of Mrs Berlinton are made in the chapter on 'Traits of Character', in which Burney contrasts a number of female and male characters. Though nominally presenting men and women, the emphasis is noticeably on the females and particularly Edgar's assessment of them. At this point in the story Camilla is already well acquainted with Mrs Berlinton, and is fashionably established in the *bon ton* as a result. In addition, as the guest of Mrs Arlbery, she is forced into Bath society on numerous occasions and, on this particular day, to another raffle.[207] Edgar, of course, watches her anxiously for potential social and moral flaws, but is distracted momentarily by the appearance of Lord O'Lerney and Lady Isabella Irby. They too notice Camilla and Lord O'Lerney points out that 'The character of her [Camilla's] countenance [...] strikes me very peculiarly. 'Tis so intelligent, yet so unhackneyed, so full of meaning, yet so artless, that, while I look at her, I feel myself involuntarily anxious for her welfare' (470). The unconscious intelligence and ingenuousness he attributes to Camilla are precisely the character traits she sees in the romantically susceptible Mrs Berlinton. Perhaps the only adjective not applicable to Mrs Berlinton, given her fashionably extravagant lifestyle, is 'unhackneyed'. Lord O'Lerney then moves on to a description of Mrs Arlbery, who he notes 'is one of the first women I have ever known, for wit and capacity. She has an excellent heart, too; though her extraordinary talents, and her carelessness of opinion make it sometimes, but very unjustly, doubted' (471). This vindication of Mrs Arlbery's merits finally puts Edgar at ease regarding Camilla's friendship with her, but the continuance of Lord O'Lerney's speech accuses all three women, Camilla, Berlinton, and Arlbery, of insensitivity:

> A young woman is no where so rarely respectable, or respected, as at these water-drinking places, if seen at them either long or often. The search of pleasure and dissipation, at a spot consecrated for restoring health to the sick, the infirm, and the suffering, carries with it an air of egotism, that does not give the most pleasant idea of the feeling and disposition. (471)

Lady Irby attempts to defend the actions of young women by trotting out the argument that they are simply doing what everyone else does, but O'Lerney insists that, when 'they do not weigh what their observers weigh for them' (471), they are, as it were, giving their censurers free reign to criticise. If, however, they stayed at home and cultivated Lady Irby's sterling traits, 'in whose manners and conversation, dignity and simplicity were equally blended' (470), they might achieve moral superiority.

After a brief commentary on Sir Sedley's character traits, Burney returns to the waiting raffle and the non-appearance of Lady Alithea Selmore and Mrs Berlinton. Lady Alithea, as a mark of superiority, sends her woman as a proxy thrower, while Mrs Berlinton sends a footman with a note to Camilla. In the letter she entreats Camilla to throw for her as she is 'in the midst of Akenside's Pleasures of the Imagination, and [can] not tear herself away from them' (474). Singling herself and Camilla out in this manner gives Edgar an opportunity to broach the subject of her influence on Camilla. In response to his tentative critique Camilla initially enthuses that it is 'impossible to resist admiring, compassionating, and loving her,' though she does concede, 'she is [not] always coolly upon her guard' (475). But Edgar presses the point and in a comparison between Mrs Berlinton and Lady Irby he manages to show Camilla how differently conduct may be interpreted. Camilla, relying on Mrs Berlinton's youth (she is only 18) and good nature, believes that, with time, she will acquire discretion; however, Edgar counters Camilla's rosy picture of Mrs Berlinton's future:

> Do you think, then [...] that the few years of difference in their age were spent by Lady Isabella in the manner they are now spent by Mrs. Berlinton? do you think she paved the way for her present dignified though unassuming character by permitting herself to be surrounded by professed admirers? (476)

Burney then records that 'Camilla was startled. She had not seen her conduct in this light: yet her understanding refused to deny it might bear this interpretation' (476). Edgar follows up with yet more examples of how Lady Isabella shuns the spotlight and admirers, while Mrs Berlinton unwittingly, perhaps, encourages adulation and speculation. The effect on Camilla is, as she notes, startling, but instead of abandoning her friendship with Mrs Berlinton she decides that she will support her friend in the hopes of guiding her away from potential evils, especially Bellamy.

In the next chapter, entitled 'Traits of Eccentricity', we are provided with a more detailed description of Mrs Berlinton. Burney describes her as one who,

> joined unhappily all that was most dangerous for herself; an heart the most susceptible, sentiments the most romantic, and an imagination the most exalted. She had been an orphan from earliest years, and left, with an only brother, to the care of a fanatical maiden aunt, who had taught her nothing but her faith and her prayers, without one single lesson upon good works, or the smallest instruction upon the practical use of her theoretical piety.[...] whatever was enthusiastic in theology, formed the whole of her idea and her belief with respect to religion. (487)

And Camilla, much to Edgar's dismay, refuses to abandon her friendship with this 'dangerous' woman. Unfortunately, Mrs Berlinton proves Edgar right and not only goes into debt gaming, but, spurred on by the so-called virtuous desires expressed in Bellamy's letters allows him to visit her in London, and, even after his marriage to Camilla's sister, Eugenia, agrees to a private tête-à-tête in the countryside. Camilla finds out about the intended rendezvous and warns Melmond, who then intervenes with his sister. Interestingly enough, it is his appeal to her fanatical religious upbringing that saves her, because reminded of the eternal nature of rewards and punishments in heaven she breaks down in remorse and maintains her virtue. Bellamy, meanwhile, in a failed attempt to extort more money out of Eugenia, is killed when their carriage driver thinks he is about to shoot Eugenia and fires on him first.

All of this may seem very far removed from Rowe's life, and it certainly is, but there are nevertheless elements of Rowe's contested 'Life' story in Mrs Berlinton's character construction. Despite the argument I have been presenting regarding Burney's distaste for Rowe's fictional letters, there is a case to be made for Burney using her personal ambivalence about enthusiastic literature, Rowe, and Rowe's works as a way of elucidating her own didactic aim. A primary concern of the novel is the way people misread the actions of others and similarly misread and misapply letters, heroic literature, and even sermons. Perhaps the spirit of perverseness and contrariety which appears throughout the novel is Burney's concession to a writer she purposefully misrepresents. As Camilla protests at the end of the novel, she too has been the subject of 'continual misconstruction' (896) by Edgar, and what to him often appears flighty is actually the result of reasoned deliberations. Likewise,

Rowe's romantic language and improbable plots need not be read as her own enthusiastic religious beliefs, but as an effective appropriation of enthusiastic poetics and amatory narratives in the name of virtue and religion. The avowed purpose, after all, of *Friendship in Death* and *Letters Moral and Entertaining* was to impress the 'Notion of the Soul's immortality' – precisely what saves Mrs Berlinton from ruin – and to do so using an entertaining method.

Uses and reception of Rowe's work

The afterlife of Rowe's literary endeavours is noticeably less volatile than that associated with her reputation or image. Her works, including *Friendship in Death, Letters Moral and Entertaining*, and *Devout Exercises*, maintained a strong and lasting presence on the book market throughout the eighteenth and nineteenth centuries. In his study, *The Reading Nation in the Romantic Period*, William St Clair remarks that Elizabeth Rowe must have been one of the most popular authors in the latter half of the century given the number of editions her works went through.[208] Combined printings of *Friendship in Death* with *Letters Moral and Entertaining in Three Parts* appeared, in London alone, at least 27 times after Rowe's death in 1737.[209] As the book market expanded so too did Rowe's popularity: editions of the combined letters were printed and sold in Dublin, Edinburgh, Glasgow, Newcastle, Plymouth, Berwick, Birmingham, Romsey, Germany, Sweden, New York, Boston, New Haven, and Philadelphia throughout the same period. *Devout Exercises* also made frequent appearances on booksellers' lists and seems to have gained a substantial following in America as well as provincial towns across England with over 56 imprints listed on the *ESTC* and *ECCO*. The last printing of the combined letters in 1818 (London) means that Rowe's letters were continuously in print for almost ninety years, and the last edition of *Devout Exercises,* in 1830 (London), indicates a run of just over ninety years. *The History of Joseph* had a less stunning showing in its own right and was only reprinted 12 times; however, it also appeared in seven of the later collected editions.[210] The *Miscellaneous Works* fared worse but still had a respectable life in print with five editions: 2nd edn 1749, 3rd edn 1750, 4th edn 1756, and 5th edn 1772, as well as new imprints in 1770 (Edinburgh), in 1795 as *The Poetical Works of Mrs Elizabeth Rowe,* in 1796 as the important *Works...in four volumes,* and in 1820 as *The Poetical Works of Mrs Elizh* [sic] *Rowe. Joseph'*s 12 editions and the *Work's* nine editions may account for the smallest portion of Rowe's printed output but, given the number of authors who never made it past a first edition, even these less popular works should be considered successes by eighteenth-century standards.

Documenting Rowe's bibliographical history in this cumulative manner reveals the impressive breadth and longevity of her appeal. From American colonists, English provincials, and London's social and intellectual elite, to translations into German and Swedish, Rowe's popularity defies easy categorisation. Scholars have documented the elite's patronage of Rowe's works, particularly the Countess of Hertford and the Thynne family in general, but there has been less focus on her general readership, especially those many eighteenth-century readers who kept her in print for almost a century. Moreover, due to Rowe's lifelong practice of circulating works in manuscript as well as using print, the attention of such luminaries as Matthew Prior and Alexander Pope as early admirers of her manuscript poetry has deflected interest away from later writers whose praise was almost entirely contingent on her printed works. Encomiums from Elizabeth Carter, Samuel Johnson, John Duncombe, and Anna Barbauld were based on works such as *Friendship in Death*, and her life and letters in the *Miscellaneous Works*, but there were also a number of less distinguished and unknown figures who applauded Rowe and her works.

Jane Turrell (1708–35), the American daughter of Benjamin Colman, had, according to her biographer, 'the Fear of God before her Eyes', and modelled her life and writings on Rowe.[211] Her 14-line poem 'On reading the Warning of Mrs. Singer' constructs Rowe in prophetic, Old Testament terms:

> the fair Reprover of a guilty Land.
> You vie with the fam'd Prophetess of old,
> Burn with her Fire, in the same Cause grow bold,
> Dauntless you undertake th'unequal Strife,
> and raise dead Virtue by your Verse to Life.[212]

Turrell's religious turn of mind is 'what the Pious will esteem and praise' and this 'enthusiastic' strain is clearly what American Nonconformist circles admired in Rowe.[213] Anna Aikin (later Barbauld) also linked herself to Rowe in her first publication, *Poems* (1773). In her 'Verses on Mrs. Rowe' Aikin very quickly notes Rowe's role as a 'chaster Sappho' (l.1) and praises her 'spotless life' (l.4).[214] However, Stuart Curran shows that Aikin's poem is substantially influenced by Carter's careful rehabilitation of Rowe in more rational terms.[215] For John Duncombe, Rowe *was* Philomela. In his poem *The Feminiad* (1754) he depicts the

'Nymph' warbling her 'ecstatic song' and 'wish'd for, death' in 'Frome's embroider'd vale', but his classical staging still sounds as epiphanic as her own meditations.[216] His footnote refers to the well-known 'Life' and his problematic combination of heightened language and moralising message suggests that his source is the conflicted Grove/Rowe life, rather than the early poetry of 'Philomela'.

Samuel Johnson foregrounds Rowe's popular prose followers in a 1756 review of *Miscellanies on Moral and Religious Subjects, in Prose and Verse*, published by Elizabeth Harrison but 'written by many hands'. He notes, 'The authors of the essays in prose seem generally to have imitated, or tried to imitate, the copiousness and luxuriance of Mrs. Rowe. This, however, is not all their praise; they have laboured to add to her brightness of imagery, her purity of sentiments.'[217] Johnson's observation that they tried to imitate Rowe was an understatement, some of the letters are virtual copies of Rowe's fictional letters from the dead. The text appears to have been aimed at a middle-class audience, especially women, and was printed in an affordable octavo size, with fine paper available for more affluent subscribers.[218]

For the most part, however, editors did not bother commissioning imitations of Rowe's luxuriant correspondence when they could simply reproduce the original letters. Reprints first surfaced in 1745, in the practical work, *An useful and entertaining collection of letters upon various subjects*, which included her real letters from the dead. This was followed by literally dozens of appearances in instructive letter manuals including the widely reprinted *Elegant Extracts* (1st edn 1783) from Vicesimus Knox, as well as texts targeted specifically at schools, such as *Models of letters, for the use of schools and private students* (1794). It would not be an overstatement to claim that the afterlife of the letters outperformed the memoirs of her life in print and yet it was Elizabeth Rowe's biographical exemplarity that eventually silenced this prolific literary afterlife.

Despite widespread earnestness towards everything to do with Rowe, she still disappeared from later literary accounts of the period. The question we need to ask is: how and why someone so popular could vanish so effectively from literary history? The answer is manifold, but a primary cause may be found in Rowe's choice of genre: the letter. Women's contributions to the republic of letters have gone largely unheeded, especially ones that deal with religion, and Rowe is no exception. Her fictional letters may have gained her a little more shelf-time, but the declining interest in didactic literature and lack of attention to the specific literary allusions in Rowe's work relegated her to the periphery of literary studies. Additionally, the conflation of Rowe's life and works caused irrevocable damage to the learned image she fostered. Her works may have referred to some of the most intellectually sophisticated writers of her day, but her biographers chose instead to focus on her natural genius and saintly, bucolic life. Biographical exemplarity overshadowed the achievement her education represented. Here was a woman whose life spanned the seventeenth and eighteenth centuries, who could read and write three languages, compose respectably correct poetry and imaginative prose, and, most impressively, actively participate in the religious, philosophical, and literary debates of her time. For this reason alone Rowe deserves reassessment, but she also rewards the reader willing to engage with her letters by offering a diverse, but inclusive view of a vast range of eighteenth-century literature.

3
'The new and untrodden path': Catharine Cockburn, Philosophy, and the Republic of Letters

> M.ʳˢ Cockburn deserveth the first Rank among the best Moral Writers. In Strength & Clearness of Reasoning in force & propriety of Language few have been her Equals. Her Manner & Matter are greatly superior to all the Performances of the Whole Sex in all Ages and Places of the Whole World. Some memorial should be preserved of so extraordinary a Person. The following Account, tho' very imperfect, is the best we have been able to procure.[219]

Catharine Cockburn (1674?–1749), dramatist, poet, philosopher, religious controversialist, and prolific writer of both fictional and familiar letters has, like Elizabeth Rowe, been characterised as a manifestly exemplary female writer. She never enjoyed the lasting popularity that *Friendship in Death* and *Devout Exercises* accorded Rowe, but was nevertheless a consistently good writer in prose, whether epistolary, dramatic, or didactic. For many literary critics, Cockburn's importance rests on her dramatic career and her appearance as one of the small group of female playwrights who wrote directly after Aphra Behn. Her poetry, though less well known, is also of interest because of what it tells us about her literary processes: much of it is incidental, coterie-produced, and courts patronage through political encomium. However, Cockburn's most significant claim to fame is that she was an extraordinarily well-versed and educated philosopher and polemicist, and gained the praise of numerous prominent contemporaries for her able defences of John Locke and Samuel Clarke. In addition, the interest of the ecclesiastical and academic communities in Scotland and Cambridge confirm her centrality in debates now seen as crucial to the Enlightenment controversies underway at those universities and colleges.[220] Cockburn, as the encomiast quoted above notes, deserves a significant rank in the list of moral writers of the period and wider acknowledgment as one of England's foremost Enlightenment women writers of the early eighteenth century.

The learned lady and biography

Catharine Cockburn, née Trotter, was the youngest daughter of David Trotter, a Scottish naval captain during the reign of Charles II, and Sarah Ballenden, who was related to several noble Scottish families. According to evidence found by Anne Kelley, the author of the new *ODNB* article on Cockburn and the recent critical biography on her life and works, Cockburn's birth date is five years earlier than that provided by Thomas Birch in his eighteenth-century biography, falling on 16 August 1674 and not 1679.[221] Despite the singular difference of dates, both biographies offer a similar outline of her life: her father's death and the family's subsequent financial problems; her precocious early education; her literary and patronage connections; her successful publications; her religious conversions; her marriage to Patrick Cockburn (1678–1749) in 1708; her extensive letter-writing network; and her struggle to get many of her works into print.[222] Where they differ is in their contrasting views about the critical representation of Cockburn. Kelley, as her subtitle – 'an early modern writer in the vanguard of feminism' – suggests, is interested in Cockburn's proto-feminism. Such feminist rehabilitation and focus is important; Cockburn is long overdue for rediscovery, and Kelley covers an impressive amount of often-overlooked material (letters included) in her study. However, her tendency to dismiss Birch's and subsequent writers' construction of Cockburn as one that touts 'the exemplary, rather austere, learned lady' is problematic.[223] Cockburn *was* a rather austere, learned lady, and the fact that she wrote from a fundamentally religious and philosophical perspective need not be equated with being unfeminist. Indeed, the fact that she was being held up as an eminently qualified philosophical polemicist suggests that her male encomiasts were actively supporting 'feminist' claims to learned equality. We need not take the word of male biographers alone in this. Her friend and patron, Sarah, Lady Piers, frequently comments on Cockburn's strict notions of honourable and virtuous action as the most rigorous, but therefore valuable, aspect of her friendship.

Cockburn, like many early modern women interested in Stoicism and Christian morality, consciously sought to master the art of rational self-government. Therefore, while this sometimes means that contemporary descriptions of her life appear complacent about her curtailed existence, it is also a powerful message about the exemplary woman who is ruled by virtuous and rational knowledge, rather than passionate emotions or, indeed, enthusiastic inspiration. Yet even this account is skewed, because exemplarity, austerity, and learning were not the exclusive attributes assigned to Cockburn. Her extreme rationalism often contributed to the wit and audacity behind many of her polemical attacks. Birch and others describe her 'vivacity of imagination', 'wit', 'chearfulness', and unaffected modesty and diffidence.[224] Kelley does a fine job recovering and dissecting Cockburn's obscure, diverse, and, therefore, quite difficult oeuvre.[225] However, her emphasis on delineating a proto-feminist import in all of Cockburn's writing is limiting given the larger discursive claims that can be made for her work.

Thomas Birch, in 'The Life of Mrs. Catharine Cockburn' that prefaced her two-volume works, had this to say about his subject:

> Posterity at least will be solicitous to know, to whom they owe the most demonstrative and perspicuous reasonings, upon subjects of eternal importance; and her own sex is intitled to the fullest information about one, who has done such honour to them, and raised our ideas of their intellectual powers, by an example of the greatest extent of understanding and correctness of judgement, united to all the vivacity of imagination. (*Works* I: i–ii)

For Birch, the grounds of Cockburn's exemplarity are predicated on her 'demonstrative' intelligence, as well as her active and visible contributions in the service of reason and religion. To reinforce this claim he offers her unpublished, but circulated, manuscripts as evidence of her lifelong commitment to and interventions in the world of philosophical and religious polemics. An action that reveals the multiple levels of public and private authorship, one of which was posthumous, that the female exemplar could factor into her writing career at this time.

Cockburn had a long and varied career during her own lifetime and, even though Birch and her supporters sought to extend her afterlife in the final version of *The Works of Mrs. Catharine Cockburn* (1751), Birch reminds us that the publication was not intended as a posthumous commemoration. Begun by Cockburn and some male mentors, it was a group effort to get as many of her unpublished manuscripts into print as possible. The project was underway in the early 1740s, while Cockburn was still actively involved in the construction of her public image: a series of unpublished letters in the Birch archive document her involvement in the planning, as well as the specific advice and direction provided by her male mentors.[226] Henry Etough appears to have been the prime instigator, but William Warburton, Edmund Keene, and Thomas Sharp also became involved in the endeavour.[227] At first, Warburton undertook the job of editor, an obvious choice given his long association as Alexander Pope's editor, as well as his acquaintance with Cockburn through previous epistolary debates. However, with the escalating demands of bringing out his edition of Pope's works (accomplished in 1751), Warburton apparently forgot about Cockburn's papers; she died in the spring of 1749, before the subscription could be of any direct benefit. Etough, still eager to bring out her works, then sought someone whose name would not only help the subscription (the proceeds of which were now destined for Cockburn's daughter), but who was a more efficient and, according to Etough, proper editor, than the 'great man' Warburton. Thus the project was handed over to Birch sometime after September 1749.[228]

Social contexts in manuscript and print circulation

One of the most important reasons for studying Cockburn's career is the example she provides of a learned woman author who, though a productive writer in manuscript, had a fraught relationship with print publication in the first half of the eighteenth century. In print Cockburn had an intermittent and moderately successful public career; if we combine that output with the extant manuscripts (including her letters), it becomes clear that she maintained a steady presence as a commentator on literature, morality, virtue, religious extremism, and benevolent affection in various generic forms her entire life. It would seem, therefore, that Cockburn was not served well by print publication. Fifteen of the twenty poems we know of were still in manuscript at her death; a series of imaginative fictional epistolary works remain unpublished to this day; many of her 'Letters', 'Remarks', or 'Defences' on contested philosophical and religious points failed to make it into print until years after the debates had subsided, and a number had to wait for the posthumous works. A lack of capital made it difficult for her to finance the printing of her own pamphlets and therefore explains in part her relative anonymity to those who might otherwise have been aware of the significance of her work. Additionally, when she did receive help in getting her pieces into print, specifically the projected multi-volume *Works*, male mentors influenced the specifics of the publication, including deciding which pieces to include, whether prefaces needed to be added, advising where it should be printed, who should be the projected audience, and even choosing to whom it should be dedicated. However, this is the only recorded instance of such extensive input by others and no doubt stems from Cockburn's age (late seventies) and infirmities (she was having significant problems with her sight and asthma) during the last planning stages of the *Works*.

The apparent obscurity and impotency these generalities convey is, on many levels, still a false representation of Cockburn's writing career. She remained involved and implicated in many intellectual debates throughout her lifetime, as evidenced in the voluminous collection of her familiar letters now in the British Library, and philosophers continued to refer to her work after her death. Birch, by virtue of editing the collection, was the first scholar to recognise and reveal that Cockburn's correspondences with various friends, family members, divines, and philosophers typified not only her sustained engagement in the republic of letters and contemporary discourses, but also a thread of continuity between her published works and the many pieces that circulated only in manuscript.

However, the fact that Cockburn did not always publish in print does not mean that she eschewed a public reputation, or that her works were not worthy of publication. Cockburn used manuscript circulation as a method for gaining patronage and support before publication, but she also used it as a way of honing her critical position and arguments. For instance, many of Cockburn's controversial tracts and letters were passed around and admired in manuscript. She often credits the viewing of her works by a network of valued judges and learned figures as the reason they do make it into print. As Gilbert Burnet put it in his preface to Cockburn's *A Guide in Controversies* of 1707 (a work which started off as a series of private letters):

> [It] falling into the Hands of some very good Judges, as well Divines as others, the publishing of them was very much desired, both for the Strength and Clearness of the Reasoning, and for the Shortness of them; many Readers being encourag'd to seek for Information in Pieces of this Size, who have neither the Mind nor the Leisure to go thro' large Volumes.[229]

Years later William Warburton's preface to her *Remarks upon the Principles and Reasonings of Dr. Rutherforth's Essay on the Nature and Obligations of Virtue* (1747) argued the same benefits when he wrote: 'you have, in the Confutation, all the Clearness of Expression, the Strength of Reason, the Precision of Logic, and Attachment to Truth, which make Books of this Nature really useful to the common Cause of Virtue and Religion'.[230] Though Warburton argued against many of Cockburn's propositions, she nevertheless sent him her work for both critical feedback and as a potential sponsor. Burnet and Warburton recognised her niche and so too did Cockburn, always producing short letters that eschewed extraneous disputation for a single practical end. The emphasis in almost all the manuscript and print commentaries on Cockburn's work falls on the conciseness and clarity of her reasoning, and it was this unspeculative, unenthusiastic, but certainly not unimaginative aspect of her writing that gained her so many admirers in intellectual circles of the period.

Nevertheless, many of her works were not printed, and the powerful draw of the publishing model as a marker of feminist importance has meant that Cockburn is routinely described as producing most of her writings before 1708, publishing nothing between 1708 and 1726, and afterwards contributing only philosophical writings.[231] A brief look at Birch's edition of the *Works* and the manuscripts in his collection at the British Library immediately makes it clear that presenting Cockburn's writing from this print-oriented perspective is unfaithful to her lifelong programme of reading and writing on literary, religious, and philosophical issues.

For the most complete reconstruction of Cockburn's manuscript output, including unfinished pieces, we necessarily have to rely on Thomas Birch's archive. An eighteenth-century wonder of scholarly industry, Birch was an indefatigable collector and compiler of lives, histories, and the *General Dictionary*. In the process of putting together the two-volume *Works of Mrs. Catherine Cockburn, Theological, Moral, Dramatic, and Poetical* (1751), Birch acquired almost all of Cockburn's manuscripts which, with all his other collections, he left to the British Museum, now the British Library. In these collections are original and transcribed letters from Cockburn and her many correspondents, fair manuscript copies of some of her miscellaneous pieces, manuscript copies and transcriptions of her poems, annotated (in Cockburn's hand) copies of print publications, as well as Birch's many notes and memoranda on Cockburn's 'Life', and Henry Etough's and John Cockburn's correspondence with him about it. The collection, I wish to argue, validates the significance of Cockburn's literary contributions, placing her alongside and within a library (Birch's) that embraced the full spectrum of eighteenth-century intellectual life. Not only was Birch responsible for biographies and editions of John Tillotson, Ralph Cudworth, and Thomas Secker, but his archive collection also contains manuscripts relating to the founding of the British Museum, as well as manuscripts and transcripts by or about a variety of contemporaries, including: Elizabeth Carter, Edward Cave, Anne Finch, the Countess of Winchelsea, Catherine Talbot, Frances Thynne Seymour, the Countess of Hertford, and Charles and Phillip Yorke (the future lord chancellor and Earl of Hardwicke, respectively).

One of the most interesting elements of the collection is a selection of fictional and familiar letters by Cockburn that have never been printed. Cockburn's very first publication in 1693 was a novella entitled *The Adventures of a Young Lady* (her anonymous contribution to Samuel Briscoe's *Letters of Love and Gallantry and Several other subjects, all written by ladies*, in two volumes, 1693–4).[232] The work was republished by Briscoe in 1718, at which time he attributed it to Cockburn. This work has generally been represented as Cockburn's only foray into epistolary fiction, but Birch's collection reveals some unfinished attempts. These letters, identified in Birch's archives as 'Volume 1/ Cockburn/ Letters of Aspasia/ Camilla/ Serena/ 1725', have dates between 1717 to 1725 recorded on them, a period for which we have no manuscript works (familiar letters or otherwise) and no print publications.[233] Whilst the question of whose manuscript hand the letters are in is problematic (I cannot positively say it is Cockburn's), Birch's attribution at the outset is significant.

The *Works* and Birch's archive also reveal that much of Cockburn's poetry relied on coterie literary practices and patronage. The five poems that appeared in print before 1751 include: the verses, 'To Mrs. Manley. By the Author of Agnes de Castro' (1696);[234] an Epilogue to *Queen Catharine, or the Ruines of Love* (1698);[235] her tribute to Dryden, 'Calliope: The Heroick Muse' (1700);[236] two poems to the Duke of Marlborough, 'A Poem on His Grace the Duke of *Marlborough*'s Return from his *German* Expedition' (published 1705, but composed in 1704) and 'On His Grace the Duke of *Marlborough*, after his victory at *Ramellies*, in 1706, a poem' (1706); and her '*Verses*, occasion'd by the *Busts* in the *Queen's Hermitage*, and Mr. *Duck* being appointed Keeper of the Library in *Merlin's Cave*. By the Authoress of a Treatise (not yet publish'd) in Vindication of Mr. *Lock*, against the injurious Charge of Dr. *Holdsworth*, in his Defence of the Resurrection of the Same Body' (written in 1732 and published in 1737). This last poem was intended to be presented, along with a new defence of Locke's Christian principles, to Queen Caroline, but the refusal (Chancellor King) and sickness (Duchess of Hamilton) of her potential patrons meant that it was never delivered. All but one of these works made it into print through patronage, either by means of other writers or aristocratic patrons, and the last, on the Queen's

Hermitage, was finally published as part of a solicited competition in Edward Cave's monthly *The Gentleman's Magazine* (1731–1868).[237] This pattern of publication almost exclusively through patronage continued to be Cockburn's modus operandi for getting her work into print until her death, marginally successful though it proved to be.

With Cockburn's input the *Works* were able to feature ten more poems: 'Mr Bevil Higgons, on his sickness and recovery from the Smallpox' (1693); 'The Vain Advice'; 'The Caution'; 'Calliope's directions how to deserve and distinguish the Muses inspiration'; 'The Platonic'; 'The Needless Deceit'; 'To Mr. Congreve, on his Tragedy, the Mourning Bride' (1697); 'The Relapse'; 'The Fair Insensible'; and 'The rapture of an affectionate soul to *Jesus* on the Cross... paraphrased'. The *Works* also included a revised version of her verses on the queen's Hermitage (she was displeased with the changes made by the editor in the *Gentleman's Magazine*), and her two poems to Marlborough. Five more poems are still available only in Birch's manuscript collection. These include one dated from York, 7 December 1694, called 'Advice to Poets'; another 'To Mrs Reresby';[238] an alternate poem 'On the Death and Funerall of the incomparable Mr. Dryden'; 'A Copy of verses Sent to a Lady with Mr. Granvill's play called Heroick Love'; and 'The Epitaph Of A young Gentleman who dyed for Love of A Married Lady'.[239]

A cursory look at the remaining unpublished poetry reveals that much of it was prompted by social networks and the exchange of manuscripts. In Cockburn's title note to 'Calliope's directions how to deserve and distinguish the Muses inspiration', she indicates that it was written at the private request of some correspondents from Ireland.[240] Likewise, the poems entitled 'Advice to Poets' and 'To Mrs Reresby' are clearly written for the benefit of the local Yorkshire people whom she features; the verses sent with Granville's play are a polite way of elevating the sharing of books and seek to cultivate the addressee's reception of the play. In general, Cockburn's poetry tends to offer advice and instruction about how to read and write. She hones this faculty in the philosophical and religious polemics she produces between 1701 and 1749. The generic mode of these polemics ranges from familiar letters to public 'Defences' and 'Remarks' and are preoccupied with language, interpretation, and instruction for the benefit of her audience.

The piece that launched that polemical career was *A Defence of the Essay of Human Understanding, written by Mr. Lock* (1702).[241] Concurrent with this publication, all of Cockburn's other writings, especially her letters, rise to a level of focused seriousness that she maintains until her death in 1749. For example, Cockburn's letters to and from

Thomas Burnet of Kemnay commence at a time when her prose style was under Locke's formative influence and reflect her growing command and deployment of the language of philosophical and religious disputation. Similarly, five years later, and after an intense period of study, Cockburn produced her refutations of Catholicism (later published as *A Guide in Controversies*, 1707) in terms highly reminiscent of those she had been shaping in her discourse with Burnet of Kemnay. During this period we also have her letters to Patrick Cockburn (though not his replies), covering the summer and autumn of their courtship in 1708. All of the existing letters to Patrick, and a heavily edited selection of the ones to Burnet of Kemnay appear in the *Works*. The similarity of tone, argumentative style, and content between the 'public' works and these 'private' letters reveals a degree of stylistic dissemination that is not often acknowledged in relation to women's letters.

Still in manuscript are a number of Cockburn's letters to female patrons and literary friends. There are a series of letters from Sarah, Lady Piers, circa 1697 to 1709, in addition to a few from a correspondent identified as 'E.B.' or 'ESB'. Medoff sees similarities between 'E.B.'s' tone and style and that of Elizabeth Burnett; however, Kelley makes a convincing case against her authorship.[242] In one letter 'E.B.' disputes the merits of a book against Bishop Stillingfleet that they believe is responsible for Cockburn's continued divorce from the Church of England. In another they discuss the variable discourses in which a letter can engage (that is, religious controversy or light comedy), as well as the performances of Delarivier Manley's plays: the comedy, *The Lost Lover, or, The Jealous Husband* (1696), and the tragedy, *The Royal Mischief* (1696).[243] The discussion of the plays securely dates the letters in 1696 and there is evidence that Elizabeth Burnet was single and living in Lincoln's Inn at this time.[244] She was also in the process of conducting her own correspondence with John Locke about the Stillingfleet controversy, and had previously been much engaged in Roman Catholic controversy with the family of her first husband. Cockburn also lived in Lincoln's Inn during this period; one of Lady Piers's letters of 1698 is directed to Cockburn at an address in Lincoln's Inn. On the other hand, as Kelley notes, the writer seems to be someone more involved in literary circles, and possibly even male. She points out that in one letter 'E.B.' gives Cockburn the standard male compliment that she may 'dispute the Lawrell with some of the most noted of Our Sex'.[245] (Though this could be a reference to the 'most noted' female writers.) She also draws attention to a 1702 letter from Burnet to Locke in which Burnet claims to have only a slight acquaintance with Cockburn.[246] Whilst this letter in particular makes Burnet's authorship unlikely, the 'E.B.' letters still point to Cockburn's social/intellectual networks as the driving impetus behind many of her non-dramatic works.

Female colleagues, patronage, and male mentors were also important to Cockburn's early dramatic career. Kelley makes the valid point that Cockburn's drama is underrepresented in Birch's edition, but so too are most of the letters from this period of her life. It would appear that this era in Cockburn's career – the period which now features prominently in literary studies – was not viewed with the same degree of importance as her polemical and poetic works.

Cockburn wrote five plays between 1695 and 1706: the tragedies *Agnes de Castro* (performed in 1695, and printed in 1696), *Fatal Friendship* (1698), *The Unhappy Penitent* (1701), *The Revolution of Sweden* (1706, though work was begun on it in 1703), and the comedy, *Love at a Loss; or most Votes carry it* (1700). While Birch discusses her plays and dramatic career in some detail in the 'Life', the final edition of the *Works* only includes one play, *Fatal Friendship*. However, there is evidence that the *Works* was originally projected at three volumes, with the design of including all the plays and poetry in one volume. Publishing costs eventually prevented Birch from fulfilling such an ambitious plan. The fact that some printed copies of her plays had only just been found but not verified as authentic before Cockburn died may also have been a factor in their exclusion from the final volumes.[247]

The printed texts of her five plays showcase a wish to court patronage and political ties: *Agnes de Castro* was dedicated to the Lord Chamberlain, Charles, Earl of Dorset and Middlesex; *Fatal Friendship* to Princess Anne; *The Unhappy Penitent* to Charles, Lord Halifax; *The Revolution of Sweden* to Harriet Godolphin – daughter of the Duke of Marlborough; and *Love at a Loss* to Lady Piers. She also developed working relationships with other female dramatists, including Delarivier Manley and Mary Pix, and provided commendatory poems for their plays (as they did for her). Critics note that Cockburn's plays reveal her as an early stage reformer and moralist.[248] They also testify to the strong thematic links between her dramatic and philosophical works. Paula Backscheider argues that Cockburn's marriage plays function as 'carriers of revisionary ideas from other discourses', and, in line with Mary Astell's contemporary critiques, herald 'women's point of view and the ideas of women as "rights bearing individuals"'.[249] Despite early twentieth-century criticism that dismisses Cockburn's plays as dull, therefore, Jacqueline Pearson declares:

> This, however, will not do. The emotional dilemmas she depicts are vivid and convincing, her moral vision subtle and ironic, her

characterisation and plotting skilful. She is especially optimistic about the abilities of women and their moral and intellectual powers. As such she is not a historical curiosity but an accomplished dramatist in her own right.[250]

Cockburn's drama, therefore, is both of its moment and of a piece with her larger discursive aims.

For the period from 1717 to 1725, which is roughly commensurate with the period of Patrick Cockburn's refusal to take the oath of abjuration (1714–26), and therefore his loss of any Church living, I have already identified her work on the 'Letters of Aspasia, Camilla and Serena'. As noted above, these have never been printed and no attempt appears to have been made to finish or find a place for them in the *Works*. There is also evidence that Patrick (though possibly Catharine) attempted translation work in 1717. In the Rawlinson papers in Bodley there is a manuscript note indicating a 1717 subscription appeal for a translation of Louise-Françoise de la Baume Le Blanc's (Mademoiselle de la Vallière) *Reflexions sur la Miséricorde de Dieu*, first published in Paris in 1680.[251] The head note identifies the translator as 'Patricius Cockburn' but, given the text's status as 'a devotional staple of Francophone Catholicism', Catharine seems a more compelling candidate as translator.[252] I have found no evidence the subscription ever came to fruition and English readers would have to wait until Charlotte Lennox's translation of the work in 1774.[253] At the latter end of this period, in 1724, Cockburn started writing *A letter to Dr. Holdsworth, occasioned by his sermon preached before the University of Oxford* (1726), and, in response to his printed reply of 1727, wrote *A Vindication of Mr. Locke's Christian Principles, from the injurious Imputations of Dr. Holdsworth*, and, later, an additional part, *A Vindication of Mr. Locke on the Controversy concerning the Resurrection of the same Body*, both of which remained unpublished until they appeared in the *Works*.[254] There was a second edition of *A Guide in Controversies* printed in Edinburgh in 1728.

Remarkably, Cockburn also produced a stream of writings in the 1740s (she was in her late sixties), and forged new epistolary relationships, both mentoring and being patronised by a younger generation. She wrote *Remarks upon some Writers in the Controversy concerning the Foundation of Moral Virtue and Moral Obligation; Particularly the Translator of Archbishop King's Origin of Evil and the Author of the Divine Legation of Moses. To which are prefaced some Cursory Thoughts on the Controversies concerning Necessary Existence, the Reality and Infinity of Space, the Extension and Place of Spirits, and on Dr. Watts's Notion of Substance* (1739–40); this was printed anonymously in *The History of the Works of the Learned* in August 1743 through the means of one of her son's friends.[255] Her last publication, *Remarks upon the Principles and Reasonings of Dr. Rutherforth's essay on the Nature and Obligation of Virtue: In Vindication of the Contrary Principles inforced in the writings of the late Dr. Samuel Clarke* (1747), was published by William Warburton, who also supplied the preface. At the same time she was conducting an epistolary debate with both Warburton and Edmund Law between 1746 and 1748; this was later reprinted in the *Works*. In addition to these polemical pamphlets are numerous miscellaneous pieces – mostly short letter essays – later included in the *Works*. There are no dates of composition for these pieces; however, based on the varying topics, they seem to span a considerable time period. There are also lengthy correspondences with her niece, Anne Arbuthnot (née Hepburn), from 1732 to Cockburn's death in 1749, and Thomas Sharp, Archdeacon of Northumberland, from 1743 to 1749. The four correspondences (with Arbuthnot, Sharp, Warburton, and Law) provide evidence of Cockburn's unflagging interest in philosophical, religious, and literary concerns right up until her death.

As this combined catalogue of her print and manuscript output shows, Cockburn's literary life was relatively consistent in terms of output yet, in its rich diversity, indicative of both a creative and a highly analytical mind. Nevertheless, her reputation is plagued by the aura of the unfinished, marginal, and tenuous status associated with manuscript production both by contemporaries and current scholars. While there is growing awareness of the continuation of coteries engaged in manuscript exchange, as well as exemplary studies of the perilous life of 'Grub Street' hacks in the early to mid-eighteenth century, work on early women writers has continued to offer generalisations about their contribution to and/or exclusion from print culture.[256] An account of Cockburn's two-pronged career provides an antidote to this trend and conclusive evidence for the continuing role of epistolary and manuscript exchange alongside print publication as a means of practising the life of the mind, as well as gaining patrons, mentors, and publishers.

At the same time, Cockburn's career reveals the social, economic, and geographical factors which could significantly constrain attempts to engage with both potential patrons and print culture. Cockburn's first theatrical and fictional publications were at least partly contingent on her London connections with people like Sarah, Lady Piers, Delarivier Manley, George Farquhar, William Congreve, and William Wycherley, while her more esoteric forays were encouraged by her Salisbury and London network of philosophical and religious acquaintances, including

Elizabeth Burnet, Bishop Gilbert Burnet, John Locke, Damaris Masham, and Thomas Burnet of Kemnay. While living in the south of England, therefore, Cockburn's print output appears consistent and her patrons numerous. Around the time she marries Patrick Cockburn, however, a number of her important friends and patrons die: Masham in 1708; Elizabeth Burnet in 1709; and Bishop Burnet in 1715. At the same time, she becomes estranged from Delarivier Manley who publicises the break in *The New Atalantis* (1709) and *The Adventures of Rivella* (1714).[257] She also has her first child in 1709, her second in 1712, followed by what must have been the most significant impediment to pursuing the muse, the financial distress of Patrick's non-juring years (1714–26). This period has traditionally been written off as Cockburn's child-rearing years but it seems just as likely that the sudden loss of a number of friends and colleagues formerly associated with her print career also contributed to her lack of publications, as too did the absence of the financial wherewithal to cover printing costs.

The scale of her career was further affected by her move to Aberdeen in 1726 and Long Horsley in Northumberland in 1737. Not only was she physically isolated from her southern acquaintances but, due to the vagaries of the postal service, she was also unable to correspond for large portions of the year. Cockburn overcame these obstacles and forged new epistolary networks, often with younger correspondents like her niece, but also with northern divines such as the Archdeacon of Northumberland, and titled patrons like Lady Betty Gordon.[258] Of note too is her late foray into periodical culture; it foregrounds Cockburn's continued interest in engaging in philosophical disputation and religious edification. She readily embraced the magazine format and ethos of Edward Cave's *Gentleman's Magazine*; its brief question and answer format perfectly suited her philosophical prose style, and its populist appeal was in line with her pragmatic approach to moral philosophy. As might be expected, Cockburn's geographical distance from London precluded her becoming a regular contributor like Elizabeth Carter, Thomas Birch, or Samuel Johnson, but she took the opportunity presented by Cave's solicitations to readers to contribute answers to queries and to submit poetry.[259] In one instance she even uses the magazine to advertise her still unpublished pieces. The title to her verses on the Queen's Hermitage specifically refers to her philosophical treatise against Winch Holdsworth: '*Verses*, occasion'd by the *Busts* in the *Queen's Hermitage*, and Mr. *Duck* being appointed Keeper of the Library in *Merlin's Cave*. By the Authoress of a Treatise (not yet publish'd) in Vindication of Mr. *Lock*, against the injurious Charge of Dr. *Holdsworth*, in his Defence of the Resurrection of the Same Body.'[260] Which begs the question: why was Cockburn not more proactive in sending other pieces to the periodicals or independent printers? The answer seems to be that geographical distance, a wariness of editorial intrusion, and a certain amount of personal diffidence inhibited her sending more works. She was clearly unhappy with the editorial freedom with which Cave and others had treated her pieces and most of her early input into the projected *Works* was reversing the changes effected on her earlier printed texts. She also felt that her literary rank fell somewhat below her current idols; she identifies herself as from 'the middle class of writers', and, despite her long-time admiration for Alexander Pope, she was unable to bring herself to send the fan-letter she had composed for him. Written circa 1738, the letter offers a critical appraisal of Pope's works, praise of his epistolary style, and a wish to forge a correspondence with him. She also notes that a friendship with him would be a qualification for happiness in the afterlife.[261] Instead of sending it, she vainly hoped that Warburton's approbation of her *History of the Works of the Learned* essay would bring her to the attention of the then dying Pope. The writer who had routinely sent her plays to the likes of Congreve and Wycherley now styled herself as one 'in a manner dead long before them'.[262]

And yet the writings that eventually turn up in Cockburn's two-volume *Works* appear both timely and potentially marketable. Her 'Letter of Advice to her Son' draws on a long tradition of didactic literature aimed at young adults and 'Sunday's Journal' appears marketed at a similar moralising culture. Perhaps the fate of Samuel Johnson's *Rambler* papers (1750–2) goes some way towards explaining her inability to get these pieces into print. The 'failure' (in terms of contemporary popularity) of Johnson's moral essays has often been attributed to the highmindedness and difficult language he refused to tone down (something Cockburn was also accused of by correspondents), but a number of Johnson's circle of ardent supporters also blamed the moral turpitude and apathy of the times. Nevertheless, to assume that Cockburn wrote for print again imposes a modern notion of authorship on someone still straddling two viable modes of literary publication. We have no evidence that Cockburn ever envisioned these works for a print market and it is just as likely that circulating them amongst her social network was the extent of her publishing/publicising aims.

In order to consider the range and extent of Cockburn's compositions I want to turn first to the familiar letters and printed works Cockburn produced around the turn of the eighteenth century. These years cover her dramatic career, her most famous printed work, *A Defence of the Essay of Human Understanding*, her letters to and from Thomas Burnet of Kemnay, *A Guide in Controversies*, and her letters to Patrick Cockburn and another suitor, the Reverend Fenn.[263] These contemporaneous writings reveal that her explorations of virtuous action, Locke's epistemology, church dogma, the grounds of moral obligation, and the discourse of the affections permeate all of her work, regardless of its 'private' or 'public' nature. The correspondences also exemplify the use she made of her familiar letters in honing her compositional skills.

Performing passion

Cockburn's drama is significant and unique in the emphasis it places on the importance of reason as the foundation for virtuous action and also for its exemplification of friendships (both female and male). Her plays and, as we will see later, her letters concentrate on the rational analysis of emotional problems and, whilst this might suggest that her plays are cold and formulaic this is not the case; melodrama, even bad melodrama (a baby is kidnapped by pirates at one point in *Fatal Friendship*), abounds. The purpose of the exaggerated plots, language, and passions, however, is the exploration of one of Cockburn's favourite subjects: the efficacy of individual moral agency in a less than ideal world.

As Heather King has convincingly shown, Cockburn was fascinated by friendship, specifically the potential of female friendship to act as both a 'moral mirror' for other women and as a 'collective force for good'.[264] Staves points out that Katherine Philips's introduction of the ideal of friendship to women's poetics was a critical and original development in the promotion of ideas about women's capacity for disinterested self-governance. Mary Astell later helped to institutionalise the concept in her *Serious Proposal to the Ladies* (1694), where she brought friendship together with education and virtue as founding principles for women's collective improvement.[265] These authors and their texts form an important source and tradition in Cockburn's drama and letters, as they do later for Carter and the Bluestockings.

The historical context surrounding the performance of Cockburn's first play is also significant for women's literary history and collective exemplification. *Agnes de Castro* (based on Aphra Behn's novella) premiered in the first full season after the secession of the lead actors from Christopher Rich's United Company in 1694. For their inaugural season both companies – the Patent Company under Rich at Drury Lane and the Actor's Company at Lincoln's Inn Fields – offered a large number of new plays.[266] One of the extraordinary outcomes of their competitive scramble for new talent was that four female playwrights premiered works during the 1695/6 season: Cockburn, Delarivier Manley, Mary Pix, and the still untraced Ariadne. This was the first time since Behn's death in 1689 that plays by women dramatists had appeared on the Restoration stage. The women were also mutually supportive; indeed, Manley claims to have been 'Fired by the bold Example' Cockburn set.[267]

Pearson's statistical data in *The Prostituted Muse* shows that *Agnes* 'concentrates on women characters to a remarkable extent. Women open the play, wholly dominate the first act, and speak more than half the lines'. However, 'there is a steady movement away from this emphasis on women. In only her first three plays do women speak first and allow us to enter their world through their eyes. In neither of her last two plays are women on stage when the curtain rises, and they speak neither first nor last lines.'[268] Nevertheless, despite the decline in terms of lines spoken Cockburn's last two plays (*The Unhappy Penitent* and *The Revolution of Sweden*) contain her most positive expressions of individual women's capability for rational self-governance. Ann, in *The Unhappy Penitent*, is a steadfast guide and exemplar to the equivocating Margarite. Constantia, in *The Revolution of Sweden*, is, apart from the historical hero of the plot, Gustavus, the most politically virtuous character in the play.

All of Cockburn's plays assert the primacy of reason over passion, but the dramatic potential or rather necessity of virtue undone by love drives the plots of her tragedies. In her dedication to *The Unhappy Penitent*, Cockburn excuses the 'defect of the Plot' (that is, the focus on love) as a 'Compliance with the effeminate taste of the Age'.[269] She insists that '[t]he most that can be allow'd that Passion is to be the Noblest frailty of the Mind, but 'tis a Frailty, and becomes a Vice, when cherished as an exalted Vertue'.[270] Throughout her plays, characters who allow their actions to be influenced by passion suffer, whilst those who act for the love of virtue find, if not happiness, equanimity. As Ann, in *The Unhappy Penitent*, puts it, 'We owe our care first to be justify'd / To our own Thoughts, next to the Worlds'.[271] This stoical stance is always about more than self-abnegation, it is about the relation of the self to the world and the individual agency available to every human being.[272]

Cockburn was equally philosophical and didactic in her one comedy. Backscheider argues that *Love at a Loss* (1700) is a complex exploration of the institution of marriage in relation to individual's capacity or, as Cockburn depicts it, incapacity to change.[273] Given that, 13 months later, Cockburn appeared to change careers, it is important to recognise the continuity of ideas between her dramatic works and her polemical and epistolary prose.

God, Locke, and Cockburn

In 1689, at the age of 57, John Locke published his magnum opus, *An Essay concerning Human Understanding*, which, in the words of Peter Nidditch, 'has long been recognized as one of the great works of English literature of the seventeenth century, and one of the epoch-making works in the history of philosophy'.[274] Over a decade later, in 1702, a 27-year-old Cockburn wrote a defence of Locke's *Essay* which, whilst neither an epoch-making philosophical treatise nor widely disseminated and read, was nevertheless a well-crafted and original performance that displayed a sound knowledge of the matters under debate, as well as the considerable wit and perspicacity of its author. It caught the attention and approval of Locke and a number of other philosophers and divines at a time when the critical responses to Locke's *Essay* were outnumbering the defences.[275] Despite the lapse of time, the debates upon key points in Locke's epistemology and ontology were intensifying, no doubt partly as a result of his refusal to engage with most of his attackers, but also as part of the growing fear of the deistical and, worse, atheistical tendencies in the new science and philosophies of the time. Cockburn's decision to enter the lists at this time was by no means a belated or untimely foray into a forgotten controversy, therefore, but an active response to the growing roster of dissenters from what she saw as Locke's valuable analysis of human understanding and support for revealed religion. Just as important for women's literary history, it represents an intervention by a female writer in the male-dominated field of philosophical polemics in the early eighteenth century, an intervention that engages on a variety of levels with some of the most fraught issues in the fields of epistemology, moral philosophy, and religion.

Cockburn's *Defence* was written in response to a series of attacks by Thomas Burnet (not to be confused with Thomas Burnet of Kemnay) between 1697 and 1699.[276] Locke's *Essay* was a popular target in the seventeenth and eighteenth centuries and the impressive scope of his philosophical inquiry meant that there were abundant and various epistemological issues for his opponents to contest.[277] There were, of course, other contested issues associated with Locke – for example, opposition to authoritarianism, toleration (that is, religious freedom), liberalism – and Cockburn does expound on some of these issues in her other works and letters;[278] however, she does not seem to have been compelled to 'Remark' publicly on these subjects, or their respective texts. What Cockburn was interested in defending were primary arguments that related to the foundations of religion and moral theory: most notably, innateness, verity, knowledge, belief, and the efficacy of self-reflection.

What is important to take away from the evidence of the *Defence* and subsequent essays is that whether Cockburn defends or actively joins an author, 'she is not merely representing the views of another to whom she defers, but thinking them, clarifying them and grounding them upon reasons that she herself has invented'.[279] And this single-minded engagement with the issues at hand is signalled from the outset in her dedicatory epistle to Locke. Cockburn's remarkable tone – confident, rational, witty – asserts her autonomy as a polemicist in the republic of letters. Published anonymously, the *Defence* presents its argument in the body of the essay in a non-gendered way; however, in the prefatory epistle she reverses the gender roles and characterises herself, the author, as a man; indeed as a male lover who is defending Locke's female honour.[280] Using language borrowed from the Restoration stage she claims that she is an 'offender' against Locke's excellence, because, 'like a rash lover, that fights in defence of a lady's honour, the juster his cause is, the more reason he has to fear her resentment, for not leaving it to assert itself by its own evidence; and the more it secures him of success against his adversary, the less pretence he has to her forgiveness' (I: 45). Yet, as Victor Nuovo has pointed out, the lady here is not Locke but Truth herself.[281] Locke's work and Burnet's critique of him is merely the opportunity to engage, to perform her own disputation and explication of the issues. She continues, 'But, Sir, *The Essay of Human Understanding* is a publick concern, which every one has a right and interest to defend' (I: 45). Asserting the public's claim on the work is aligning the work and her remarks in that rational-critical sphere of the republic of letters.

Dramatic tropes and a dialogic process are revisited in the course of the *Defence*, and, though the vindication draws on the epistolary form in which Thomas Burnet framed his remarks, Cockburn is more concerned with presenting her response in a dialectical method of presentation, investigation, and refutation. In the course of this exercise she iterates the centrality of reflection in the discovery of those innate natural principles that inhere to us by virtue of our being human beings, and finds in Locke's principles a practical basis for morality, unabstracted, and relevant to society. She also constructs Burnet's 'proofs' or opinions (a pejorative term in Locke's and her own epistemology) as dogmatic arguments at variance with the empiricist concern for experiential knowledge. As a result, she consistently notes the importance of the meaning/reading/misreading of words in the *Defence*, and it is often through her opponent's misuse of crucial terms that she is able to rebut his epistemological points, whilst displaying her own dramatic flair for witty repartee. We see this same concern for defining one's terms in all of her letters, and, though this tactic is inevitable given the fraught nature of the concepts she is dealing with, her skill at identifying, questioning, counter-subverting, and ultimately clarifying the use of those terms foregrounds her analytical and didactic abilities. It was this clarity and the pedagogical uses it could be put to which endeared Cockburn to theologians and philosophers eager to influence a wider market of readers and which also cemented her learned image for many of those later readers.

But how did the *Defence* influence her own theories of epistemology, and how did it continue to resonate in her works and letters after 1702? Martha Brandt Bolton has provided the most thorough account of Cockburn's philosophy to date and, though generically marginalising Cockburn's works as rebuttals and therefore not original philosophy, has nevertheless persuasively argued that Cockburn's treatises, especially the *Defence* and *Remarks upon some Writers in the Controversy concerning the Foundation of Moral Virtue and Moral Obligation* (written 1739–40, but not printed until 1743), are far from derivative commentaries.[282] She notes that, on the whole, Cockburn's arguments in the *Defence* are consistent with Locke's principles, but points out that a few of her answers go far beyond anything Locke discussed in the *Essay*. For instance, Bolton argues that Cockburn's main challenge is to show 'that Locke's principles of knowledge are adequate to ground *certainty* with regard to a nonvoluntarist account of moral good and that Locke's remarks concerning the source of duty is consistent with such an account', but that she fails to prove that Locke endorsed the same moral theory as herself. That is, Bolton believes that Locke's theories are potentially voluntaristic, implying that there is no possibility of a fixed notion of moral good and evil and that God is free to alter things at will.[283] Bolton likewise contends that the germ of Cockburn's so-called Clarkean theories of moral obligation and the foundations of morality are evident in her first defence and, therefore, something she had come up with independent of Clarke's theories, which were not published until 1704 and 1705. She counters some earlier critics, such as Leslie Stephen, who accuse Cockburn of inconsistency in defending both Locke and Samuel Clarke, and argues instead that it was simply a case of Cockburn anticipating the positions of Clarke in her defence of Locke.[284] More to the point, Cockburn's pragmatic approach to controversy meant that her sole purpose was to target critics of Locke and Clarke who, however unintentionally, weakened general theories about the foundations of morality through their dogmatism and hence opened up the floodgates to deism.

Cockburn's agenda was squarely on the side of active religious defence and this reached its zenith in her 1707 letters, *A Guide in Controversies*. Cockburn was a Catholic at the time of her *Defence*, but based on her own adherence to and development of Locke's experiential theory of knowledge she found herself drawn to rethink her belief in the customs and superstitions of the Roman Catholic Church. This led to the decision that reasonable religion could only be based on a personal interpretation of scripture and a thorough understanding of the theory of natural moral obligations as expounded by Clarke and his followers. She re-converted to the Anglican faith in the belief that it was the most amenable to such a rational and individual interpretation of religion. That she originally enacted this reflective and reasonable process through a series of private letters points up again the importance of this medium in an environment which privileged, above all, the Protestant right to private judgements in faith.

Locke, as an empiricist, emphasises the absence of innate ideas (though, importantly for Cockburn, not the absence of natural principles or natural laws), and contends that the basis of all knowledge lies in sensation and reflection. Cockburn focuses almost exclusively on the internal experiences derived from reflection, rather than the external, sensory aspect, and repeatedly delineates the ways in which reflection helps us to progress towards the knowledge of moral obligation, revealed religion, and personal identity. This individualistic (and Protestant) approach to knowledge is of enduring interest on a psychological as well as epistemological level and confirms Bolton's thesis that Cockburn had already begun to develop a notion of the inherent problems between investigative reasoning and practical morality. That it found its public manifestation in the private crisis at the heart of the *Guide in Controversies* – privately reasoned faith has to be put before traditional beliefs – alerts us to the fact that for Cockburn and many of her contemporaries the most important debate was still the religious one.

What I find equally intriguing, though, are the competing tropes of reflection/interiority and dramatic/public exchange that Cockburn transfers from her *Defence* of Locke into her familiar letters. On the one hand, she forgoes a scientific and concretely external basis for knowledge, and relies instead on the associative abilities of the mind born out of reflection and right reasoning. Yet she also engages in a debate on the problems of meaning when disputants will not agree on or stick to the terms under debate. Deployed in her letters, the reflective trope manifests itself as a didactic concern to control the acceptable parameters of philosophic examinations, whilst her attention to words finds a witty and entertaining outlet in her not so subtle trouncing of others' arguments. Significantly, it meant that she was particularly cogent at dissecting the philosophic stylings of Lord Shaftesbury, her niece's favourite philosophical author.

The pupil and later antagonist of Locke, Anthony Ashley Cooper, third Earl of Shaftesbury, initially gained Cockburn's approval based on the apparent similarities in his notions of moral virtue with those of Clarke. She wrote to her niece that 'Lord *Shaftesbury's* notions of moral virtue are certainly very noble and very just, perfectly agreeable to Dr. *Clarke's* doctrine, in his *Evidences of natural religion*, and through all his sermons' (II: 268, 2 March 1732/3). She continued, however, that she thought her niece hardly needed Shaftesbury because Clarke's writing would have sufficiently shown:

> how morality may be capable of demonstration, as it is founded on the very nature of things; and our obligation to it on that relation, in which we stand to God and our fellow creatures. This is properly called natural religion, from which indeed morality may be distinguished, when the consideration of the author of our being is left out of the scheme, for that is what makes it religion. (II: 268)

Her understanding of the nuances of religious and philosophical discourse allowed her to see through Shaftesbury's numinous language and she immediately recognised the potential pitfalls in his wholly personal evocation of virtue and natural religion (something we do not see in Rowe's more literary appreciation of him). She was a careful enough reader to point out to her niece:

> But such a scheme will be very defective, because many moral duties arise from our relation to God; nor can virtue have the force of law without that regard, how highly soever the beauty and tendency of it to the happiness of mankind may be extoll'd and admired. And you see Lord *Shaftesbury* excuses himself, by his design of giving those, who doubt of a supreme being, some notion first, that there is such a thing as real goodness, that they may be led by that to seek for the perfection of it, the author of order and beauty. However, I am sorry, that many

Christians have given too great a handle to Deists, to treat of moral virtue, not only as distinct from, but opposite to, religion. (II: 268)

At one point in her letters to Anne she goes so far as to direct her reading by making clear the full implications of his deistical and 'interested scheme'.

> The objections you make against a *disinterested benevolence*, are, I believe, owing to your not being thoroughly acquainted with the scheme of those, whom the advocates for it oppose, which makes you not see the drift of our reasoning. You say, our concern for our offspring has much of an instinctive nature in it. Why, that is the very thing, which we contend for, and which they deny. They pretend, that all the appearance of benevolence, that is in the world, is owing to an early associating the *idea* of doing good to others, with that of our own interest [...]. All we contend for is, that God has given to man such a disposition to benevolence, as should lead him to virtue; should teach him, that he was designed to seek the good of others, as well as his own; and that self-love, or an artificial association of ideas, are not the sole ground of benevolence, or the proper foundation of virtuous practice, as the gentlemen of the interested scheme maintain. (II: 340–1, 29 September 1748)

She also diligently catalogues Shaftesbury's purposeful misrepresentations of Locke and wrongheaded undermining of reasonable and solid religion in the hopes of showing how his language of ridicule could upset the very tenets of moral obligation that he pretended to promote (II: 341–2). What Cockburn still took away from Shaftesbury, though, was an appreciation for his use of the affections when talking about the moral virtues and humans' relations with their creator. She avers, 'His notions of virtue are indeed very sublime; but he seems to be defective in his foundation' (II: 294).

Cockburn's emphasis on the foundations of knowledge and morality are significant for another reason, however. Throughout her *Defence* and familiar letters there is a distinct lack of Pauline 'fear and trembling' in her search after the nature of the 'Supreme Being', moral obligations, and rewards and punishments. This has important consequences for her later exemplification by people such as Thomas Birch, Catherine Talbot, and Elizabeth Carter. Unlike Elizabeth Rowe, Cockburn's judicious and reasonable performances could safely be referenced as 'learned' treatments of religious concerns, unsullied by the aura of enthusiasm. For even later critics, however, this rational approach has been equated with rigidity and an outmoded adherence to an untenable ontological stance. Nevertheless, in her own time it placed her squarely within the ranks of Enlightenment anti-dogmatism, and thus her letters generated considerable interest amongst the academic community in the late 1740s and 1750s.[285]

Correspondences

As the brief look at the letters to her niece reveal, Cockburn's familiar letters contain detailed discussions of her philosophical and religious views. This preoccupation is evident from the beginning of the century through to later exchanges with Sharp, Warburton, and Law. For example, in early letters to three of her suitors we not only see her engaging with the discourse of the affections, but we can also see the work of Locke's *Defence* and her epistolary practices merge in the most creative way.

In the previous chapters I noted the concerted editorial effort of Elizabeth Rowe to create a sustained spiritual tone, the better with which to inculcate the joys of religious contemplation. Her works, despite relying on the philosophical and religious ideas of many important male authors of the period, channel instead the heightened prose of enthusiastic writers. Cockburn's letters are a complete contrast stylistically, though not morally. Though Cockburn's early letters and epistolary fiction show some similarities with Rowe's letters of the 1690s and early 1700s, and both writers show signs of being influenced by Madame de Sévigné's writing-to-the-moment approach, the parallels end there. From 1701 Cockburn's epistolary prose takes a completely different trajectory to Rowe's, and, except for the aberrant fictional letters of the 1720s and an interest in French Quietism, uniformly evince a rational, didactic, and, most importantly, polemical style. Nevertheless, they both sought to shape (Rowe) or define (Cockburn) effective methods for conceptualising and promulgating the same concerns: the grounds of moral obligation and the performance of virtue. In the Introduction I outlined the importance, to all three of the women in this study, of contemporary theories regarding affection and benevolence, and how this in turn formed part of their own conceptualisations of earthly happiness, or 'theatre of happiness'. In Cockburn's case, this results in a two-pronged approach to her correspondents involving: first, a concern to maintain her affectionate epistolary community and display her tolerance for any Christian who engages in benevolent affection with God; and second, her active promulgation of the foundations of morality as she saw them, through polemical and didactic means.

A useful method for charting the evolution, or rather concentration, of content (affection and the foundations of morality) and style (rational, didactic, and polemical) in her epistolary oeuvre is an analysis of the letters she wrote to a number of male suitors between the years 1701 to 1708. What we see during the course of these letters is a growing confidence and sense of her epistolary role in relation to her male addressees, and, at the same time, a coming to terms with her own views on a number of fraught issues in philosophy and religion. This has a direct correlation and analogue in her printed works of the period, at the beginning of which she wrote her *Defence* of Locke and, at the end, her letters, *A Guide in Controversies*.

The most obvious difference between the printed works and the familiar letters is that Cockburn is able to differentiate her audiences, and her friends are treated with much more latitude than any of her rhetorical foes. My argument that Cockburn develops a polemical style in her familiar letters does not mean to imply that she becomes a confirmed controversialist; rather, she uses the skills developed in her printed works (such as the dialectical process), but adjusts the tone to maintain the experience of an affectionate and shared approach to religion and philosophy. In her letters to Thomas Burnet of Kemnay and others, she resolutely refuses to debate the specifics of any controversy, remains on the most general terms, and turns many of the conversations around to discussions of similarities rather than differences. What this suggests is that it is Cockburn who controls the terms upon which the letters function and it is her correspondents who must adapt.

i. The suitors: Thomas Burnet of Kemnay, Patrick Cockburn, and Reverend Fenn

Cockburn received numerous letters from male admirers throughout her career, many of which did not go beyond the polite parameters of traditional encomium, but she was also subjected to quite a few pleading, prodding, and pompous letters from suitors eager to attach themselves to an intelligent and reputedly witty woman. A number of the most extreme and nonsensical of these letters are tucked away in the back pages of Birch's manuscript volumes and, though they make for some entertaining if puzzling reading, they remain unpublished.[286] Three highly charged correspondences Cockburn engaged in with male suitors before her marriage do appear in the *Works*, including the letters exchanged between her and Thomas Burnet of Kemnay, three letters she wrote to a Church of England clergyman, Mr Fenn, and her letters to her future husband, Patrick Cockburn. All of these texts deploy tightly structured and dense narratives that call into play various ideas about affection and friendship, religious tolerance, the nature of the exemplary life, and the image of the learned woman. Clearly aware of the various roles she could play as well as the variations in reception she could expect from her audience, Cockburn both plays with and seeks to control the terms upon which she engages with her male correspondents.

In the correspondences with Mr Fenn and Patrick Cockburn we have only Cockburn's half of the exchange, but with Thomas Burnet of Kemnay there are so many of his letters that Birch was unable to find room for all of them in the *Works*. Thomas Burnet of Kemnay (d.1729), misidentified as George Burnet by Birch and not to be confused with the Thomas Burnet who Cockburn attacks in her 1702 *Defence*, was a Scotsman who, during his travels in Europe and time away from London, wrote long and detailed accounts of his personal and business affairs to Cockburn. Their letters span an important period of publication and personal change for Cockburn, covering the years 1701 to 1708. Whilst providing invaluable incidental evidence about Cockburn's early social connections, including Sarah, Lady Piers, Elizabeth Burnet, and Damaris Masham, these letters are more instructive for the insight they give into Cockburn's rhetorical abilities in managing the emotional and religiously intolerant Burnet. A persistent disputant against Catholicism, Burnet frequently takes Cockburn to task for her 'Popish' connections. He also presumes to advise her on the content and presentation of her earliest forays into polemical writing, while denigrating her interest in fiction and poetry. Cockburn maintains her own against these onslaughts and turns the tables on Burnet by criticising his own veneration for the Calvinists in Geneva, and challenging his preconceptions about women's writing. For instance, when Burnet implies, in passing, that Locke helped Lady Masham write her philosophical letters to Leibniz, Cockburn jumps on the accusation, stating:

> It is not to be doubted, that women are as capable of penetrating into the grounds of things, and reasoning justly, as men are, who certainly have no advantage of us, but in their opportunities of knowledge. And as Lady *Masham* is allowed by every body to have great natural endowments, she has taken pains to improve them; and no doubt profited much by a long intimate society with so extraordinary a man as Mr. *Locke*. So that I see no reason to suspect a woman of her character would pretend to write any thing, that was not entirely her own. (*Works* II:190)

Cockburn signifies her support of Masham's intellectual integrity, and alerts us to women's lack of educational 'opportunities'. This exchange also reminds us that Masham's correspondence with Leibniz (which was never published in her lifetime) was known and discussed in contemporary circles. Whether or not contemporaries viewed it as an exchange on Locke's behalf, or as an original performance, it is clearly a publicly recognised critical debate under the auspices of a transnational republic of letters.

Burnet viewed Cockburn's letters in a similar transnational and public context. Though he is frequently at a loss in the correspondence when the issue is human affection (his barely disguised purpose in attempting to convert Cockburn back to Protestantism is so that he can marry her on his return to England), Burnet was not just a lovesick antagonist. He was instrumental in ensuring Cockburn's name was known in Europe: he showed her *Defence* to both Leibniz and Electress Sophia, and tried to convince Cockburn to translate the work into French.[287] He also took a genuine interest in her philosophical and religious studies (this was the type of literature he read for pleasure), and felt this was her destined route to fame, being the one most amenable to her abilities.

> I am exceedingly glad you have made so good use of your retirement for a contemplative study, and should be yet gladder, to hear you had found opportunity for quitting fictitious and poetical study, for the more serious and solid, especially knowing perfectly the strength of your genius that way; and that particular inclination and fame both together seem to invite you to raise your reputation, by this new and untrodden path. (II: 160, Paris, 18 February 1702)

Though his advice sounds patronising, and Cockburn, as a rule, barely ever acts on or acknowledges his objections on literary issues any more than politeness dictates, his opinions are probably indicative of what many contemporary readers of religious works expected. In the same letter he offers advice about how she might expect to be perceived by publishing a work of this nature (that is, the defence of Locke).

> [A]ny thing upon such a nice and important subject, especially from one of your sex, and years, and in defence of such an aged philosopher, and whose notions have not been thought by many to have done the best service to religion, I know not what to say, that may be cautiously enough contrived for taking off all suspicion of vanity, novelty, or too great curiosity of examining sacred things[...].
> In all events I would have you insert something of a strain of

orthodox sentiments in theology: otherwise your single silence (upon occasions of mentioning any thing relative to the immateriality and immortality of the soul) may be construed as incredulity. (II: 160–1)

Cockburn would come to realise the wisdom of this last statement especially as she expended so much energy in defending Locke precisely because Locke refused to insert the appropriate orthodox sentiments. However, Burnet's suggestion that she might be suspected of 'vanity, novelty, or too great curiosity' in affairs beyond her scope was overly cautious. Cockburn seems only to have benefited from the exercise as the favourable responses of contemporaries show.

Further references to Locke and, along with him, Leibniz and Lady Masham, are sprinkled throughout the Burnet correspondence and, if Burnet's knowledge is anything to go by, Cockburn and Lady Masham were on familiar terms. At one point Burnet asks Cockburn if she 'would be so kind as to convey this letter to my Lady *Masham*, which hath all the news of learning and other kind here, I leave it open, that you may read them' (II: 202). Aside from these social accounts of their acquaintance, there is no record of any letters or conversation on each other's Lockean writings. Nevertheless, as Karen O'Brien's excellent study of *Women and Enlightenment in Eighteenth-Century Britain* suggests, Masham and Cockburn clearly shared similar moral concerns. O'Brien, following Brian Young, usefully categorises these interests as a '"late Latitudinarian" Anglican preoccupation with the uses and limits of reason, the happiness that comes from a moral life, the possibility of human progress, and the salvation that comes, not only from faith, but from active, good works'.[288] She also notes that Young's thesis, that the English Enlightenment was often an internal battleground between various Protestant interests (Anglicanism, Dissent, Whiggism, and radicalism), 'helps to make sense of the evolving debate about the nature and role of women'; a topic I will return to in chapter 4.[289]

Despite Burnet's reservations, Cockburn's *Defence* clearly placed her in another sphere in his eyes, and he made every effort to add to her fame through his championing of her to Leibniz and others. Cockburn showed her appreciation of his efforts, but was diffident about the usefulness of her work in the long term. She was fully aware of the transitory importance of her remarks in the ongoing debates surrounding Locke's work; her brief contribution was only meant to silence one who she felt was not engaging with Locke on his own terms – a particular preoccupation of all Cockburn's controversial writing.

Another preoccupation of Cockburn's was the practical potential of her interventions in philosophical and religious debate. For example, though she considers the possibility of countering what she sees as some erroneous arguments in John Norris's *Essay towards the Theory of the Ideal or Intelligible World* (1701 and 1704), she decides that 'to oppose another's notions in matters merely speculative, which, whether true or false, are of no necessary importance to religious or moral truths, is perhaps an employment scarce worthy of a wise person' (II: 190–1, 12 November 1705). Cockburn, in other words, seeks experiential knowledge over the chance offerings of uncertain metaphysical speculations.

There are numerous valuable discussions of her writings throughout this correspondence, but some of the most revealing views Cockburn shares are those regarding epistolary prose. In the course of a discussion about the merits of the Electress Sophia's light conversational style which Burnet had related to her, she declares, 'The most solid subjects should not, in my opinion, be treated of in conversation, as one would write of them' (II: 188, 7 July 1705). She goes on to differentiate letters/serious writing from sociable converse, and opines that 'long grave speeches' belong only in letters (II: 188). As a final deprecatory aside, she notes that she does not have the conversational skills many of her friends do, and describes herself as not tedious, but 'sufficiently dull' and that 'nature has disposed me more for the *serieux*' (II: 188). Here is Cockburn agreeing with and promoting the image of herself as a dull, but serious, author to someone who she knows talks about her in international intellectual and social circles.

Perhaps the most entertaining debate Burnet and Cockburn engage in is the one ostensibly concerned with the competing merits of Protestantism versus Catholicism, but which was clearly emotionally biased given Burnet's underlying agenda. It should come as no surprise that the most edited correspondent in the *Works* is Burnet. Burnet's many politically sensitive passages about the wars in Europe are excised, but so too are many of his emotional effusions and even some of his excessively intolerant religious ones.[290] It would appear too that the editor in many instances is Cockburn.[291] Some of the originals are still filed with the transcriptions, and allow us to piece together the words with which Cockburn and Burnet acted out their epistolary non-courtship. It was a contest in which Cockburn gained the ascendancy through the iteration of the nature of the terms upon which their friendship was formally founded. She repeatedly reminds Burnet of the importance of religion as the grounds of their mutual affection (she often invokes the concept of the Christian community), and counters his stereotypical views of Catholics with a personalised account of how a true catholic understanding of religion amongst Christians would eradicate the irreligion of which he despairs.

For example, in a letter written in reply to two of Burnet's in which he seeks to impress upon her the strong presence she retains in his heart and mind and his continuing hopes of her conversion, Cockburn is cheerily precise about the status of their friendship and places the blame for any perception of complications back on Burnet's conscience. In his letter of 4 January 1703/4 O.S. (not included in the *Works*) he expresses his best wishes for her current and past fortunes; this inevitably leads him into a discussion of scripture, and the hope that she has seen the 'clear cristal glasse of Revelation' and 'That you may be even a Reformer amongst the Reformed', a clear reference to reformist Calvinists within the reformed, i.e. protestant, church.[292] Another letter written shortly after this one, on 14 January 1704 O.S., is included in the *Works* but is provided in a significantly edited version by what appears to be Cockburn's hand. Cockburn cuts out Burnet's impassioned expressions of 'Oh May you be gained' and, more to the point, 'loosing you will be the bereaving my soul of its most desyrable expectations'.[293] In response to these two declarations of renewed interest in her religion and personal affairs Cockburn offers what will become her epistolary hallmark of a highly contained, rational, and yet affectionate style. In what is clearly a personally edited version of her original letter, she replies, 'I Received your obliging letter with much satisfaction, both as it gave me an assurance of your health, and of your remembrance and concern for me, which, I assure you, I have always had a grateful sense of' (II: 164–5). After telling him what she knows of the town news, including the discovery of her authorship of the *Defence*, and her own improving health, she segues into a discussion of their religious differences with an acknowledgement of the providence they are both subject to (the topic he opened his first letter with). She writes:

> As for my other affairs, I can only tell you at this distance, that I have had my share of uneasinesses, which, in the circumstances of my fortune, I must still expect to struggle with: yet I keep a sufficient chearfulness of spirit, having the comfort of some years experiences of the gracious care of providence for me. (II: 167)

This is a standard enough expression of their similar probationary states, and her circumspection is explained away as a question of distance. However, Cockburn adds:

> I am sorry, Sir, the difference there is between us in the controverted points of religion, should abate any thing of the little happiness you

could find in my company. For my part, I consider nothing in the opinions of my friends, but what is likely to influence their morals; and provided they worship the true God, and acknowledge the doctrine and authority of *Jesus Christ*, I think we are sufficiently united in *religion* for all the ends of friendship. (II: 167)

She continues at some length on the subject of respecting everyone's interpretation as long as they believe in Jesus Christ, and offers the following piece of advice:

> I have employed myself much in considering the proofs, and defending the truth of the *Christian* religion; which has so entirely engaged my concern, that when I am with those, who sincerely submit to the authority of *Jesus Christ*, what sense soever they understand him in, I am satisfied, and really think myself with one of my own communion. Thus you see, Sir, there will be no obstacle on my part to that satisfaction, which an agreement in matters of religion gives. (II: 168)

By containing Burnet's expressions within a Christian framework of benevolent affection, Cockburn is able to acknowledge their friendship whilst ignoring his romantic subtext. It is likely owing to careful responses such as these that Cockburn's literary executors found these letters unexceptionable enough to print given that both parties were unmarried at the time the letters were sent.

However, if there was a letter that could epitomise and exemplify the difference between Rowe's 'operatic' style and Cockburn's stentorian tones it is the one she wrote to Burnet on 8 August 1704. Replying to two more letters in which he persistently, almost passionately, seeks assurances of her undivided loyalty and affection towards him, while denigrating her religion and friends of Catholic persuasion, she replies to him in the calm, measured style that characterises all her letters from this point forward.[294] The text below is from the *Works*, and matches the edited version in what appears to be Cockburn's hand in manuscript (the original is not included in the collection).

Sir,
I Received both yours of the 5th and 17th of *July*, with much satisfaction to find you keep your health so well, in all the troubles and fatigues you have gone through;[295] and that you remember me so obligingly both in your misfortunes, and in the happiness and

honour you receive by the favour of two princesses, whom you with such reason admire. I have all the sense I ought of your concern to secure my friendship, and do assure you, that no new acquaintance has deprived you of the share you had in it; for, as I think there is a due esteem and gratitude for every degree of merit and kindness we observe in our friends, I never suffer one to dispossess another of my friendship, but endeavour to divide it, as impartially as I can, among all, who have the goodness to set any value on it. It is only that niggard passion, which is distinguished by the name of love, that excludes all but one object from having a part of it, and is not satisfied without monopolizing the affections of the heart. Friendship is more just and more beneficent; and you may depend upon finding me willing to contribute all I can to your satisfaction, and that I shall always use your confidence in me with the sincerity and faithfulness becoming a friend, and a *Christian*;[...] (II: 174–5)[296]

Her definitive statement on this issue is reiterated in her letter of 7 July 1705:

> though your concern for me is very obliging, I cannot but wonder, that in an engagement of friendship only, you should think the difference between us will deprive you of whatever satisfaction you can propose it; especially since I have so freely declared to you, that I cannot think myself at a great distance from the communion of any *Christians*; esteeming an agreement in the duties of practice, in the worship of one God, and faith in Christ, the only essentials sufficient to establish an union of friendship, though our worship is not performed in the same place, or the same manner, which, as the world is divided, must be confined to some one. This easy principle is one reason, why I am not inclined to engage with any friend in controversy; and if I were, I should not chuse this way, so much has been published and written with long reflection by eminent hands, that I should rather refer to those authors, who have set the subjects in dispute among us in the truest light. [...] I know not whether this reasoning will so far satisfy you, as to excuse my not answering the particulars of your letter; but indeed, the only point I am zealous to have you agree with me in is this one article, that all good *Christians* are of the same religion; a sentiment, which I sincerely confess, how little soever it is countenanced by the generality of the church of *Rome*. And if you could be of the same opinion, there would be no contest between us. (II:186–7)[297]

While she refuses to engage with Burnet on questions of church practice and doctrine, she is nevertheless adamant when it comes to the larger question of what constitutes the Christian community and the degree of tolerance which such a view affords. For Cockburn, duty, worship, and faith – in whatever Christian form they take – are all that should be required.

The year 1707 marked the end of the contest between them and was an important personal turning point for Cockburn. She returned to the Church of England and marked the conversion with the publication of two private letters in *A Guide in Controversies*. The letters were, according to Birch, originally addressed to Mr Bennet, a Roman Catholic priest, and Mr H____, but their circulation was much wider as Mr H____ had sent Cockburn an answer from a correspondent who was apparently a stranger to them both.[298] Elizabeth and Bishop Burnet, as well as Samuel Clarke, were also privy to the manuscript letters, and it was probably through Bishop Burnet's instigation (he provided the anonymous preface) that Cockburn decided to publish the work. *A Guide in Controversies* is therefore another product of Cockburn's early letter-writing community.

Kelley rightly notes that *A Guide in Controversies* marked Cockburn's 'admission to a field of debate that would have been inaccessible to her had she remained a Catholic', and adds that it 'demonstrates a consistency of concern with her other philosophical writing, in particular her rejection of the dogmatic adherence to conventions'.[299] This 'consistency of concern' is evident not just in the published writings, but also in Cockburn's letters and the miscellaneous works which remained unpublished until 1749.

After her return to the Church of England Burnet was out of the matrimonial picture; this was the year she met (or at least began writing to) her future husband, Patrick Cockburn. She also received overtures from another young clergyman, Mr Fenn. Burnet was privy to all these developments, and might have been responsible for introducing Catharine and Patrick (a friend and countryman of the Scottish Burnet). While Burnet's own hopes of marrying Cockburn were by this time disappointed, the correspondence with him continued for a year after her marriage. In one of these letters Cockburn laid out her notions on the role of affection in her marriage to Patrick Cockburn.

> You was not, you see, mistaken in apprehending, that our intimacy would turn to love: but, I hope, you was, in supposing it would convert us from the love of God. We are much mistaken in our own

hearts, if that was not the ground of our affection for one another; and if our chief aim was not to improve that, and to assist each other in performing the duties, that flow from it, when we engaged in this union. (II:206, 10 September 1708, London)

This statement is pregnant with the idealised language of benevolent affection, as Cockburn describes their feeling for one another as something that partakes of the 'flow' of duties between the faithful and their God. A brief glance at Catharine's letters to Patrick Cockburn reveal that the godly and selfless portrait of their union which she provided to Burnet was constructed in slightly different and wittier terms when Patrick was the recipient of her letters.

After this letter there are no further exchanges between Burnet and Cockburn which survive in either manuscript or print, and it is his rival and ultimately the successful suitor, Patrick Cockburn, who engrosses Cockburn's attention. Cockburn's letters to Patrick Cockburn present a much more self-consciously literary speaker than is usual with Cockburn, and as a result her letters to him are among the most fascinating in the *Works* and her letter collections. One of the reasons for this was her use of fictional characters as a cover under which she could discuss herself and Patrick in the third person, passing along judgement and advice in the process. Unsurprisingly, affection, therefore, becomes a much more fraught issue. Whereas previously Cockburn was able to rationalise it as a matrix of sociability within the Christian community, she is now forced to confront 'that niggard passion, which is distinguished by the name of love, that excludes all but one object from having a part of it, and is not satisfied without monopolizing the affections of the heart' (II: 174–5, 8 August 1704).

So how does she deal with this religious and philosophical problem in her affairs? She creates an alternate cast to act out the drama. The fictional cover is a complicated one; the characters she uses are from her tragedy *The Revolution of Sweden* (started in 1703, performed in February 1706), which charts the fortunes of Gustavus, the future king, and his friends in arms as they fight to overthrow the tyrannical rule of the Danes. In the course of the play, Constantia, the wife of Gustavus's best friend Arwide, is taken hostage, and Arwide, in a display of passionate true love, offers himself in exchange, jeopardising the Swedish cause. A whole series of counterplots ensue, but the outcome is that, despite defying reason at every turn, Constantia and Arwide are happily reunited and *alive* at the end of the play. In the play, it is the man, Arwide, who frequently allows his heart to dictate to his head, and Constantia who must remind him of the greater cause that they both serve. There is a fourth character, Christina, who is responsible for freeing Gustavus before the time period of the play, and of establishing Arwide's innocence at the end. She, however, dies for her contribution to the affair. In the familiar letters, the main issue is the status of Constantia and Arwide's rocky relationship. Here, Arwide appears to have a prior attachment to a woman identified by Cockburn as the character Christina. As a result, Constantia is at a loss whether to continue entertaining the attentions of Arwide, or to commit instead to the unexceptionable Gustavus. The twist, of course, is who these characters actually stand for. Cockburn represents herself throughout the letters as Constantia's friend and mouthpiece to Patrick, who in turn is represented as the friend and voice of Arwide.[300] Unfortunately, we do not have Patrick's letters to see how he personally figured himself, but based on the internal evidence Constantia and Arwide are clearly Catharine and Patrick.

What these fictional characters seem to indicate is Cockburn's need to create a performing other when she is forced to confront the language of the passions outside of a dramatic or polemical context. By displacing her discussion of affection onto Constantia, Cockburn is able to objectively discuss fears about love and marriage (something she had previously explored in *Love at a Loss* (1700)), while persuading Patrick that there is no conflict between his Christian beliefs and the possibility of earthly happiness with another person (he fears that it will lessen his affectionate ties to God).[301] Again, like her letters to Burnet, it is she who is in control of the lovers' discourse by framing it in her own terms, in her own drama in fact. As controlling as she could be, Cockburn was also susceptible to subjective angst equivalent to that exhibited by Rowe's enthusiastic letter-writers and it is useful to compare Rowe's deployment of affection, the passions, and enthusiasm with Cockburn's construction of the same discourse in her letters to Patrick.

I noted at the outset the notion of a theatre of happiness in relation to the discourse of affections in these two writers' works and I would like to revisit this idea in an attempt to offer a contextual basis for their joint deployment of this important eighteenth-century idea. Isabel Rivers, in the first volume of *Reason, Grace, and Sentiment*, identifies a useful binary for understanding the theological basis behind their representational techniques. Essentially she posits a nonconformist/puritan tradition in which a direct appeal to the passions or affections was seen as the most effective method of gaining the heart and therefore souls of the congregation. This method emphasised 'God's acts and man's passivity', and tended to concentrate on how individuals respond affectively to sensory or imaginative appeals.³⁰² Against this tradition she argues for an Anglican emphasis on human rationality. Thus for Anglican writers, the way to the heart was first through the mind. Though these dichotomies initially suggest that the proselytising warmth of the nonconformists was being pitted against the reasonable proofs of the Anglicans, her analysis goes on to note that both sides used each others' linguistic arsenal in manifold ways. What obtains though is the argument for two ways of moving the affections: first, 'by the senses and imagination' working on the heart, and second, 'by reason and judgement' informing the mind how to direct the heart.³⁰³

The prose works and familiar letters of Rowe and Cockburn confirm this basic difference in emphasis. Rowe, the daughter of a dissenting preacher, the wife of a nonconformist, and the central literary figure in a network of dissenting divines predictably displays the sensory overload of the nonconformist tradition. Though as I revealed in my example of her reading and poetic interpretation of a Shaftesburyan enthusiast, she had a much more complicated and individualistic approach to religious literature than either religious camp could safely classify. Unlike the dissenting Rowe, Cockburn switched religious allegiances a number of times. Raised an Anglican, she converted to Catholicism in her youth but later rejoined the Church of England (at the age of 33). Despite these conversions, she maintained an Anglican bias throughout her writings by appealing to reason as the director of the affections. For her, the 'principle of reflection' constitutes a God-given guide and obliges all Christians to engage in benevolent affections with both their maker and all those who submit to the authority of Jesus Christ. This has important consequences in her epistolary prose where she talks at great length about the benevolent form that reflection should take and it is here that she specifically counters Shaftesbury's picture of philosophic contemplation. Cockburn, like many commentators on religious affections, takes pains to consistently assert the necessity of a divine law (rather than universal presence) for the effective working of affection in social interrelations – something Shaftesbury was ready to do without.

Returning to the Cockburn courtship correspondence, it becomes clear that she is torn between the rigours of reflection and the inevitability of doubts without sufficient evidence of a feeling ('warm') heart engaged in the service of affection. She deploys her alternates to present a seemingly rational and controlled response to potential rejection. She writes:

> If you find *Arwide* inclined to conceal from *Constantia* any thing, that passes betwixt him and *Christina*, or the state of his heart towards

either, pray advise him to deal faithfully in it, whatever effect he may apprehend it will have on *Constantia*: for I dare answer for her, that she will not think she has lost any thing, if, instead of a divided lover, she finds in him a sincere entire friend, and that on those terms he may be secure of her friendship, whatever becomes of the softer foolish part. (II: 217, 3 June 1707)

As controlling as she could be, Cockburn was also susceptible to subjective angst. At one telling point she writes in a manner that appears to be stream of consciousness transcribed:

> I will not undertake to convince *Constantia*, that she wronged *Arwide* in her opinion of his affection; for, notwithstanding his excuses, I cannot but see, that she would have a great deal to object, if she thought fit, which I believe she would not, at least as her mind was disposed when I saw her last. She must keep it calm she said. (II: 219, 16 June 1707)

Like Rowe assuming the role of an agreeable enthusiast, displaying and concealing the signs of inner feeling, Cockburn takes on a dramatic persona in order to act out passions she cannot directly confront, whilst ostensibly carrying on a discussion about her future in reasonable and Christian terms. Instead of appearing coy, it comes across as an entertaining way of airing her insecurities without admitting the full implications of what she means. These letters offer the clearest evidence of her awareness of the representational and dramatic possibilities of epistolary communication. They also offer an antidote to the image of the dull and prudish vicar's wife. Cockburn's imaginative construction of her courtship reveals a writer at playful and painful variance with herself.

The affections were not the only subject Cockburn wrote about to Patrick. She also specifically addressed the problems inherent in the notion of the exemplary life. For her, exemplarity was manifestly a religious construct and, in an interesting twist, it is actually Patrick's concerns about leading such a strict existence which prompts Cockburn's discussion of the matter. In reply to a letter in which he presumably expressed doubts about his own ability to maintain a high standard, Cockburn writes:

> your apprehension of drawing hatred and persecution on yourself, if you live up to the character you have framed, alarms me much; though

I can imagine no reasonable ground for it, and must beg of you to explain yourself upon it. All the duties of that character seem to me of such a nature, as, if well discharged, force a reverence and esteem, even from the most profligate. The strictness it requires is, I think, only in abstaining from all that is vicious, or vain, and the most exact practice possible of every *Christian* virtue; which indeed is an obligation common to all, and very lovely in itself; and that which is their peculiar, the care of instructing others, if it be done with prudence, with meekness, and compassion to their infirmities, it will seldom be ill received, especially coming from one of an exemplary life: an expression, that abates the fear I am inclined to, that the character you have framed, is something too singular, aiming at things, which (if any perfection) are not practicable by all, as what is exemplary must be; [...] I am not of opinion, that pleasure is inconsistent with a serious frame of mind. (II: 217–18, 16 June 1707)

Cockburn's insistence that exemplarity is 'practicable by all' is probably the most representative statement of her pragmatic approach to moral virtue. But she also cites two other key elements in her ethics: a belief in the importance of pleasure (happiness) and in learned seriousness (reflection). This takes us back to the idea of the 'theatre of happiness' which, for both Rowe and Cockburn, was a way of figuring forth their optimistic beliefs in the efficaciousness, sociologically and everlastingly, of religious exemplarity. Rather than attribute benevolent actions and human happiness to abstract philosophical associations, they both ground it in the tangible links forged in the social world. Cockburn's stress in the above letter is decidedly on the active part exemplarity can play in a social environment and, further, that it is precisely those actions which attract others to the notion of exemplarity. Cockburn's and Rowe's more than active circulation of ideas and representative exemplary lives bears out their adherence to this hypothesis.

Unfortunately, their notions and achievements were still construed as out of the ordinary by many people. In Cockburn's letters to Mr Fenn, her other would-be suitor, she chides him for scaring other ladies away from her with his exaggerated compliments about her learning. Cockburn writes:

you said the ladies here were afraid of me. Pray on what grounds is this? I believe I must chide you for it, if it be so; for I am sure I past for a very harmless animal among them before, as indeed I am, and much value that character; nor shall easily forgive you, if you have

robbed me of it; for I think every thing impertinent in a woman, that
makes her unfit for the conversation of her own sex, whatever fine
names may be given it. (II: 253, 31 August 1707)

She does, however, acknowledge the reciprocal aspect of exemplarity
and, in the first of the three letters she sends to him, she observes:

> It is very natural to be pleased with the esteem of a worthy friend,
> though beyond what we deserve [...] if it quickens our endeavours to
> be, what we are thought; which is an effect I promise myself of the
> satisfaction I take in your thinking so obstinately well of me. (II: 246,
> 18 July 1707)

Ostensibly a self-deprecating repudiation of his admiration, her response
actually affirms his role in perpetuating and elevating her own image.
Her letter goes on to soften the blow of her refusal of his romantic attentions
(perhaps even a marriage proposal) by explaining how his image
of her is better actuated in the guise of friendship and the exchange
of benevolent Christian affections. What Fenn was unaware of during
this time was that she was already carrying on a courtship with Patrick,
a relationship in which her more passionate affections were engaged.
Taking charge of the situation she counsels Fenn:

> In the mean time, since I have engaged to be your real friend, and
> that, as such, you desire my advice, I must not deny it, how little
> soever you may need it. I believe the best method you can take to
> keep your heart in good order, whilst thus uncertain, is often to
> reflect, how little we know what is truly best for us; how frequently
> we desire such things, as, if obtained, have proved in themselves,
> or been occasions of great misfortunes to us; and to practice, in this
> case, that resignation to the will of God, which no doubt you have
> often resolved on. (II: 247, 18 July 1707)

Reasoned reflections are encouraged to facilitate resignation to the
uncertainties of some types of knowledge and our grasping desires. She
even suggests that seeking to define the feelings of others is much the
same as searching after tangible proofs of God's infinite mysteries. In
the end, though, she displays a keen understanding of the strength of
feeling that can be engaged where human affections are concerned. She
concludes, 'Whatever I do, I assure you I shall never give you reason
to complain, that I dealt ungenerously with you; and perhaps may so

act, as to convince you, that your happiness is not so much, as you imagine, in the power of, Sir, Your sincere friend, and humble servant, C.T.' (II: 248, 18 July 1707). Happiness, in her construction, is latent in the actions of the individual and she tries to reveal to her suitor that one can mediate and, therefore, control the scope of that happiness through the verbal actions one engages in with the world. In her negotiations with her three suitors Cockburn uses the processes of her philosophical tracts: the reflective method, dramatic figures, and a rigorous defining of terms, to direct the terms upon which her textual theatre of happiness functioned.

Given contemporary biases against single, young women engaging in correspondences with men, it is striking that a volume of letters from a reputed female exemplar includes three correspondences dealing with exactly the sort of fraught exchanges moralists sought to prevent. Even more remarkable is the obvious creative and rhetorical supremacy of Cockburn in these encounters. In one instance she writes, 'Considerations of this kind [whether to give up personal control to marry and the existence of unequal affections], with some others, have made me long think it best for me, always to live as I am [i.e., single]' (II: 249, n.d.). Such statements showcase her independent spirit and, latterly, the tacit support her opinions and practices received from her male editors and posthumous audience. We will later see Elizabeth Carter deploying the exact same argument and being respected in her choice. Cockburn's literary and personal authority as practiced in her public polemics and private dilemmas reveals that she expected and received a degree of latitude we do not often assume was accorded to women in the early years of the eighteenth century. She makes it clear, however, that she thinks all women should try to function along similar lines and her letters to her niece, Anne Arbuthnot, carry on the directorial but inclusive mode she inaugurated in the letters to her suitors. Before I review these letters I want to briefly address the writings which bridge the 'gap' in Cockburn's multifaceted career and reveal that her domestic concerns did not preclude a continued engagement in literary endeavour, though a preoccupation with themes of courtship and benevolent affection did.

ii. Apocrypha

I have previously noted Rowe and Cockburn's debts to Madame de Sévigné's epistolary style, but there was a far more famous French celebrity from whom they both undoubtedly drew inspiration: Louise-Françoise de la Baume Le Blanc, Mademoiselle de la Vallière (1644–1710), mistress of Louis XIV and later Soeur Louise de la Miséricorde of the Carmelite order. De la Vallière is, according to John J. Conley, another female writer/philosopher whose 'romantic' biography has overshadowed 'her status as an author'.[304] Her one published work, *Réflexions sur la miséricorde de Dieu* (1680), was written in 1671 after de la Vallière had recovered from a dangerous illness and is constructed as a series of apostrophising devotions from a penitent sinner to a merciful God. The book was a huge success in France, going through five editions in its first ten years alone, and became 'a devotional staple of Francophone Catholicism for centuries'.[305] Conley argues, however, that the book also expounds a unique moral philosophy in which the study of the theological virtues of faith, hope, and charity can help one transform unruly passions into emotionally invested devotions.[306] As we have seen in Cockburn's 'courtship' letters to Patrick, the discourse of the passions or affections was a fraught one for many seventeenth- and eighteenth-century intellectuals. Further, it was one in which women's contributions were copious, popular, and of significant merit. Conley's superb study, *The Suspicion of Virtue: Women Philosophers in Neoclassical France* (2002), supplies the continental forerunner and counterpart to my work on women philosophers engaging in this discourse in Britain, and confirms that there is an even more prominent group of female *philosophes* expounding on the foundations of morality in France. That is why it is so exciting when the paths of intellectual history cross and we see a writer like Cockburn drawing on, availing herself of, and learning from the writings of someone like de la Vallière. It not only suggests her own gendered awareness of literary and philosophical history, but also implies a wish to align herself with an important and successful female forebear in the philosophy of virtue ethics. This link adds to Jane Stevenson's account of the fluidity of national boundaries in matters of philosophical inquiry and also reminds us of the religious diversity of the participants.

The borrowing in question arises from my discovery of a 1717 subscription proposal to translate de la Vallière's work.[307] The handwritten note identifies the proposal as Patrick Cockburn's, but given Catharine's Catholic background, her philosophical interests, the gender of the writer, and what Conley identifies as the very gendered construction of the devotee in the text, Catharine seems the more able candidate for translator. A letter from Thomas Burnet of Kemnay, on 8 July 1707, also contains possible hints of Catharine's interest in French mystics. In the course of a letter discussing the trial of some '*French* prophets', Burnet appears to mock Patrick's and Catharine's lack of 'perfection in mystical devotion'; however, he notes that this will be remedied since she has 'an instructor in *Latin*' and has taken a 'Grammar for the *French*'.[308] Even if Patrick was the potential translator, Catharine certainly would have been reading the text and no doubt helping him with the work of translation given her intimate knowledge of Catholic doctrine and devotional life. Though there is no evidence that the work ever made it to press, another female writer who aligned herself with the intellectual and exemplary tradition would translate it in 1774. Charlotte Lennox's translation added the all-important 'Life' and is entitled, *MEDITATIONS and PENITENTIAL PRAYERS, Written By The celebrated Dutchess DE LA VALLIERE*. James Dodsley was Lennox's printer for this edition and one wonders if this was Dodsley's attempt to counter Rivington's printing monopoly on Elizabeth Rowe's popular devotional texts.

Rather like Rowe, de la Vallière's intellectual credentials have often been overlooked; she was well versed in Aristotle's and Descartes's theories through salon debate and had intimate knowledge of libertine ethics as a result of her years at court. The strong dialectic in her work reveals that she used her knowledge of these worldly debates, but grounded her own response on the mystical writings of people like St. Teresa of Avila and Thomas à Kempis. Cockburn's published writings do not reflect this mystical strain to the extent that Rowe's *Devout Exercises* does, but her unpublished series of letters between Aspasia, Camilla, and Serena do.

While it is helpful to find writing from a lost period for Cockburn, the style and tone of these letters are at such odds with any of her writing after 1700 that the letters pose more problems than they solve. They are certainly more reminiscent of her early letters, such as those to Mr Walsham in the Birch archive and the fictional ones from Olinda to Cleander in her 1693 novella, but the dates identify them as much later works, written when Cockburn was at least 43 years old.[309] The period between 1714 and 1726 was a time of uncertainty and hardship for Cockburn and her husband, rendering it not implausible that Briscoe's publication of the second edition of her novella in 1718 would prompt her to start writing in this popular genre again. However, the letters also appear to have been written in concert with a friend, and the most likely candidate is Sarah, Lady Piers. In fact, the letters match Piers's epistolary tone much better than Cockburn's and seem to reflect an attempt on Cockburn's part to write in a more heightened, even romantic, strain for the benefit of an aristocratic audience. They also include many inset verses, similar to Rowe's letters in *Friendship in Death* and *Letters Moral and Entertaining*, and mirror Rowe's and Hertford's joint productions. More importantly, they consciously construct a gynocentric community being torn apart by the gradual erosion of their spiritual and affectionate ties and the libertine conduct of one of the members, exactly what prompted de la Vallière's renunciation of the court of Louis XIV. As the series is incomplete and not always internally consistent it is difficult to conclusively tie it all together. I also do not want to imply that de la Vallière's strict devotions inspired the work. Rather I find it helpful and not a little interesting that the personal history and literary ethos of de la Vallière is intertextually present in the fictional letters Cockburn and Rowe are producing at the same time.

The name Aspasia also held special resonance for female sociability: the famous queen of the Bluestockings, Elizabeth Montagu, was called 'The Modern Aspasia' and Hannah More, in her paean to Bluestocking discourse, *The Bas Bleu; or, Conversation* (1786), refers to Aspasia as the first 'bas-bleu' and cites her symposium where Socrates and Pericles, her lover, engaged in rational conversation as a precursor to Montagu's salons.[310] Undoubtedly Cockburn was aware of this classical allusion (there are many references to oracles and Delphi scattered throughout the letters), but in her own construction Aspasia appears to be the problematic figure of the group. What is consistent with these and all of her familiar letters, though, is the emphasis on philosophical reflection, resignation to the vicissitudes of life, and personal integrity and indifference against the onslaughts of a 'calumniating' world. At a time when the scandal fictions and romantic novels of Eliza Haywood and Delarivier Manley were inundating the print market, it is notable that Cockburn chose to create an imaginative epistolary network which propounded an ethos of platonic spirituality and was held together by the bonds of benevolent affection.[311]

Of the 15 extant letters, two are between unidentified figures, six from Camilla to Aspasia, Seraphina, and another woman, and seven from Serena to Aspasia and one unidentified man.[312] Aspasia's replies are not included. The letters from Serena and Camilla alternate between extolling Aspasia as their philosophic guide (professing that, 'Methinks w[he]n Aspasia talks, I see things in a different Medium, she by Her power o'er my Mind can Calm ye wild disorders there: how do I Wish we Dayly might Converse'),[313] and threatening to withdraw their unreciprocated affections. The vexed nature of the letters seems to stem from the changing fortunes of the heroines as a result of the influence men have on their virtue and their futures. Marriage proposals and unequal fortunes and stations figure prominently but are generally repudiated by Camilla and Serena. The dominant theme in contrast to that of the men, marriage, and domesticity which threatens to end their friendships is the eternal world in which they can escape the 'gross Matter' of 'Bodies feminine' and be 'transmigrated to Birds, or Fishes' or even vegetables, as long as it is free from the pursuit of 'Happiness, unattainable on [this] side Eternity'.[314] One of Serena's letters to Aspasia on this subject is almost identical to Rowe's fictional apostrophes:

> my greatest pleasure at present is, to contemplate ye beautys of ye creation; wch ye more we viue [sic] ye more we must admire, ye author of so Stupendious a Work, for even y^s lower World, a Small part comparitive to ye mighty whole, is so artfully fram'd, ye Minutest creature ^wou'd is so take ten times ye age of man, e'er he cou'd comprehend, ye Springs by wch it moves; how presumtious [sic] y^n is it for any to pretend, to solve by Mecanism, to solve all ye doubts arissing, in y^e search of Nature; perhaps you'll think me vain, in presuming to seek after misterys, w^n I beleive [sic] a thorough certainty not in y^s world not attainable; you know most people things are most esteem'd where y^e persuit [sic] is difficult, tis y^e frailty of humane nature, to be fond of $w^{t's}$ above us, while we are too apt to despise $w^{t's}$ in it self Valuable, because in our power.
>
> I've even now beheld y^e fields illustrated by y^e sun beams, y^e trees ^whose boughs will e'er will ^e'er aford a pleasant shade, adds to y^e prospect wch so Delights my eyes; y^e breezes of y^e wind, aid'd by y^e tunefull Notes of birds, charms my ears; all wch has so captivat'd my fancy, I cou'd almost become poetic.[315]

As in the writings of Rowe, the emphasis is placed on the capacity of the female mind to contemplate the beauties of God's creation as well as the awareness that, in so doing, she is securing her own everlasting happiness. The romantic entanglements and unexplained disruptions in the friendships are likewise unimportant when each of them can calmly renounce the transitory problems of this world for the unmitigated delights of the next. Ultimately, it is the shared experience of each other's sufferings which contributes to the continuation of their epistolary friendships and as Camilla writes to Aspasia, 'The perusal of yours gave me Pleasure & Pain Alternately Pleasure on Consideration of my being Blessd wth a generous $F,^{nd}$ to whom I can unbosom my self w^{th}out fear of Pervertion, Pain w^n I reflect y^t $F,^{nd}$ is not Happy as [I] cou'd Wish & you Merit.'[316] Reciprocity in the form of rational conversation and engaged affections is as important in the female community as it is when Cockburn corresponds with learned men and potential suitors, and she carries this programme through in her familiar, but philosophic, letters to her niece.

iii. Letters to her Niece

We have already seen some of the philosophical directives Cockburn sent to her niece on the subject of Shaftesbury's moral theory, but the correspondence was much more expansively literary as well as religious in its scope. The exchange spanned over two decades, though we only have extant letters beginning in 1731 and ending in late 1748, and they cover varied literary, religious, philosophical, domestic, and social topics. Almost all of Cockburn's letters to Arbuthnot in Birch's possession are reprinted in the *Works*, but are subjected to a number of substantive changes in the case of editing out some accounts of familial and social gossip as well as domestic affairs. Only two of Arbuthnot's letters are printed, though Birch has 19 catalogued in his collection.[317]

Kelley's biography criticises Birch's intrusive 'editing' of Cockburn's familiar letters. In particular, she laments his 'omission of most of the references to family and domestic matters in the published correspondence' and complains that this 'reinforces the impression of a learned lady, whose intellect dominated all spheres of her life, even into old age'. She adds that 'the manuscript letters reveal a much more rounded picture, of a woman who accorded equal value to her emotional and her intellectual life' and praises the 'comfortable blend of philosophy, literary criticism amid more homely concerns' that she finds in the manuscript versions.[318] In my own work with the manuscript sources it is apparent that the personal references Birch omits are those dealing with the private lives of people still alive, and that there are as many representative 'homely' concerns left in the printed versions as are excised.[319] Birch was an intrusive editor – almost all eighteenth-century scholars were – but given that Cockburn was involved in the early process of choosing letters, it is necessary to consider her own agency in constructing the epistolary image that appears in the *Works*.

It is also important to keep in mind the fluid status of many familiar letters of this period, particularly those by literary-minded writers. As I have argued elsewhere, the category of 'miscellaneous' printed text is often the familiar letter redesignated as 'Remarks' or 'Essay'.[320] Early periodicals such as *The Tatler* and *The Spectator* suggest this slippage in their free use of the letter-essay, many of which retain the formal signs (for example, dates, superscriptions, and so on) of epistolary communication in order to reproduce polite sociability on the textual page. These texts also suggest the fiction of their private (that is, familiar) status by hiding personal details with dashes and visibly selective editing. We saw a similar example of this in Rowe's moral letters which successfully disguised the real within the fictional through highly selective editing.

Some private letters became printed texts. Mary Astell's almost year-long correspondence with John Norris eventually became *Letters Concerning the Love of God* (1695); John Toland claimed that his *Letters to Serena* (1704) were prompted by the queries of a real lady. More often than not, many of these learned exchanges remained in manuscript letter books, but occasionally they were also printed in volumes of familiar letters. The editorial life of one of Cockburn's letters to her niece reveals the ease with which reclassification was possible. Originally projected as one of the 'miscellaneous pieces', the letter was later moved to the 'familiar letters' section of the *Works*.[321] The change to the volume's order probably came about as a result of Cockburn's death. Whilst alive, Cockburn's reason for publishing her letters would have been to foreground the philosophical or religious issues they contained. Even if this preliminary manuscript arrangement were posthumous, the same reasons could obtain.[322] However, once Birch was able to collect even more of Cockburn's familiar letters for the final version of the *Works*, he clearly 'restored' the letter to its 'proper' place chronologically with the rest of the letters to her niece. The generic transmutation of letters is, therefore, not just a question of content (whether personal, literary, scholarly, polemical, or didactic), but their variable modes of distribution (manuscript, print, posthumous) and address (whether 'public' or 'private').

In her exchanges with Arbuthnot, Cockburn comes across as, and certainly is, the mentor, but by the late 1740s her niece starts to explore and defend her own positions, albeit in order to show how they are conformable to Cockburn's. What is clear, though, is that during the course of their exchange Cockburn manages to get Arbuthnot to the point where she is able to reason and debate on her own terms, rather than to simply comply with Cockburn's views.

In these letters, Cockburn engages in polemical discussion via an instructional framework which casts her replies as friendly advice, but which are in fact in-depth critiques of the writers under question. Hence, the reason the unrealised version of the *Works* placed one of the letters to Arbuthnot in the section of miscellaneous philosophical pieces. For Birch, her private explanations were on a par with her public performances and, though Arbuthnot was not a necessary part of the equation in his eyes, Cockburn obviously found their exchange important enough, and sought to shape the ideas behind it, as often as she could find the time. The emphasis in the letters is always on clarifying terms, defining the role of the passions, and instilling a belief in the demonstrable foundations of morality, but there is also a repeatedly broached concern about gender. This elicits some very interesting comments from Cockburn about the common perceptions of women's social and intellectual personas. In one tongue-in-cheek response to Arbuthnot's apologies for keeping a book so long due to her domestic responsibilities, Cockburn replies, 'I should be loth to have any thing I send you for the entertainment of your leisure hours, prove a hindrance to your good housewifry, which is certainly a very commendable quality (though not the only virtue) in our sex' (II: 267–8). At another point she defends the poet, Elizabeth Thomas, against those who spoke 'slightingly' of her 'with a kind of insult on her unhappiness', and refutes the accusation against her writings being too 'romantic', for as the 'letter was there for every body to judge of, I could not but acquit it of that character' (II: 299). In Cockburn's eyes the trials of Thomas's life conferred virtue and demanded pity, not contempt, from readers. She even points out that Pope amended his entry on Thomas in the *Dunciad* once he realised her personal unhappiness.[323]

The 'Letter to her Niece upon Moral Virtue', or rather the familiar letter of 2 March 1732/3, is the all-encompassing letter, and is transcribed in its entirety, domestic news and all, in volume two of the *Works*.[324] It begins with the above quotation that 'good housewifry' is not the only virtue of the female sex and goes on to deliver a detailed analysis of Shaftesbury's moral theories, a tirade against religious fanaticism, and finally attests to the compatibility of our natural notions of moral virtue with Christian revelation as found in the New Testament. Cockburn concludes the letter with a characteristic inclusive gesture by noting that if there is anything Arbuthnot still does not understand, or if objectors protest against any of the arguments, 'you may communicate them; for I shall be glad of an occasion to *clear my own thoughts* from any confusion or ambiguity' (II: 271, italics mine). Cockburn's self-deprecating comment that she would wish to clarify her 'own thoughts' encourages dialogue and debate from her correspondent and inculcates the reasoning and refining process which she sees as intrinsic to the philosophic process. Likewise, when her *Remarks* are printed in the *History of the Works of the Learned*, she sends Arbuthnot a copy with the caveat, 'I shall expect to know your sentiments, especially on the principal subject' (II: 314). As Staves points out, 'in contrast to the single-voiced treatise, the letter, unpublished or published, becomes a favored form of enlightenment discourse, in part because it suited contingent inquiry and the exchange of ideas and experiences'.[325] More importantly, the dialogic nature of epistolary communication fostered a sense of reciprocal endeavour and shared worth.

This reciprocity could manifest itself in more personal ways, too, especially when it helped to cement or bulwark the social bonds of benevolent affection. After the death of Arbuthnot's husband in the spring of 1741, Cockburn sent her a bracing letter about the need for 'reasonable and religious resignation', as well as the following observation:

> We may sometimes be apt to reflect, that others are allowed to enjoy the blessings we are deprived of, when those very persons may have some cross, which we would find harder to bear. To have a good husband early snatched from us, is indeed a grievous affliction; but to live long with a very bad one, might be much worse, which is the lot of many, and numberless other more grievous evils this life is subject to. (II: 302)

Constant reminders about the larger picture serve to reinforce the notion of their shared probationary state, but she also reminds Arbuthnot that the only way to access the comfort and support of the larger community is to correspond with friends who 'willingly contribute to lighten your affliction' (II: 303). These exchanges recall the terms upon which she placed her friendship with Burnet of Kemnay, and show that she treated male and female correspondents, young or old, to the same rules of engagement.

Other letters cover the works of Clarke, the *Turkish Spy*, Henry Prideaux's *Historical Connection of the Old and New Testament*, Samuel Shuckford's *The Sacred and Profane History of the World* (1728), Joseph Butler's works, as well comparative discussion of Alexander Pope's and Anne Dacier's translations of Homer's *The Iliad* and *The Odyssey* (II: 274, 278). In all of them Cockburn is meticulous in attending to the details of her niece's letters and, much like the way she defends Locke, goes through the letters point by point in her own replies (which is probably why Birch found it so easy to do without Arbuthnot's side of the correspondence). The full range of Arbuthnot's manuscript letters, on the other hand, reveal the steady development of her own philosophical ideas, as well as the confidence to voice them; by 1747, Arbuthnot can offer informed praise about Cockburn's piece against Rutherforth and insert a few comments in defence of Shaftesbury too

(II: 325-9). Birch must have felt she held her own here: this is one of the two letters he includes in the *Works*. Cockburn's trust in her grew as well, and she begins to delegate the education of her daughters to Arbuthnot, and, near the end, includes her in the excitement leading up to the publication of her works. The posthumous completion of those works meant that not only were her correspondences with male writers made available to a new audience, but also her intellectual exchanges with Arbuthnot in the form of the familiar letters. They provide her female readership with a model for how intellectual exchange and Christian ideals could be practised between women, as well as men.

iv. Letters to Thomas Sharp and Edmund Law

Correspondences with Thomas Sharp and Edmund Law provide additional examples of Cockburn's continued engagement in polemical discourse and develop a number of the issues I have already discussed. As with the letters to Arbuthnot, they went through numerous editorial migrations and generic transformations. For example, the Sharp exchange appears as both 'familiar letters' and 'tracts' in various publications. In manuscript, the letters first appear after the 'miscellaneous' grouping containing Cockburn's 'Letter to her Niece upon Moral Virtue'. In the *Works*, they appear as the last set of letters in the section, 'Letters between Mrs. Cockburn and several of her Friends'. Four years later, they were published in *The Works of Thomas Sharp, D.D.* as *'Tracts on Various Subjects'*.[326] The second title page then designates them as 'Letters on Moral Virtue and Moral Obligation', and finally the table of contents refers to them as 'Letters between Dr Sharp and Mrs Cockburn, on the Subject of Moral Virtue and Moral Obligation'. Despite their 'relegation' to familiar letter status in the *Works*, Richard Price later drew attention to their importance in his remarks on the foundation of morality. He specifically notes their attempt to clarify ambiguous or contentious terms and propounds natural law arguments similar to Cockburn's.[327] Price's late use of their correspondence shows that their quibbling over terms – particularly 'foundation' – was seen as a useful intervention and clarification. In a footnote to his point that 'a great deal of... perplexity, arising from the ambiguity of words, has attended the subject now before us? and particularly it seems that the word, *foundation*, admits of various senses, which, if not attended to, cannot but produce endless disputes', Price directs his readers that, 'The letters which passed between the judicious and candid Dr. *Sharp* and Mrs. *Cockburn*... deserve to be consulted here.'[328]

In the course of the exchange with Law, Cockburn reiterates comments made years before to Burnet of Kemnay about her lack of skill in conversation. Though she responds favourably to his request for a 'personal conference', she warns him that, 'My companionable capacity (if I may so speak) has entirely left me, readiness of thought and expression, so necessary in conversation, are no more' (II: 348). However, she assures him of her 'desire to continue a correspondence' (II: 348–9). Law's replies are not included in the *Works*, but his two autograph letters in Birch's archive reveal a scholar who not only respected Cockburn's status as a polemicist, but who was also eager to facilitate her continued intervention in the debates underway at Cambridge.[329] In the first letter of 22 December 1746, he thanks Cockburn for her 'extraordinary candour and civility' in her published work against him. (She critiqued his notes to the translation of William King's *Essay on the Origin of Evil* (1731) in her *Remarks upon some Writers in Controversy* (1743).) He notes, however, that his work, the *Enquiry into the Ideas of Space and Time* (1734), set out to advance a Lockean position, and, therefore, it was the 'greater concern to me to see it disapproved by a Lady who was so well acquainted with his [Locke's] Principles, & who had shewn herself so very able to support some of y^m [them] at a time when so few men were capable of understanding him'.[330] Cockburn's reply (cited above) is included in the *Works*, but the addressee's name is edited out. She readily engages with Law on disputed points, but the true scope of their debate is cryptic in its printed form. Reading Law's manuscript letter alongside Cockburn's reveals not only the thoroughness of her response in relation to his points, but also shows her comparative understanding of both Locke and Clarke. It also puts her authoritative tone in context. Her junior in respect of age (he would have been in his forties *c*.1746), Law was nevertheless the Archdeacon of Carlisle and a noted polemicist; yet Cockburn is very quick to call him to account for running away with unsubstantiated ideas. In response to his critical remarks against Clarke's a priori arguments regarding the foundation of morals and metaphysics, Cockburn writes:

> When you talk of *his argument* a priori, *both in morals and metaphysics, being of pernicious consequence*, this is such strange language to me, that I am ready to apprehend indeed, that either you, Sir, or I, are under the influence of some strong association of ideas, which hinders one of us from seeing the force of the other's reasoning. You esteem Dr. *Clarke's* argument to be a fallacy, and I think I have shewn the pretences against it to be nothing else. (II: 347–8)

The conciseness and precision of her summation insists on more substantial evidence. In response Law sent Cockburn a detailed explanation of the sequence of debates, disagreements, and publications between himself and John Jackson (a follower of Clarke's Newtonian physico-theology), and attempts to clarify Jackson's confusion of himself and Daniel Waterland in certain texts. He also sent her a number of his own works to aid further debate between the two of them. In Cockburn's last letter to Law she aligns herself with John Balguy (another follower of Clarke), and suggests that his arguments are so correct and forceful that 'I would rather suppose you had not read it [Balguy's *Foundation of Moral Goodness*], since you seem at a loss for an origin of our moral maxims, without recurring to a *sense* or a *habit*' (II: 350). Adamant to the last in her view on the innate foundations of morality, Cockburn was clearly not convinced by Law's or even Sharp's arguments. Nevertheless, in the spirit of enlightened dialogue she always stressed her desire to continue the debate in the hopes of reaching deeper understanding if not agreement.

There are, in fact, too many letters and too many unpublished works for me to do justice to in this study. Exploring just a few of the familiar letters and published polemics reveals that Cockburn's writings, regardless of the mode, were always concerned with the same philosophical, religious, and social problems. Further, delving into her manuscript archive brings to light an account of Cockburn's career which shows a sustained presence and real engagement with the republic of letters throughout her long life. Whether that engagement manifested itself in print or not, should not discourage the feminist literary historian from recognising the true scope of this particular woman writer's exemplary life of the mind.

4
'[H]ow Obscure her Lot': Catharine Cockburn's Double Afterlife

> She was a remarkable Genius, & Yet how Obscure her Lot in Life! It seems grievous at first, & such Straitness of Circumstances as perplexes and Cramps the Mind, is surely a Grievance, [...] methinks those who knew Such Merit did not do their Duty in letting it remain so Obscure.[331]

On 13 May 1751 Catherine Talbot wrote the above lament in her journal. One of the many subscribers to Thomas Birch's two-volume edition of *The Works of Catharine Cockburn*, Talbot was particularly upset at what she saw as the similarities in situation between Cockburn and her friend Elizabeth Carter. Talbot continued, 'E[lizabeth]: C[arter]: is her Superiour – Alas will not she live & die perhaps as Obscurely, & What Alas can I do to prevent it?'[332] The result of Talbot's Socratic questioning was that she then encouraged Carter to embark on the most significant act of her literary career: the translation of all the works of Epictetus, a feat completed in 1757 (published in 1758) and which garnered Carter lifelong financial independence.[333] Talbot was obviously a sympathetic observer of the plight of learned women, but what she crucially realised was that the lack of an effective patronage/friendship support system meant that Cockburn's contributions to the republic of letters never won her the sort of remuneration (in terms of wealth and fame) she deserved, and that her productions were wrought in unfairly constrained circumstances. Talbot and, arguably, many of the men behind the subscriber edition belatedly recognised that, had some champion of female learning and the arts stepped forth earlier, Cockburn's interventions in literary and philosophical affairs might have been more widely available from the start. As it was, it was only at the very end of her life, when missing patrons and friends signed up for the subscription to the collected works, that Cockburn finally re-emerged in print, and thus the annals of literature, as the erudite defender of Locke and Clarke and a pillar of female exemplarity.

Cockburn's afterlife is a little more complicated than her late rescue from obscurity suggests, though, for she had something of a double afterlife in print: one in life and the other posthumous, as well as an apocryphal one consisting of those works that have not survived, or were never started, yet constitute our sense of her unfulfilled life of the mind. Robert Douglas-Fairhurst, in his engrossing monograph on *Victorian Afterlives*, discusses the ambiguity which exists around the term after-life.[334] For him, the term is a useful way of delving into the ways in which nineteenth-century writers dealt with issues of influence, but it also serves as an evocative reminder of metaliterary concerns such as survival, whether that meant personal immortality or textual materiality. The *OED* entry for the term offers fruitful lines of development and/or contradistinctions when applied to Rowe's, Cockburn's, and later Carter's, sense of their literary and metaphysical afterlives.

> **After-life. 1.** A subsequent or future life.
> *a*1593 MARLOWE *Hero & Leander* (1598) (Ded.) sig. A2, The impression of the man, that hath been deare unto us, living an after life in our memorie, there putteth us in minde of farther obsequies...
>
> **2.** The later period of one's life.
> *a*1678 H. SCOUGAL *Life of God* (1726) 204 The lessons which afflictions teach us, are then most advantageous when we learn them betimes, that we have the use of them in the conduct of our after lives...

The definition of 'after-life' as a 'subsequent or future life' is primarily the one I have drawn on so far in this study. Rowe's posthumous print career is one of 'impressions', literal and figurative, which helped her live on in the memory of later writers. The second definition, that 'after-life' can be used to designate 'the later period of one's life', is one which helps to excuse and elucidate my method in regards to Cockburn.

Her dual heritage in print stems from her early decision to forgo a strictly literary output for the rarefied heights of philosophical and religious polemics. Notably, though, what many commentators have seen as her decisive switch from dramatic and poetic literature to philosophy and theology is a symptom of Cockburn's own representation of that change. In the letter never sent to Alexander Pope she notes with regret

> that you [Pope] did not come sooner into the world, or I later; for I flatter myself, I should then have had the pleasure of your acquaintance by the means of one or other, who have had a share in your friendship, to whom I was not unknown, Mr. *Wycherly, Congreve, &c.* But they are all gone before me, though I was in a manner dead long before them. You had but just begun to dawn upon the world, when I retired from it. Being married in 1708, I bid adieu to the muses, and so wholly gave myself up to the cares of a family, and the education of my children, that I scarce knew, whether there was any such thing as books, plays, or poems stirring in *Great Britain*.[335]

As Chapter 3 made explicit, this is not a true statement of her literary habits in the period, but it was one she nevertheless felt compelled to disseminate. What this version of events does accord well with, however, is the way Catharine Trotter, the youthful and dramatically gifted prodigy, recreated herself as the didacticising polemicist. In the process of creating this alternate persona she clearly alienated a circle of former friends, most notably Delarivier Manley, and thus acquired a second, or subsequent life as the unfaithful female wit who had abandoned her company of female muses for the staid prudery of protestant theologians and philosophers. This is surely what most irks Anne Kelley in her attempt to reconstruct the 'radically feminocentric' writer, but does not invalidate her overall claim to prove Cockburn's 'concern to empower women by encouraging them to develop their intellectual and moral strength'.[336] Instead, it confirms the protean nature of authorship, and the transformative effects of different social networks in the period. The correspondent of Lady Piers, Delarivier Manley, and William Congreve was contextually and materially different from the correspondent of Elizabeth Burnet, William Warburton, and Thomas Sharp. Because of this, Cockburn's career, based as it was around the letters of those networks, appears sharply divided and ill-managed. Of course, Cockburn's social networks had the capacity to be as integrative as her authorial roles, but the way her life was subsequently represented suggests that some contemporaries and most literary historians have presumed otherwise.

In addition to these competing formulations regarding the sociocultural aspects of Cockburn's afterlife, is the important fact of the continuation of interest in her contributions to philosophical discourse and learned inquiry in general. Birch's two-volume *Works* is a crucial tool in later constructions of Cockburn's image, most evident in the excerpts of his 'Life' which crop up in various texts throughout the remainder of the century. This chapter will revisit his and Henry Etough's biographical and editorial choices in order to ascertain what version they (and Cockburn too) wanted to perpetuate regarding her life and her life's works.

Independent of Birch's and Etough's biographical and scholarly tasks, however, was the purely critical interest in Cockburn's works evinced by writers still engaged in the polemical battles she had entered into during the first half of the century. The philosopher and religious writer Richard Price was one such writer, and his 1758 text, *A Review of the Principal Questions and Difficulties in Morals*, takes advantage of Birch's edition to offer a response to Cockburn's and Thomas Sharp's letters on the foundation of morality. Allied to his interest is the general attention paid to her work by the academic communities in Cambridge and Scotland. Her supposedly esoteric interests had much in common with the type of dissertations being advanced and defended at the forward-thinking universities of the period.[337] Her intellectual affiliations to those universities which embraced curricula in line with Enlightenment enquiry, rather than the Aristotelian scholasticism commonly derided by freethinkers, point to her status as the pre-eminent female thinker of that still trenchantly debated cultural phenomenon, the English Enlightenment. The primary reason for this notable aspect of her intellectual life remaining obscured is the tenuous hold the idea of an English Enlightenment currently maintains in academic discourse. It might be easier to claim for her a place in the widely regarded Scottish Enlightenment (and I do to a certain extent), but part of the very reason for her dismissal as an 'inconsistent' theoriser and hence 'disappearance' from intellectual histories of the period is that her works are caught up in the revolving arguments regarding the very existence of an English Enlightenment project. Positioning Cockburn within the wider context helps to clarify her philosophical acumen and also provides evidence for her unique status as one of, if not the foremost female philosopher of England's Enlightenment.

Literary identity: wit versus learning

The first person to hint at a necessary division of roles between the literary and the philosophical/religious was Thomas Burnet of Kemnay when he encouraged Cockburn to quit 'fictitious and poetical study, for the more serious and solid' (II: 161). His position was later bolstered by the salacious attacks of Delarivier Manley, who pilloried Cockburn's approach to literary identity in the *New Atalantis* (1709) and *The Adventures of Rivella* (1714). In these works Manley attacks enough former acquaintances and famous figures that Cockburn's appearance is negligible. Nevertheless, it required a response from Birch in his 'Life' and today constitutes an important 'source' and 'construction' of Cockburn by a contemporary.

Manley's 'secret memoirs' and 'histories' of her life and times have inevitably tantalised literary historians with the opportunity of presenting the possibility that Cockburn had a far more exciting, even subversive, life than the one delivered by herself and Birch.[338] Yet in the *New Atalantis* there is not much Manley adds, or even invents, that significantly changes what we know about Cockburn's early patrons, financial petitioning, religious conversions, and marriage. Critics have identified the figure of Daphne in volume two of the *New Atalantis* as Cockburn and the narrative, minus the slanders, conforms to the events of Cockburn's life and the writings she published before 1709.[339] However, Manley does take the opportunity to inject sexual deviance into the narrative and suggests that Daphne/Cockburn engaged not only in lesbian relations with her female patrons, but in numerous affairs with everyone from John Churchill, the Duke of Marlborough, to 'as many of the Town as found her to their Taste, and wou'd purchase' (184).[340] She then throws out her most common accusation against supposedly exemplary women by exclaiming that Daphne's virtue is only '*Virtue pretended*' (184), and further that it is Daphne who slanders people: 'ever eloquent (according to her stiff manner) upon the *Foible* of others' (184). Manley has nothing more concrete than this accusation and appears rather piqued at the supposed advantages Cockburn enjoyed; in particular, the early acquaintance with the Churchills and her 'air of *Youth* and *Innocence*, which has been of excellent use to her in those occasions she has since had to impose upon the World, as to Matters of Conduct!' (183).

Manley's desire to impugn Cockburn's name raises another question though: did Manley know or is there reason to believe Margarette R. Connor's argument for the existence of a son and an early 'quasi-legal marriage'.[341] If there was ever a writer more likely to hunt out this sort of information and reveal it, Manley was surely the one, yet there is no hint of it in either the *New Atalantis* or *The Adventures of Rivella*.

Perhaps the most interesting, if tangential, piece of information is a detailed physical description which notes how 'her *Shape* would be well *turned*, if something of a certain *stiffness*, which suffers no part of the Person to move without the whole, were not unbecoming, to all' (182–3). Even the rendering of this physical quirk is questionable in its evident bias in presenting Daphne/Cockburn as the overly stuffy/stiff prude. The problem, of course, is that there is no record of Cockburn ever repudiating, responding to, or rewriting Manley's aspersions. The only comments that come close are the constant iterations in the familiar letters of her distaste for party politics; otherwise, nothing has turned up in manuscript or print attributable to her.[342] The most we can say is that she let this version of her life exist uncontested in print, allowing her early London career to be the 'secret life' Manley made of it. In an interesting extension, Manley's construction of a duplicitous colleague is mirrored in Cockburn's own crisis of literary identity during her courtship with Patrick Cockburn. Her complicated interplay of dramatic *double entendres* (from her own plays) and the consciously erudite and Christianised stoicism in her epistolary exchange with him hints at a professional irresolve reflected in the dispersive range of her writings. Given her subsequent vacillations between works of fictional prose (the Aspasia letters) and philosophical disputation, it is unsurprising that contemporaries were at a loss to pinpoint her generic niche. Whether this affected her ability to market her works to publishers is difficult to assess, but it may explain the number of unfinished, unrealised, and unpublished pieces.

At the end of her life, Thomas Sharp, William Warburton, Henry Etough, Thomas Birch, *et al.* firmly established her position as the learned and exemplary woman of a philosophical and religious bent. Kelley claims, 'The image of the erudite scholar is confirmed by the particular selection of texts reprinted in the *Works*, which virtually ignores Trotter's literary writing in favour of philosophy and theology.' She adds, 'Over the centuries, most readers would have had access to her texts only through the Works, so it is easy to see how a distorted view of her writing has been perpetuated.'[343] I would like to suggest an alternative point of view with regard to Cockburn's eighteenth-century editors: one that, I hope, considers the constraints as well as aims of these men in a less condemnatory light.

The publishing history of Cockburn's *Works*, like her life, was beset with patronage and money woes and, crucially, the finished product actually included less 'philosophy and theology' than Cockburn had intended. A series of letters between Etough and Birch reveal that the fraught process of getting her manuscripts into print resulted in the male editors failing the specific intellectual ambitions of their subject, whilst, paradoxically, revealing for posterity the truly wide-ranging extent of those ambitions. A number of factors play into this. First, the blame for the posthumous printing of the *Works* can be apportioned entirely to Warburton. He held onto her various manuscripts for so long (presumably he was too busy attending to Pope's oeuvre) that

Cockburn died before anything material had been accomplished. He was also, it must be remembered, one of her opponents in the debates on the foundation of morality and Etough pointedly states that, when the work passed into Birch's control, 'ye affair will be transferred from ye most improper, into ye most proper hands'.[344] Second, as a result of Cockburn's death and their frustrated wresting of the project away from Warburton, Etough and Birch came into the possession of Cockburn's familiar letters, including those sent to some of the prominent philosophers she defended or attacked. These letters were seen as so material to rendering an accurate history of her philosophical thought that they were willing to cut other pieces in order to feature them. So too the decision to cut rather than enlarge the volumes depended on costs. When Thomas Secker, Bishop of Oxford, and Sharp queried whether the cost of the subscription would have to be increased, Birch and Etough reassured them that they would simply remove an out-of-date section of the original proposal. The text chosen was Cockburn's pet project, the defence of Locke against the charge of Socinianism. Despite Cockburn's reiterated attempts to advertise and print it, her last unprinted philosophical/religious apologetic may have been left out of the *Works*.[345] However, by including her letters, they foregrounded the personally exemplary woman as well as the exemplary work – the image Cockburn had all along tended to use to promote herself. Thus Elizabeth Carter, on reading the *Works*, could write that she saw in Cockburn a 'clear understanding and excellent heart'.[346] Conflating the life with the work was evidently deemed the most effective method of displaying the moral life of the mind and subsequent literary women, such as Carter, would draw upon and uphold the model in an even more exacting way.

However, to return to Kelley's point about the literary scope of the *Works*, specifically the lack of dramatic and poetic pieces, Birch and, before him, Warburton and Sharp fully intended a volume of poetry and plays.[347] Volume two actually offered the most complete collection of her poetry to date and the number of dramatic works was curtailed due to costs and because correct copies could not be obtained. Contemporary interest in her writings was decidedly biased in favour of her religious and philosophical works, adducible from the long list of academic and clerical subscribers, and, when it came time to pare down the volumes, this is what Birch delivered.

> [I]t were to be wished, that these two volumes, conditioned for by the terms of subscription, could have contained all her dramatic writings, of which only one is here published. But as that was found

impossible, the preference was, upon the maturest deliberation, given to those in prose, as superior in their kind to the most perfect of her poetical, and of more general and lasting use to the world. (I: xlvi)

It is unlikely that Cockburn's dramatic writings would have captured as broad an audience; her strength and usefulness to mid- and late-century didacticists was as a learned woman, not a versifying one. Importantly, the prose works Birch speaks of as 'superior in kind' are the familiar letters which cover the entire span of her writing career. Instead, it is early twentieth-century criticism which reads the *Works* in an uncontextual manner; and it is scholars such as Leslie Stephen, Edmund Gosse, and Myra Reynolds who turn Cockburn into the entity Kelley resists.

In a text otherwise meant to celebrate the accomplishments of *The Learned Lady of England*, Reynolds opines:

> that [Cockburn's] editor's confident prediction of her fame has been discredited by time, that she is in reality hardly so much as a name to-day, is due partly to the oblivion that has overtaken her subjects, but also, and even more justly, to the dead level of her excellence. She has no wit, no fancy, no imagination, no sprightliness of thought, no humour. Mary Astell and 'Sophia' were occasionally roused to picturesque indignation. But not so with Mrs. Cockburn. She is as cold, as orderly, as unstimulating as a formula.[348]

Reynolds's assessment simply does not square with the 'sprightliness of thought', the 'wit', and the 'imagination' which are everywhere evident in Cockburn's prose. Stephen and Gosse are similarly uninspired, though prolix, on the subject of Cockburn's forgettable topics, amateur style, and mistaken opinions, and marshal incorrect evidence in their quest to validate her warranted obscurity. Stephen damns her philosophy and Gosse belittles her life (whilst getting it mostly wrong), and ends with a gesture of polite condescension by offering up the prayer: 'I hope her thin little lady-like ghost, still hovering in a phantom like transparence round the recognised seats of learning, will be a little comforted at last by the polite attention of the Royal Society of Literature.'[349] Douglas-Fairhurst, drawing on the paranormal possibilities of textual afterlives, delineates the nineteenth-century obsession with ghosts, sound waves, and the many other ephemeral and aerial forces haunting the palimpsest of poetic composition, but Cockburn's early twentieth-century detractors had no such inspired motive behind their portrayal of her as the diminutive, dismissible phantom disturbing the otherwise admirable progress of eighteenth-century literature.

Such depressing assessments are at a far remove from that provided by Birch in his comparatively encomiastic 'Life'. For Birch and Etough, Cockburn was neither the pathetic ghost of failed female endeavour (a peculiarly Victorian image), nor the dull sideshow of a forgotten controversy. She was simply another neglected intellectual light in a publishing environment rife with them, and Birch, who loved getting his hands on another collection of manuscript writings, readily accepted Etough's request to take on the task Warburton would not or could not find the time to complete. Etough was canny in his choice of Birch. Not only was he relying on Birch's editorial and historiographical skills, of which he thought quite highly, but he also banked on Birch's intellectual, political, ecclesiastical, and social connections furthering the appeal of the work. Allying Cockburn to Birch was, in effect, a way of securely placing her at the epicentre of contemporary scholarly interest. The collection Birch left to the British Museum, now the British Library, is tangible proof of a widespread academically minded scribbling culture and Cockburn's manuscript remains comprise at least five large folio volumes in the archive. For Etough, then, Cockburn deserved to be recognised along with the many other ecclesiastical and scholastic figures Birch wrote about routinely.

For both men, though, the larger task was the biography. Biography of all ages seeks to narrativise, and therefore selectively re-sequence, reconstruct, and even revision the life story(s) of its protagonist. When that protagonist is a learned women and perceived role model to young girls in search of the life of the mind the narrative is doubly important. The 'Life' by Birch was quite clearly constructed with these things in mind; female exemplarity in the form of intellectual excellence and moral seriousness is paramount in his narration. However, these exalted characteristics had their sources in material which preceded and significantly influenced Birch's account. The most important of these were the familial accounts which Cockburn herself passed along: the unsent letter to Alexander Pope which reveals her complicity in the retiring scholarly image, and John Cockburn's familial 'memoir' of his mother. Henry Etough also solicited reminiscences of Cockburn from family, northern divines, and friends and his 'imperfect memoir' provided Birch with most of the material that eventually went into the 'Life'.[350]

The satiric legacy also provided a similar figure to posterity, as we have seen with the Daphne/Cockburn persona propounded by Manley and a character deployed by the anonymous author of the 1697 play, *The*

Female Wits: or, The Triumvirate of Poets at Rehearsal (printed in 1704). This comedy, 'Acted several Days successively with great Applause', lampoons the three female playwrights, Manley, Mary Pix, and Cockburn, who had made the 1696 theatrical season such a success. Manley is the main target as the exasperatingly bad playwright trying to get her piece rehearsed, whilst Pix and Cockburn are parodied in lesser roles as Mrs Wellfed and Calista respectively. Calista is described, rather presciently, as 'A Lady that pretends to the learned Languages, and assumes to her self the Name of a Critick'. In her few appearances on stage she discusses her latest translations and boasts of reading Aristotle in his own language.[351] In terms later adapted by Manley she is also described as 'the vainest, proudest, senseless Thing, she pretends to Grammar, writes in Mood and Figure; does everything methodically'.[352] In other words, like Manley's satire, these descriptions reinforce a uniform image of Cockburn as a learned and serious writer though, in their characterisations, an affected one. Jeslyn Medoff may claim that Cockburn 'was successful in suppressing her early, risqué reputation', but contemporary evidence suggests that there was not much risqué business to hide.[353] Slander and notoriety were not, of course, the type of attention someone seeking an unblemished and morally superior reputation hoped to attract but, as Birch argued, 'such a pen as Mrs. *Manley's* can injure no reputation but her own' (I: xlvii), and, for good measure he adds, 'The collection now exhibited to the world is so incontestable a proof of the superiority of our author's genius, as in a manner supersedes *every thing*' (I: xlviii, italics mine).

Nevertheless, Birch and others wanted the world to realise the magnitude of what Cockburn had accomplished in spite of the penury, the slanders, and the 'near twenty years [...] spent in the cares of a family' (I: xlviii). Part of the exemplary image, then, was the notion of perseverance in spite of social restrictions and Birch's admiration for her dogged dedication to philosophical inquiry and literary endeavour tended to make him exaggerate the duration and surmountability of those obstacles. In the last paragraph of his account he paints a study of Cockburn's life as one of stark and dramatic contrasts.

> [H]er abilities as a writer, and the merit of her works, will not have full justice done them, without a due attention to the peculiar circumstances, in which they were produced; her early youth, when she wrote some; her very advanced age, and ill state of health, when she drew up others; the uneasy situation of her fortune, during the whole course of her life; and an interval of near twenty years, in the vigor

of it, spent in the cares of a family, without the least leisure for reading or contemplation: After which, with a mind so long diverted and encumbered, resuming her studies, she instantly recovered its intire powers, and in the hours of relaxation from her domestic employments pursued, to their utmost limits, some of the deepest inquiries, of which the human mind is capable. (I: xlviii)

At first sight, this encomium appears to be another typically inflated tribute, but the monumental struggle which Birch manages to convey tips Cockburn's achievement into a grander category. At the same time, it is astonishingly sensitive to determining contexts and sympathetic to the plight of a learned woman in the early years of the eighteenth century. Passages like this show Birch to be a friend, in a very modern scholarly sense, to women's involvement in the republic of letters. Etough, the less equanimous of the two, was absolutely enraged by the neglect and wrote in his memoir that, 'The Total neglect of such a Couple fixed in such a manner in their Diocess [sic] is greatly to the Dishonour of the Bp of Durham. how happy would the smallest Preferment belonging to their Patronage have made this Family!'[354] But he also notes that, far from putting herself in fame's path, 'She is so far from Conceit & assuming that her Diffidence is very Remarkable': an exact reiteration of the persona Cockburn evinces in her letter to Pope.[355]

These passages also explain why the rather sparse textual afterlife Cockburn enjoyed was predominantly in works celebrating female endeavour (if not success) for the benefit of a female readership. In poems like John Duncombe's 'The Feminiad' (1754), she is recalled under the terms Birch sought:

> Tho' long, to dark, oblivious want a prey,
> Thy aged worth past unperceiv'd away,
> Yet Scotland now shall ever boast thy fame,
> While England mourns thy undistinguish'd name,
> And views with wonder, in a female mind,
> Philosopher, Divine, and Poet join'd![356]

In the popular *Poems by Eminent Ladies* (1755), which went into numerous editions and had many imitators, the editors specifically chose to highlight Cockburn's works which stemmed from manuscript exchange, reinforcing her particularised niche and obscure life.[357]

One of the most telling instances of Cockburn's appropriation as an exemplar is the use to which she is put in Anne Fisher's *A new English exercise book. Calculated to render the construction of the English tongue, easy and familiar, independent of any other language* (1770). In a template letter for a young girl to write to an older brother who has accused girls of leading lives of vanity and triviality, Cockburn's name is one of those invoked as an example of women who have attained standards of learning above and beyond men. The young girl writes to her brother:

> You seem, indeed to have a mean Opinion of our Sex [...] and to have entertained a Belief that we are incapable of Learning, and have Capacities only for Dress, for Trifling and Impertinence: But I assure you that my Person is not of such Importance to myself as you imagine; and, as to my Mind, if you will give yourself the Trouble to be my Instructor, I will thankfully accept of any Improvement you will give me; and will do my best to convince you, that your Advantages, as a Boy, is merely accidental. Did Miss Carter fall short of any of her Brothers in Learning? Or does Madame Dacier's Works, Mrs Cockburn's, Lady M.W. Montague's, or Mrs Macauly's, proclaim any of that incorrigible Ignorance the Gentleman lays to our Charge?[358]

Besides these poetical and didactic renditions, Birch's 'Life' was often reprinted verbatim, or in brief, in various biographical dictionaries featuring notable women, and/or eminent British figures. Again the emphasis tended to be placed on the subject's poverty and in-the-face-of-all-odds achievements. If we recall Catherine Talbot's complaint, quoted at the beginning of this chapter, it merely confirms that this was how the *Works'* intended audience were meant to 'read' her. Evidence that such a 'reading' could then help to inspire the patronage, promotion, and support of a new generation of learned women is instructive of the power the exemplary image held.

In the end, the representation of Cockburn effected in the *Works* functions similarly to Rowe's public construction as the enthusiastic poetess. The image of the austere learned lady served a didactic end for a particular buying public. The list of subscribers in the *Works* is telling in this instance. As a barometer of who and what was being supported, the list squarely places Cockburn in an ecclesiastical, aristocratic, scholastic, and (burgeoning) professional framework. Whilst we may credit a lot of the names and professional connections to Thomas Birch, the predominance of female aristocrats and gentlewomen is important, especially as they were conceived to be the work's primary audience.

The Etough/Birch letters document the degree of social networking needed to secure enough subscribers to make the venture profitable and it is significant that they relied on the help of a number of influential women. First among these was Lady Isabella Finch.[359] Etough tells Birch:

> Lady Isabella Finch who is our Heroine in this affair, is already grown impatient for a sight of You & of them [Cockburn's manuscripts] I do not know which she is most desirous of seeing. When you are in a capacity for waiting on her, please to direct To The Right Honble Lady Isabella Finch at ye Palace at Kensington, desiring to be informed what time will be proper to present Yourself & Mrs Cockburns Papers. She will speedily dispatch & return them with Observations.[360]

Lady Isabella is further documented as dealing directly with Knapton (the printer) about subscription receipts and advises Etough how best to secure the full payment from the forgetful 'great and fashionable' of Great Britain. He likewise notes the help of Catherine Talbot and a Mrs. Walkinshaw in obtaining subscribers and publicising the endeavour, and also includes Talbot in the correspondence relating to Warburton's relinquishment of control.[361] But the real 'hero' of the affair is unquestionably Etough. His vigorous and stubborn pursuit of every potential market reveals the astonishing amount of social intrigue and intellectual clout needed to secure every guinea from potential subscribers.[362] He laments forgetting to annex to the subscription proposal the names of all the fashionable figures who had already paid, aware that this would have inspired imitators, and decides to print an extra 50–100 copies in the event that aspiring society types will purchase them. Aware too that, since Warburton and Sharp's proposals had been circulated, the non-appearance of the *Works* had caused interest to flag, Etough decides that a new proposal trumpeting Birch's involvement is necessary to generate both curiosity and confidence in the new edition.[363] He then specifically identifies a number of people whom he thinks will subscribe as long as personal applications are made and allocates various members of the 'team' to secure their interest. He instructs Birch:

> When I come up I will contribute my full proportion. In ye mean while I take ye liberty to suggest ye measures to be pursued by Mr C[ockburn]: & Yourself. Dr Tom: Green is in Town he is well disposed & perpetually with ye Great People of both Sexes. If You or any other proper person applieth to him, he can & will give good Assistance. Particularly he can procure from ye Bps of Chichester Ely

& ye two new ones but certainly from Cornwallis. Mr & Lady Mary Jennings are in Town he can certainly procure from One of them, for they have promised & he is better with them than I am. There are many others he knoweth better than I who they are. Perhaps he is acquainted with ye ArchBp of Yorke; are not You? I do not know him. Mr C[ockburn]: should remind Lady Bell Finch to speak to ye Bp of Bristol. Mrs Sherlock has given me a Guinea, ye Bp I fancy would do ye same on seeing ye new Proposals if a proper Applier could be found. Mr Wray is well acquainted with Mr Read, as they are well with considerable People they must be now reminded. You can speak to the speaker Ld Ch[arles]: Cavendish & Cha: Stanhope Mr Yorke & Mr Charles. Mr Yorke will be ye most proper to recommend ye affair to ye Master of Christs. But if he is averse what cometh from You will be equally effectual, to him to ye M^r of Maudlin, & above all to Dr Midleton. Mr Cockburn should send Proposals & receipts to ^y^e Vice chancellor & ye M^r of St Johns who is well disposed & can do service in his College. Dr Rooke has interest in Trinity, but it will be proper Dr Bentley should hear from You. it was Lady Bell Finchs proper advice & management to get ye whole Guinea, where we can [...]. The old General as it is for a Womans works & as he is a Brother of ye R[oyal]: Society would surely be a subscriber, & might make it a fashion for other officers.[364]

Of particular interest, however, are his comments about the fraught nature of the subscription at Cambridge. He frequently mentions that he has been advised to stay well away from the university men in his quest for subscriptions, and that the nature of the controversies was still so fresh that Cockburn's writings were likely to spark unfriendly flames despite the charitable nature of the *Works*. Etough writes that, 'The Great People will not allow me to interfere at Cambridge. I have been there only once this winter. The feuds & jealousies which subsist among friends, are a very unpleasing entertainment Notwithstanding what I am to do for ye subscription, & many other charities.'[365] Men from within the university took charge of the advertising and collecting of subscriptions, therefore. In the end, Etough and his team still managed to get 442 subscribers. Sarah Fielding, an experienced practitioner of the subscription method, netted 440 for *The Lives of Cleopatra and Octavia* (1757).[366]

Many of the eventual subscribers were, interestingly enough, men and women who had aided the literary career of the financially independent Rowe: Frances, Duchess Dowager of Somerset (that is, the

Countess of Hertford), the Countess of Northumberland (Hertford's daughter), the Duchess of Portland (long-time friend and correspondent of Hertford), and Theophilus Rowe (the brother-in-law and editor of Rowe). Another contingent were those associated with the Birch, Talbot, and Carter circle: Edward Cave, Thomas Secker, Mrs Talbot, Miss Underdown of Deal, Dr Lynch (Dean of Canterbury), William Duncombe, Marchioness Grey, and the Yorke brothers. Warburton's connections also secured a few more names: Ralph Allen (the friend of Henry Fielding and uncle of Warburton's wife), Thomas Balguy, and Richard Hurd (future Bishop of Worcester). Thomas Sharp undoubtedly secured many of the northern subscribers, of which a group of women signing themselves as from Durham College are particularly interesting, suggesting as it does the presence of a more advanced women's college in the northern town. Particularly prominent, however, are the number of high-ranking church divines who subscribed. No less than 12 bishops appear in the list of subscribers: including Joseph Butler (Bishop of Durham), Benjamin Hoadly (Bishop of Winchester), and the Archbishop of Canterbury, Matthew Hutton. On the scholastic front, the members of the University of Cambridge managed to overcome internal squabbles, or were just eager to find out what Cockburn had to say about their former alumni and the ongoing disputes they engendered: forty college members, two college libraries, many past alumni, and even the Vice-Chancellor of Cambridge, Edmund Keene, ordered the *Works*. The interest Cambridge men took in Cockburn's contribution to philosophy and religious commentary provides compelling evidence of Cockburn's prominence as the most significant female philosopher of what Brian Young refers to as 'England's peculiarly clerical Enlightenment.'[367]

Did women have an Enlightenment?

Feminist scholars have already questioned whether women had a Renaissance, and answered in the affirmative. More recently, with the publication of *Women, Gender and Enlightenment*, the editors and their many contributors have made apparent the breadth and variety of women's involvement in the Enlightenment. Whilst no one in this volume discusses Cockburn – a significant and glaring lack – contributors do explore questions relevant to her engagement with the ideas, participants, and means of exchange in this still hotly debated historical construct/movement. Indeed, the focus on 'the media of Enlightenment' confirms my arguments thus far regarding Cockburn's diverse, but nevertheless typical, oeuvre in relation to her continental and seventeenth-century forebears, as well as her late eighteenth-century successors.

As many of the essays in the volume reveal, however, unlocking the ideologies, influences, and networks requires an attention to particularities which can often seem reductive when applied to the age of light. It would, of course, be grand to claim for Cockburn an international agenda and scope given her early contacts with well-known continental figures. At present, however, it is much more productive and illuminating to consider her in relation to a national, that is, British, Enlightenment, and the effect present-day debates regarding the conceptual parameters of that movement have had on our attempts to contextualise and 'place' the British Enlightenment woman. Thus, whilst it is fairly easy to show that women took full advantage of the intellectual fruits of a 'knowing' age, the more difficult question to answer is the degree to which they were aware of and specifically influencing the distinctive currents and counter-currents of enlightened discourse. For instance, the degree to which scholars have accepted the hegemony and compatibility of John Locke and Sir Isaac Newton's ideas on their English and European followers has an important bearing on Cockburn's reception and longevity. Drawing on Brian Young's important revisioning of the heretofore harmonised and highly politicised approach to Lockean and Newtonian confluences in Enlightenment thought, I argue that the status of Cockburn's intellectual legacy is ineluctably caught up in the complicated tangle of opposing, as well as criss-crossing, theological polemics which constituted an important component of the philosophical discourse of the English Enlightenment.[368]

Whilst an understanding of Cockburn's intellectual relevance is best captured by exploring the male-dominated sphere of controversial polemics in which she chose to engage, her lasting importance to literary history is to be found through a consideration of her own awareness and championing of women's involvement in enlightened public discourse. Emma Jay's recent work on Queen Caroline's importance to British literary culture explores some of these issues through Caroline's interaction with and support for English Enlightenment figures.[369] Cockburn herself recognised, celebrated, and hoped to take advantage of this feminine influence, and her 'Poem, occasioned by the busts set up in the Queen's Hermitage,' conspicuously claims for Caroline and herself a philosophic and religious directive.[370]

In 1727 Queen Caroline ordered the building of a hermitage at Richmond which served to project 'an image of herself as a promoter of enlightened ideas',[371] whilst also signalling those thinkers she placed at the forefront of the English Enlightenment. Of Caroline's decision to place the busts of Clarke, Locke, and Newton in her hermitage (Cockburn conveniently neglects to mention her adversary Wollaston and also Boyle), she adduces that 'each new honour, added to their name,/ Shall back reflect on her's a brighter fame' (II:572). Even more to the point, she argues that it is Caroline's choices which should now dictate the subjects men write about. Directing her lines to Stephen Duck, the thresher poet installed nearby in Merlin's Cave, Cockburn advises him:

> The venerable busts, that honour'd stand,
> Plac'd by thy royal patroness's hand,
> Instruct thee in her taste, and bid thee raise
> To subjects worthy her thy future lays:
> By them stupendous truths thou may'st be taught,
> Thy maker's awful works excite thy thought,
> His wisdom in their structure to rehearse,
> And deep philosophy inform thy verse. (II: 573)

Not only does Cockburn here imply that Caroline's artistic monument acts as a barometer of the queen's erudite interests, but that she specifically singled out a trinity of (anti-trinitarian) intellectuals in order to influence the religious and philosophical substance henceforth applied in poetic composition.

Cockburn, however, has her own directive to promote in the form of a lesson about unpatronised and therefore undirected learning in female writers. Contrasting the restraints placed on women with that experienced by the queen's rural bard, Cockburn writes:

> Learning deny'd us, we at random tread
> Unbeaten paths, that late to knowledge lead;
> By secret steps break thro' th'obstructed way,
> Nor dare acquirements gain'd by stealth display.
> If some advent'rous genius rare arise,
> Who on exalted themes her talent tries,
> She fears to give the work, tho' prais'd a name,
> And flies not more from infamy than fame. (II: 573)

First describing women's attempts at learning in a manner reminiscent of eighteenth-century depictions of the judgement of Hercules,

Cockburn echoes Shaftesbury's moral painting but replaces the polite gentleman with the learned woman climbing the rock-strewn path towards virtue.[372] Even once she passes this test she is still faced with the problem of whether to court public recognition ('infamy' and 'fame'), which leads Cockburn to ask, 'Would royal *Caroline* our wrongs redress' (II: 573). That is, would the queen actively patronise and protect in her own name the names of women writers in the marketplace. Cockburn then returns to specifics and constructs herself as one abandoned not only by fame, but by her own country (and by extension the queen): 'I alas! in northern climes grown old,/ No more my native country shall behold' (II: 574), and implores the queen to indulge her with even the faintest praise, 'Tho' in the lowest class, of *Merlin's* cave' (II: 574). Her *coup de grâce* is the assertion that should Caroline choose to bestow her considerable influence upon the world of women's writing, and, specifically, her own works, she would impart a reforming influence capable of transforming British women's literary history.

> Then, as this happy isle already vies
> In arms with foes, in arts with her allies;
> No more excell'd in aught by *Gallia's* coast,
> Our *Albion* too should of her *Daciers* boast. (II: 575)

Invoking the well-worn comparison with France and Madame Dacier, Cockburn essentially challenges the queen to stand up for English women writers and, in the process, the nation.

In her own day Cockburn was often regionalised as the 'Scots Sappho', or, as Sophia, the Electress of Hanover, coined it, 'la nouvelle Sapho[sic] Ecossoise', rather than a specifically English writer.[373] True, she had considerable Scottish connections. Her mother's and husband's families, and even her early suitor and champion, Thomas Burnet of Kemnay, were all Scottish. She also resided in Aberdeen and near the Scottish border for almost a quarter-century. Scotland contained some of the most intellectually forward-thinking universities and philosophers of the time, so it would seem fitting if Cockburn could be heralded as the leading female light in the widely regarded and more advanced Scottish Enlightenment. And, to an extent, this is possible. The esteem in which she was held in the 1740s was a reflection of the growing recognition and respect being accorded intellectuals from the northern universities. It also explains the trajectory of some her interests. Compare Cockburn's works with those of her Scottish contemporaries (many of whom are now heralded as significant contributors to the moral-sense, or common sense, school of Scottish philosophy) and she fits right in. Take, for example, George Turnbull (1698–1748), a tutor at Marischal College, Aberdeen, who was an early advocate of dissent, freethinkers, and Shaftesbury, but later became an Anglican clergyman. His *The Principles of Moral and Christian Philosophy* was a defence of Clarkean physico-theology. His *Observations upon Liberal Education* (1742) draws on Locke and advocates the use of a liberal education for inculcating the moral virtues and, therefore, ensuring responsible, happy citizens in a free society. Turnbull's early christianising of Shaftesbury is echoed in Cockburn's letters to her niece, as is the later repudiation. Francis Hutcheson (1694–1746) also wrote on similar themes, but Cockburn disagreed with his theory of the moral sense. Nevertheless, further consideration of the debates with which she was engaged unquestionably locates Cockburn's contribution in English Enlightenment terms given her focus on and fusion of Lockean and Clarkean ideas. In a related side note, just as Cockburn's afterlife fizzles out after the brief resurgence at mid-century, so too did Caroline's paean to the English Enlightenment: the hermitage was pulled down to make way for an observatory in the 1760s.

In an effort to revisit the historical reasons which led to the queen's concerted publicisation of English Enlightenment thinkers, scholars such as John Gascoigne and Brian Young have, over the past two decades, sought to elucidate what the precise terms of that English Enlightenment were, both in contrast to the Scottish experience and within the movement itself. There are still considerable gaps in both of their narratives, though, and, unsurprisingly, one of them is the woman question. Thus, we return to the question of whether women had an Enlightenment, or, more specifically, whether they had an English one?

Based purely on the evidence of Cockburn's philosophical incursions and epistolary connections the answer is yes. Anyone who wants to look farther afield than this study has the time or space to do will find many more candidates in Knott's and Taylor's *Women, Gender and Enlightenment*, and O'Brien's *Women and Enlightenment*. My focus is on Cockburn and manuscript/scribal publication, however, so it should come as no surprise that I also argue that the primary mode in which English women participated in Enlightenment discourse was through the exchange of learned letters. The list of women who corresponded with, and were admired by, prominent philosophers of the Enlightenment is considerable. There is likewise evidence that they often exchanged letters amongst themselves or used their male mentors as intermediaries. Continental precursors as well as contemporaries include the writers

Anna Maria Van Schurman, Elisabeth of Bohemia (who famously corresponded with Descartes), Sophia, Electress of Hanover (correspondent of Leibniz), and the French salonnièrres: Madeleine de Scudéry, Madeleine de Sablé, Madame de la Sablière, Madame de Maintenon, Madame Deshoulières, and Mademoiselle de la Vallière. Their seventeenth-century English counterparts include: Anne Conway (whose exchange with the Cambridge Platonist Henry More has been called 'the first correspondence course in Cartesian Philosophy'),[374] Mary Astell (with John Norris), Elizabeth Burnet (with Locke) and Damaris Masham (with Locke and Leibniz). All of them participated in philosophically influenced religious debate through private correspondences with famous academics and/or clerics of the period. A discussion of the full extent of their philosophical incursions in European, Scottish, and English Enlightenment polemics awaits a future study. For now I want to point out that, in England, only Masham and Burnet (for) and Astell (against) seriously engaged with one of the fathers of the English Enlightenment, John Locke, whilst the other figurehead of the period, Isaac Newton, had to wait until later in the century for a similar league of opposition and defence through the followers of Samuel Clarke. Cockburn, in what has been characterised as a failing, was the only female philosopher of the first half of the eighteenth century to actively write in support of both Lockean and Newtonian (through Clarke) ideas.

She can also, through the subscription list of the *Works*, be identified as one of the chosen writers of the clericy and academy, the university-trained elite at the heart of the English Enlightenment movement. This is important for two reasons. As Young points out, it was primarily in the 'universities and the Dissenting academies that much of the controversial life of the eighteenth-century intellect was exercised', and, though women were, of course, not yet allowed into the universities, this exclusion did not ultimately hinder someone like Cockburn from making an impact or becoming known precisely because of the epistolary nature of polemical discourse in the period.[375] Secondly, it has been argued by Gascoigne, among others, that Cambridge, like the Scottish universities, was an early reformer in the realm of science and philosophy and it had managed, in a period of radically changing political and ecclesiastical loyalties, to carve out a niche for itself as a place that facilitated the link between Anglicanism and science, forging the so-called 'holy alliance'.[376] Contrary to popular clichés about university insularity and an anti-Enlightenment ethos, therefore, Cambridge was notable for its outward-looking climate and had more in common with the Scottish universities than with its old rival, and the alma mater of

Locke, Oxford. Gascoigne notes that, at Cambridge, classical logic gave way to mathematics and the study of Locke's epistemology, and at both Oxbridge universities scholastic natural philosophy was supplanted by the 'new philosophy' inaugurated by Descartes and then reformed by Newton.[377] Members of Cambridge were well versed in the non-establishment approaches of someone like Cockburn, therefore, and, in any event, were more interested in her very specific moral theories precisely because of their academic and religious biases. The number of them who subscribed to her works is an astonishing display of institutional support for someone from outside the fold and, despite the short-lived nature of this interest, it is clear her acumen was valued.

But this was not a one-sided and entirely uncritical engagement. Just as many members of the university sought out Cockburn's work in order to refute her arguments, Cockburn turned her sights on the academy itself and took stock of their function and relevance in the 'holy alliance'. In her brief essay, *On the Usefulness of Schools and Universities, for the Improvement of the Mind, in right Notions of God*, Cockburn assesses the primary advantages a liberal education can bestow and to what purposes those advantages ought then to be directed.[378] Her unequivocal conclusion is that a liberal education will, 'by opening and enlarging our minds,... bring us to the knowledge of a supreme being, upon the most solid and rational grounds' (II:125). This is in direct opposition to the type of free-thinking assault on academia and 'priestcraft' typified in Shaftesbury's works and Cockburn specifically takes that sort of scepticism to task in favour of the rational approach.[379] She writes:

> How poor a logician must he be, who, whilst he reduces reasoning to an art, and considers the progress of his own understanding, does not see, that all this active thought cannot be the effect of heavy senseless matter; and is not from thence led to the necessary consequence of admitting an eternal, self-existent mind, from which all other thinking beings must be derived! (II: 125)

Not content with warning the sceptics, she also turns her attention to the various new sciences making such an impact at the universities and in intellectual discourse of the period. Of the astronomer she notes:

> How idly would the astronomer be employed, who in calculating the motions of the heavenly bodies,[...] should only divert himself with the agreeable amusement, without reflecting what that power must be, which can sustain such ponderous orbs, prevent their interfering

with each other, and keep them in a constant course, so contrary to the known laws of bodies set in motion! (II: 125–6)

Likewise with the philosopher, who she warns against consigning means and ends to mere 'undesigning chance', and against the practical scientist (that is, moral philosopher/ethicist), who she sees as deficient unless he considers the laws of nature and the duties of society in tandem with consideration of a supreme being (II:126): a notion which is at the basis of all her moral philosophy. Essentially the essay is concerned to argue the merits of the moral virtues, but what is peculiar to Cockburn is that she prefaces it with the idea that these things can only be inculcated through courses in moral philosophy tempered by the rational approaches of the natural sciences.

Remarks in Cockburn's familiar letters reveal that she was practising the same sort of programme in the education of her own and others' children. Her letters to her niece act as their own correspondence course in early eighteenth-century moral philosophy and natural religion, and reiterate over the years her position that morality is as capable of demonstration as anything in the natural sciences. Further evidence regarding her interest in the foundations of education emerge in Cockburn's recommended readings, for instance Charles Rollin's, *The Method of studying and teaching the Belles Letters* (II:273),[380] or her adamant stance that her daughter be taught geography despite her own inability (due to failing eyesight) to teach it.[381] Earlier, in 1709, Sarah Piers had solicited the Cockburns on behalf of a gentleman who needed somewhere to send his young female ward to be educated; he disliked 'Common schools for her', and Cockburn was seen as the best candidate for the job.[382] This suggests that not only was she aware of systems and institutions from which we would normally assume her excluded, but that she had formulated alternatives to those systems and institutions through her own studies and private teaching.

These educational interests are one of Cockburn's most valuable legacies and align her with later educationalists such as Elizabeth Carter (who schooled her younger brother and nephew, successfully, for entry to Cambridge and Oxford respectively), Hannah More (who taught at the Bristol girl's school founded by her father and wrote numerous works on women's education), and Anna Barbauld (who, with her husband, opened the Palgrave school for boys and also wrote educational tracts). What all of these women were engaged in, in one way or another, was the Enlightenment reform of the foundations of learning. These scholastic interests may also explain their lack of advancement. University patronage happened through appointments and posts within the academy or clericy, and men within the academy were unlikely to sponsor learned women at the expense of their own students and lesser clergy. It was, as Cockburn had realised in her appeal to Queen Caroline, up to female aristocrats, including the queen, to confer 'posts' (that is, pensions) and sponsor women. The road to recognition and recompense was still through private patronage or public subscription.

However, to return to Cockburn's Enlightenment role in Britain, questions remain as to whether her writings embody a significant current of thought in the history of ideas of the time, and if she managed to affect subsequent work in any way. The answer to both is yes, sort of. First, because her writings represent the difficulty in explicating the ultra-particular yet relatively open-minded fusion of philosophical and religious ideals in works of the period, she is a useful barometer of what Brian Young has identified as the prevailing state of clerical Enlightenment discourse: that is, its internal disjunction. For Young, controversial discourse was waged *within* the clerical culture, not primarily between the clergy and freethinkers and, as a result, the actual subject of controversy is to be found within the ranks and in the latitude accorded intellectual debate on religious subjects.[383] The real enemy was 'dogmatism, the authorisation of tradition and history as guarantees of religious truth', whilst anti-dogmatism, or latitudinarianism, became the prevailing mode of Enlightenment thinkers.[384] Further, Young points out that even within this anti-dogmatic movement there was internal dissension, between those that espoused a Newtonian brand of physico-theology and so-called Lockean divines who wrote against Newton's Arianism and metaphysical propositions. Samuel Clarke was one of the greatest champions of Newton's metaphysics and natural philosophy, but many of Locke's followers, and even some of Newton's, took exception to the extreme metaphysical theory involved in Clarke's defences and sought instead a rational, and more 'secure', basis in scripture.

Cockburn was no different. I previously mentioned her decision not to engage in metaphysical disputation with John Norris, and her own appreciation of Clarke was founded squarely on his rational defence of scriptural interpretation. However, her decision to point out what she saw as crucial loopholes in his opponents' arguments led her to being credited with a wholesale belief in Clarke's ideas.

Bolton has given a superb explication of the roots of this philosophical and religious misidentification in Cockburn's works and, in so doing, confirms Young's later thesis about the unrecognised religious focus of the English Enlightenment. Bolton outlines Cockburn's consistent (from the time of her Locke defence to her late works on Clarke) concern in proving that 'what our nature and society requires, we are obligated to do, and that in turn shows that God commands us to do it'.[385] Cockburn, therefore, affirms Clarke's belief in the evidence for moral truths as eternal objects of God's knowledge, whilst still adhering to Locke's idea that our knowledge of human nature is the ground for our knowledge of moral good.[386] She then uses both of these propositions in defending the motivating source of moral obligation, arguing that the motive to be moral is in human nature but that that antecedently obligates us to God's commands which we realise through our very nature.[387] She bases moral obligation on a belief in natural law theories about human nature, which is entirely consistent with both Locke and Clarke. What she specifically wanted to attack in Locke's and Clarke's opponents, though, was their dogmatic adherence to orthodoxy, which not only aided the sceptics, but was entirely against the Enlightenment ethos of a rational approach to religion. Bolton notes that Cockburn's 'vanishing act' as a philosopher stems from her decision to go after the 'obscure' religionists propounding what she saw as a dangerous theistic voluntarism, rather than any weakness in her own arguments.[388] However, as Young has since pointed out, this is precisely what makes her philosophical-religious incursions uniquely in line with the English/clerical Enlightenment. Where Bolton differs from Young is in her conclusion that Cockburn did this for political reasons. I tend to agree with Young that stronger reasons lie in the religious tendencies of the time, and it is only because Whig history has so effectively been aligned with Enlightened discourse that the political bias has appeared uppermost. Cockburn was a religious proselytiser but hardly ever a political one, and trying to insert her, at last, into whiggish interpretations of literary history does an injustice to her idiosyncratic but determined belief in the efficacy of her mode of philosophically grounded religious apologetic.[389]

There is one other aspect of Cockburn's philosophical afterlife to consider: her influence on later thinkers. As I noted in Chapter 3, the philosopher and libertarian Richard Price (1723–1791) included a note in the first and second editions of his book, *A Review of the Principal Questions and Difficulties in Morals*, recommending the letters between Cockburn and Thomas Sharp, as well as referring the reader to her *Remarks* (1743).[390] Through the notes, he specifically aligns her with men like Bishop Butler and other moral philosophers who have influenced his thinking on the foundations of morality, and he echoes many of her own statements. His views on the non-voluntarist foundation of morals owe much to Cockburn's analysis and has been insufficiently noted in discussions of his moral philosophy (he uses the argument Bolton identifies as Cockburn's unique contribution: that of the antecedent obligation to God's laws through natural law).[391] He also shares his critique of the moral sense theories of Hutcheson with Cockburn. Perhaps prompted by Price's use of the letters, Thomas Sharp issued them as part of his own collected works in 1763.[392] Price's late evocation of Cockburn reminds us again of the catholic nature of religious polemic within Enlightenment England – the fact that Price was a dissenter and theist did not preclude his approbation of her opinions. Of tangential note, but interesting nonetheless, are Price's connections with both the Scottish Enlightenment and women writers of the later eighteenth century. He was awarded a doctor of divinity degree by Marischal College, Aberdeen, in 1767, he had peripheral connections to Elizabeth Montagu and the Bluestocking group, and he was a major influence on Mary Wollstonecraft.[393] It may seem like playing at six degrees of separation, but these links are suggestive of Cockburn's continued presence/relevance/influence in moral discourses of the second half of the eighteenth century, including that conducted by radical libertarians, the Bluestockings, and later feminists such as Wollstonecraft.

Apocryphal lives

I have discussed a number of reasons why Cockburn's exemplary and learned life is of such interest for the literary historian and most of these stem from the manifold issues surrounding manuscript and print in the period. Possibly the most intriguing aspect of her legacy, though, are all the tantalising claims and evidence for even more unpublished manuscripts than made it into the *Works*. A response to John Norris, the 'Letters of Aspasia', the de la Vallière translation, a reply to the author of an 'Essay on Virtue'; all of these incomplete starts must still be factored into Cockburn's career, as they grant us a farther insight into the scope of her intellectual and artistic ambitions. However, Etough, in his 'Imperfect Memoirs of Mrs. Cockburn', concludes:

> She [Cockburn] has many Valuable things in [manuscript]. They must be very considerable for she spends several hours every day in Reading and Writing. A Large Defence of Mr Locke from the Charge of Socinianism has been many years ready for the Press. There is no doubt of its being an Accurate Performance, but the Publication

cannot be advised, Forty or Fifty Years ago, such a Work would have been regarded, but the Subject has been Many Years out of Date.[394]

Etough's assumption that her hours of 'Reading and Writing' are producing 'valuable' manuscripts is indicative of the high esteem in which he held Cockburn's perspicuity, but his assumption that these pieces are likely out of date is a consideration which plagues her unrealised or, rather, unrecognised career. Literary treasure hunts aside, we want to know whether what she was doing was relevant to others in the field and, more importantly, whether her piecemeal literary legacy represents something significant for women's literary history. It does, both through the *idea* of the apocryphal writings and her actual life and literary contributions.

The missing writings and incomplete versions of her life are crucially important in a consideration of her literary afterlife for a number of reasons. First, they indicate the extent to which financial circumstances (including lack of patronage) limited Cockburn's material output, which in turn highlighted that neglect to future patrons and friends of female learning. Second, they offer a useful outline of the broader scope of her literary interests, including her interest in devotional literature and metaphysical disputations but pragmatic distrust of their usefulness. Third, the very notion of an apocryphal life, the one not-lived or only half-lived, is a construct which lies at the very heart of the female experience of literary history. Virginia Woolf's *A Room of One's Own* (1728) and, over sixty years later, Catherine Gallagher's *Nobody's Story: The Vanishing Acts of Women Writers in the Marketplace, 1670–1820*, are only two of the most prominent studies which delineate this sense of lack in women's literary history. It is precisely this (not always accurate) construct of aporias, gaps, and silences in the female tradition that has provided the primary impetus to recover and record female authors going back to at least the end of the fourteenth century.[395] Every era seems to have had its group of proto-feminists bemoaning the absence of a female literary pantheon and subsequently producing tomes of female worthies to make up the defect. Yet with each passing century the problem has appeared afresh, and female champions again come out with their 'Feminiads' and 'Memoirs' in answer to a perceived or actual lack. This repetitive reclamation project should not always be taken as proof, therefore, of the wholesale 'vanishing... of women writers', but rather as the necessary cultural bulwark against that possibility. The contemporary discussions surrounding the reintroduction of Cockburn should be seen in this light. Put in the simplest terms, she never 'vanished'; she merely used other means of publication and distribution than the print market and we need to acknowledge that this is something she shared with a vast number of other literary and intellectual women in the seventeenth and eighteenth centuries. The life of the mind could be practised in manifold ways, as fully or partially as a women's circumstances (as too a man's) directed. Revisiting those circumstances with as much contextual disinterest as possible reveals that the repetitive rehearsals of female exemplarity by its male and female champions ensured that women entered rather than vanished from the eighteenth-century marketplace.

5
Elizabeth Carter: 'a very extraordinary Phaenomenon in the Republick of Letters'

> This lady is a very extraordinary Phaenomenon in the Republick of Letters, and justly to be rank'd with the Cornelia's, Sulpicia's, and Hypatia's of the Ancients, and the Schurmans and Daciers of the Moderns. For to an uncommon Vivacity and Delicacy of Genius and an Accuracy of Judgment worthy of the maturest Years, she has added the Knowledge of the ancient and Modern Languages at an Age, when an equal Skill in any one of them would be a considerable Distinction in a Person of the other Sex.[396]

Elizabeth Carter (1717–1806) was one of the most acclaimed female writers of her day. Given the equivalent of a university education by her father, the perpetual curate of Deal Chapel, Carter's early literary precocity and learning prompted Samuel Johnson to claim that 'she ought to be celebrated in as many different languages as Lewis Le Grand'.[397] By the time her poem, 'Ode to Wisdom', had been enshrined in Samuel Richardson's *Clarissa* (1747-8), Carter had already established a solid literary reputation based upon her poetic contributions to the *Gentleman's Magazine*, a small volume of poetry entitled *Poems on Particular Occasions* (1738), and two translations: *Sir Isaac Newton's Philosophy Explain'd for the Use of the Ladies* (1739)[398] (from the Italian of Francesco Algarotti) and *An Examination of Mr Pope's Essay on Man, From the French of M. Crousaz* (1739). Carter's subsequent translation from the Greek of *All the works of Epictetus* (1758) garnered her critical acclaim and financial independence. Her second volume of poetry, *Poems on Several Occasions* (1762), further secured her status as one of the most eminent women of letters of the latter half of the century.

Like Rowe and, to a lesser extent, Cockburn, she managed a successful career by negotiating the media of manuscript and print, attracted patronage through the help of aristocratically connected friends, and maintained an impeccable record for virtue, domesticity, and humility throughout her very long life. She also irrevocably affected the image of the learned lady. Where Rowe produced some translations from French and deployed the philosophical theories of Pascal and Shaftesbury, and Cockburn sparred with religious and philosophical controversialists on the foundations of virtue, Carter vied with the academic establishment itself in her erudition and language abilities in Latin, Greek, and Hebrew. As her friend Catherine Talbot would state, Carter was a 'university of ladies',[399] and her professional status suggests the culmination of an Orindan tradition of learned, respectable, and conservative female writers.

Despite such valorisation and esteem, Carter's literary and biographical legacies offer a significant counterpoint to the careers of Cockburn and Rowe. Carter complicates many of the polarising distinctions that contemporaries and current scholars tend to make about women writers of the long eighteenth century. For that reason, she presents a very useful challenge to the way we view the agency and implicit project of women writers in the period.

Many receptions of Carter have tended to assume an essential distinction between her learned image and her poetic career. From the late eighteenth century to the present, the critical respect accorded her learning is treated as separate from appraisals of the poetry that garnered her the attention in the first place. Unlike Rowe, whose learning was subsumed by the image of the enthusiastic poetess, Carter's early persona as the precocious female versifier gave way to a more enduring identity as a public intellectual/moralist and private domestic exemplar. The latter roles, whilst often allied to the period when Carter nominally ceased to produce work of an obviously literary or learned bent, are nevertheless the guises that frame her most prolific letter-writing years. Ironically, our awareness of Carter's epistolary efficacy in the second half of the eighteenth century also stems from a nineteenth-century memoir and editions of her correspondence that many fault with undermining her literary career.

As with Rowe and Cockburn, the biographical and critical tradition are not wholly to blame for the image revision: Carter herself helped to create and, in fact, lived out her literary afterlife as Britain's most learned lady long before her biographer or later critics reinforced the role. More so than the other women I have discussed in this book, Carter lived for posterity. Cockburn may have claimed she was 'dead long before' Pope and Congreve, and Rowe determinedly left the realm of the living before her death, but neither of them were quite as conscientiously image-driven and 'afterlife'-aware as Carter appears to have been. On her eighteenth birthday Carter was hinting at some of those present and posthumous desires; her poem, 'In Diem Natalem' (1735), praises God for moulding her into a joyful and well-tempered being, but she also dwells on a future immortal state, where her soul will 'live when Earth and Skies shall be no more' (*BF* II: 342–4, ll. 18). More to the point, she acknowledges her time on earth as 'Life's Stage' and hopes that 'I my Part sustain,/ And at my Exit thy Applauses gain' (ll. 57–8). A poem 'To Mrs Montagu' (1776), published over forty years later, constructs a similar dramatic exit for her friend:

> For wider Glories, for immortal Fame,
>   Were all those Talents, all those Graces given:
> And may thy life pursue that noblest Aim,
>   The final Plaudit of approving Heav'n. (*BF*, II: 372–4, ll. 57–60)

Conventional metaphors, perhaps, but Carter's choice of theatrical imagery for her accounts of earthly happiness and final applause suggests her sense (and awareness) of a watching world.

In the present and following chapter, though I begin with a reconstruction of some early aspects of her literary career, the need to rely on her heavily edited letters makes it necessary to consider the 'afterlife' more immediately than in previous chapters. Like the poems just cited, Carter's epistolary exercises were largely concerned with afterlives, both literal and figurative, and her entire corpus has an aura of futurity that is suggestive of her posthumous pretensions. Her emphasis on an exemplary life for the purposes of this final reward will be contextualised more fully in chapter 6.

In spite of Carter's attention to the future she is often seen as a regressive participant in the culture of ideas of her time. To historians concerned primarily with the secularising movements of the period, Carter's championing of High Church Anglicanism appears to express outdated religious biases. Similarly, her allegiance to earlier traditions of manuscript circulation and continental humanism relegates her to the side of the ancients in our preoccupation with identifying the 'modern' in the eighteenth century.[400] Nevertheless, Carter's approach towards her own career and posterity was distinctly modern. She was able to harness secular ideas, particularly the periodical press and the discourse of polite sociability, for her own ideological purposes. Her dual manuscript and print careers also reveal that she was making integrative, 'modern', decisions about the deployment of manuscript traditions alongside print advancements.

Since the 1990s, Carter's impressive intellectual achievements and celebrity status in her own time have drawn increasing interest from historians and literary critics. Sylvia Harcstark Myers, Harriet Guest, Judith Hawley, Karen O'Brien, Elizabeth Eger, Betty Schellenberg, and Nicole Pohl have redrawn the map of Carter's career and significantly changed the way we approach the Bluestockings more generally. In contrast to some of the available literature on Rowe and Cockburn, these scholars have already teased out many of the socio-historical complexities of Carter's contemporary scene, manuscript history, and critical aftermath. The reception and manuscript history of these three writers suggest an intellectual and textual continuum in the mode and manner of their participation in the republic of letters. Carter, however, offers a unique example of a writer actively engaged with this implicit republic and with her own distinct ideas about the trajectory of a literary career.

Biographical fragments

Carter was born on 16 December 1717 in Deal, Kent, the eldest child of Nicholas Carter (1688–1774) and Margaret Swayne (d.1727/8). Her mother, an heiress who brought £15,000 to the marriage, died after an apparent decline brought on by the loss of her fortune in the South Sea Bubble in 1720. There were four other children from this marriage and all of them were educated to the same high standard as Elizabeth.[401] Nicholas's second marriage to Mary Bean, in 1729, produced four more children whose education was placed in his eldest daughter's hands. Most notably, Carter tutored Henry or Harry (b.1739), the youngest, for entrance to Corpus Christi College, Cambridge. He matriculated 2 July 1756 and later became a rector.

At an early age Carter began sending riddles, epigrams, and poetry to Edward Cave's *Gentleman's Magazine*, and went on to produce the translations and poetry already mentioned. She fostered a diverse network of friendships, most famously amongst those women later designated as the Bluestockings, including Catherine Talbot, Hester Mulso Chapone, Elizabeth Robinson Montagu, and Hannah More, but also with male luminaries such as Samuel Johnson, Samuel Richardson, Horace Walpole, and many others. She never married, despite a number of offers, and frequently expressed an aversion to any such curtailment of her autonomy. Likewise, though she sometimes travelled and visited with Montagu, Talbot, William Pulteney, the Earl of Bath, and other friends in Canterbury, she always chose to rent private rooms during her winters in London. She owned a house in Deal (paid for by the subscription revenue from *Epictetus*) and spent her summers there with her father. She outlived most of her contemporaries and died, at the age of 89, in 1806.

Carter and the life of writing

Carter first appeared in the pages of the *Gentleman's Magazine*, at the age of 17, when she submitted a riddle on fire, and she continued to contribute occasional pieces to the magazine for over a decade.[402] One of her most well-known works for the magazine was her elegy on the death of Elizabeth Rowe, which first appeared in the April 1737 issue, and provided an early link between Carter and the female exemplars of the past century. However, Carter's association with Cave and his Grub Street hacks, as well as the London literary scene in general, would transform the picture of the professional woman writer in ways that neither Rowe nor Cockburn could have effected, because Elizabeth Carter wrote, not only with a moral agenda and intellectual authority, but for fame and for money.

In 1734, when her first poem appeared in print, she was still living at home in Deal, Kent. It is possible that her supportive father, who was a friend of Edward Cave, encouraged his daughter to send in that first composition.[403] Carter's father had no qualms about sending the young Elizabeth to London either, and Sylvia Myers, in her important survey of the early Bluestockings, notes that, 'the Revd Carter seems to have encouraged her to think of herself as an independent person capable of taking risks'.[404] One of these risks was associating herself with the circle of writers who worked for Cave, including Thomas Birch, and later Samuel Johnson and Richard Savage.[405] Carter did more than associate with them, she became one of them, and was soon contributing riddles, epigrams, translations of Latin and Greek odes, poetry, and, like Johnson, was also producing longer works of translation for Cave to publish separately. She was to all intents and purposes a proper Grub Street hack. Sir George Oxenden, her father's patron, perhaps on the lookout for such popularising signs, suggested to Carter's father that Elizabeth was cheapening her work by appearing too often in the pages of the *Gentleman's Magazine*, implying that her works would be valued more if they were less available.[406]

Years later, when Catherine Talbot was trying to get a seemingly unwilling Carter to send Dodsley some poems for the new volume in his miscellany, *Collection of Poems by Several Hands*, her exasperation would lead her to point out:

> Things will steal abroad some time or other; is it not better they should appear in the dress you wish them, and in proper company? But you and I don't always agree what is good company and what not. Some of your tuneful choir had warbled in Magazines among many unclean birds, when you was scandalized at finding your Owl on Clarissa's harpsichord. But I hope you are cured of these pruderies. Dodsley's Miscellanies are better far than any others; I would have them still improve. Why should not Miss Mulso and you now and then throw in a few gems without any other name than by a lady? I do not press this as an air of consequence, but I cannot help naming it as what for many reasons I wish – for the honor of poetry, of the nation, of the sex.[407]

Carter, in reply, explained:

> If I ever writ any thing worth printing, I should rather chuse to publish them myself than have them published by any body else. If I ever do appear in a Miscellany, I should chuse it should be in a Miscellany of Ladies. One may venture to say this with regard to the lady writers of the present age, though it would not have been much to one's credit perhaps in the last. As to the Magazines, my being very young then, and my personal acquaintance with and esteem for Mr. Cave, must be my excuse. The poor man had a hearty *twinkation* once for suffering me to appear in bad company.[408]

These two very different responses regarding the need to publish as well as the variable value of print are indicative of the wide range of assumptions writers and readers brought to bear on any number of print publications. The gendered focus of this discussion is even more notable though. Conservative ideas about publication are evident, yet they actively debate the issue by exploring the merits of following a course of inclusion (in the male-dominated Dodsley *Collection*) or of highlighting and celebrating difference by publishing individually or collectively with other women writers. Whilst Talbot advocates the moral efficacy of reaching a large audience through Dodsley, she nevertheless reminds Carter of her questionable, because popular, literary beginnings in Grub Street. Like Oxenden, she disdains the indiscriminate inclusiveness of periodicals like the *Gentleman's Magazine*, and encourages Carter instead to ally herself to the dominant tradition of male poets.

It is uncertain whether Carter's appearance in Dodsley's volumes was ever voluntary. A letter to William Duncombe in 1750 states that she did not give Dodsley permission to print her first two poems (these appear in the second edition of Dodsley's *Collection* (December 1748)).[409] Presumably publication of the later two, 'Ode to a Lady in London' and 'To Miss ****', in the fifth and sixth volumes issued in 1758, were agreed given their previous appearances elsewhere.[410] She may have been concerned with furthering her individual cachet but she was equally invested in the idea of her importance to the female tradition. Her sense of their collective identity, in terms of both their growing numbers (they could fill a miscellany) and moral importance (in contrast to the lady writers of the last century), suggests a fundamental change in the identity of the professional woman writer.

Guest argues that the 'moral authority or personal worth that [were] attached to labor, and particularly to specialised professional careers' gave Carter a sense that she was valued for her contributions and also belonged to a group of female writers of some significance.[411] Many of those writers were friends, and Carter has since become famous for her female friendships. Montagu Pennington (1762–1849), Carter's nineteenth-century biographer, editor, nephew, and heir, reinforced this aspect of her career and went so far as to suggest that she had a decided bias in favour of female writers, choosing to read any book from a virtuous female on principle. Whilst this does not appear to have been entirely accurate – she frequently confesses ignorance at Talbot's mention of many contemporary female writers – Carter nevertheless supported a number of female associates by subscribing to their works, contributing to their productions, encouraging various solo literary endeavours (Montagu, 1769), posthumously editing their manuscript writings (Talbot, 1772), and embarking on philosophical, religious, and literary-minded correspondences with them (Montagu, Chapone, and More, to name just a few). Most of this activity took place in the latter half of the century. It is problematic, if not erroneous, however, to attribute a specifically female-gendered allegiance to Carter. Throughout the eighteenth century she appeared in countless miscellanies and anthologies featuring the canonical male poets and collaborated more often with male colleagues than with women writers. Nevertheless, her iteration and theorisation of the benefits of female collectivity and her constant attention to the particularities of a female career, specifically the most efficacious professional ethos (exemplarity), signifies a writer overtly concerned with authorial identity, tradition, the female author, and professionalisation.

The overall picture with Carter is that of a writer taking advantage of multiple personal opportunities whilst also functioning as an enabler or supporter of fellow writers. The list of Carter's contacts and collaborators is extensive: university men, bishops, aristocrats, London publishers, provincial women writers, continental intellectuals, and adventurers. It is evident that in all of these interactions Carter's intellectual authority was encouraged, recognised, and celebrated. Here again correspondence networks and manuscript exchange were the primary means behind the transmission and promulgation of ideas and works, and Carter's careful balancing of the older tradition alongside a print career presents a viable variation of how the female exemplar could construct a writing self as well as a life of writing.

An important factor in her construction of a writing self was an authorial identity, and Carter (with the early guidance of her father) sought to distinguish her literary niche in a very calculated manner. Carter almost always signed her poems 'Eliza' in the *Gentleman's Magazine* but, as she did not have exclusive 'rights' to the name, other writers could use the same signature, and this occasionally meant less than acceptable works being attributed to Carter. An excerpt from one of Nicholas Carter's letters on the subject of the multiple Elizas highlights the lengths to which Elizabeth and her father were willing to go in order to secure the right name with the right works. Nicholas Carter writes, 'It is generally believed by all who know Eliza, that that riddle was wrote by you, because signed *Eliza*. An advertisement in the Magazine asserting only a matter of fact (that the Eliza in the Magazine is not the Eliza in that Almanack) I think would not savour of ostentation, but be very right and prudent.'[412]

For Carter and her father, the importance of linking her authorial identity with a certain calibre of work was a necessary first step in her literary career and suggests a very modern sensibility towards authorship. Surprisingly, therefore, her first three solo publications were signed not with 'Eliza', the name she had so carefully cultivated in the periodical world, but were anonymous. In these instances, Carter appears to have been availing herself of the older patronage tradition and was unwilling or was advised against making her work publicly available without a patron to 'protect' it. Her first volume of poetry, *Poems on Particular Occasions* (1738), was printed almost solely for the purpose of providing copies to potential/actual patrons. Her father recommended '[t]hat you ought to print some few of your Verses, with that [the poem on Q. Caroline's death], and make a Present of a Dozen Copies of them to your Patron. I would not print them to Sell, but only about twice that Number, only to give away.'[413]

The following year Carter attempted to secure the Countess of Hertford as a patron for her Algarotti translation and, though Hertford declined the dedication of the work, she later corresponded with Carter. Hawley notes that the application to Hertford was made at Birch's instigation and, after that failed, he 'gave the translation a glowing review in the *History of the Works of the Learned*', thus making her authorship public knowledge.[414] The sequence of events leading from anonymity to public approbation may be read as a symptom of Birch's officiousness, but this does not negate Carter's active role in the process. Birch sought patronage and published critical commendations for many male colleagues during the same period and it is possible that Carter, once she realised she had no patron to advertise and protect her work, utilised her *Gentleman's Magazine* colleague to advance her literary stock. Henry Etough relied on Birch for the same reasons when he sought his help with Cockburn's works.

Possibly the most important factors to reconsider in the reconstruction of her career are her social networks, the legacy of manuscript circulation, and her early experience with the professional writers at Cave's periodical. To illustrate this, a few representative exchanges, collaborations, and comparisons from the 1730s to 1750s offer a useful barometer of the breadth of her interests and abilities.

The first example stems not from literature, philosophy, or religion, however, but from the world of science. In the late 1730s, Cave published a number of works by Carter that engaged with Newtonian science. In 1739, he published her two translations on scientific matters, Francesco Algarotti's explanation of Isaac Newton's theories and Jean Pierre de Crousaz's critique of Alexander Pope's understanding of them.[415] The year before, Carter's poem, 'While clear the Night, and ev'ry Thought serene', appeared in the *Gentleman's Magazine* (June 1738); it displayed her knowledge of astronomy and also paid public tribute to Newton's protégé John Theophilus Desaguliers (1683–1744), and to the astronomer (and her tutor) Thomas Wright of Durham (1711–86).[416]

Her poem charts constellations and ponders life on other worlds ('Where ev'ry star, that cheers the gloom of night/...Perhaps illumes some system of its own', 315, ll. 11, 13), but it also reminds readers of the important religious function of scientific discovery.

> Let stupid atheists boast th' atomic dance,
> And call yon beauteous worlds the work of chance;

> But nobler minds, from sense and passion free,
> [...]
> Survey the footsteps of a ruling god, (316, ll. 27–32)

She had, according to Pennington, been interested in astronomy and mathematics from a young age and visited William Haley with Thomas Birch and her father in 1738. In an undated letter in the *Memoirs* (which Pennington dates to 1737/8), one of Carter's correspondents accuses her of forgetting her mortal friends in favour of the stars, so engrossed is she in her night-time studies. Echoing the unhappy Cartesian marriage of the soul and the body expressed in Carter's poem, 'A Dialogue' (*GM* 11, January 1741), her correspondent continues, 'Your mind and your body, I understand, have quarrelled lately, and are separated, which I suppose is, in plain English, your wits are gone a wool gathering'.[417]

A correspondent who encouraged this obsession, however, was Wright. A mathematician, astronomer, antiquary, landscape gardener, tutor and 'visionary',[418] Wright was 'a good example of how a scientifically minded man could make his way in the eighteenth century through appropriate patronage and... a range of activities'.[419] He adapted his skills to the needs of his patrons and seems to have been moderately successful in attracting resources. He was also responsible for introducing Carter and Talbot, and a letter from him prefaces the Carter–Talbot correspondence. Hampshire claims that Wright exchanged over one hundred letters with Carter and Pennington states that she 'used to send him her schemes and solutions to be corrected'.[420] Though not much is known about the nature of this scientific correspondence course, Hampshire's estimate of a large quantity of letters suggests an exchange of some importance. Nevertheless the examples available present only the social aspect of their relationship and give no indication of any more abstruse discussions. Wright's one remaining letter to Carter is brief and practical. Dated 14 January 1741, it assures Carter that Talbot is 'as desirous of seeing you, and as impatient as you can possibly be of seeing her' but that he is still trying to fix an actual interview date.[421] In her reply, Carter reveals more about the social milieu in which they were operating. After complaining about the obstacles to meeting Talbot she moves on to a request from her hostess, Mrs Rooke.

> If your conjurorship's worship is not engaged to-morrow in the afternoon, Mrs. Rooke bids me tell you, she desires your company to hold a consultation upon the screen, and hopes you will bring half the

stars in the firmament along with you to fix upon it, not forgetting the sun, moon, and other planets.[422]

Wright, the public intellectual, is sought as entertainment for Mrs Rooke's afternoon salon, and Carter, the female prodigy and astronomical enthusiast, is employed to secure his attendance. Carter, who stayed with Mrs Rooke in London, was not as reliant on patronage as Wright (though she did seek it) and it is possible that his peripatetic and almost too diverse series of professions gave Carter an adverse impression of paid posts with aristocratic patrons. We know that she turned down many attempts by Talbot and Montagu to secure a place for her at court, and seems to have been as averse to patronage as she was to marriage.[423] This brief glimpse of an early correspondence/mentorship/friendship shows that Carter was cognisant of the world of social networking, patronage, and public life from the outset of her career.

My second example is drawn from the world of Latin scholarship and is based upon a small manuscript collection held by Trinity College, Cambridge. These papers, bequeathed to Trinity by Isaac Hawkins Browne (1706–60), a graduate of the college, include letters to Browne from Carter, William Duncombe, Thomas Herring (then Archbishop of Canterbury), and James Harris (the well-known Greek scholar). In addition, there are letters addressed to his son, Isaac Hawkins Browne (1745–1818), after the father's death, from William Warburton, John Hoadly, and Joseph Highmore. The letters from Duncombe, Herring, and Harris are complimentary epistles on the upcoming publication of Browne's Latin poem *De animus immortalitate* (1754), and those from Warburton, Hoadly, and Highmore comprise thanks for the new edition of his father's poems and further encomiums on the elder Browne's compositional skills. Whilst all the letters confirm these writers' shared celebration of Latinate learning and scholarly endeavour, it is Carter's letters that are specifically concerned with the practicalities of poetic composition in Latin. Invited by Browne to help correct his manuscript of *De animus immortalitate*, the English translation of which she had already declined, she clearly took her reviewing task seriously, and sent pages of notes and corrected print copy to Browne over the spring to autumn of 1752.[424] Though she often avers that there is nothing to correct except what Browne himself highlights as doubtful, she nevertheless sends a number of detailed corrections, along with additional comments from her father.[425] However, seeing this correspondence within the context of the complete collection of letters, her role in contemporary Latin scholarship/poetics is thrown into greater relief.

Amidst the fulsome praise offered by Duncombe, Herring (the poem's dedicatee), and Harris on the imminent publication of Browne's poem, Carter's letters clearly delineate her role as the colleague, the professional, and the critic. She not only functions as one of the 'learned men' who offer support and praise to Browne, but her exchange is distinct as the one in which professional expertise is of primary importance. The letters also confirm the sense of privilege and priority Carter associates with manuscript circulation.

> Though I am afraid any Remarks which I am capable of making will be of very little Signification. I am too great a gainer by the Honour your good opinion does me to quarrel with it for being more favorable to me than I deserve, & setting me a Task for which I am so little qualified, as it procures me the noble Entertainment of reading your Poem sooner than I could otherwise have done.[426]

She later adds, 'I send you a few Remarks that I may be intitled to a sight of the third Book which I ~~am~~ shall expect with Impatience.'[427]

Carter's exchange with Browne was not a unique or exclusive example of her contemporary appeal as a Latin scholar, literary critic, poet, and correspondent. Of Browne's correspondents listed above, Carter also wrote to and socialised with Harris, Duncombe, Highmore and his daughter Susannah, and knew Herring through her father.[428] Harris later helped Carter with some difficult Greek passages in *Epictetus* and Duncombe managed to convince Carter to contribute Ode XV in Book I of his *Works of Horace in English Verse* (published in 1757–9, but Carter's poem was written in 1751).[429] Carter later assisted Elizabeth Montagu on the subject of classical tragedy whilst the latter was working on her essay on Shakespeare. Of particular interest are a number of letters about writing she sent to Susannah Highmore, the future wife of John Duncombe. In one she protests that she is unable to produce verse or prose on request, declining an offer to contribute to the prefatory pages of Mary Leapor's collected works. She avers, 'you pay me much too great a Compliment in Supposing me capable of writing upon any Subject that is proposed to me'.[430] She further claims that she is not familiar enough with Leapor's writing and, therefore, suggests that others will do her memory better justice. However she does ask for the subscription notice to be sent to her. This example of Carter's repudiation of the hack-for-hire, or, as Brean Hammond styles it, 'hackney for bread' image, hints at her uneasy relationship with the mechanical requirements of professionalisation.[431] It also suggests that she was not always the fervent supporter of women's writings that Pennington claimed.

All of these writers were part of a larger social network that, today, tends to be seen as radiating from Samuel Richardson's familial circle, but which was also founded on more professional reasons than the popular model of conversational fellowship suggests. Though a useful example of another one of Carter's reciprocal professional collaborations, the Richardson connection is also important for the lasting influence he has had on Carter's literary 'stock'. She has long been associated with Richardson and his literary ethos but, whilst Carter praised the morality of Richardson's works, she actually preferred the novels of Henry Fielding and thought herself the better writer when she and Richardson contributed to Johnson's *Rambler*.[432] She also took issue with his views on women and took particular delight in Hester Mulso's epistolary debate with him regarding a daughter's prerogative in the choice of a marriage partner.

Carter may have been introduced to Richardson as early as 1739 when he printed the second edition of Rowe's collected works, which included Carter's encomiastic poem on her; however, it seems a regular acquaintance did not begin until after Richardson's unauthorised printing of her 'Ode to Wisdom' in the first volume of *Clarissa* (1747–8). The printing of this poem was a direct result of scribal copies having 'stolen abroad' to such an extent that she had lost control of the copies being made; in fact, her name was no longer being appended to it. As with the moniker 'Eliza', Carter was careful about the types and quality of work being attributed or, as the case was here, not being attributed to her; when she felt someone else was encroaching on her territory she hastened to protect her own writings and image by asserting her authorial rights. Carter's opening sally to Richardson proclaims her disappointment at his unauthorised use of her poem:

> I was, very lately, extremely surprized on receiving an account that you have thought proper to print an Ode, which, I apprehend, no one had a right to publish, if I did not choose to do it myself. To print any thing without the consent of the person who wrote it, is a proceeding so very ungenerous and unworthy of a man of reputation, that, from the character I have heard of you, I am utterly at a loss how to account for it[.][433]

Carter's 'twinkation', as she called it, of Richardson is not the response of a writer worried about her private image; rather, it is the voice of an author who valued her body of work and asserted her right to distribute it as she determined.[434] She exhibits, in fact, a distinctly modern notion of intellectual property by refusing to allow that anyone has a right to her writing without her consent. She held her correspondents to the same strict terms, and friends had to sue for permission to circulate and/or make amended copies of her letters.

Richardson's apology explained the provenance of his copy.

I have a worthy kinswoman, Miss Elizabeth Long by name, who shewed me the Ode to Wisdom, as a piece she knew I should admire. She had obtained the promise of a copy of it, when in Wiltshire a few weeks before (at Mr. Long's, I think); and one was accordingly sent her.

I wanted not matter for the piece I had then ready for the press [i.e. *Clarissa*]. I had a redundance of it, and, after it was written, parted with several beautiful transcripts from our best poets, which I had inserted in order to enliven a work (my characters being all readers), which perhaps is too solemn. But, the Ode being shewn me as written by a lady, and the intention of my work being to do honor to the sex, to the best of my poor ability, I was so pleased with it, that I desired my kinswoman to give me what light she could as to the author, and to write down into Wiltshire, to be informed, whether any exceptions would be likely to be taken if I should insert it.

She said, she had herself, when in Wilts, been desirous of knowing who the author was, but had no other intimation given her, than that the Ode was really written by a lady, and by one whom she had had the honor once to see. Whence she conjectured the lady to be a descendant of the famous Mr. Norris, of Bemerton.

She wrote, however, but could get no farther light; but said, that, as there were more copies of it, as it had been given to her without restriction; as I thought the piece excellent in itself, and that the inserting it with the distinction I talked of, could bring no disreputation on the author – no name to be mentioned – she was of opinion, that no offence could be given or taken.

By this time my little work was so far advanced at press, that I was obliged to resolve one way or other; and I ventured to insert it. I presumed not to make my character, though, the principal one, claim it, only doing intentional honour to it, by setting it to music, which is done in a masterly manner. I caused it to be engraved and wrought singly, the more to distinguish it. And all this trouble I might have spared, and the expense with it, as, though the Ode would have been an ornament to any work, and an honour to any character, it was not expected.[435]

Prolix as always, Richardson nevertheless highlights two key points in relation to Carter's literary practices and image. First, the circulation of her anonymous manuscripts was a primary factor in the cultivation of her contemporary popularity. Richardson specifically notes that Mrs Long forwarded the poem because she knew it was one he would 'admire' and because there were numerous copies circulating 'without restriction'. However, Carter's anonymity led Long to attribute it to a metaphysically minded female descendant of John Norris (the correspondent of Mary Astell, and the same Norris who commended Cockburn's defence of Locke in manuscript).

Second, Richardson appears already to associate Carter with the programme of female exemplarity he wants to inculcate through his novels. Carter is often described as one of those responsible for disseminating/domesticating Richardson's ideals – part of his circle of admiring females – but in this early instance it is Richardson domesticating her work and not the other way around. He was using her poem, as he says, not only as a mark of his gentlemanly condescension to the ladies, but also for the aesthetic purposes it served in his novel. He casts the poem as an ornament, a diversion from the solemnity of the novel, and pays little attention to the question of active virtue and intellectual rigour which the poem propounds. In many respects, his reading of Carter's poetry is the one that still obtains.

Though she accepted Richardson's apology and allowed him to continue using the poem, Carter was not amenable to gender-specific flattery. Despite her valorisation of the virtues of contemporary female writers and her professed wish to appear in a female miscellany, she was patently uncomfortable with Richardson's division of merit and labour. In a letter to Talbot written four years later, she complains, 'I cannot see how some of his [Richardson's] doctrines can be founded on any other supposition than that Providence designed one half of the human species for idiots and slaves.'[436] Her comments were levelled at his *Rambler* No. 97, in which he advocates women's passivity and subjugation in matters related to courtship and marriage, but she hints that she has additional grounds for her accusation based on his other writings (probably the letters between him and Hester Mulso).[437] Carter believed in active not passive virtue, social versus reclusive habits, and took pains to foster this ethos amongst her female friends.

Nevertheless, Richardson's legacy is more pervasive and Carter is now associated with the domestic ideals which he propounded and which he helped to align with her image. Richardson's inclusion of her poem in one of the most popular novels of the century ensured that Carter's name would be associated with its exemplary heroine even though friends thought she was a closer fit to the feistier Anna Howe.[438] Richardson reinforced her association with virtuous wisdom and retired domesticity in *Sir Charles Grandison* (1753-4) through his exemplification of her in the character of Mrs Shirley. Though Carter was only in her mid-thirties at the time of publication, Richardson's fictional guise for her opinions and way of life was presented in the person of the most elderly character in the novel. In an odd twist, these fictional harbingers, especially the latter, predict the future personae attached to Carter's literary image. Before her nephew posthumously claimed that Carter was the repository of all that was pious, virtuous, and learned, Richardson had advertised these social and intellectual propensities during her own lifetime. In this way, Carter was witness and party to her own exemplification. Important to note, therefore, is the fact that well before *Epictetus* and *Poems on Several Occasions* were published Carter had established her literary reputation through a combination of manuscript circulation/exchange and periodical print publication.

Carter's association with Richardson was one that benefited her professionally, both in terms of her fame and in relation to practical matters such as his printing of the subscriber edition of *Epictetus*. Both were part of a network of writers and friends who advocated similar social ideals, but most of the friendships associated with Richardson were often sustained independent of him and outlasted his influence. Carter's close relationship with Catherine Talbot predated any acquaintance either had with Richardson, and that with Hester Mulso Chapone outlasted Chapone's rockier one with Richardson. Carter's iterated complaints about Richardson's views on women, and her confidence in her superior writing suggest that she was not as admiring of his domestic ideology as his younger acolytes.

In addition to the individuals Carter met through these social and scribal networks were the acquaintances she made during her years with the *Gentleman's Magazine*. Thomas Birch was the most significant of these and his influence was instrumental when it came to her choice of translations for Cave.[439] E.J. Clery points out that these translations were not 'hack-work' (if they were Carter would not have pursued patrons such as the Countess of Hertford on their merits); rather, 'They were interventions in British intellectual and literary life through the indirect route of foreign commentary.'[440] In fact, the original Crousaz and Algarotti texts were 'foreign' commentaries upon British intellectuals (Pope and Newton) and there was nothing 'indirect' about providing English readers with a translation. Carter's notes on Crousaz point out the errors of his critique of Pope due to his reliance on a bad prose translation in French of Pope's *Essay on Man*.[441] In her footnotes for the Algarotti translation Carter makes extensive use of historical and literary information from Pierre Bayle's *General Dictionary*, which Birch was in the process of translating and adapting, and she takes issue with some of Algarotti's generalisations on philosophy, as well as his use of translations of unidentified poetry.[442] In many ways, these translations represent the first public manifestation of Carter's most enduring critical legacy: her humanist learning and her association with the scholastic world of letters. The later translations of Greek and Latin odes and edition of *Epictetus* reinforced the image. However, the friendship with Birch, which some have speculated verged on marriage, did not survive the summer of 1739; instead, it was her more professional relationship with Samuel Johnson which endured. Theirs is the last exchange I would like to look at in the context of an emergent professionalisation of literary careers alongside a thriving and socially diverse manuscript republic of letters.

Eliza and Sam

The two most famous and oft-quoted remarks about Carter relate to Samuel Johnson (1709–84). The first, courtesy of Boswell, is Johnson's quip that '[a] man is in general better pleased when he has a good dinner upon his table, than when his wife talks Greek. My old friend, Mrs. Carter, could make a pudding as well as translate Epictetus from the Greek, and work a handkerchief as well as compose a poem.'[443] Roger Lonsdale considers Johnson's 'intended compliment' akin to an historical curse, allowing, indeed encouraging, her erudite and public productions to be seen as analogous to, if not merely an extension of, the domestic productions of pudding recipes and handkerchief stitching.[444] The second is recorded by Pennington. He writes that, '[Carter] used to relate with much pleasure in her own family (for no person spoke less of herself, and of her own acquirements, in company) that Dr Johnson had said, speaking of some celebrated scholar, that he understood Greek better than any one whom he had ever known, except Elizabeth Carter.'[445] Pennington's account does not conflate Epictetus with puddings but it nevertheless situates Carter's pride within a familial context and furthermore suggests that she relied on Johnson's intelligence, influence, and public prominence to validate her more private intellectual claims. Contemporary evidence and the trajectory of their literary careers complicate these easy dichotomies of public/private, influence/anxiety, male/female, though, and offer a useful comparison of gender assumptions, past and present, regarding such literary careers.

Sylvia Myers has argued that Johnson was an important influence on Carter, serving as an example of a scholar and writer in touch with the real world yet one who preserved deep religious and ethical standards.[446] Robert DeMaria, Jr and, more recently, Anthony Lee trace a less mentor-like relationship or unidirectional course of influence between the two.[447] In his critical biography of the 'Great Cham' of literature DeMaria argues that Johnson's wish to identify himself 'with a unified, late Latin European cultural heritage' has been insufficiently explored in previous treatments.[448] He further argues that the 'story' of Johnson's career is one of compromise and alienation amid the successes. Compromise because he had to produce works in English rather than in the Latin of the humanist tradition and because he never quite escaped his Lichfield origins and his father's trade. A lifelong association with the booksellers and publishers who helped to make him famous also tied him to a restricted scope of material marketable to an English audience. Within this context of an idealised European humanist tradition and scholarly compromise due to the exigencies of the English world of letters and print culture, Carter features as an ally, even exemplar, rather than follower. Lee is even more explicit. He charts a 'sibling alliance' but also rivalry between the two, where 'Carter at times took the lead, and exerted the strongest influence'.[449] Both critics suggest that Johnson was responding to and relying on Carter's already established status in literary circles, her additional expertise, her broader epistolary experiences, and her balanced social perspective.

DeMaria notes that Johnson's first production in the *Gentleman's Magazine*, an Horatian ode in defence of Cave against his rivals at the *London Magazine*, 'was the work of a writer seeking preferment'.[450] His next two productions for the periodical were to two of Cave's regular contributors, Richard Savage and Elizabeth Carter. He went on to write two more Latin poems to Carter, 'To Eliza Plucking Laurel in Mr Pope's Gardens' (*GM* 1738) and 'Quid mihi cum culta?' ('What good is refinement to me?'), which was never published in his lifetime. According to DeMaria, 'The poem suggests a young Johnson with provincial manners and a naturally rough temperament self-consciously confiding his fears in his new-found, urban intellectual companion.'[451] Pennington reminds us that Johnson was relatively unknown at this point – a letter from Carter's father on 25 June 1738 highlights his obscurity: 'You mention Johnson; but that is a name with which I am utterly unacquainted. Neither his scholastic, critical, or poetical character ever reached my ears.'[452]

Despite the fact that Johnson was eight years older than Carter, DeMaria paints Johnson's relationship with her as one where Carter held the superior, because prior, status in contemporary periodical culture and literary circles. What DeMaria's picture misses out, however, is that Carter's reasons for entering the professional scene were based on factors remarkably similar to Johnson's. Excluded by her gender from most of the careers that her education enabled her to perform, Carter ventured to display her erudition amongst the other upstart authors at Edward Cave's establishment. Johnson, also denied the career path through the lack of a degree, found himself in a similar position and must have appreciated Carter's skill at balancing Cave's persistent requests and an independent life of the mind. It is possible, therefore, to reimagine Carter's importance to Johnson as a function not only of their similarities, but also of her more assured place in that wider republic of letters to which he aspired. Rather than seeing her as a writer on the periphery or as somehow contained in private social circles, her career looks like a continuation of an older, more respected tradition of philosophical, religious, scholarly, and literary manuscript exchange. However, this is not the only prism through which Carter ought to be re-envisioned, for, in her early years, she is as involved in the world of booksellers and publishers as Johnson. Rather, by approaching the issue in an oblique manner, setting Carter against the Johnsonian trajectory, I hope to suggest the degree to which Carter controlled her own interventions in print culture, and the emphasis she placed on her right to maintain a distance from this phenomenon which broke from a tradition of letters she valued more.

In print, Johnson and Carter have quantitatively unequal publication histories, but there are some telling similarities. They both began as periodical writers, producing occasional poems, and later translations, for Cave. Lee claims that Carter had a formative impact on Johnson's poetics at this time; however, Johnson's poem *London* (1738) pushed him into another league, and garnered him a professional post at Cave's establishment worth around £100 per annum.[453] Carter appears not to have been offered anything similar and it is questionable whether she would have accepted it. Instead, she abruptly left London literary life and returned to Deal in June 1739.[454]

During the next decade Carter wrote many of her most well-known and oft-reprinted poems and miscellaneous prose. These include: 'Ode to Melancholy' (*GM*, November 1739); 'Occasioned by Hearing Miss Lynch Sing' (*GM*, November 1740); 'A Dialogue' (*GM*, January 1741); 'On the foregoing verses. Inscribed to Miss L-CH of Canterbury' (*GM*, July 1744), which Cave solicited to accompany the reprinting of Katherine Philips's poem 'To Mrs. Mary Awbrey at parting';[455] and the 'Ode to Wisdom', printed without her permission in Richardson's *Clarissa* (1747), and subsequently with permission in the *Gentleman's Magazine* (December 1747). Whilst Cave repeatedly sought new material from Carter, and correspondents to his magazine routinely celebrated her accomplishments, Carter nevertheless seems to have resisted the guise of hack-for-hire to which Johnson submitted. The poetry she eventually sent Cave was more often the result of sociable/scribal networks than anything written with publication in mind: witness how many are addressed to her Canterbury acquaintances. The story of the 'Ode to Wisdom' fluttering about Wiltshire is indicative of Carter's diffidence regarding public approbation through print means. She sent Cave a copy of the 'Ode to Wisdom' (he claimed to have been in possession of the true copy for over a year), yet did not authorise him to publish it. Why is unclear, but it does show the control she maintained over her productions. She tended to dictate publication terms to Cave whenever she sent him work; for instance, when she insisted that the 'Ode to Melancholy' be printed without a signature. As I noted above, Carter's father, Oxenden, and Talbot tried to influence Carter's interventions in print culture, but she resolutely refused to succumb to others' ideas about how her literary career should be mapped.

Johnson, on the other hand, contributed regularly to the *Gentleman's Magazine* in the 1740s. He also started to produce the biographical writings which culminated in the *Lives* (1778–81). The first of these, *An Account of the Life of John Philip Barretier* (1744), was drawn from material he had used in the *Gentleman's Magazine* in 1741 and 1742. Jean Philip Baratier (1721–40) was a continental child prodigy who, before his early death, corresponded with a number of public intellectuals in several different languages. One of those intellectuals was Carter. DeMaria argues that Johnson's account relies heavily on the letters of Baratier's father to Nicholas Carter, and undoubtedly those to Carter herself.[456] At the end of the same year Johnson produced *The Life of Savage* (1744), which DeMaria argues could have been more factually correct had he bothered to consult with either Carter or Aaron Hill, both friends of Richard Savage.[457] Though DeMaria rightly concludes that Carter did not have any direct influence on Johnson's productions, she repeatedly features as an enabling factor. Her awareness of Baratier and access to personal letters was surely one of the reasons Johnson undertook the biography. As DeMaria puts it, 'Johnson's life as a writer for hire fostered a willingness to rely on existing printed accounts of his subjects and such oral or manuscript evidence as presented itself to him.'[458]

Why didn't Carter produce *The Life of John Philip Barretier*? Perhaps she had no interest in biography, perhaps she knew Johnson was the better match for the material; whatever the reason(s) may have been it does seem evident that Carter chose to spend the 1740s focusing on family and friends, and her literary output and rate of production reflects this sociable preoccupation. Hawley notes that during 'this decade her female friendships became very important to her', and it is true that her feminocentric epistolary oeuvre, as compiled by Pennington, begins around this time.[459] The example of the Wright and later Browne correspondences reveals the lacunae in this gynocentric epistolary and social construction, and, likewise, highlights the degree to which she persisted in her esoteric studies and attachment to a realm of letters concerned with scholarship and intellectual humanism. Nevertheless, it is important to note what Carter did not do, given her abilities, her resources, and the example of friends like Johnson. Cave often complained of not having anything new from Carter. He wrote to Nicholas, 'I cannot perswade Miss to undertake any Thing – & ye World wants to know what she is about.'[460] Talbot too felt Carter was wasting her talents as a children's tutor, but no one was able at this stage to inspire her to produce a suitably canonical work or maintain a steady output for the press. The 1750s would partially remedy that.

Johnson, to continue the comparison, began the 1750s with a new venture, the *Rambler* (1750–2), which, though a commercial failure in its first guise, established him as one of the great moralists of the age and sold extremely well as a collected edition.[461] Carter contributed two essays to the *Rambler* and seems to have had more on hand which were never sent. After the demise of the *Rambler* Johnson contributed essays to *The Adventurer* (1753–4) and Carter was encouraged to do the same but declined.[462] Throughout this time Johnson was also at work on the text that would secure his fame in the world of letters: the *Dictionary of the English Language* (1755). He finished off the decade with *The Idler* (1758–60) and *Rasselas* (1759), and, in the process, proved himself one of the most significant figures in contemporary English letters. Johnson was rewarded for this body of work with a pension of £300 for life in 1762.

During these years Carter was also busy, but not quite so prolific. Part of the reason for this was her commitment to the education of all the children of her father's second marriage. This was no small undertaking; their lessons took up most of the day, and she clearly theorised and sought to differentiate her own mode of teaching from that carried out in the public boys' schools.[463] Thus, when Talbot tried to request some poetry, Carter responded, 'Between my pupils, my gossiping, and Epictetus, I have scarcely ever a minute's leisure, except sometimes to write a dull stupid letter.'[464] This was not true, she was writing coterie poetry, helping Browne with his Latin poem, sending essays to the *Rambler* and Talbot, and engaging in religious controversy on behalf of her father: in 1753 she published *Remarks on the Athanasian Creed* against dogmatism in doctrines of the Trinity. This period of intense study and teaching was significant too for the philosophical, religious, and educational debates she carried out with Chapone, Talbot, Highmore, and many others. However, the acknowledged achievement of this decade was her translation of *All the Works of Epictetus* (1758). This work, begun at Talbot's request in 1749, was accomplished after seven years' toil, and made her roughly £1,000. It also garnered her a new level of respect and prestige. The subscriber's list featured the Prince of Wales and the Dowager Princess of Wales at the head of a roll call that included 12 more pages of the great and the good of the kingdom.[465] Elizabeth Montagu sought Carter's friendship after its publication and by her means of encouragement *Epictetus* was followed shortly by *Poems on Several Occasions* (1762).[466] And there, by most accounts, ends Carter's official literary career.

Johnson goes on to produce his edition of *Shakespeare* (1765), *Journey to the Western Islands of Scotland* (1775), and *Lives of the English Poets* (1779–81), but we have nothing comparably substantial from Carter. She was not idle, however, and spent time revising old poems and writing new pieces (the third edition of *Poems on Several Occasions* (1776) includes seven new poems); she continued her own private studies of the classical Greek and Latin authors, and, of course, wrote letters by the baker's dozen. Judith Hawley argues that 'the ideology of the familiar letter is crucial to the creation of the social space in which Carter flourished as a woman writer'.[467] Indeed, the dates listed in the titles of Pennington's editions of the letters (1741–70, 1763–87, and 1755–1800) reveal Carter's sustained writing career *'upon Literary and Moral Subjects'* throughout the latter half of the century.[468] Friends like Talbot, who suggested the translation of Epictetus, or Montagu, who requested *Poems on Several Occasions*, initiated their requests as epistolary exercises for

Carter. They also repeatedly tried to obtain her a position in the queen's household – possibly the only available female equivalent to Johnson's pension – but Carter always rejected such a job as a curtailment of her freedoms. She did, however, take on a semi-public role when she acted as the secretary of the Ladies Society, a charitable institution founded by her friend Georgiana, Countess Spencer. In the late 1760s she provided critical expertise and editorial support to Montagu during the writing of her *Essay on the writings and genius of Shakespear* (1769), and in 1772 edited and published Talbot's posthumous *Works* at her own expense.

One of the great merits of Hawley's edition of Carter for Pickering and Chatto's multi-volume *Bluestocking Feminism* (1999) is the emphasis she places on the consistency of Carter's literary endeavour and output. Pennington, and most critics after him, have characterised Carter's writing as being intermittent up to her publication of Epictetus and over by 1762, the year *Poems on Several Occasions* was published. Helen Small, in her review of *Bluestocking Feminism*, attests to the 'achievement' of Hawley's edition in regards to its 'convincing demonstration that Carter's career was far more sustainedly and effectively professional than it suited her conservative clerical descendant to see', but nevertheless conflates the eight women included in the volumes when she also argues that, 'the first generation of Bluestocking women had relatively little interest in asserting the right to define themselves as scholars and writers'.[469] Small's contention, directed largely at Gary Kelly's unhelpful construction of a 'full-blown "Bluestocking program" for feminizing the culture', unfortunately forces her into generalities that do not take into account the variety of models available to a woman of letters in the mid- to late-eighteenth century, or the possibility that Carter could have been different from, whilst allied to, her 'first generation' peers.[470]

Carter *was* different and had long since defined herself as a scholar and writer who understood the requirements of the profession. Suggesting anything less would mean disregarding her determined rise from provincial poet, to periodical moralist, to celebrated translator and Britain's 'paradigmatic learned woman'.[471] This trajectory suggests a writer confident in her own abilities, her literary authority, and her public agency on learned matters.

Carter's early career at the *Gentleman's Magazine* was a crucial factor in the creation of her literary career. Not only did she meet many of the men and women who would have significant roles to play in her subsequent career, but it forced her early on to examine and determine her position(s) in relation to print culture, authorship, and the republic of letters. Brean Hammond has presented the most convincing schema for the emergent professionalism of this period.

> Professionalization, novelization, the polite: these were all broad cultural tendencies that provoked a backlash in those pockets of early eighteenth-century cultural practice that valorised the amateur, gentlemanly, classically trained, allusive model of authorship. Between, roughly, 1690 and 1720 wholly new forms of literary production and thoroughly hybridized literary kinds emerged or were in their gestation period (newspapers, literary periodicals, the novel) that provided new opportunities for workers in the writing industry. Various means of controlling this production were sought, but one pan-institutional discursive framework emerged [...]: the 'polite'. Polite discourse was a means of facilitating social inter-mingling between disparate status-groups in a society rendered increasingly mobile and fluid by the requirements of trade and commerce.[472]

Whilst this version of text production and social responses does capture the broad outlines of Carter's 'discursive framework' it does not adequately take into account 'those pockets' of writers who 'valorised' the older mode while also engaging with 'emergent' print culture. DeMaria posits Johnson as one of the aspirants after the classical, gentlemanly past, but Carter, despite her inability to fit within these gendered parameters, arguably exists as a more viable example of the hybrid amateur/professional scholar in eighteenth-century England.

In the midst of her most productive years, Carter described her state of affairs in illuminating terms.

> I now seem entirely accommodated to a state of inactivity and repose, and grow on faster and faster to my rock, and it must be a violent effort that could draw me from it. And yet besides the particular inducement that there are some very valuable people in the world whom I must be strangely stupid not to wish sometimes to see, there are more general reasons that should make one chuse to mix a little now and then in the hurry of society, in order to keep up some kind of connexion with the universal community of mankind; to enlarge and vary one's ideas, and thus become more agreeable to those with whom one is chiefly to converse, than it is possible to be in an absolute regular clock-work kind of life, where one is always moved by the same springs, and perpetually striking the same notes, and thus in time grow as tiresome to people as an old tune. From

> such considerations I should think it right, perhaps, not to live year after year upon the same spot, and the same contracted circle of conversation, if it was in my power to do otherwise. But yet that it is not in my power gives me no uneasiness. A natural indolence, which was once checked and in some degree over-ruled by the conversation of the world, now that it is set free from all restraint, seems to have got the entire possession of me, and the way of life I am in, appears to be the very way in which I am most likely to be happy.[473]

This letter attests to Carter's commitment to the improvement of the 'universal community'. It also conveys her sense of the reciprocity of that engagement: something that was possible in polite conversation, letters, and manuscript exchange, but not as clearly defined via the realm of print. Carter appears suspended, therefore, between her desire to fix her identity, her life, her future around a familiar set of variables, and her philosophical and moral beliefs about the efficacy of moving and being moved by the world at large. Her decision to undertake and then print a translation of Epictetus and to oblige Montagu with *Poems on Several Occasions* suggests that Carter briefly felt that the answer to perpetuating her personal literary agency was to confirm her worth in print. However, whilst these productions did 'fix' Carter's professional and public image, they also freed her (financially) to continue her more flexible, collaborative, and potentially more influential role as a public/private woman of letters.

Image, influence, and anxiety

> But what [...] can be said of so obscure an individual as I am? and what do you think the world will care about me?[474]

According to Pennington, the above quotation was Carter's reply to his suggestion that he write her memoir. How much credit can we give to such self-effacement? More importantly, given the proliferation of Carter's texts, image, and learned influence in the material culture of her time, in what ways did Carter and her contemporaries shape her subsequent biographies and literary credit? Though all present-day versions of Carter's life are reliant on her nephew's nineteenth-century account, Carter's textual afterlife begins with a late-eighteenth-century exemplification of her early literary career. Subsequent nineteenth- and early twentieth-century treatments of her importance rely almost exclusively on these accounts. Carter, who lived until 1806, was in a position, therefore, to influence the future scope of her literary legacy and her agency and/or diffidence on these issues is a significant factor in both her 'paradigmatic' and peripheral status today.

The most enduring image, literary function, and historiographical discourse associated with Carter during her own lifetime was that of classical scholarship (demonstrably evident in her translations, poetry, and tuition of her brothers and nephews for entrance to Oxbridge colleges). Today she is primarily known as one of the first Bluestockings, but Pennington, who reaped the benefits of Carter's scholastic legacy, tended to reinforce the classical image of his aunt and went so far as to claim that:

> In the course of her Greek studies, especially in reading the Greek historians, to whom she was very partial, Mrs. Carter took great delight in ancient geography, and made many [manuscript] corrections and alterations in the maps which she used to consult. With this indeed she was much more conversant than with modern geography, or even that of her own country, of which she had only a general, and, in some cases, merely a superficial knowledge; so that she was literally better acquainted with the meanderings of the Peneus, and the course of the Ilyssus, than she was with those of the Thames or Loire; and could give a better account of the wanderings of Ulysses and Aeneas, than she could of the voyages and discoveries of Cook or Bougainville.[475]

There is a sense that Pennington's constructions of Carter are those she may have enjoyed promulgating herself. Recalling his aunt's fame in the early nineteenth century, Pennington would have been relying on the personal accounts he had heard from Carter, the constructions in the letters, and the recollections of surviving contemporaries. The fact that Carter, her correspondents, and her contemporaries show an acute awareness of her image, her role in the world of letters, and her delight in being known, suggests that – whilst Pennington consolidated the material – Carter and her friends had already set the parameters.

Talbot especially enjoyed shaping an academic persona for Carter and the letters exchanged between 1749 and 1758, the years Carter was instructing her younger siblings and preparing the translation of Epictetus, are full of such references. In 1754, for instance, Talbot expostulates:

> For pity's sake, if you will be a tutor all your life, put on a coat and a square cap, and come and be a tutor at Oxford. You are excessively wanted there, and I could help you to a pupil that I would defy you

not to love better than you do even your own Harry. Between you both the University would be absolutely reformed in a few years, and consequently the nation in a few more. This scheme now would be somewhat worthwhile, and as it has nothing to do with matrimony or a court, I do not really see what objection you can make to it.[476]

Talbot lived in Cuddesden, near Oxford, whilst Thomas Secker was the Bishop of Oxford, and her letters display intimate knowledge of academic life, suggesting that her paralleling of Carter with an Oxford don was not without basis in fact. Her comparison also reinforces the image of scholasticism and academic poetry with which Carter often associated herself and which Talbot knew she valued.

In a letter to Talbot six years after the publication of *Epictetus*, Carter jokes that as '*a la Grecque*' is in vogue, she will no doubt be all the rage this season.[477] Perhaps she had already sat for Katharine Read's portrait, in which the simple draping of her garments along with her book and quill announces her classical propensities, but since her *Gentleman's Magazine* days she had sought to advertise her Greek and Latin learning in conscious comparison with the male tradition.[478] The epigrams on Pope's stolen laurel twig, her epitomisation as the owl of Minerva after the appearance of her 'Ode to Wisdom' in *Clarissa*, her Latin translations for the *Gentleman's Magazine* and Duncombe's edition of Horace, and her appearance in the company of the male literati in Dodsley's *Collection*, all suggest that Carter encouraged her association with the ancients, with tradition.

This image was not confined to her epistolary coteries nor, as the above list indicates, was it solely reliant on public approbation after the publication of *Epictetus* in 1758. Three years before the translation was complete, Carter appeared in George Colman and Bonnell Thornton's *Poems by Eminent Ladies* (1755). This work, which featured the poetry of 18 women – including Behn, Philips, Rowe, and Cockburn – was devised as 'the most solid compliment that can possibly be paid to the Fair Sex.'[479] This was, finally, the miscellany of ladies of which Carter wanted to be a part; however, the two pieces chosen – 'Ode to Wisdom' and 'To a Gentleman, on his intending to cut down a Grove to enlarge his Prospect' – were culled from Dodsley's *Collection* (1748), and Carter either was not asked or declined to offer more work. The biography appended to her two pieces characterises Carter in a manner that is consistent with all those that follow:

> [Carter] is now living; and is remarkable for her knowledge in the antient and modern languages, as well as the several branches of

philosophy. This Lady is no less famous for her refined taste, and excellent talent in poetry: as will appear from the following little pieces, which are all that her modesty has ever suffered to be made public.[480]

Though Colman and Thornton are wrong about the extent of Carter's publications, they acknowledge her larger interests and aims and attest to the efficacy of her life of the mind.

In the same year Edward Moore's periodical *The World* mirrored Talbot's suggestions by advancing the possibility of Carter as the warden of an Oxbridge college.[481] The essay, possibly written by Hester Mulso, is a dream-vision in which Jupiter reallocates people to positions more suited to their tastes and abilities. It is primarily concerned with the transposition of private persons to public posts and vice versa. After exploring a number of satiric prince and pauper scenarios (nobility transformed to jockeys, tailors, and fiddlers; translators, commentators, and polemic divines finding fulfilment as cobblers, gold-finders, and rat-catchers!), the author turns her attention to women. She recounts that 'The fine ladies remained as they were; for it was beyond even the omnipotence of Jupiter (without entirely changing their natures) to assign an office, in which they could be beneficial to mankind.'[482] She later reinforces this reductive formulation of female worth when she acknowledges that, of the two types of women, fashionable and domestic, the fashionable women only seek to enshrine themselves in posts where their beauty will be recognised; the domestic women go on with their daily occupations unfazed by the changes occurring around them. The suggestion is that, for the most part, the ambitions of women are fulfilled by their present, contracted lot.

However, there is an exception for some women when she considers ability as opposed to taste (for example, the nobility are interested in their horses, clothes, and music and so take on the occupations associated with them), as a factor in the elevation of private citizens to public figures. In these cases the display of Christian virtues and the moral imperative is paramount.

> [I]t was with a secret pride that I observed a few of my dear countrywomen quit their dressing-rooms and card-assemblies, and venture into the public, as candidates for fame and honours. One lady in particular, *forced by the sacred impulse*, I saw marching with modest composure to take possession of the warden's lodgings in one of our colleges; but observing some young students at the gate, who began

to titter as she approached, she blushed, turned from them with an air of pity unmixed with contempt, and retiring to her beloved retreat, contented herself with doing all the good that was possible in a private station.[483]

Though the essay does not mention Carter by name, the persona matches her own descriptions of herself. Carter often entertained her correspondents with tales of her debilitating shyness and embarrassment in public situations, describing herself as hiding behind her fan or her knitting needles and work basket.[484] This domestic image was one which she cultivated to the end of her career and in which both she and Montagu took great pride. What the essayist makes clear, though, is that Carter's exemplarity and sense of religious imperative, 'the sacred impulse', constituted the grounds for her incursion in the public sphere of male education. At the same time, her demonstrable embarrassment at public attention was a further indicator of her Christian virtues; she exhibits an 'air of pity unmixed with contempt,' and seeks to do 'all the good... possible.' Pennington elaborates:

> Fame she never courted, but was so feelingly alive to censure, as to dread the exposing herself to it, or indeed to the observation of the world at all. Her character was truly feminine, however strong the powers of her mind might be; and even to the last, she shrunk from too much notice, and felt a certain timidity in company whenever her friends brought her forward in too strong a light. (*Memoirs*, 103–4)

Carter's ethos was securely marked as virtuous and private, whilst her mind was allowed its stronger (that is, masculine) powers.

Guest notes of the essay that 'the dreamer recognises in private men and women the virtues necessary to public office'; however, she acknowledges that 'this remains an essentially conservative vision which attempts to reappropriate virtue to public identity, and to indicate that the public sphere is its natural and appropriate habitat. For that to be accomplished, women must remain private and retired, even though their ability to evince what are identified as public virtues is recognized.'[485] Carter is the embodiment of this contradictory aim. She could safely be referenced as a woman who exuded public virtues in a private life and, better yet, was so conscious and responsive to adverse publicity that she immediately retreated. Part of the issue here seems to stem from the problematic nature of public fame and the visual and oral forms which celebrity could take. The author's distaste for the fashionable ladies' avocation for display, and the tittering (gossiping/mocking) sounds from the students, mirrors many of the critical comments later levelled at Elizabeth Montagu. Montagu, it was frequently noted, courted attention whilst Carter kept her nose in the books.[486]

James Fordyce relied on this aspect of Carter's image when he alluded to her in his *Sermons for Young Women* (1765). After complaining about the lack of reasonable and virtuous accomplishments in contemporary young ladies, he nevertheless warns them against becoming abstruse 'metaphysicians, historians, speculative philosophers, or Learned Ladies'.

> I should be afraid lest the sex should lose in softness what they gained in force; and lest the pursuit of such elevation should interfere a little with the plain duties and humble virtues of life. Amiable instances of the contrary I know there are. I think at this moment of one lady, in particular, who to an extensive knowledge in philosophy and languages ancient and modern, with some portion of poetical genius, and a considerable degree of literary fame, has the sense and worth to join every domestic quality that can adorn a woman in her situation.[487]

Talbot was quick to bring this exemplification to Carter's attention. In a letter from the summer of 1766, she observes that she has been enjoying a new book, 'Sermons to Young Women', and moreover, that *'You are in, and handsomely in, but not so handsomely as you would have been, had the author known you better.'*[488] Fordyce's conduct book was not likely to appeal to Carter's sensibilities, especially in light of his views on women's role in marriage, but his appropriation and acknowledgment of her atypical status as a learned lady who actively pursued 'the plain duties and humble virtues of life' suggests that the specific nature of her achievements was widely discussed and commended. Fordyce did not know Carter, and yet he articulates in very precise terms her list of virtues: 'extensive knowledge', 'some portion of poetical genius' (elsewhere defined as sensibility), 'literary fame', and 'every domestic quality' for a woman in her 'situation' (middle-class and single). Fordyce's nod to her exemplarity overtly acts as a pre-emptive argument against women being metaphysicians, historians, and speculative philosophers: Carter, he points out, is exceptional. But his language also confuses the issue by hinting at the potentially normative aspects of her achievements as well as the criteria by which all 'domestic' (that is, English) literature should be judged. His phrases, 'some portion of poetical genius' and 'every domestic quality', suggest a certain levelling of the field as these are two of the accoutrements he determines women should aspire to as the more sensitive sex. The language also contains echoes of the notion of a providentially conferred portion in life, as if Carter is merely fulfilling her destined role as an exceptional English woman. Paradoxically, she represents for Fordyce a specific kind of diluted 'domestic' literature at the same time as fulfilling his need for an extraordinary exemplar of learning.

In the late decades of the century, Carter consistently appears in relation to a thwarted role in academia. In 1773 Montagu jokingly refers to Carter as her 'Brother Doctor' at the suggestion of a contemporary magazine which recommended that Lord North, the new Chancellor of Oxford, hand out degrees to them rather than to political supporters. Montagu quotes the unidentified author as stating that 'ye honour of a Doctors Degree had been more properly conferred on Mrs. Eliz Carter & Mrs. Montagu, than on a Parcel of Lords, Knights, and Squires, who are unlettered'.[489]

In line with the Katharine Read portrait, paintings of Carter made during the latter half of the century also helped to cultivate an image of learned as well as retiring austerity. Sir Thomas Lawrence's 1788-9 portrait of Carter (exhibited in 1790) emphasises, as Guest notes, 'the privacy of her retirement: her face is turned away, her gaze directed modestly downward'.[490] There are no emblems of her profession: no books, pen, letters, nothing, in short, to equate her with the literary world. However, the black folds of her dress look strikingly reminiscent of a university fellow's gown and her averted profile suggests a sense of gravitas in keeping with her learned image. Most famously, Carter appeared in Richard Samuel's painting, *The Nine Living Muses of Great Britain: portraits in the characters of the Muses in the Temple of Apollo* (1778). This portrait of a 'modern' coterie of exemplary women was celebratory and nationalistic, and a print of the painting was widely disseminated. Montagu wrote to Carter:

> Pray do you know, that Mr Johnson, the editor of a most useful pocket [book], has done my Prose head the honour to putt [it] into a print with yours, & seven other celebrated heads, & to call us the nine Muses.[491] He also says very handsome things, & it is charming to think how our praises will ride about the World in every bodys pocket. Unless we could be all put into a popular ballad, set to a favourite old english tune, I do not see how we could become more

universally celebrated. We might have lived in an age in which we should never have had ye pleasure of seeing our features, or characters, in Pocket books, Magazines, Museums, literary & monthly reviews, Annual registers, &c &c &c. You, who may look to future & posthumous fame, may despise the weekly, monthly, or annual registers, but for a poor Grisette of a Commentator, who only aspired to brush off a little dust & some Cobwebs with which time & filthy spiders had disgraced the Bays of a great poet, I think it an extraordinary felicity even to enjoy a little brief celebrity, & contracted fame.[492]

Carter's reply to the pocket book and *Nine Muses* print humours Montagu's enthusiasm whilst it mocks the ephemeral importance of Johnson's exemplification.

O Dear, O dear, how pretty we look, and what brave things has Mr. Johnson said of us! Indeed, my dear friend, I am just as sensible to present fame as you can be. Your Virgils and your Horaces may talk what they will of posterity, but I think it is much better to be celebrated by the men, women, and children, among whom one is actually living and looking. One thing is very particularly agreeable to my vanity, to say nothing about my heart, that it seems to be a decided point, that you and I are always to figure in the literary world together, and that from the classical poet, the water drinking rhymes, to the highest dispenser of human fame, Mr. Johnson's pocket book, it is perfectly well understood, that we are to make our appearance in the same piece.[493]

In Montagu's letter the themes of popular culture and domestic literature are invoked, rather than the high cultural modes that both women actually practised and were, theoretically, what made them eligible for honorary doctorates. However, she also suggests that 'future and posthumous fame' are the sole reward of the classical scholar. Her own Shakespeare studies are seen as secondary, reactive, and eligible only for a 'contracted fame'. There is friendly deference in Montagu's elevation of Carter's achievements, just as Carter returns the favour in her delight at their paired exemplification, but both are equally aware that contemporary print culture was a fraught place in which to gain and maintain literary credit.

Carter's reply references another sphere of influence and repudiates not only print but also the ancients ('Your Virgils and your Horaces') in favour of the local and the social ('the men, women, and children, among whom one is actually living and looking'). Her sense of importance as an actor in her immediate social milieu suggests an implicit acceptance of the domestic and private paradigm Guest finds in the periodical press of the period, but is complicated by her own earlier periodical career and her later willingness to be exhibited (in paintings and print) as an exemplary learned Englishwoman.[494] Nevertheless, her authority in the domestic arena was recognised by subsequent readers. In the Mitford manuscripts in the British Library, John Mitford (1781–1859) – who was reading the *Memoirs* at the time – gleefully records of Carter that, 'while <u>Servants</u> were in attendance at Meals, she made a Point of giving the Conversation such a turn, as might be <u>useful to them</u>. [...] they always listened to such instruction, with the utmost Earnestness. !!!'[495] Despite Mitford's ironic tone, he identifies Carter's interest in didactic exemplification, and her awareness of her role and potential spheres of influence.

For one of the remarkable facts of Carter's literary career is the degree to which she did influence those 'among whom [she was] actually living'. Mirroring her work with her younger siblings and nephews, Carter was an important figure in the education of the younger generation, her poems and essays featuring widely in school anthologies of the latter half of the century. Ian Michael, in his study of *The Teaching of English from the Sixteenth Century to 1870*, looks at texts commonly used for educative purposes in the period and finds that one of the authors most frequently represented is Carter. She appears more often than Pope, Thomson, Cowper, Shakespeare, Addison, J. Cunningham, and Milton, and ties with Isaac Watts for frequency of representation.[496] Only Oliver Goldsmith and Edward Young outnumber her in appearances. The clue to Carter's popularity can be deduced from the two recurring themes in the school texts Michael considers: 'a fear of passion, and a preoccupation with morality'.[497] Carter's correspondents and Pennington identified precisely this anti-enthusiastic bent and preoccupation with ethics in all of her letters and works.

There were also other factors that led to Carter's anthologisation. Michael attests to the fact that compilers often took their pieces from earlier anthologies and that they seldom selected from complete works. Thus poets who had collected editions in print (Pope *et al.*) were unlikely to feature as prominently in the new anthologies. Dodsley's *Collection*, the foundation text for so many that followed, did not feature any poets of the recent past; instead he consciously crafted a 'modern' canon of contemporary poets, including, of course, Carter.[498] The two pieces by Carter in *Poems by Eminent Ladies* (1755) are from

Dodsley's first edition (1748): 'Ode to Wisdom' and 'To a Gentleman, on his intending to cut down a Grove to enlarge his Prospect'. This is not to say that Carter's works did not fare well on their own. *Poems on Several Occasions* went through four editions by 1789, a French translation in 1796, and another three editions as part of the *Memoirs*. *Epictetus* went through four London editions and one Dublin printing during her lifetime, and, in addition to Pennington's posthumous version (1807), it served as the basis for popular editions throughout the nineteenth and twentieth centuries, including Everyman's Library (1955); more than respectable print runs for poetry and Stoic philosophy respectively.[499] What it does mean is that it was Carter's professional and private coterie associations of the early half of the century that promoted her longevity in the long term. Her seemingly idiosyncratic approach to publication and adherence to manuscript circulation in this era of the 'rise of print' meant that, textually at least, her works would continue to circulate and proliferate in miscellanies and anthologies dedicated to preserving the 'beauties' of English letters well after she had stopped producing them.

Just as important to that longevity, though, was the content and quality of her works. Whilst the historical variables of manuscript and print culture played a large role in the dissemination and perpetuation of her literary credit, the extraordinary intellectual and moral power of her writing was, and still is, a significant factor in the attention and admiration she receives. Like Rowe and Cockburn, the main reason we can reconstruct Carter's life in the republic of letters is because of the posthumous biography and the editions of her letters. The publication of those letters has often been viewed as the first act in the staging of her prescriptive literary afterlife, but they are also the evidence for her larger life of the mind. As the previous pages have made clear, long before Pennington formulated a plan to publish her works, Carter herself was aware of and an instrumental agent in the construction of the conservative authorial ethos and popular image. Nevertheless, Pennington plays a significant role in Bluestocking historiography and the construction of Carter's posthumous image, and his editions are a perpetual problem for critics and readers of Carter. It is a critical commonplace to criticise his eulogistic biography and editorial stewardship of the Carter correspondence, but little attention has been paid to the determining contexts or potential validity of his productions. Nevertheless, his editions *are* problematic and unreliable because, unlike Birch, Pennington was significantly less rigorous in his attention to basic historical and textual details. I want to end this reconstruction of Carter's writing life, therefore, with an account of the textual problems and history of the biography and, most importantly, the letters, which will be addressed in the next chapter.

Pennington's editions

Pennington's express aim was to show 'how far their [Carter and the Bluestockings] writings and their lives agree with each other' (*Memoirs*, 2). To this end he published a biography of his aunt entitled *Memoirs of the Life of Mrs. Elizabeth Carter with A New Edition of her Poems, some of which have never appeared Before; to which are added, some Miscellaneous Essays in Prose, together with her Notes on the Bible and Answers to objections concerning the Christian religion* (1807). The combined 'life' and works was clearly still a popular and profitable format, a second edition appeared the following year, a third in 1816. Carter's letters were a significant element of that success; pieced together into a narrative, excerpted letters make up a significant portion of the biography and Pennington claims 'he was assailed from all quarters with the most pressing solicitations to give more of them to the public' (*Letters* (1809), I:iii). He obliged with two more publications of her letters: the first, a series of letters between Carter, Talbot, and Elizabeth Vesey (1808, 2nd edn 1809); the second, a three-volume edition of letters from Carter to Montagu (1817). Once he started, Pennington could not seem to stop. In addition to publishing the *Memoirs*, the letters, and his own work, *Redemption; or, A View of the Rise and Progress of the Christian Religion, from the Fall of Adam, to its Complete Establishment Under Constantine the Great* (1811), he also issued new editions of *Epictetus* (1807) and *The Works of the Late Miss Catherine Talbot* (1809, 7th edn).[500] Carter's death had given him a job and a purpose. He even notes that the leisure of a new country living afforded him the time to devote himself to growing editorial demands. Pennington may have embarked on the first publication only interested in biography, memorialisation, and didactic exemplification, but the breadth of material he went on to publish suggests more expansive aims.

Pennington also benefited from or was responding to a market primed for the writings of his intellectual relation and her female friends. For he was not alone in his appeal to a readership hungry for the letters of the last century. That public had recently been treated to a flurry of biographies about Samuel Johnson, including Hester Thrale's *Anecdotes* (1786) and Boswell's *Life of Johnson* (1791) – both of which feature stories and quips about Carter.[501] Anna Barbauld's edition of *The Correspondence of Samuel Richardson* came out in 1804, and Pennington reminds us that the Duchess of Somerset's correspondence with the Countess of Pomfret, published in 1805, had mentioned 'Mrs. Carter in it in terms of high approbation'.[502] Hester Chapone's *Posthumous Works* appeared in 1807, prominently featuring letters to Carter and Richardson. Between 1809 and 1813 Matthew Montagu published the correspondence of his aunt, Elizabeth Montagu; many of these letters were addressed to Carter.[503] In 1812 the *Monthly Magazine* published more 'Original letters of Miss E. Carter and Mr Samuel Richardson'.

A reading public eager for tales of the private Johnson and the familiar letters of the author of the great epistolary novels, *Clarissa* and *Sir Charles Grandison*, were a ready market for the letters of writers whose social and intellectual circles overlapped with theirs. Private experience, as the history of the rise of the novel tells us, was increasingly important to eighteenth- and nineteenth-century readers.[504] The popularity of the epistolary novel as a textual space for 'testing and defining character', and for allowing human beings to 'self-consciously sift their experience, transform evanescent perceptions into personal meanings, and construct their interior realities', has important generic implications for familiar letters of the late eighteenth century.[505] Carter's letters (as well as Talbot's, Vesey's, and Montagu's) become, in this context, textual specimens: evidence for the exemplary life; they are also literary and educative tracts capable of either improving the minds of readers or enlarging the readers' sympathetic engagement with the moral lives of others. In contrast to the earlier evidence for enlightenment debate and intellectual correspondence courses, letter collections after the turn of the century appear increasingly domesticated by a novel-reading culture: collected letters forming the basis for a narrative of self-conscious introspection and examination.

Carter's life, implicated as it was with two of the greatest epistolary novels of the previous century (*Clarissa* – which contained her 'Ode to Wisdom' – and *Sir Charles Grandison* – in which she appears as the wise Mrs Shirley), becomes an exemplary tale. Aside from simply feeding the contemporary vogue for anecdotes and collections of letters from the famous, therefore, Pennington's publications evince a narrative purpose akin to that of epistolary fiction. In offering a record of Carter's life it was his hope 'that the contemplation of so much piety, virtue, and learning, may be attended with better effects than the gratification of mere curiosity; that her precepts and example may serve to rouse the indolent, while they confirm and strengthen the good' (*Memoirs*, preface unpag.). Further, he opines, the 'fervour' and 'enthusiasm' evidenced in the letters of Talbot, and the 'Christian piety, breathed in language always persuasive' in Carter's, are correctives to the 'lukewarmness' of his own age (*Letters* (1809), I: ix, xxi, and ix). Pennington's presentation of the life and letters in such an edifying context was not entirely at odds with Carter's own views on the purposes of the exemplary life and epistolary exchange. Yet he often went further and provided his readers with even more directed contexts. Numerous editorial notes function, rather like Richardson's notes to *Clarissa*, as extended essays on how to read Carter; they extol the text of some letters, qualify others, draw comparisons with classical, biblical or literary works, and parallel the upheavals of her time (the Jacobite rebellion of 1745, the Lisbon earthquake, the American and French revolutions) with his contemporary Napoleonic Wars.

The notes make it clear that Pennington felt Carter needed a mediator between her 'sequestered' but 'good and learned' existence and the exemplary narrative he wanted to tell.[506] In this sense, Pennington's memoir very obviously casts Carter in the politicised terms Nancy Armstrong formulated for the domestic heroine of the eighteenth-century novel.

> In place of the intricate status system that had long dominated British thinking, these authors began to represent an individual's value in terms of his, but more often in terms of *her*, essential qualities of mind. Literature devoted to producing the domestic woman thus appeared to ignore the political world run by men. Of the female alone did it presume to say that neither birth nor the accoutrements of title and status accurately represented the individual; only the more subtle nuances of behaviour indicated what one was really worth. In this way, writing for and about the female introduced a whole new vocabulary for social relations, terms that attached precise moral value to certain qualities of mind.[507]

Individualised as the domestic woman whose life of the mind and social accomplishments equate to 'precise moral value', Pennington contrasts Carter's life with those of the 'Statesmen, Heroes, and Monarchs' of the public political sphere (*Memoirs*, 1). Though Pennington seems to suggest that he is the first to draw attention to her significance on the subjects of morality and literature, and her importance to the nation, Carter, her contemporaries, and her successors were more than aware of her importance as a symbol of national virtue and learned merit. Frequently mentioned in the newspapers and monthly magazines, painted as one of Britain's nine *living* muses, and alternately extolled or satirised by a younger generation, the historical record of Carter's public life is difficult to square with Pennington's portrait of a retiring and constrained individual.[508] From a young age Carter projected her writing and imaginative life onto a national stage and, like the other women I have looked at, enjoyed availing herself of the performative license her learned and exemplary status gave her. Despite Pennington's claims about Carter's conservatism, it is worth questioning whether the insecurities, retiring image, and restrictive domestic ideology are not the unconscious symptoms of Pennington's own peripheral status and situation in life. We might also question whether the Carter bequeathed to us by Pennington is not simply an earlier manifestation of Gosse's brand of 'thin little lady-like ghost' whose 'phantom like transparence round the recognised seats of learning', requires the charity of a religiously minded male intellectual to revive her forgotten dust.[509] I do not think this is necessarily the case with Pennington; if anything he was in awe of Carter's erudition (he makes frequent references to his inability to assess her scholastic achievements because he is not competent in many of the languages or fields of inquiry she mastered), but it is often how he is read.

The ideological constructions in Pennington's editions may be transparent but his editorial practice and textual interventions are less easy to evaluate. They appear to stem from Pennington's quandary regarding the moral validity of publishing Carter's letters. By his own account he went against the express wishes of his subject in printing her letters. He avers that 'Mrs. Carter expressed a wish to her executor, that her letters should not be published', and adds,

> In two letters to friends now deceased she gives the following reasons for it: – 'I do not deem any opinion of mine of consequence enough to be brought as an authority, and you have more than once heard me declare my great aversion to being quoted, or having any part of my letters seen by anybody.' This was in 1766. (*Memoirs*, 13–14)

Intent upon recounting her aversion to the publication of her opinions or the assertion of her 'authority', he creatively ventriloquises Carter's 'two letters' as if they are a single statement. Whilst Carter did duplicate information in letters to her correspondents, the particularity of the subject makes it doubtful that two recipients received the exact same account and even more unlikely that she would have been discussing the problem of printing her letters as early as 1766. The quotation seems to hint, rather, that an opinion Carter had expressed in a letter is being used against someone in a public/social situation and that she is withholding her permission for it to be used out of context. Pennington goes on to conflate this quotation with anecdotal evidence:

> Another reason which she frequently gave in conversation, was the want of judgement and delicacy, so apparent in many collections of letters [...]. Not that this could here be the case, for Mrs. Carter was incapable of disguise. As she thought she spoke, and as she spoke she wrote. Some few of her Letters, therefore, either explanatory of her opinions, or illustrative of her life, the Author of these Memoirs thinks he may be allowed to insert: and in doing this, he will be solely guided by what he believes would have been permitted or forbidden by herself. (*Memoirs*, 14)

Even eighteenth-century reviewers found his justifications here rather spurious. If she had expressly forbidden the publication of her letters, they argued, then whatever Pennington believed 'would have been permitted or forbidden by herself' had already been established: everything was forbidden.[510] Pennington eventually overcame all scruples, however, and in the apologising preface to his second publication, the Carter, Talbot, and Vesey correspondence, he states he received no 'positive directions', nor had he 'given a promise' not to publish the letters (*Letters* (1809), I:iv). He adds, 'the correspondence between her and Miss Talbot was found regularly arranged and bound up in volumes, with all such names carefully erased by herself', as if waiting for him to publish them (I: iv).

But Pennington's use of the letters is more complicated and controversial than the act of publication alone. His deployment of them in the *Memoirs* is selective, without context, and often out of chronological order. Fragments from various letters are woven together with his own narrative additions to create a variously autobiographical and didactically biographical narrative. As the example of the 'two letters' above shows, his piecing together and creative rewriting or recontextualising of epistolary fragments raises more questions than answers about Carter's opinions and life. In the editions of the correspondence one would assume that he was less casual about his treatment of letters, but comparisons between the autograph copies of the letters we still have access to and Pennington's highly reconstituted editions reveal that we cannot rule out his considerable intervention in most of the printed correspondence.

Gwen Hampshire's 1972 B.Litt. thesis discusses the discrepancies between the surviving manuscript letters and Pennington's editing in detail.[511] She confirms that in all of his editions he misdates numerous letters and likewise calls attention to the many careless errors in his notes. For example, he implies that an allusion to a play in one of her letters indicates a lost piece of dramatic writing. Cross-referencing this information with other letters Pennington would have had in his possession, Hampshire reveals that Carter never wrote a play; rather she is alluding to her own performance in one during a stay at a friend's house in Canterbury.[512]

Hampshire's main concern, however, is with his use of the letters in the *Memoirs*, where, '[q]uotations from them, usually fragmentary and undated, and references to them, are worked into a narrative'.[513] By excerpting from some letters and splicing together others (often written years apart), he renarrativised Carter's life using a representative selection of letters in the *Memoirs* and then supplemented that narrative with the additional correspondence editions. Such selective transcribing and fusing is a constant frustration for scholars used to modern notions of editorial integrity; however, in Pennington's defence, he openly claimed to be attendant on this editorial policy. For instance, in his preface to the letters from Carter to Montagu, he explains that he joined together letters 'too short to form a separate letter' precisely because he wanted to reinforce the literary and moral aspects of the letters (*Letters* (1817), I:xv). He wanted people to find and/or attribute value (literary/monetary) to his aunt's familiar letters because he suspected, and possibly knew, that they had been written with that goal in mind.

Hampshire also finds fault with Pennington's excising of the human element in the letters. Particularly illuminating is her transcription of one of Nicholas Carter's letters written during the 1745 rebellion. She provides the full letter, but underlines the sentences Pennington uses in the *Memoir*, demonstrating the degree to which he edited out the descriptive elaboration and family details with which Nicholas and his children imbued their letters.[514] Nicholas's letter appeared in the highly selective *Memoirs*, but if we compare it with many of Carter's to Montagu we can see evidence of the same excising of information. Again, Pennington readily admits his role in reshaping the letters. Statements such as 'Nothing has been added to any of the Letters, but a good deal has been left out of trifling chit-chat and confidential communications' (*Letters* (1809), I:v) are standard in eighteenth-century letter-collections, but do appear to be at odds with his biographical intent to convey Carter's life through her own epistolary writings. In Pennington's defence, his policy of editing out 'the human element' is not much different to that which Birch practises in his edition of

Cockburn's letters. As I argued in chapter 4 Birch's editing is neither unfaithful nor invasive because it accurately reflects the epistolary and editorial ethos of Cockburn; it foregrounds the literary, philosophical, and moral purport of the letters which was so important to their author. Carter used her letters for similar ends to Cockburn and rewrote familiar missives as public essays (in the *Rambler*), and allowed particular letters (especially those which dealt with morality and theology) to be circulated after private information was scored out or excised from new transcriptions.

Hampshire usefully summarises the provenance of manuscript material, particularly letters, and the scope of what has been lost. She records 2,750 letters in her calendar (including manuscript letters, published letters, those in biographies, and those that can be deduced), but this is only a fraction of the total Carter wrote. Hampshire cites the example of Carter telling Talbot that hers is the 13th letter that day, yet we are still missing the other 12.[515] Pennington reports that, at Carter's request, a series of letters between her and the Earl of Bath were burnt, 'as they were for the most part on confidential subjects and family concerns' (*Memoirs*, 150). Hampshire also attempts to trace the history of the volumes bound and arranged by Carter and which Pennington used, but they have never since been located. She charts Pennington's duplication of letters from the *Memoirs* to the correspondence editions, something he claims not to have done except where explicitly noted.[516] Finally, she allows that Pennington may have 'softened' by the time he produced the volumes between Carter and Montagu, because he tends to leave more in the letters than just the serious or literary.[517]

Leonore Helen Ewert's slightly earlier doctoral thesis – a selected edition of Elizabeth Montagu's letters – reveals more fully Pennington's splicing and erratic dating of the Carter to Montagu correspondence.[518] A comparison of Ewert's transcriptions of Montagu's autograph letters with Pennington's edition of Carter's replies (1817) makes it apparent that Pennington had little interest in chronological and historical accuracy. Ewert states:

> Pennington is totally unreliable as to dates; by comparing the printed letters with Mrs. Montagu's manuscripts one can often determine without doubt where Mrs Carter's letters 'fit in' – and it becomes equally clear that Pennington frequently splices together parts of letters written ten or more years apart, and presents them as a single epistle under a very specific date. On other occasions Mrs. Carter's answer to a query predates the question.[519]

This causes considerable problems if one wants to, for instance, make a chronological list of Carter's reading. Based upon Pennington's edition, it would appear that she reread much of the same material a decade after her initial attempt, or that she read a number of contemporary works very belatedly. It also obscures the fact that the two women would often read works in tandem so that they could share their critical opinions and, in Montagu's case, seek clarification and acquire additional scholarly commentary from Carter. Pennington's splicing also makes for some oddly disjunctive comments on the domestic and revolutionary changes in the political sphere at this time. Observations on the struggles in America and France are messily merged with national parliamentary squabbles on very different issues from an earlier period. Unsurprisingly, Carter appears to shift from one topic to another in a random manner: a function again of Pennington's cut-and-paste technique. Any attempt to understand his editorial rationale is singularly frustrated by his frankly odd sense of what constitutes effective epistolary narrative.

However, Ewert's claim that her practice of excerpting from Montagu's letters did not significantly change the epistolary style of her subject offers a potential corrective to our sense of Pennington's editorial injustices. Ewert explains:

> In selecting the 267 excerpts for this edition, I have culled out all references to books, literary personages, critical issues, or literary gossip. Passing references to ephemeral publications may not be important in themselves, but they help to indicate the broad range of Mrs. Montagu's reading. In addition I have permitted myself to include some passages which throw an interesting light on Mrs. Montagu's personality, or on the nature of her relationship with Mrs. Carter. There are also comments on the bluestocking salons, education, and similar topics of related interest to scholarship in the eighteenth century.
>
> Doubtless such a planned program of excerpting would wreak havoc with the epistles of some letter writers, but Mrs. Montagu's letters suffer less from such treatment than may be thought. Her letters – unless she is showing off to a new acquaintance – rarely have a strong organic unity; they are instead episodic, for she will often jump from one subject to another with bewildering abruptness. Her strength lies in apt phrases and striking similes, rather than in larger units of composition.[520]

Ewert's editorial comments, with some caveats, reflect those Pennington espoused in his introduction to the Carter to Montagu correspondence. This is an exchange upon literary and moral subjects and, regardless of contextual contingencies, the underlying narrative is one concerned with a timeless critical perspicacity.

All of this suggests that, at their worst, Pennington's biography and editions of the correspondence are the textually inaccurate and critically naïve manifestations of a nineteenth-century cleric's sociological baggage about learned and exemplary women of the eighteenth century. At their best, they are precisely the same things. Textually rich, historically complex, and ideologically loaded, they reward any sustained effort with a palimpsestic understanding of the degree to which the interweaving, layering, and erasing of the manuscript heritage informs print productions of women's letters and biography well into the nineteenth century.

The problem that remains, though, is that little of the biographical information we have about Carter's early family life, aspirations, habits of mind, writing practices, and so on, is verifiable from sources independent of Pennington. Leaving us almost wholly reliant on his editions of the *Memoirs* and correspondence for much of her unpublished writings, his 'gate-keeping editorship' has been seen as a significant barrier against which feminist scholars must batter.[521] What critics often find, however, is that Pennington's weak edifice presages the larger difficulties of Carter's own conservatism and diffidence. Unsurprisingly, letters here become even more susceptible to abuse as biographical appendages, a problem exacerbated by Pennington's idiosyncratic editorial method. For these reasons close readings of the letters are extremely tricky and interpretation liable to endless caveats and equivocations. Nevertheless, this fragmentary piecing together of Carter's life from her own literary constructions does allow for autobiographical agency on the part of Carter. Even as he intrudes and corrupts the texts, Pennington lets Carter do a large part of the writing herself.

Despite much twentieth-century discrediting of Pennington's ideologically driven memoir and unscholarly editing of the letters, therefore, his version of his subject is no more problematic than the other memoirs I have discussed in this book. His construction of his aunt in exemplary religious terms is not dissimilar to Theophilus Rowe's, Henry Grove's, Henry Etough's, and Thomas Birch's versions of Rowe and Cockburn. Like these memorialists, he actively created biography out of literary effects, notably using letters as particular specimens of the confluence between the life and the writings. He presents Carter's letters, as opposed to her works, as the truest expression of her 'eminently beautiful' writing style, her intellectual and religious strivings, and her useful and entertaining opinions. He also foregrounds their self-regulating and instructive nature, drawing attention to their practical efficacy as exemplars to be imitated. At the same time, he also published many of her poetic and scholarly works which were still in manuscript in the *Memoirs*. Attaching the biography to a given corpus of work necessarily conflates the life and writings, but it also encourages the kind of textual connections I have been drawing despite generic categorisations of letters as weak siblings to literature per se. The abundance of writings, whether epistolary or otherwise, created a corpus and helped to create the impression (indeed reality) that there was more to the life than a reputation for female exemplarity. Ballard's *Memoirs of Several Ladies of Great Britain* (1752) was, perhaps, so poorly received precisely because it did not sufficiently establish the literary credit of his subjects. Ballard provided an eclectic mixture of fragmentary secondary evidence (from manuscript letters, funeral sermons, epitaphs, monuments, and so on) in place of the published work that had earned the women the right to be included in his work. Like Rowe's and Cockburn's collected works, the lives and letters only made sense in the larger context of their poetic, dramatic, fictional and polemical writings.

For all Pennington's faults, his depiction of his aunt's career as one of sustained integrity has also contributed to the attributions of professionalism which critics today find 'in spite' of his celebratory interment of her. Judith Hawley has observed that Pennington, 'like those other worthy nephews, Matthew Montagu and James-Edward Austen-Leigh, in memorialising his aunt,[...] also embalmed her reputation and insulated her to some extent from further scrutiny'.[522] There was undoubtedly an element of pride in commemorating the family's most illustrious member, but Pennington also made her available for scrutiny in a manner that privileged her own writing. It is the existence of his editions of her correspondence that has ensured that her 'reputation' in the world of letters persists. Whether the 'reputation' he supplied her with was beneficial or not to her long-term image is now a moot point; of interest is how much his editions built on the legacy she had already established in the course of the eighteenth century.

6
Elizabeth Carter and the *Theatrum Mundi*

> I was much obliged by your Court intelligence, which was the first of any kind that I have received since I left London, and I longed to know a little how the world was going. Though I am very little a party in the said world, few people I believe are more attentive to it as a spectator, or receive more amusement from the shifting scenes. People whose interests and passions are engaged in the bustle have very little leisure to attend to the spectacle which affords such an entertainment to quiet uninterrupted observers, who content themselves with seeing the drama without any wish for the plumes and the tinsel, and the long trains of the actors.[523]

> We are led to form much too magnificent ideas of our own powers of action, and by this means, to overlook, with foolish contempt, the proper occasions for exercising them. It is not in the study of sublime speculations, nor amidst the pompous scenery of some imaginary theatre of action, that the heart grows wiser, or the temper more correct. It is in the daily occurrences of mere common life, with all its mixture of folly and impertinence, that the proper exercise of virtue lies. It is here that the temptations to vanity, to selfishness, to discontent, and innumerable other unwarrantable affections arise; and there are opportunities for many a secret conflict with these in the most trifling hours, and it is our own fault if the business of life is ever at a stand.[524]

The previous chapter revealed the variety of literary means and the moral agency Elizabeth Carter deployed in her literary career. It also detailed the degree to which she was aware of her own image and influence in the public sphere, as well as the figurative and literal melding of her literary life and 'afterlife'. This chapter is concerned with texts and contexts: the literary and moral arguments Carter made for the intrinsically social and religious nature of happiness; the efficacy of her conservative ideologies; and the continued importance of letter-writing as a medium for intellectual exchange and social cohesion in the female literary tradition.

Carter is generally identified as a social and political conservative; however, I think it is possible to recontextualise her moral prescriptiveness and religious conservatism as a means to a different end.[525] Barbara Taylor has argued that women of the revolutionary period, particularly Mary Wollstonecraft, came to their political thought through their religion rather than in spite of it.[526] Taylor writes that the 'cult of feminine sensibility', that is, the 'affirmation of women's capacity to apprehend and identify with the divine,[...] was so fundamental to women's sense of ethical worth, and so far-reaching in its egalitarian implications, that it can properly be described as one of the founding impulses of feminism'.[527] Whilst Taylor looks at a woman who is readily identified as a politicised feminist, her central point, that religion shaped not only *how* these women thought, but *what* they thought, is crucial to understanding Carter's influence, both positive and negative, on succeeding generations of women writers.

Guest has made similar arguments regarding the importance of religion to women writers' sense of intellectual and political entitlement. She points out that it was precisely Carter's reputation for domesticity and piety which licensed her fame, and, more importantly, that her 'significance to notions of the national character' (in her guise as a learned *English* woman) politicised her as a subject.[528] Carter was cognisant of an observant world and her concerted attempt to choose the terms upon which she engaged with and was seen by the public suggests something more fundamental in her authorial ethos than just a wish to align herself with an emergent professionalism. The model of authorship advanced in the previous case studies clearly develops from, as Hammond says, a seventeenth-century 'gentlemanly' paradigm; however, what we get by the time of Carter is an articulated sense of a female tradition. Carter's sense of her individual agency is evident in her practice of circulating manuscripts/letters and selectively publishing authoritative works, yet she did so with a moral agenda that is directly attributable to a collective identity founded on religious and feminist ideals. Pennington admits as much when he concedes that, 'She was much inclined to believe that women had not their proper station in society, and that their mental powers were not rated sufficiently high.' However, he goes on to differentiate her feminism from the

> detested [...] principles displayed in Mrs. Woostonecraft's [sic] wild theory concerning the 'Rights of Women,' and [she] never wished [women] to interfere with the privileges and occupations of the other sex, yet she thought that men exercised too arbitrary a power over them, and considered them as too inferior to themselves. Hence she had a decided bias in favour of female writers, and always read their works with a mind prepared to be pleased. (*Memoirs*, 447–8)

Subsequent scholars have, for the most part, agreed with Pennington on the issue of Carter's conservative stance. The concluding section of this chapter will consider the ways in which Carter's complex feminism results in her historical divorce from a female literary tradition that she attempted to perpetuate and validate.

To begin with, however, I would like to return to scenes of textual production. The theatre of moral virtue and earthly happiness that has figured in the works of the two previous authors in this study is likewise a significant element in the metaphorical imagination of Elizabeth Carter. It captures the rhetorical framework upholding the literary, philosophical, and religious concerns of all of these women, whilst gesturing towards the acute sense of the metaliterary in their textual and actual lives. Nevertheless, the intellectual and moral seriousness of Carter's letters, and that of the Bluestockings in general, often levels the dramatic quality of much of their writing; instead, it is in their ethics and in the critical construction of their works that the theatrical trope continues to be articulated. 'Each of these authors is preoccupied with the necessity of reading and being read by other people', and this awareness of an audience, whether in manuscript, print, or real life, informs all of their writings.[529]

Epistolary performance and friendship

The letters of Carter and her female friends are a continual trope on the life of writing, but they also bear witness to larger aesthetic and ideological ideas – some of them antithetical. The 'theatre of happiness' I have rehearsed in previous chapters finds an experienced playwright and actor in Carter, and displays, yet again, the contemporary currency of her discursive aims. Carter's moral philosophy was informed by her belief in the importance and efficacy of social ties, particularly female friendships. One area of continuity or mediation between the domestic and the public that has often featured in accounts of the male literary life and their pursuit of civic happiness is that of friendship – specifically same-sex friendship between men. From classical texts through to the works of American transcendentalists, the discourse of friendship has provided countless male writers with an ethical framework in which shared meaning can be created and sustained in the face of diverse social and political relations. Until the seventeenth and eighteenth centuries women did not feature in the discourse.[530]

As I noted in chapter 3, the influential linking of female friendship and virtue established in the poems of Philips, consolidated in the polemical prose of Astell, and further tested on the stage by Cockburn was an important construct for women's collective self-regulation and agency. Carter and the Bluestockings inherited this female tradition, and their letters celebrate female friendship as a formative space for generating the intellectual imaginary necessary for women's writing.

At the same time, as religious conservatives, Carter and her female correspondents believed in 'a divinely-ordained, hierarchical society, in which the place of the individual is determined by mutual obligation and dependence', that is, conformity to the law of nature.[531] Sylvia Bowerbank persuasively argues that the writings of many pious early modern women express a critical tension between the status quo of a gendered hierarchy and their active cultivation of a better self and society.[532] For Bowerbank, their letters, diaries, and devotional writings represent 'instruments for self-direction and self-reformation' in line with 'an abstract concept of good nature', 'understood – alas – as a transcendent hierarchy'.[533] At the same time, their works also show 'techniques of self-fashioning' that showcase the potential of individual female subjects.[534] In Carter's exchanges, the tension between status quo and potential most often manifests itself around the subject of writing.

The performative aspect of letters also attains new resonances when considered alongside Adam Smith's contemporaneous and influential treatise, *The Theory of Moral Sentiments* (1759). In it, Smith argues for a spectatorial theory of morality that encapsulates the self-consciousness, self-projection, and complex individual morality we see in Carter's letters to her female friends. His influential theory of sympathy, in particular, captures a moral ideal that is mirrored in the processes of epistolary communication. Leslie Stephen captured these scenes of reciprocity best when he noted that Smith's sentimental moral 'theory becomes complex as it is worked out. [...] we must imagine two opposite mirrors, reflecting images in indefinite succession. We must consider A's sympathy for B, and then B's sympathy with A's sympathy, and then A's own sympathy with B's sympathy with A's sympathy for B.'[535] The epistolary medium offers the perfect framework for constructing this hall of mirrors. Forced to become spectators of their own behaviour on the page, and then to witness the effect of that self-projection on another in the form of a reply, was a tangible way of staring into Smith's mirror of opinions.

Smith also provides readers with a series of portraits in order to paint a picture of the complexity of moral actions and moral judgements.[536] His array of demonstrative moral characters is not dissimilar to what we find in the Bluestocking letters. When Pennington solicited the advice of his literary friend, Sir Egerton Brydges, regarding the content of the letters, Egerton replied: 'What I consider the most worthy of selection are opinions on books, life, and morals; and even if a private character is drawn with power, eloquence, and nicety of distinction, it becomes valuable and instructive.'[537] Carter's perceived role in reproducing, circulating, and moralising the private characters of her high society associates was obviously a significant factor in her potential appeal. However, whilst Egerton sought 'opinions on books, life, and morals', Carter's own sense of epistolary appeal seems to have been more subtle.

The confluences between Smith's projection of imaginative sympathy and the letter's ability to create a virtual meeting place of hearts and minds offers a constructive interpretive framework for exploring Carter's complex and self-conscious presentation of self in her familiar letters. For Carter, letter-writing, indeed all writing, was a personal, authoritative act which enabled her to construct her own terms of engagement and moral worth with the word and world. Guest affirms this when she writes that 'a part of the value of learning to women is that it gains them moral authority; it is perceived as a substantial property, analogous to landed estate in its ability to confirm the moral worth of its owner'.[538] Evidence that her readers/correspondents understood (sympathised) and reciprocated this reflexive authority is apparent in both manuscript and print texts. But Carter was not simply constructing a self-centred theatre, acting and directing as Rowe and Cockburn were wont to do. Carter's letters have enjoyed such success because they are so clearly written from the vantage point of a professional writer knowingly constructing her writing life for her correspondents. Unlike Rowe who created a performing 'other' or Cockburn who sought to control the semantics of her epistolary exchange, Carter quite clearly enjoyed disseminating and sharing her sense of authority and authorial identity.

Carter's letters advertise her awareness of the epistolary construct's essential literariness and elevate it beyond its typical conversational and practical parameters. In addition, the fusion of authority and authorial identity in her letters brings what Hammond would recognise as a public/professional ethos into the so-called 'private' world of manuscript circulation. Conversely, the posthumous publication of those very letters reversed that public/private dichotomy, revealing that the ideology of domesticity which had categorised female virtue as private, was, in Carter's case, actually founded on the public/professional identity she had cultivated in the 1750s.

From the very beginning of her epistolary career Carter was self-consciously elaborate about her compositional methods. Her early letters to Mrs Underdown exemplify the friend and correspondent who iterates and mocks her burgeoning literary role and potential fame, but explicitly seeks both.[539] The following letter, written in 1738, is a perfect example of Carter's literary projections of the self. It begins with the usual sally about never hearing from her correspondent, and, after thanking Underdown for her 'concern' at Carter's decision to remain in London all winter, continues:

> For any Thing I know to the contrary I shall have the Pleasure of seeing you at Deal in the Spring, & when I am once there it may be a pretty while before I leave it again. In the mean Time when you happen to be alone of a Clubb night, as you are tolerably well acquainted with my manner of thinking in most Cases, you need only set up the poker (which I by these presents authorize & appoint to be my Representative) & propose it a Subject & it will be easy for you to imagine my Answers [...]. I think tis Time for me to conclude for I am certainly putting a most unmerciful Violence upon your Eyes which have hardly recovered the Fatigue of reading, or rather decyphering my last Letter. As most Things improve by practice I find my self every day make a greater Proficiency in the Art of bad-writing, & I have vanity to think I shall soon be distinguished for it, so without the Trouble of a long Superscription you need only direct to me Eliz: Carter Scrawler in great Britain.[540]

Carter's assumption that she has easily identifiable and therefore reproducible discursive tendencies, as well as the social graces of a poker, relies on Underdown's intimate knowledge of her opinions and way of life, but it also suggests her sense of humour about her own aspirations. At this early stage it was known, in Kent at least, that she had ambitions as a writer and conversationalist and, moreover, that she was envisioning those ambitions on a national scale. In another letter she mocks her image and her learning when, after a garbled sentence, she writes 'excellent English this for a Scholar & all that'.[541] And a third letter from London records:

> Female Scribbling goes on most successfully. St. John's Gate is hourly attacked by whole Vollies of Rhyme from a jingling Club. There came one curious piece last Week in which I had the Honor to be mentioned; I think it not proper to be exposed to vulgar Eyes & therefore have deposited it among the Rarities in my Cabinet. To say Truth it was wrote in a Way I do not at all like. I showed it to Miss Wilbraham who put a comical Way of Revenge into my Head by advising me to have it printed in the farthing News paper,[542] & then inclose one of the Copys to the Authors. I must not however conclude my Account of these poetical Gentry without doing them the Justice to own they sometimes write prettily.[543]

Her eagerness to share her growing celebrity is evident in the passage. Even more interesting, though, is the dialectic she sets up between 'Female Scribbling' and a respondent 'jingling Club' of male writers. In this instance, her construction of success is reliant on the reciprocal practicalities of manuscript exchange, rather than on the monetary or entrepreneurial rewards we would expect.

Other early letters display the notion of the letter as a vehicle of affective pleasure. In his *Rambler* essay on the art of letter-writing (No. 152) Johnson wrote that, 'Wherever we are studious to please, we are afraid of trusting our first thoughts, and endeavour to recommend our opinion by studied ornaments, accuracy of method, and elegance of stile.'[544] He continues, 'Pleasure will generally be given, as abilities are displayed by scenes of imagery, points of conceit, unexpected sallies and artful compliments.'[545] Long before he identified this practised element of epistolary discourse, and its importance to the truly conversable eighteenth-century letter, the letters of Carter and Talbot exhibit the abilities of the ladies to create these literary effects. The inaugural letter (16 August 1741) in the correspondence between Carter and Talbot details problems related to epistolary composition and the metaphoric possibilities of their textually based relationship. Carter begins with a complaint regarding the twin curses of writing: stupidity at invention and lack of time. Noting that 'this Letter has begun under the influence of some very dull planet, for it has cost me at least half an hour's laborious study to compose the Introduction', she goes on to exhibit how creative she can be with a fanciful disquisition on the benefits of receiving a letter rather than a visit from Carter's ghost.

> I believe you will the sooner pardon the present trouble I give you, when you know that if I do not satisfy my present inclination in writing, it is very probable I may haunt you, for I have drawn Mr. Wright into the scheme of a romantic voyage to the Goodwin sands, where it is one to a hundred I may be drowned, and you will readily compound for the impertinence of a Letter, rather than run the hazard of being surprized by a posthumous visit. However, if this should happen to be the case, I promise to accost you in the most agreeable manner possible, in the dress and attitude of Mrs. Rowe's etherial beings, or, (what would make me appear to still greater advantage) like one of your own beautiful ideas put into form. (*Letters* (1809), I: 4–5, Deal, 16 August 1741)

Her evocative rendering of the 'present trouble' (the letter) as a metaphor for the troubled spirit (Carter) who would have to haunt Talbot in its attempt to fulfil its unexpressed potential is revealing of Carter's view of the letter as a physical and metaphysical representative of herself and her mind. It also attests to the influence of Rowe's epistolary 'others' who provide Carter with a familiar reference point for her prospective haunting.

As the correspondence continues, Talbot and Carter show an attentiveness to phrases and narratives which they then weave into subsequent letters. Talbot's reply to Carter's letter above expands upon the topic of composition:

> If it cost even Miss Carter herself half an hour's study to frame the Introduction to one who she might be sure would receive any thing of her writing with a great deal of pleasure, I will give her leave to imagine that I have been racking my brains for an answer ever since I received it, and then I need make no further excuse for not acknowledging the favor sooner. (*Letters* (1809), I: 6, Cuddesden, 15 September 1741)

And Carter returns to the theme of ghosts and apparitions in her letter of 24 May 1744, evocatively subscribed as written at 4 a.m.[546] The *theatrum mundi* in Carter's letters is thus not always of this world but often of the next.

The legacy of Elizabeth Rowe's ghostly scenes on Carter's epistolary imagination was more than a useful fictive trope; their mutual faith in the superior intellectual delights and sphere of action available to them in the hereafter served as an impetus to all of their corporeal endeavours. Rowe's brand of numinous enthusiasm and fictive proselytising was, of course, problematic, and prompted Nicholas Carter to warn his daughter against following in the mode of the other-worldly writer. Carter's letters to Talbot show that Carter conformed to her father's advice and that she repeatedly counselled Talbot out of a similar propensity. In one particularly Rowe-esque letter, Talbot writes:

> There are times when even the magnificence of the sky, the fair extensions of a flowery lawn, the verdure of the groves. The harmony of the rural sounds, and the universal fragrance of the balmy air, strike us with no agreeable sensations,
>
> 'What does of their sweetness those blossoms beguile,
> That meadow, those daisies why do they not smile?'[547]
>
> nothing surely but the ungrateful perverseness of one's own humour. This reflection throws human happiness in a most mortifying light. If these most beautiful, most innocent enjoyments, are so very imperfect, so sadly unsatisfactory, where shall the fugitive be found? There only where it shall no longer be fugitive or uncertain. You see I am in a sermonizing humour, and do what I will I fall into the style every moment. (*Letters* (1809), I: 63–4, Cuddesden, 27 June 1744)

Talbot's 'sermonizing', or in Bowerbank's terms: her 'cultural labor of harmonisation' of nature, signals the lengths to which Talbot pressed her piety.[548] Talbot's disappointment at her own lack of an enthusiastic response to nature was an important indicator of her state of mind and was something with which Carter empathised.

In response to such asceticism Carter presents the case for a more practicable and sociable model.

> Where indeed below the stars shall happiness be found, if it flies from a mind like your's! If I might venture to dispute any point with you, who understand every thing so much better than myself, I should be inclined to philosophize a little with you upon this melancholy reflection. Give me leave however, dear Miss Talbot, most sincerely to wish, you may very seldom, if it were possible never, feel any stronger argument against human happiness than such an accidental flagging

of the spirits as an hour's enlivening conversation, or a hundred varied amusements might easily conquer. These transient fits of *oscitation*, and inactivity, are perhaps no more than a necessary relaxation to the mind, and serve to quicken its faculties to a more lively sensation of returning pleasure. (*Letters* (1809), I: 66–7, Deal, 20 July 1744)

The good humour and subtle hints in Carter's reply take into account Talbot's chronic depressive tendencies, but it is clear that she is deeply concerned about Talbot's inability to find happiness in her present lot. At the same time, there is a definite sense that Talbot's flowery, commonplace constructions of nature are an attempt to generate a sympathetic response in Carter akin to those she had read in Rowe. The nature of their correspondence required just such of flow of sympathetic projections (especially failed ones) in order to signal the constructive and benevolent nature of their exchange to themselves and others.[549]

Such monitory self-reflexivity lends the Carter/Talbot exchange a defeatist air at times, especially when the two women seem to find so little to value in their present selves/situations and are so diffident about their own abilities and scope of action. On a more positive note, they recognise this aspect in themselves and seek to counter it by constantly keeping in view the larger sphere of action available to them through their belief in heaven and immortal bliss. It is thus their 'posthumous' ambitions which compel them to perform and conform to the ethical system offered to them by way of revelation and scripture. The intense moral 'worth' and love which Carter and Talbot attached to their friendship helped them to envisage it on a similar plane as the immortal love of God, and to therefore imagine what immortality might entail. Carter explains to Elizabeth Vesey that, 'Through all the various stages of our existence, our friends are given us to aid our virtue, to heighten our enjoyments, and to lessen our cares: and with equal regard to our advantage are they at several periods removed, to instruct us that our hopes of perfect happiness must depend wholly on *the Friend who never dies*' (*Letters* (1809), III: 269, Clarges Street, 15 January 1766). In this case, friendship mediates, not just between the domestic and the public, but between life and death – or, as Rowe framed it, *Friendship in Death*.

When Carter questioned her role and the status quo, her sense of active virtue battled with her contemplative habits.[550] Writing to Talbot, she complains:

> If you talk of the insignificancy of your life, what is to be said of such a wretched trifler as I am? Sometimes indeed I have the grace

to be ashamed, and really think I am living to no kind of purpose; at others I look round the world, and see most folks in it as foolishly busied, and take comfort. This, however, is a species of comfort so dangerous, and wants so many qualifications and restrictions, that one may almost as well be without it. At one time I think it must proceed from voluntary dilatoriness that I do so little, at another the whole fault is thrown upon some natural defect, some unavoidable slowness of constitution. At last, tired with all these various conjectures and speculations, and not pleased nor perfectly satisfied with any of them, I make the shirts I have to make, hear the lessons I have to hear, and upon the whole, go on in the same daily track tolerably well contented. If it be considered that with these petty employments, these idle amusements, which in some views we are apt to look upon as so trifling and insignificant, and below the dignity of our nature, are necessarily interwoven innumerable occasions for the improvement of it; that in the most ordinary occurrences of conversation there is always some irregularity of temper to be corrected, some impropriety of behaviour to be avoided, some good disposition to be called forth, we shall find no reason to treat the daily exercises of life as low and contemptible, even where there are no opportunities from great and distinguished talents, and advantages, of rising to remarkable degrees of excellence. (*Letters* (1809), II:54–5, Deal, 21 October 1751)

In characteristic fashion Carter finds an important lesson about religious orthodoxy in her own plight: the link between duty and happiness. Carter believed that, by fulfilling her providential duty, she could be secure in the knowledge that she was conforming to the law of nature and of God. Or, as John Tillotson succinctly decreed, 'Surely nothing is more likely to prevail with wise and considerate Men to become Religious, than to be throughly [sic] convinced, that Religion and Happiness, our Duty and Interest, are really but one and the same thing considered under several Notions.'[551] Carter believed that engaging in social activities, regardless of their intellectual benefit, was an important part of fulfilling one's duty precisely because it necessitated the examination and regulation of one's actions and ideas in a variety of social roles. This does not make her letter an ode to conservative ideologies about women's restricted sphere of action; rather, it is a message about the personal empowerment a Christian Stoic can effect in her own life and over her own mind regardless of external constrictions.

The problem with Carter's figuration of the moral merits of village domesticity was that she was no longer simply a private actor, and had readers and friends who associated her with more rigorous pursuits and more public displays of them. They were also determined to effect her return to the world stage and not all of the plans had to do with publication. Talbot was instrumental in devising most of the schemes which made the 1750s such an important decade for Carter: the translation of Epictetus, the contributions to *The Rambler*, the sense of religious vocation, and the court prospects can all be traced to her influence. Importantly too, their letters, and Talbot's constant iteration of their usefulness, clearly had an impact on Carter's sense of purpose.[552]

A productive decade: *The Rambler* and theological controversy

Despite all of her protestations, the 1750s were a significant and prolific decade for Carter. During this period, Talbot and others worked especially hard to get Carter to produce a number of works for the public. Talbot had already asked Carter for a private translation of Epictetus (c.1749), and suggested other projects, including a book of instructive fables for 'farmers and spinners, and weavers' to 'teach them useful sentiments in an amusing lively way' (*Letters* (1809), I: 88, Cuddesden, 6 January 1745). Thomas Hayter, Bishop of Norwich, wanted Carter to contribute essays to *The Rambler*.[553] Carter, therefore, was partly on the defensive with her theory about the moral efficacy of doing very little.

The problem with Carter's contracted vision of her sphere of action and influence was that others clearly saw her exemplary private life as one of the primary reasons for her taking on a more public role. 'Indeed such a one as you, were Providence to call you into the world, might be of such vast use in it, that I cannot bear to hear you talk in this way' (*Letters*, (1809), II: 80, St Paul's, 13 June 1752), Talbot proclaimed. Talbot, and later Elizabeth Montagu, tried to assist Providence by negotiating a place for Carter as a governess at court (this was years after Nicholas Carter's unsuccessful attempt to place his daughter); unsurprisingly, Carter refused again. Nevertheless, Carter acknowledges that she has reason to be 'ashamed' at her lack of productivity, and even suggests that she feels she has something of value to contribute to her world. That it was her epistolary and social community which prompted the renewed attention to public productions is indicative of the importance of letter networks to women writers.

Equally important are contemporary contexts in print culture. Talbot, Carter, and others found new or rather renewed worth in their exchanges when they compared them with print publications which foregrounded the same moral concerns and did so in similar epistolary or essay modes, such as Samuel Johnson's *Rambler* papers and the letters of Catharine Cockburn. A brief look at Carter's and Talbot's relationship with *The Rambler* and comments upon Cockburn highlight yet more of the theological and epistemological continuities between their familiar letters and print productions in the period.

i. *The Rambler* papers

The literary and fictive possibilities of Carter's and Talbot's epistolary universe were given new contexts and purpose upon the arrival of Johnson's bi-weekly paper, *The Rambler* (1750–2). First published on Tuesday 20 March 1750, it appeared every Tuesday and Saturday until Saturday 14 March 1752. A month into its run, on 28 April 1750, Talbot enquired of Carter, 'I hope you are fond of *the Ramblers*', and from that point forward they take a keen interest in the fledgling periodical (*Letters* (1809), I: 343). More important to my discussion than the contemporaneous accounts of *The Rambler* in the letters of these two women are the analogous moral preoccupations of the two works. The comparable concerns of the letters and the *Ramblers* do not begin, however, with the women themselves, but rather with the appropriation of the letters by Pennington. Pennington published his aunt's letters during the Napoleonic Wars, and his conception of the moral laxity of his nineteenth-century readers led him to press the sanctity, seriousness, and corrective nature of them. *The Rambler* began its life as a series of periodical essays devoted to moral improvement, and, as Pennington stressed, the familiar letters of Carter, Talbot, Vesey, and Montagu were missives concerned with the moral efficacy of lives and works. Paul J. Korshin argues, however, that Johnson saw *The Rambler* as something bigger from the start and maintains that he projected it 'as an entrepreneurial undertaking that would rival the other great collections of English essays, Bacon's *Essays Civil and Moral*, and Addison and Steele's *The Spectator*'.[554] Whilst Carter's and Talbot's letters were clearly not written with any such grandiose aim, they would, in the end, be read by the public in the same format as Johnson's essays, that is as a collected edition. Korshin suggests that, based on the modest sales of the original papers (less than 500 copies per issue), and the subsequent success of the collected editions, 'most eighteenth-century readers of *The Rambler* first made an acquaintance with the work as a complete collection'.[555]

The Bluestocking letters, indeed any edition of letters, shares the same history: the originals are subsumed into a larger organisational structure and enforced narrative and their autonomous material status is reinscribed for the benefit of wider audience. The majority of readers experience the once autonomous texts for the first time as a collected corpus.

In Carter's, Talbot's, and Montagu's case this recontextualisation of their letters significantly affected their posthumous reputations. However, I would like to consider what the publication of their manuscript essays and letters in *The Rambler* did for their own sense of epistolary and literary agency, and explore the possibility that a recontextualisation occurred long before Pennington was in possession of their papers. Despite the existence of numerous letters of the 1740s which evince a *Rambler*-like ethos, there is a notable increase in the moral seriousness of Carter's and Talbot's letters during and after *The Rambler* years. I do not believe that this newly charged tone and content was entirely dependent on Johnson; however, I do think that his style validated its broader use in their letters and occasional tracts. Tellingly, many of Carter's correspondents started to request her epistolary intervention on issues relating to religious doubt, practical morality, and exemplary living after this period.

Carter submitted two essays to *The Rambler* (Nos 44 and 100), the largest contribution by any of Johnson's six outside correspondents. Amongst the other contributors were two more female members of the Bluestocking coterie: Catherine Talbot, who contributed No. 30; and Hester Mulso, who wrote the four billets included in No. 10. The remaining contributors were all male: David Garrick provided some of the material for No. 15; Joseph Simpson, the second letter of No. 107; and, most famously, Samuel Richardson provided the best-selling No. 97.[556] The female contribution is unique; not only did three women write for one of the most important periodicals of the period, but it also provided a public forum for topics which they had already been exploring in their familiar letters.

The letter/essay which became *Rambler* No. 44, for instance, predated the periodical and, according to Talbot, required a number of emendations to make it acceptable for a general readership. She wrote to Carter:

> The Vision is much approved with its present preface, and will make an excellent *Rambler*, only it is wished there were something added. Being writ with the sole intention of raising depressed spirits

into cheerful gratitude, wrong-headed people may draw inferences from it favourable to a life of mere amusement and good-humour; therefore now that it is intended for general use, something should be mentioned of the serious and active duties of life, and its proper restraints, and caution given, lest by too entirely attending to the duty of enjoying a beautiful world, people should neglect the government and improvement of the heart, and miss the happiness that is intended them. (*Letters* (1809), I: 348)

Talbot's preoccupation with the hereafter and her perception of the lack of seriousness in the world lead her to suggest zealously cautious corrections. The topic is a familiar one for Carter, though, and whether or not she adopted Talbot's corrections, we know that she had traversed similar ground before. One of her many powerful letters to Talbot during one of the latter's crises is that of 20 June 1748.[557] The reason for Talbot's grief is not given (it is likely the death of Mrs Secker), but the letter is indicative of Carter's arguments and style:

I was most sincerely affected, dear Miss Talbot, when I reflected on the distress I knew you would undergo, and yet it seemed so just and proper, that I could not tell how to wish you might not in some degree feel it. But alas! you will feel it too long, and the mournful set of images in which you indulge yourself, will I am afraid fall in too naturally with the general disposition of your mind, for you to endeavour effectually to throw them off. You will be inclined to think, that reason and religion are the only proper methods of relief; but to beings such as we are, these are no more to be depended on of themselves for removing the painful sensations of the heart, than for the cure of the fever. They are, no doubt, highly and indispensably necessary, to form a decency of behaviour, to calm the extravagancies of passion, and convince one that every thing is right, but with all this conviction, and the most perfect resignation imaginable may end in nothing better than a quiet unruffled melancholy. Neither religion nor reason can alter the constitution of human nature, which however patiently it may suffer, will not be argued out of feeling while it dwells upon the object that gives it pain. To prevent this some dissipation is absolutely necessary, and an endeavour to interest oneself a little with what passes in the world. This is a remedy to which I know you will be very averse, as you have so industriously reasoned yourself into the persuasion of its being a duty to keep the mind entirely free from any real attention to any agreeable objects that surround it. I have certainly a higher opinion of your understanding than of that of any one person upon earth, and yet I cannot help thinking you carry this virtue of indifference too far. You have a set of notions highly adapted to a more perfect state of being, but perhaps it may not be right, to endeavour to disengage yourself from a connection with that to which you at present belong, nor to resolve against every engagement with the pleasures of human creatures, because they are not the pleasure of angels. I often feel a real concern in thinking where these refinements may end; too probably I fear in depriving you of all the enjoyments of life, and leaving you sensible only of its pains; for whether you will always allow it, or no, sensibility in a high degree you most certainly have. (*Letters* (1809), I: 262–4)

As in Smith's *Theory of Moral Sentiments*, Carter's letter opens by constructing her advice as a sympathetic projection of fellow-feeling. Smith, in his chapter on sympathy, argued that, 'As we have no immediate experience of what other men feel, we can form no idea of the manner in which they are affected, but by conceiving what we ourselves should feel in the like situation [...] and it is by the imagination only that we can form any conception of what are his sensations.'[558] He further points out that there is pleasure in this exercise of mutual sympathy and that it is generally an intuitive rather than a reasoned response. Carter develops this same theme in arguing that the remedy for Talbot's sorrow is not to be found in stoical doctrines or reasonable religion, but rather in the affectionate theatre of society. She goes so far as to remonstrate with Talbot, 'yet I cannot help thinking you carry this virtue of indifference too far', and tries to encourage her to lower the pitch of her feelings in an effort to help her attain a state of emotional equanimity. Carter's benevolent theory of regulation is echoed in Smith when he writes:

> Society and conversation, therefore, are the most powerful remedies for restoring the mind to its tranquillity, if, at any time, it has unfortunately lost it; as well as the best preservatives of that equal and happy temper, which is so necessary to self-satisfaction and enjoyment. Men of retirement and speculation, who are apt to sit brooding at home over either grief or resentment, though they may often have more humanity, more generosity, and a nicer sense of honour, yet seldom possess that equality of temper which is so common among men of the world.[559]

A comparison of Carter's letter with *Rambler* No. 47, 'The proper means of regulating sorrow', reveals the contemporary currency of these ideas amongst writers interested in disseminating efficacious moral philosophy. The advice against stoic indifference that Carter claims Talbot will try to affect, is also refuted in Johnson's essay when he argues that 'an exact compliance with this rule might, perhaps, contribute to tranquillity, but surely it would never produce happiness'.[560] Carter was writing for a dear friend, and Johnson for a general reader, but the overall shape, tone, and content of the two arguments is almost identical.

Though the above letter from Carter, Johnson's *Rambler* No. 47, and Smith's *Theory of Moral Sentiments* all attempt to provide a secularised version of how benevolent affections work in society, the arguments of the two former are fundamentally religious in perspective.[561] It is this religious basis which differentiates them from Smith's intuitive theories, as they both still subscribe to Lockean notions about the fixed foundations of morality (natural law theories) and that 'moral judgment and moral motivation are forms of rational inference.'[562] Like Cockburn, Carter and Johnson could not accept a worldview that divorced human action and potential from the wisdom, goodness, and happiness associated with the divine attributes and it is only when writing to someone as strict as Talbot that Carter would temper her religious prescriptions. Thus, despite Smith's comparable rendering of the function and form of social affections, his lack of reference to scripture and revelation as guiding principles would not have made his moral theories popular with someone like Carter. Nevertheless, Carter's letters show that she was incorporating moral sense theories into her own writings, and further that Smith's notion of an impartial spectator, captures her own sense of self-consciousness in the social theatre.

ii. Theological controversy – the Athanasian Creed

During the summer and autumn of 1752 Deal and, even closer to home, Carter's father, became embroiled in a religious debate. The theological basis of the dispute was belief and adherence to the Athanasian Creed, one of the authoritative creeds of the Anglican Church which concerns the coeternal and coequal status of the three figures of the Trinity, and to which Carter's father did not subscribe. Nicholas Carter was called before the corporation of Deal on the issue, published a sermon in defence of his views, and finally avoided further problems by employing someone to read the creed in his place. As a result of this local controversy, however, a number of polemical pamphlets were published including Elizabeth Carter's own *Remarks on the Athanasian Creed*

(1752/3?). This was not an insignificant engagement or controversy – you could still be criminally prosecuted for professing this heresy and, if you were a university scholar or clergyman, be forced from your post.[563]

During the furore, Carter observed to Talbot:

> such scenes as those of which I have been for some time an uneasy spectator, may furnish one, if properly applied, with many an instructive lesson. A view of the errors on both sides is a surer guide than the very best formal treatise of morality, as pictures are generally more striking than descriptions.[564]

Invoking her own species of Shaftesbury's 'moral painting' Carter positions her unhappy but impartial self at a remove from the distressing scenes of potentially internecine clerical wars. Her spectatorship did not prevent her polemical intervention in the affair, however, and, as the following excerpts show, Carter did not assume the conservative response. Instead she was adamant in her opposition to the orthodox position and to the tone of the controversy in general. Her stance was one later attributed to liberal reformers such as Joseph Priestley, but was a significant movement within the establishment from the likes of the Cambridge Platonists, Herbert of Cherbury, and John Locke.[565] Moreover, it is as close as Carter gets to the rationalist polemical mode and Anglican enlightenment battles that Cockburn engaged with. Carter's critical attitude in relation to the controversy is indicative of her enlightenment values regarding the primacy of practical reason and private judgement in religion and society, but it is also, as Guest argues, attributable to her belief in human affections and her 'emphasis on Christ's humanity' in matters of faith.[566]

The *Monthly Review* of November 1752 excerpts from and describes a few of the pieces already in print. Though it presents pamphlets from both sides of the argument it clearly champions the anti-trinitarian position. William Hopkins's anonymous *An Appeal to the Common Sense of all Christian people* convinces the reviewer that:

> The *Athanasian* doctrine of the Trinity, and the worship founded upon it, are such gross insults on the common sense and reason of mankind, so expressly contradict the plainest declarations of our Saviour and his apostles, and are so foul a reproach on our established church, that it is just matter of wonder and astonishment to the considerate part of mankind, that no vigorous effort has hitherto

been made to reform what is amiss in this respect, and to wipe off such a stain from our ecclesiastical constitution.[567]

As J.N.D. Kelly observes, many orthodox Church of England followers, including Carter, found 'repellent' the creed's 'unquestioning assumption that our eternal destiny is poised on adhesion or non-adhesion to the detail of a highly technical, man-made formulary'.[568]

Carter's contribution, which takes the form of a letter to Mr Randolph, the rector of Deal, is itself a reply to two further tracts, indicated in the full title of her work: *Remarks on the Athanasian Creed; on a Sermon Preached at the Parish Church of Deal, October 15, 1752; and On a Pamphlet, lately published, with the Title, "Some short and plain Arguments, from Scripture, evidently proving the Divinity of our Saviour." In a Letter to the Rev. Mr. Randolph, Rector of Deal*. Despite the existence of numerous, and even competent – according to the *Monthly Review* – defenders on both sides of the controversy, Carter chose to join the public fray (albeit anonymously).

Unlike Hopkins's pamphlet, where he professes 'to have done his best to adapt it [the creed and scripture relating to it] to the Capacities of Common Christians, for whose Use it [his arguments against] is intended', Carter's pamphlet is an individualised polemic that insists on a personalised response from Randolph.[569] Throughout the text she uses personal pronouns, 'I', 'me', rather than the male-gendered pronouns and generalised address of Hopkins. The importance of this small difference is apparent when we consider one of the orthodox replies to Hopkins. In *A Sincere Christian's Answer to the Appeal to the Common Sense of all Christian People* (n.d./1751?), the Rev. Thomas McDonnell specifically frames the debate as a learned affair that should remain within the scholarly clerical community. He chastises Hopkins for claiming to present a text that is 'made level' to the understandings of everyone and yet frequently has recourse to the evidence and 'Authority of the Learned'. McDonnell asserts, 'It is evident then, that the Subject-Matter of his Appeal is not simply cognisable by those, to whom he hath appealed. The Necessity he was under of introducing Evidence, which only the Learned can comprehend, plainly confines the Decisions to them.'[570] Carter, in joining this fray, claims a place among the learned who understand the primary texts (in Greek and Hebrew) and, therefore, have a right to question Church authority.

Her argument is succinctly laid out in the introduction:

Not to waste your Time by a tedious Introduction, The Design of this Address is to ask the Favour of you [Randolph] first to instruct me how to understand the *Athanasian* Creed consistently with the Principles and Deductions of Reason: how it is to be reconciled with all those Passages in the *New Testament*, which either directly or by fair Consequence ascribe Supremacy to God the Father only; and how the several Parts of it may be interpreted in a Sense, so as not to be repugnant to each other. (1–2)

Sounding remarkably like Cockburn, whom she had read just the year before, Carter makes similar claims about the primacy of personal agency (reasoning) in matters of practical religion.[571] She assures the reader and her opponent that, though she is 'sincerely attached to the Church of *England*', she bases it upon 'the Right of private Judgement, and the Principle, that the holy Scriptures are the only Rule of necessary Faith' (3). As McDonnell makes clear, private judgement, particularly if it is outside academe, is suspect. Carter then proceeds to show her intellectual credentials by listing the various inconsistencies between Church creeds and scripture, drawing on her knowledge of Hebrew and Biblical history in the process. Paramount in her argument is the importance of scripture and the exercise of reason rather than inflammatory rhetoric in the discussion of points of faith.

> Whatever Veneration you, or which is more, the Church, has for this Confession of Faith, neither the Church, nor you I suppose, pretend to equal its Authority with that of the holy Scriptures. A Christian then may be allowed to have some Doubts and Difficulties concerning it, without immediately deserving Censure. And it will always be much more to a Clergyman's Credit, as it is agreeable to his Office, as well as to the Benevolence of the Gospel, to endeavour, in the Spirit of Meekness, to satisfy such Doubts, and clear away such Difficulties, than it is to run eagerly into unbecoming Reflections, abusive Language, and open, or secret Persecution. (3–4)

As in Cockburn's letters to Thomas Burnet of Kemnay, Carter stresses the lack of benevolence in her opponent's discourse and highlights the semantic problems which undermine his arguments, not just in the terms of his abusive language, but in the creed itself.

Carter's single, but reiterated point throughout the letter is the dogmatic and illogical theology of the creed in comparison to the clear tenets of the New Testament. She cites the creed's numerous phrases which show that the Father, the Son, and the Holy Ghost are three distinct persons, and argues that its insistence on their unity is irreconcilable with scripture, common sense, or reason.

> But if you think another Sense, which leaves Supremacy to God the Father, may fairly be put upon these Clauses, you will do an acceptable Service, if you can clearly point it out, and demonstrate by what Rules of Grammar, and Examples in the Use of Words, such other Sense may well be understood to be the Intent of them. And should you Sir, who are a Scholar, find Difficulties in this Attempt, then I must again, and again beseech you to give Us a clear Insight into the Prudence, the Benefit, and the godly Simplicity of your so eagerly insisting upon the Use of a Creed, which, upon this Supposition, is to the far greater Number of those who are ordered to repeat it, incomprehensible. (11–12)

The authority and assurance with which Carter states the problem may seem uncharacteristic of this usually modest writer, but she was nothing if not positive about the grounds of her faith. Just as Cockburn originally stayed with the Roman Catholic church because she felt that as long as it 'teaches all necessary truths... it is better to continue in it, than to make a noise in the world with changing' (*Works*, II: 187), so Carter endeavoured to reconcile people to the orthodox faith in an effort to stem further sectarianism in the Anglican Church. However, this did not mean that Anglicans should unquestionably accept what they did not understand or could not reconcile with scripture. Carter writes:

> And let them [i.e. teachers] exert a double Diligence to extirpate the absurd as well as fatal Opinion, that Christians please God by *solemnly* professing to believe, what they understand not, and by censuring, hating, and persecuting others, who in Conscience dare not imitate their Example. Let no Christian contend for Faith in a Manner subversive of Equity, and Charity, and let him not call any Thing Faith, religious Faith, which he is unable to explain, and which he makes Confession of, either for secular Advantages, or in mere Compliance with Custom. (28–9)

In fact, Carter found many of the creeds and articles related to the profession of faith in the Anglican Church problematic and spent time counselling and persuading others of the importance of privileging private faith over public profession. Pennington includes some of these letters in the 'works' section of the *Memoirs* but others remain in manuscript.

One of these manuscript letters, written in 1773 for the benefit of one of Countess Spencer's friends, deals with just the sort of public versus private dilemma evident in the Athanasian controversy. Carter writes:

> By your Ladiships description of her Terrors about receiving the Communion, they do not seem to arise so much from What she meets in the Bible, as from ~~the~~ our church offices, & from the Catechism – Before I go any further give me Leave to premise, that I truly reverence the church of England, & think the Service on the Whole a most Excellent Composition. But all human Compositions are imperfect, & it is from Scripture alone that we are to be determined in those points, Which that alone has made a Duty.[572]

She goes on to counter two points which the correspondent finds problematic; in this case the phrases, 'Eating & drinking Damnation' and a '<u>lively Faith</u> in God's Mercy through Christ'. Carter dismisses the former on the grounds that it was 'very injudiciously inserted into our Communion offices' and the latter because '[t]his Expression does not occur either in our blessed Saviour's Institution, nor in St Paul's Account of it, but is taken from our Church Catechism: therefore she has no need to be alarmed, or discouraged any farther than as it agrees with Reason & Scripture'.[573] Once past these minor quibbles, Carter proceeds to the chief complaint: the ramifications of receiving 'Communion under an <u>absolute</u> <u>disbelief</u> of Christianity, & only out of mere decent External Compliance with popular Custom, & from a wish of recommending her self to the world.'[574] Carter, as we might expect, replies that, 'such a Motive would indeed be unwarrantable, & might be charged as Hypocrisy. But this I hope is by no means a description of her Case.'[575] She continues:

> we will only suppose, that after weighing the Arguments on Each Side, the Result amounts to no more than her finding the proofs for & against so nearly Equal that she cannot determine but ~~ha may be~~ that it may be true. Now in this doubtful State if she complies with the External Duties from a sincere principle, that if the Gospel be indeed a Revelation of the will of God, she is perfectly disposed to submit to it, such a disposition surely cannot subject her to his displeasure. With Regard to the Sacrament in particular, if she commemorates

the death of Jesus Christ with such sentiments of piety, that if he is in Reality the Son of God, & appointed by Him to be the Saviour & Redeemer of the world she willingly consents to receive Him as such, & thankfully accepts of that new & gracious covenant of pardon & Salvation ratified in his Blood: & if she performs this, & all other External Means in the Hope of receiving Assistance & Confirmation, if Christianity should prove to be the Truth, - surely there can be nothing like Hypocrisy, or profanation in such Dispositions as these.[576]

Similar in thesis to Pascal's gaming wager, Carter's advice assumes a propensity to belief and builds on this foundation by constructing an image of how her correspondent's external compliance, given the right degree of sincerity, may be sympathised with by the Almighty. Moreover, Carter suggests that the internal monitor/spectator is the real theatre of action and carefully recommends the heart and not the mind as the most efficacious actor in seeking divine assistance.

When there has been a long Habit of doubting, it is very difficult to regain the power of decision: & therefore instead of Combating her doubts, she should use her utmost endeavours to stifle them, & apply her Thoughts only to the positive proofs. Above all, you can tell her, for you know & feel it, that christianity is infinitely more concerned in the Heart than in the Head. If by carefully examining the Gospel she cultivates those internal sentiments of piety, & endeavours to keep up that perpetual Intercourse between God & her Soul which it every where prescribes, there is no Doubt but she will receive all the Instruction she needs. – It cannot I am sure, to you, be necessary for me to vindicate my self from any enthusiastic Meaning in any Expression I have used. Upon no principle of true Religion can a constant Reference of all our Thoughts Words & Actions (so far as human Infirmity will allow) to that Being to whom we are accountable for them, be liable to such a charge.[577]

The benevolent flow of affections between God and self reclaims one to the theatre of happiness in Carter's optimistic paradigm. Of course, she distances herself from the potentially enthusiastic connotations her language suggests, but nevertheless resolutely attests to the importance of such an 'intercourse' in overcoming worldly doubt. In her mind the struggle of the faithful was a private one and, whilst an exemplary life could convince society of the eudaemonic benefits of virtue and piety, the final point of reference was always meant to be personal: 'the human mind, at once the theatre and spectator of the wonders of the Omnipotence'.[578]

In her *Remarks on the Athanasian Creed* and letters to the countess, Carter's expressed belief in Godly supremacy does not mean that her adherence to this particular hierarchical paradigm translated into an unquestioning acceptance of the socio-religious forms of a patriarchal church; indeed, it patently contradicted them. The direct access which Carter maintains the pious may enjoy with God is not just a palliative to help one overcome doubt, it is concerned with advocating and instilling a sense of personal agency. In her work on the confluences between Wollstonecraft's feminist politics and her religious beliefs, Barbara Taylor identifies this trend regarding the religious imperative in women's writing as part of the 'cult of feminine sensibility': where 'preachers of all stripes could be heard arguing that female religious feeling was intrinsically more powerful than that of men: a view reinforced by the idealization of pity as the primary Christian sentiment'.[579] Carter, in her own work, tries to downplay the enthusiastic element of such an argument, and certainly would not have identified her affectionate approach to religious doctrine as, in Taylor's terms, 'one of the founding impulses of feminism'.[580]

Carter was not a feminist, but her individualistic spirit and the purposefulness of her legacy meant that she became an enabling example for later feminist writers. It is, of course, a shame that Carter's work did not reach a wider public given her intellectual authority and literary talents. Nevertheless, her personal and reasoned approach to church creeds, ceremonies, and the nature of faith, ensured that an exemplary tradition of female writing was transmitted intact, if still problematic, to the next generation. Virginia Woolf may have claimed that 'Letters [do] not count', but she nevertheless noted that George Eliot should have 'done homage to the robust shade of Eliza Carter – the valiant old woman who tied a bell to her bedstead in order that she might wake early and learn Greek'.[581]

Conclusion

The perpetuation of numerous aspects of Rowe's and Cockburn's material, contextual, and biographical history in certain elements of Carter's career establishes the final link in my chain of female exemplarity; however, the story does not end here. These three graces, or as Gosse would have it, 'phantom like transparences', shared a belief in the efficacy (that is, in order to attain immortality) of a Christian life based on the law of nature learned from the male philosophers of the Enlightenment.[582] This religious and philosophical ethos was given a particularly gendered import by the coterie (epistolary, manuscript, didactic) nature of their literary endeavours and their growing sense of their collective influence. As Guest argues, it was precisely their 'commitment to a life excluded from politics' – in this case, Habermas's public sphere of commodity owners – which reinforced 'the sense in which this group of educated women [here the Bluestockings] define[d] themselves increasingly as a distinctively gendered collective, and not only as members of the educated class'.[583] I have argued that the legacy goes farther back than the Bluestockings, and Taylor shows us its future in Wollstonecraft and Hays; and, though I have only explored the writings of Rowe, Cockburn, and Carter, there are many other intellectual women whose manuscript letters are waiting to be discovered or re-examined.

My focus on manuscript and epistolary communication as formative as well as alternative modes of engaging with the eighteenth-century republic of letters has tended to stress continuity rather than change. Partly this stems from Rowe's and Cockburn's contemporaneousness – they were both functioning within fairly similar patronage and publication traditions – but also because the evidence suggests that despite the 132 years between their births and Carter's death, their practise of literary production and circulation altered very little. In many respects, therefore, these case studies are an effort to understand a particular tradition of women's writing in the context of recent reconsiderations of print's hegemony and progressiveness.[584]

The three case studies have also emphasised similarities in my effort to foreground a tradition of women's writing that is concerned with advocating a social theatre of benevolent action, a rational and religious impulse after moral truths, and a professional ethos of exemplarity. In terms of habits of mind, Rowe, Cockburn, and Carter were all products of an 'Age of Reason'; a period born out of a Reformation focus on rational individualism, self-examination, and, most importantly, faith. They were also intellectuals who readily engaged with the innovatory scientific, epistemological, ontological, and moral theories of the early modern period. Like many of their male contemporaries, therefore, these learned women were forced to incorporate or rethink many traditional modes of thought, whether religious, political, philosophical, or social. They were also part of an influential new class – the middle class, or gentry – which helped to legitimate their public and private gender roles.[585] Though alternately 'conservative' or 'progressive' in their approach to faith, philosophy, class, gender roles, or literary production, these women nevertheless embody enlightenment modes of thought and practise that were influential with contemporary and subsequent writers.

It is important to note the existence of patterns and similarities; however, I have also shown the differences amongst these writers of the exemplary tradition. From Rowe's spectral scenes, to Cockburn's controlled stagings, and Carter's social theatre, the sheer variety of genres and discourses with which they engaged has revealed that adherence to manuscript exchange and exemplarity was not, in artistic, intellectual, or moral terms, a constraining mode of practice. The intermittent appearances of Rowe's, Cockburn's, and Carter's print productions have often meant that the exemplary image is seen as an inhibiting construction, but I hope this book has revealed that this is merely a symptom of our own incomplete picture of authorship in the period. Similarly, whilst their male biographers and editors may have delivered encomiastic versions of their 'Lives', and intrusively edited their literary remains, these eighteenth- and nineteenth-century male scholars are important allies in our attempts to reconstruct the varied nature of Rowe's, Cockburn's, and Carter's manuscript writings and literary lives. If it had not been for Montagu Pennington and his like we might never have known about Elizabeth Carter's bell, or, more importantly, never have realised the full scope of her extraordinary life of the mind.

Notes

1. For an overview see Paula Findlen's survey in 'Ideas in the Mind: Gender and Knowledge in the Seventeenth Century', *Hypatia: a journal of feminist philosophy* 17:1 (Winter 2002): 183–96; also Sarah Knott and Barbara Taylor, eds., *Women, Gender and Enlightenment* (Houndmills, Basingstoke: Palgrave Macmillan, 2005); Paula McDowell, 'Consuming Women: The Life of the "Literary Lady" as Popular Culture in Eighteenth-Century England', *Genre* 26 (1993): 219–52; and Susan Staves, *A Literary History of Women's Writing in Britain, 1660–1789* (Cambridge: Cambridge University Press, 2006).
2. Kathryn Sutherland highlights this oversight in 'Editing for a New Century: Elizabeth Elstob's Anglo-Saxon Manifesto and Aelfric's St. Gregory Homily', in *The Editing of Old English: Papers from the 1990 Manchester Conference*, eds. D.G. Scragg and Paul E. Szarmach (Cambridge and Rochester, NY: D.S. Brewer/Boydell and Brewer, 1994), 213–37, and in 'Writings on Education and Conduct: Arguments for Female Improvement', in *Women and Literature in Britain, 1700–1800*, ed. Vivien Jones (Cambridge: Cambridge University Press, 2000). Staves also remarks on the emphasis placed on 'transgressive' writers as opposed to 'the party of virtue' in *A Literary History*, 7 and 9. In addition to the works just cited, excellent assessments of learned and virtuous women can be found in: Paula R. Backscheider, *Eighteenth-Century Women Poets and Their Poetry: Inventing Agency, Inventing Genre* (Baltimore: The Johns Hopkins University Press, 2005); Carol Barash, *English Women's Poetry, 1649–1714: Politics, Community, and Linguistic Authority* (Oxford: Clarendon Press, 1996); Sylvia Bowerbank, *Speaking for Nature: Women and Ecologies of Early Modern England* (Baltimore: The Johns Hopkins University Press, 2004); Norma Clarke, *The Rise and Fall of the Woman of Letters* (Pimlico: London, 2004); Elizabeth Eger, *Bluestockings: Women of Reason from Enlightenment to Romanticism* (Houndmills, Basingstoke: Palgrave Macmillan, 2010); Harriet Guest, *Small Change: Women, Learning, Patriotism, 1750–1810* (Chicago and London: The University of Chicago Press, 2000); Sylvia Harcstark Myers, *The Bluestocking Circle: Women, Friendship, and the Life of the Mind in Eighteenth-Century England* (Oxford: Clarendon Press, 1990); and Karen O'Brien, *Women and Enlightenment in Eighteenth-Century Britain* (Cambridge: Cambridge University Press, 2009).
3. For recent general histories that have begun to flesh out the careers of virtuous women writers see Marilyn L. Williamson, *Raising Their Voices: British Women Writers, 1650–1750* (Detroit: Wayne State University Press, 1990); Paul Salzman, *Reading Early Modern Women's Writing* (Oxford: Oxford University Press, 2006); Betty Schellenberg, *The Professionalization of Women Writers in Eighteenth-Century Britain* (Cambridge: Cambridge University Press, 2005); and, in particular, Susan Staves, *A Literary History*.
4. In the interest of consistency I refer to Elizabeth Singer Rowe as Elizabeth Rowe and Catharine Trotter Cockburn as Catharine Cockburn.

5. Samuel Johnson, 'Enthusiasm', *A Dictionary of the English Language*, 2 vols (London, 1755) For a history, see R.A. Knox, *Enthusiasm: A Chapter in the History of Religion* (Oxford: Clarendon Press, 1950).
6. Shaun Irlam, *Elations: The Poetics of Enthusiasm in Eighteenth-Century Britain* (Stanford: Stanford University Press, 1999), 5–6. See also Jon Mee, *Romanticism, Enthusiasm, and Regulation: Poetics and the Policing of Culture in the Romantic Period* (Oxford: Oxford University Press, 2003).
7. Irlam, 7.
8. Elizabeth Clarke, 'The Perdita Project Catalogue 1997–2007', Perdita Manuscripts, 1500–1700. Available at: http://www.perditamanuscripts.amdigital.co.uk/Introduction/Content/EssayContent.aspx [accessed 23 April 2012]. Access to this valuable digital archive is by subscription. The catalogue currently stretches to 1723, but only includes letters if they are part of a larger text such as a letterbook. Only one letterbook, Mary Evelyn's, is listed.
9. Catherine Talbot, BL Add. MS 46688, f.22r.
10. Ibid., f.27r.
11. She goes on to say that she will show the original letter to Berkeley.
12. Susan Staves, 'Church of England Clergy and Women Writers', in *Reconsidering the Bluestockings*, ed. by Nicole Pohl and Betty A. Schellenberg (San Marino: Huntington Library, 2003), 81–103. (Also published as vol. 65, nos. 1 and 2 of the *Huntington Library Quarterly*.)
13. Jennifer Summit, *Lost Property: The Woman Writer and English Literary History, 1380–1589* (Chicago and London: University of Chicago Press, 2000) and Margaret Ezell, *Writing Women's Literary History* (Baltimore and London: The Johns Hopkins University Press, 1993), especially 66–103.
14. Ezell, *Writing*, 15.
15. Staves, *A Literary History*, 4.
16. Margaret Ezell, *The Patriarch's Wife: Literary Evidence and the History of the Family* (Chapel Hill and London: University of North Carolina Press, 1987), 62.
17. Ezell, *Writing*, 6. Elaine Showalter, *A Literature of their Own: British Women Novelists from Brontë to Lessing* (Princeton: Princeton University Press, 1977) and Sandra M. Gilbert and Susan Gubar, *The Madwoman in the Attic: The Woman Writer and the Nineteenth-Century Literary Imagination* (New Haven: Yale University Press, 1979).
18. Ezell, *Writing*, 15.
19. Ibid., 25.
20. Ibid., 26, 27.
21. Ibid., 27.
22. Ezell observes that, 'Katherine Philips's appeal is rather diminished when Pearson declares that she was one of the few women "fortunate enough to find favour with the male establishment. ... She led a blameless life, avoided risqué subjects, did not explicitly question conventional notions of women, and above all did not seek for publication. Consequently she... seemed unthreatening to men and thus retained their respect." In this presentation, however, she loses ours', 27.
23. Staves, *A Literary History*, 7.
24. McDowell, 'Consuming Women', 235.
25. Virginia Woolf, *A Room of One's Own* (London: Hogarth Press, 1929). Woolf is misleading in her polemical opening chapters; she claims that, were she to try

to talk about women and fiction, her only reference points would be Burney, Austen, the Brontës, Mitford, Eliot, and Gaskell (5). In chapter two, she writes that she cannot locate any books about women *writers* in the British Museum (40), nor find women who wrote in the Elizabethan age or the seventeenth century (62). She contradicts her own evidence, however, by revealing an awareness of Finch, Cavendish, Osbourne, Behn, and even Carter (88–98). Melinda Alliker Rabb refers to Woolf's 'now-discredited assumptions' about seventeenth-century women writers in 'The Work of Women in the Age of Electronic Reproduction: The Canon, Early Modern Women Writers and the Postmodern Reader' *A Companion to Early Modern Women's Writing*, ed. Anita Pacheco (Oxford: Blackwell Publishing, 2002), 348.

26. Marilyn Williamson, in *Raising Their Voices: British Women Writers, 1650–1750* (Detroit: Wayne State University Press, 1990), argues that 'Orinda was a better model for other women writers than she was a creative artist,' 78.

27. There has been a facsimile reprint of her earliest volume of poems by Ashgate (2003); she appears in Paula Backscheider's and John J. Richetti's anthology, *Popular Fiction by Women, 1660–1730: An Anthology* (Oxford: Oxford University Press,1996); important scholars of early modern and eighteenth-century women's writing, including Sharon Achinstein, Paula Backscheider, E.J. Clery, Kathryn King, Sarah Prescott, and Susan Staves, among others, have published articles and chapters on her. See Sharon Achinstein, 'Romance of the Spirit: Female Sexuality and Religious Desire in Early Modern England', *English Literary History* 69:2 (Summer 2002), 413–38; Paula R. Backscheider, *Eighteenth-Century Women Poets and Their Poetry: Inventing Agency, Inventing Genre* (Baltimore: The Johns Hopkins University Press, 2005); Norma Clarke, 'Soft Passions and Darling Themes: from Elizabeth Singer Rowe (1674–1737) to Elizabeth Carter (1717–1806)', *Women's Writing* 7:3 (2000), pp. 353–71; E.J. Clery, *The Feminization Debate in Eighteenth-Century England: Literature, Commerce and Luxury* (Houndmills, Basingstoke and New York: Palgrave Macmillan, 2004); Stuart Curran, 'Romantic Women Poets: Inscribing the Self', in *Women's Poetry in the Enlightenment: The Making of a Canon, 1730–1820*. Eds. Isobel Armstrong and Virginia Blain (London: Macmillan Press Ltd., 1999), pp. 145–66; Robert Adams Day, *Told in Letters: Epistolary Fiction Before Richardson* (Ann Arbor: The University of Michigan Press, 1966); Marlene R. Hansen, 'The Pious Mrs. Rowe', *English Studies* 76:1 (1995), 34–51; Kathryn King, 'Elizabeth Singer Rowe's Tactical Use of Print and Manuscript', in *Women's Writing and the Circulation of Ideas: Manuscript Publication in England, 1550–1800*. Eds. George L. Justice and Nathan Tinker (Cambridge: Cambridge University Press, 2002), pp. 158–81; Sarah Prescott, 'Provincial Networks, Dissenting Connections, and Noble Friends: Elizabeth Singer Rowe and Female Authorship in Early Eighteenth-Century England', *Eighteenth Century Life* 25:1 (Winter 2001), 29–42 and *Women, Authorship and Literary Culture, 1690–1740* (Basingstoke, Hampshire and New York: Palgrave Macmillan, 2003); John J. Richetti, 'Mrs. Elizabeth Rowe: The Novel as Polemic', *PMLA* 82:7 (December 1967), 522–9; and Susan Staves, *A Literary History* (2006).

28. King, 'Elizabeth Singer Rowe's Tactical Use of Print and Manuscript', pp. 158–81.

29. Cockburn's dramatic works have fared respectably – in addition to a smattering of articles, Fidelis Morgan's reintroduction of her as one of *The Female Wits* (1981) has given way to more recent anthologisation in *The Broadview Press Anthology of Restoration and Early Eighteenth-Century Drama* (2001). See Paula Backscheider, 'Stretching the Form: Catharine Trotter Cockburn and Other Failures', *Theatre Journal* 47:4 (December 1995): 443–58; Heather King, '"Be Mistress of Your Self, and Firm to Virtue": Female Friendship in Catharine Trotter's *The Unhappy Penitent* (1701)', *Eighteenth-Century Women: Studies in their Lives, Work, and Culture*, ed. Linda V. Troost, vol. 3 (November 2003): 1–23; and Susan Staves, *A Literary History* (2006). On the philosophy front, Victor Nuovo, Martha Brandt Bolton, Jacqueline Broad, Karen O'Brien, and others have given sustained attention to Cockburn's interventions in English Enlightenment thought. See also Sherry O'Donnell, 'Mr Locke and the Ladies: The Indelible Words on the Tabula Rasa', *Studies in Eighteenth Century Culture* 8 (1978): 151–64; Eileen O'Neill, 'Disappearing Ink: Early Modern Women Philosophers and their Fate in History', *Philosophy in a Feminist Voice: Critiques and Reconstructions*, ed. Janet A. Kourany (Princeton: Princeton University Press, 1998), pp. 17–62; Kathryn J. Ready, 'Damaris Cudworth Masham, Catharine Trotter Cockburn, and the Feminist Legacy of Locke's Theory of Personal Identity', *Eighteenth-Century Studies* 35:4 (2002): 563–76. Selections from Cockburn's defence of Locke appeared in Margaret Atherton's anthology of *Women Philosophers of the Early Modern Period* (1994) and Broadview Press's philosophy section has also recently published an edition of some of Cockburn's philosophical writings (2006). Anne Kelley is the only scholar to have published a monograph on the full range of Cockburn's writings, *Catharine Trotter: An Early Modern Writer in the Vanguard of Feminism* (Aldershot, Hampshire: Ashgate, 2002). As the title suggests, this work privileges a proto-feminist reading – an approach which I argue distorts the contemporary contexts within which Cockburn lived and wrote; however, Kelley's study of Cockburn has established an enabling platform upon which future work can build.

30. In addition to Sylvia Harcstark Myer's important history, *The Bluestocking Circle: Women, Friendship, and the Life of the Mind in Eighteenth-Century England* (Oxford: Clarendon Press, 1990), there is an excellent introduction on Carter from Judith Hawley in, *Bluestocking Feminism: Writings of the Bluestocking Circle, 1738–1785*, gen. ed. Gary Kelly, *Volume II: Elizabeth Carter* (London: Pickering and Chatto, 1999), which, incidentally, makes a point of featuring a number of Carter's letters. The importance of Carter's letters is further confirmed with the appearance of Gwen Hampshire's edition of previously unpublished correspondence, *Elizabeth Carter, 1717–1806: An Edition of Some Unpublished Letters* (Newark: University of Delaware Press, 2005). Critical work on Carter is also growing: see Norma Clarke, *The Rise and Fall of the Woman of Letters*; E.J. Clery, *The Feminization Debate*; Elizabeth Eger, *The Bluestockings*; and Harriet Guest, *Small Change*. Numerous articles on her translations, poetry, letters, and essays are also now in print.

31. Harold Love, *The Culture and Commerce of Texts: Scribal Publication in Seventeenth-Century England* (Oxford: Clarendon Press, 1993, rpt. Amherst: University of Massachusetts Press, 1998); A.F. Marotti, *Manuscript, Print and the English Renaissance Lyric* (Ithaca, NY: Cornell University Press,1995); and

H.R. Woudhuysen's, *Sir Philip Sidney and the Circulation of Manuscripts, 1558–1640* (Oxford: Clarendon Press, 1996).
32. See David Vieth's introduction in *The Complete Poems of John Willmot, Earl of Rochester* (New Haven: Yale University Press, 2002); Stephen Karian, *Jonathan Swift in Print and Manuscript* (Cambridge: Cambridge University Press, 2010); James Sambrook's *ODNB* entry on William Walsh (1662–1708); and Rosemary Sweet, *Antiquaries: The Discovery of the Past in Eighteenth-Century Britain* (London and New York: Hambledon and London, 2004).
33. *Women's Writing and the Circulation of Ideas: Manuscript Publication in England, 1550–1800*, eds. George L. Justice and Nathan Tinker (Cambridge: Cambridge University Press, 2002).
34. Katherine Philips, *Poems* (London, 1667), sig.Av. For an account of the 'pirated' edition, the publisher's notice of withdrawal, and the letters that passed between Philips, Cotterell, and Dorothy Temple about the edition see Patrick Thomas's introduction in *The Collected Works of Katherine Philips, The Matchless Orinda: Volume 1 – The Poems*, ed. Patrick Thomas (Stump Cross, Essex: Stump Cross Books, 1990).
35. Preface to *The Lucky Chance* (1686). See Jeslyn Medoff, 'The Daughters of Behn and the Problem of Reputation', in *Women, Writing, History, 1640–1740*, eds. Isobel Grundy and Susan Wiseman (London: B.T. Batsford Ltd., 1992), 35.
36. See *Paper Bodies: A Margaret Cavendish Reader*, eds. Sylvia Bowerbank and Sara Mendelson (Peterborough: Broadview Press, 2000), 11.
37. Barash, 8.
38. *Works II*, Letter XLV, 29 January 1664, 129.
39. Woudhuysen, 13–14; J.W. Saunders, 'The Stigma of Print: A Note on the Social Bases of Tudor Poetry', *Essays in Criticism*, 1 (1951): 139–64; and, for a contrasting argument, Steven May, 'Tudor Aristocrats and the Mythical "Stigma of Print"', *Renaissance Papers*, 10 (1980): 11–18.
40. Saunders, 141.
41. Ibid., 142.
42. Woudhuysen, 13–14.
43. Margaret Ezell, *Social Authorship and the Advent of Print* (Baltimore and London: The Johns Hopkins University Press, 1999), 7.
44. Ibid., 12.
45. Ezell, *Patriarch's Wife*, 70. See also Love's exploration of male writers and scribal publishing in *The Culture and Commerce of Texts*.
46. Ezell, *Patriarch's Wife*, 99.
47. King, 'Elizabeth Singer Rowe's Tactical Use of Print and Manuscript'.
48. Eve Tavor Bannet, *Empire of Letters: Letter Manuals and Transatlantic Correspondence, 1688–1820* (Cambridge: Cambridge University Press, 2005) and Clare Brant, *Eighteenth-Century Letters and British Culture* (Houndmills: Palgrave Macmillan, 2006). Brant refers to her study as 'cultural poetics' rather than 'cultural history', p. 3.
49. Bannet, *Empire of Letters*, from the dustjacket.
50. Bannet mines British, Scottish, and American letter manuals for their textual differences.
51. Brant, *Eighteenth-Century Letters*, 1.
52. For example, the conversational trope or Samuel Richardson's famous writing-to-the-moment.

53. Clare Brant, 'Varieties of Women's Writing', in *Women and Literature in Britain, 1700–1800*, ed. Vivien Jones (Cambridge: Cambridge University Press, 2000), 285–305, 285.
54. Staves, *A Literary History*, 4.
55. Bruce Redford, *The Converse of the Pen: Acts of Intimacy in the Eighteenth-Century Familiar Letter* (London: University of Chicago Press, 1986) and Cynthia Lowenthal, *Lady Mary Wortley Montagu and the Eighteenth-Century Letter* (Athens, GA: University of Georgia Press, 1994).
56. See Howard Anderson, Philip B. Daghlian, Irvin Ehrenpreis, eds., *The Familiar Letter in the Eighteenth Century* (Lawrence: University of Kansas Press, 1966); Cynthia Lowenthal, *Lady Mary* (1994); Bruce Redford, *Converse of the Pen* (1986); and Keith Stewart, 'Towards Defining an Aesthetic for the Familiar Letter in the Eighteenth Century', *Prose Studies* 5 (1982): 179–89. For a more theoretical discussion of the fictional aspects of the form see Janet Gurkin Altman, *Epistolarity: Approaches to a Form* (Columbus: Ohio State University Press, 1982).
57. Redford, 2.
58. David Marshall, *The Figure of Theater: Shaftesbury, Defoe, Adam Smith, and George Eliot* (New York: Columbia University Press, 1986).
59. Brian Southam quoting Kathryn Sutherland, '*Mansfield Park* – What did Jane Austen Really Write? The Texts of 1814 and 1816', in *British Women's Writing in the Long Eighteenth Century: Authorship, Politics and History*, eds. Jennie Batchelor and Cora Kaplan (London: Palgrave Macmillan, 2005), 88–104, 90.
60. Jane Stevenson, 'Still Kissing the Rod? Whither Next?', *Women's Writing*, 14:2 (August 2007): 290–305, 291.
61. Ibid., 290.
62. See also M. Bigold, 'Letters and Learning', in *The History of British Women's Writing, 1690–1750*, ed. Ros Ballaster (Houndmills, Basingstoke: Palgrave Macmillan, 2010), 173–86.
63. Knott and Taylor, xvii.
64. Ibid., xvi–xvii.
65. Dena Goodman, 'Letter Writing and the Emergence of Gendered Subjectivity in Eighteenth-Century France', *Journal of Women's History*, 17.2 (2005): 9–37, 11. See also Anne Goldgar, *Impolite Learning: Conduct and Community in the Republic of Letters, 1680–1750* (New Haven and London: Yale University Press, 1995).
66. Clifford Siskin, *The Work of Writing: Literature and Social Change in Britain, 1700–1830* (London: The Johns Hopkins University Press, 1998), 5–6.
67. Thomas Birch, *History of the Works of the Learned*, Art. XXXI (1 June 1739), 392.
68. For an excellent study of the political aspect of the republic of letters see Dena Goodman's *The Republic of Letters: A Cultural History of the French Enlightenment* (Ithaca and London: Cornell University Press, 1994).
69. Stevenson, 292.
70. O'Brien, 1–2.
71. Sarah Prescott, 'The Debt to Pleasure: Eliza Haywood's *Love in Excess* and women's fiction of the 1720s', *Women's Writing* 7:3 (2000), 427–45.
72. Sharon Achinstein, 'Romance of the Spirit: Female Sexuality and Religious Desire in Early Modern England', *English Literary History* 69:2 (2002), 413–38.

73. Sarah Prescott, *Women, Authorship and Literary Culture, 1690–1740* (Basingstoke, Hampshire and New York: Palgrave Macmillan, 2003), 165. See also Sharon Achinstein, 'The Politics and Aesthetics of Dissent', *The History of British Women's Writing, 1690–1750*, ed. Ros Ballaster (Houndmills: Palgrave Macmillan, 2010), 81–95, and '"Pleasure by Description": Elizabeth Singer Rowe's Enlightened Milton', in *Milton and the Grounds of Contention*, ed. Mark R. Kelley, Michael Lieb, and John T. Shawcross (Pittsburgh: Duquesne University Press, 2003); Peter Walmsley, 'Whigs in Heaven: Elizabeth Rowe's Friendship in Death', *Eighteenth-Century Studies* 44:3 (Spring 2011): 315–30.
74. Prescott, *Women, Authorship and Literary Culture*, 148. Rowe's poems appeared in *The Athenian Mercury* between 1693 and 1696.
75. The third edition of *Friendship in Death: in Twenty Letters from the Dead to the Living. To which are added, Letters Moral and Entertaining, in Prose and Verse. In Three Parts. By the same Author.* 3rd edn (1733) was the first time all three parts were published together.
76. Henry F. Stecher, *Elizabeth Singer Rowe, the Poetess of Frome: A Study in Eighteenth-Century Pietism* (Frankfurt: Peter Lang, 1973), 14.
77. Rowe's poem, 'Upon the death of her husband' is a notable exception. Written between 1715 and 1717, the poem was reprinted throughout the eighteenth and nineteenth centuries. The composition dates of many of her other works are unknown and there is reason to believe that a number of the poems and fictional letters were written long before they appeared in print.
78. Later called the first part of *LME*. When referencing part one, I have relied on the first edition throughout. Hereafter cited as *Letters* (1729).
79. The last two books were added at the Countess of Hertford's request.
80. Editions of the combined letters were printed almost every year from 1733 to 1818, with only a few gaps of two or three years later in the century.
81. An excellent source on the manuscript evidence is Kathryn King, 'Elizabeth Singer Rowe's Tactical Use of Print and Manuscript'.
82. Jeremy Gregory, 'Secker, Thomas (1693–1768)', in *Oxford Dictionary of National Biography*, ed. H.C.G. Matthew and Brian Harrison (Oxford: Oxford University Press, 2004); online edition, ed. Lawrence Goldman, May 2008, http://www.oxforddnb.com/view/article/24998 (accessed 2 July 2009). Secker was educated at a dissenting academy but later conformed to the Church of England, and eventually rose to the position of Archbishop of Canterbury.
83. H. Bunker Wright, 'Matthew Prior and Elizabeth Singer', *Philological Quarterly* 24:4 (October 1945): 71–82.
84. *Ibid.*, 76. The letter is dated 16 November 1703.
85. Staves, *A Literary History* 128.
86. J.F. Maclear, 'Isaac Watts and the Idea of Public Religion', *Journal of the History of Ideas* 53:1 (1992): 25–45, 25.
87. MS 110, Letter 68, f. 174: 'I read Mr Watts Sermons with sincere Delight, but I did not Commend them to you for fear you shou'd think me more partial to the Dissenters then I realy [sic] am.'
88. MS 110, Letter 97, f. 234, and *MW*, II:134.
89. Knox, 1.
90. *Devout*, iv and 13–14.

91. Stecher, 200. Madeleine Forell Marshall agrees, arguing that the work of Watts and Rowe evidences '[t]he influence of German piety and poetry on English hymnody', 2. See, 'Teaching the Uncanonized: The Examples of Watts and Rowe', in *Teaching Eighteenth-century Poetry*, ed. Christopher Fox (New York: AMS Press, 1990), 1–24.
92. Stecher, 208, and H. N. Fairchild, *Religious Trends in English Poetry*, 2 vols. *Volume II: 1740–1780, Religious Sentimentalism in the Age of Johnson* (New York: Columbia University Press, 1942), 198.
93. Despite my focus on letters, it is important to note that Rowe's poetry, particularly her long poem, *The History of Joseph*, and her devotional text, *Devout Exercises*, went through multiple editions and were extremely popular into the nineteenth century. *Devout Exercises* also has interesting manuscript origins (see Chapter 2).
94. Notable exceptions from the early modern period to the nineteenth century include: Jane Couchman and Ann Crabb (eds), *Women's Letters Across Europe, 1400–1700* (Aldershot: Ashgate, 2005); Julie D. Campbell and Anne R. Larsen (eds), *Early Modern Women and the Transnational Communities of Letters* (Farnham: Ashgate, 2009); James Daybell, *Women Letter-Writers in Tudor England* (Oxford: Oxford University Press, 2005) and (ed.), *Early Modern Women's Letter Writing, 1450–1700* (Basingstoke: Palgrave, 2001); Rosemarie Bodenheimer, *The Real Life of Mary Ann Evans: George Eliot, Her Letters and Fiction* (Ithaca and London: Cornell University Press, 1994); and, for the eighteenth century, Brant, *Eighteenth-Century Letters* and Clarke, *Rise and Fall of the Woman of Letters*.
95. See Nancy Armstrong, *Desire and Domestic Fiction: A Political History of the Novel* (New York and Oxford: Oxford University Press, 1987); Robert Adams Day, *Told in Letters: Epistolary Fiction Before Richardson* (Ann Arbor: The University of Michigan Press, 1966); J. Paul Hunter, *Before Novels: the Cultural Contexts of Eighteenth-Century English Fiction* (New York and London: W.W. Norton, 1990); Ruth Perry, *Women, Letters, and the Novel* (New York: AMS Press, 1980); John Richetti, *Popular Fiction Before Richardson: Narrative Patterns, 1700–1739* (Oxford: Clarendon Press, 1969; rpt. 1992); Jane Spencer, *The Rise of the Woman Novelist: From Aphra Behn to Jane Austen* (Oxford: Blackwell, 1986); Cheryl Turner, *Living by the Pen: Women Writers in the Eighteenth Century* (London: Routledge, 1992); and William Warner, *Licensing Entertainment: The Elevation of Novel Reading in Britain, 1684–1750* (Berkeley, Los Angeles and London: University of California Press, 1998).
96. King notes the lack of work on the letters, 177n. 13.
97. See King, 177n. 13 and Prescott, *Women, Authorship and Literary Culture*, 174.
98. BL Add. MS 46688 (Catherine Talbot's journal), f. 8–37r (f. 22, 9 November 1753, and f. 27, 22 November 1753).
99. See MS 110, Letter 86, f. 213.
100. The countess clearly profited from Rowe's influence. For instance, her poem, '[To the Countess of Pomfret: Life at Richkings]' (1740), was circulated in a letter to her correspondent and offers a portrait of retirement where the domestic, the pious, and the intellectual easily cohabit. In Roger Lonsdale (ed.), *Eighteenth-century Women Poets: An Oxford Anthology* (Oxford: Oxford University Press, 1989), 109.
101. Ezell, *The Patriarch's Wife*, 70.

102. Germaine Greer, *Slip-Shod Sybils: Recognition, Rejection and the Woman Poet* (London: Viking, 1995), 51 quoted in Chantal Lavoie, *Collecting Women: Poetry and Lives, 1700–1780* (Lewisburg: Bucknell University Press, 2011), 44.
103. Marie De Rabutin Chantal, Marquise De Sévigné (1626–96). Her letters circulated in manuscript as early as 1673; they appeared in print in Roger de Rabutin, comte de Bussy's, *Les Memoires de Messire Roger de Rabutin, comte de Bussy* (Paris, 1696); and first appeared in an English translation in 1727 (*Letters of Madame de Rabutin Chantal, Marchioness de Sevigné* [sic], 2 vols).
104. Mary (Thynne) 'Aunt Howe', wife of Sir Richard Howe, Bt. The Howes employed Robert Dodsley when he was still a footman. He wrote three poems commemorating one of Hertford's visits, see 'Verses Occasioned by A Visit expected from the Right Honourable the Countess of Hartford, to the Honourable Lady Howe, at *Compton*, in *Gloucestershire*', in *A Muse in Livery* (1732), 34–8.
105. Unidentified.
106. For the full poems see Patrick Thomas (ed.), *Collected Works of Katherine Philips*, I: 159–62 and I: 145–7 respectively.
107. Mary, Lady Brooke (née Thynne, d.1720), married William Greville, 7th Baron Brooke, and was Frances Thynne's younger sister.
108. Uncertain readings are included in small braces: { }. See also Letter 54, f. 151, Letter 56, ff. 153–64, Letter 67, f. 170, and Letter 71, f. 178.
109. Rowe wrote to Hertford that her 'Character of Henry in the Pastoral suited so well to Lucius that I added it to that Letter I have not Shown it to any Mortal But if I should Hear it so much admir'd as Rosella was I shou'd have ^had a great temptation to do y^u justice', MS 110, Letter 130, 6 September 1732, f. 314r. This suggests that Hertford contributed the sequel to the Rosella story in Part II, Letter XII, and the paragraph on the character of Lucius in Part III, Letter II.
110. *Letters* (1729), Letter I, 139. Cf. MS 110, Letter 58, ff. 156–8.
111. Thomas Tickell, *A poem, to His Excellency the Lord Privy-Seal, on the prospect of peace* (London, 1713). The poem was published in October of 1712, the pamphlet is dated 1713.
112. MS 110, Letter 67, f. 170.
113. Goldgar, 102.
114. For a comprehensive examination of the philosophical and religious debates which informed contemporary literature, and the print histories of such productions, see Isabel Rivers, *Reason, Grace, and Sentiment: A Study of the Language of Religion and Ethics in England, 1660–1780. Volume I Whichcote to Wesley* (Cambridge: Cambridge University Press, 1991) and *Volume II Shaftesbury to Hume* (Cambridge: Cambridge University Press, 2000). Hereafter cited as *RGS* I and II.
115. The Countess of Warwick's biography is likely that of Mary Rich (1624–1678); it included a funeral sermon by Anthony Walker and was entitled, *Eureka, eureka. The virtuous woman found, her loss bewailed, and character examined in a sermon preached at Felsted in Essex, April 30, 1678, at the funeral of ... Mary, countess dowager of Warwick, the most illustrious pattern of a sincere piety, and solid goodness his age hath produced* (1678). Rivet's biography is *The last houers, of the right reverend Father in God Andrew Rivet.... Faithfully collected translated* [sic] *by G. L.* (Hague: Samuel Broun, 1652). Rivet was

a Dutch divine who tutored Prince William of Orange and also corresponded with Dorothy Durie on women's role in the protestant church. See M. Greengrass, 'Durie [King], Dorothy (c.1613–1664)', in *Oxford Dictionary of National Biography*, ed. H. C. G. Matthew and Brian Harrison (Oxford: Oxford University Press, 2004); online edn, ed. Lawrence Goldman, October 2007, http://www.oxforddnb.com/view/article/55437 (accessed 13 July 2009).
116. MS 110, Letter 63, f. 166.
117. I am assuming that Theophilus is using 'natural' to mean both innate and unreflective. See the first entry in the *OED*: '1. Existing or present by nature; inherent in the very constitution of a person or thing; innate; not acquired or assumed.'
118. Isabel Rivers, *RGS*, II:15 and 'Shaftesburian Enthusiasm and the Evangelical Revival', in *Revival and Religion Since 1700: Essays for John Walsh*, eds. Jane Garnett and Colin Matthew (London and Rio Grande: The Hambledon Press, 1993), 21–39, 29.
119. *MW*, II: 266–71.
120. Mee, 54. See note 6.
121. Anthony Ashley Cooper, third Earl of Shaftesbury, *Characteristicks*, 2nd edn rev., 3 vols (1714), II: 344–5.
122. Rivers, 'Shaftesburian Enthusiasm', 21–3.
123. Stecher makes a similar point when he observes that, 'Like Shaftesbury, Elizabeth felt herself able to commune with the spirit of divinity in and through nature. She too enjoyed philosophizing in solitude and manifested an ecstatic appreciation for natural beauty', 29.
124. MS 110 contains, 'An Epistle from Lady Jane Grey To Lord Guilford Dudley suppos'd to be written the night before Their Execution', ff. 91–3; 'To Mr Prior on reading his Solomon', f. 93; and 'A Poem ocasion'd [sic] by reading a Discourse of Lord Shaftsbury's Call'd the Moralist', ff. 94–5.
125. For the recycled lines see MS 110, Letter 13, f. 64: '[A]s there are no Shades in these Desolate Regions, of greater Consequence than my self nothing happens remarkable enough to bear a recital; when I was alive I never was very fond of talking of my self But being the greatest novelty in this place I am now forc'd upon the Subject for want of som'thing more considerable.'
126. Marshall, 1.
127. *RGS*, II: 115.
128. John Barker, *Strange Contrarieties: Pascal in England during the Age of Reason* (Montreal and London: McGill-Queen's University Press, 1975), 196.
129. Ibid., ix.
130. Ibid., 36.
131. Ibid., 20 and 13. He also notes the interest in Pascal amongst seventeenth-century nonconformists such as Andrew Baxter and Samuel Clarke, 14–15.
132. Ibid., 114.
133. Ibid., 259, n. 20.
134. Ibid., 80 and 82.
135. Insertions in square brackets are the words and letters changed from the 1678 *Pensées*. Blaise Pascal, *Pensées De M. Pascal Sur La Religion et Sur Quelques Autres Sujets, Qui ont esté trouvées après sa mort parmy ses papiers. Nouvelle Edition, Augmentée de plusiers pensées du mesme Autheur* (Paris,

1678), 6. The underscored passage is in the Bodleian copy, Shelfmark Vet. E3. f.305 (1).
136. The translation is from Basil Kennet, *Thoughts on Religion, and other Curious Subjects. Written Originally in French By Monsieur Pascal. Translated into English by Basil Kennet, D.D.* 2nd edn (1727), 5–6.
137. Barker, 51–2, 106, 128.
138. Ros Ballaster notes that men, not women, were the principal purchasers of amatory works in the period. *Seductive Forms: Women's Amatory Fiction from 1684–1740* (Oxford: Clarendon Press, 1992), 41.
139. Barker, 196.
140. Cf. *MW*, Letter XXVIII, II: 68–9.
141. Kennet, 190.
142. Pascal, *Pensées*, 199.
143. Kennet, 192–3.
144. Nancy Sherman, *The Fabric of Character: Aristotle's Theory of Virtue* (Oxford: Clarendon Press, 1989).
145. Ibid., 3.
146. MS 110, Letter 13, f. 64.
147. See MS 110, Letter 82, f. 196 in which she states that Letter XIV in *Friendship* puts her in mind of Lady Brooke – the countess's recently deceased sister.
148. Brian Young, 'Theological Books from *The Naked Gospel* to *Nemesis of Faith*', in *Books and their Readers in Eighteenth-Century England: New Essays*, ed. Isabel Rivers (Leicester: Leicester University Press, 2001), 79–104.
149. I am referring to the title of Ballaster's book, *Seductive Forms*. See Prescott, 'The Debt to Pleasure', on Rowe's similarities with amatory novelists.
150. MS 110, Letter 13 (c. 1717), f. 64.
151. See, for example, MS 110 Letter 24, f. 86; Letter 54, f. 151; Letter 56, f. 164; and Letter 67, f. 170.
152. William Law, *A Serious Call to a Devout and Holy Life* (1729), 33–4.
153. Cf. *Letters* (1729), 158–61.
154. *Friendship* contains three poetic excerpts and one prose, and the three parts of *LME* contain 72 poetic and prose excerpts from various authors, plus 15 original poems from Rowe.
155. For other instances of Rowe introducing verse, see Letter IX, 35 and Letter XX, 64.
156. Samuel Johnson, *A Dictionary of the English Language*, 2 vols. (1755), s.v. 'Enthusiasm'.
157. James Boswell, *The Life of Samuel Johnson*, ed. George Birkbeck Hill, rev. edn L.F. Powell, 6 vols (Oxford: Clarendon Press, 1934), I: 312.
158. Ibid., I: 312.
159. Rowe was forced to express this opinion because she was refusing, yet again, to leave Frome and visit the countess at Marlborough.
160. See Prescott, 'The Debt to Pleasure', 436–42.
161. This letter appears indebted, in theme and tone, to Pope's *Eloisa to Abelard* (1720) and to *Five Love-Letters from a Nun to a Cavalier* (1678), which was very popular throughout the eighteenth century. On *Five Love-Letters*, see Ballaster, *Seductive Forms*, 62–6 and 100–13.
162. Richard Rambuss, *Closet Devotions* (Durham and London: Duke University Press, 1998), 2.

163. Wesley was, of course, a Church of England clergyman.
164. Information kindly communicated by Isabel Rivers.
165. For discussions of the discourse of enthusiasm and nonconformism in both fictional and non-fictional works see Clement Hawes, *Mania and Literary Style: the Rhetoric of Enthusiasm: From the Ranters to Christopher Smart* (Cambridge: Cambridge University Press, 1996); Mee; and Rivers, *RGS* I and II.
166. Barbauld, however, did not distance herself from Rowe's life.
167. *GM* (March 1737), 188. The *GM* always appeared the month following, thus March 1737 would have been issued in April.
168. *GM* (March 1737), 183.
169. There would be at least three more attempts in print, in *GM* (March 1739), in Rowe's *MW* (1739), and in her own *Poems on Several Occasions* (1762).
170. *GM* (May 1739), 261. Norma Clarke attributes the abridged life to Carter in *The Rise and Fall of the Woman of Letters*, 79.
171. Theophilus excises almost all references and letters to himself when he prints Rowe's letters.
172. Margaret Ezell, 'The Posthumous Publication of Women's Manuscripts and the History of Authorship', in *Women's Writing and the Circulation of Ideas: Manuscript Publication in England, 1550–1800*, eds. George Justice and Nathan Tinker (Cambridge: Cambridge University Press, 2002), 121–36, 122.
173. Ibid., 124.
174. Mary Kathleen Madigan, 'Forever Yours: The Subgenre of the Letter from the Dead to the Living with Thematic Analyses of the Works of Elizabeth Singer Rowe and Meta Klopstock', PhD Diss. (The University of North Carolina at Chapel Hill, 1988), 2–3.
175. Stecher concurs, noting, 'they contain some of the finest expressions of Mrs. Rowe's personal thoughts on friendship, death, and immortality, and indicate the sincerity and conviction with which she must have composed her other writings on these subjects', 166.
176. *MW*, xxxvii.
177. Samuel Richardson, *Clarissa, or the History of a Young Lady*, ed. Angus Ross (London: Penguin Books, 1985), 1361.
178. Bannet explores compiler's and publisher's aims with regards to letter manuals and their exemplary letters.
179. Mee, 5.
180. See Michael Edson, '"A Closet or a Secret Field": Horace, Protestant Devotion and British Retirement Poetry', *JECS* 35:1 (2012): 17–41, 27.
181. The dedication is entitled, 'To ******* An Intimate Friend of Mrs. ROWE', sig. A2r. Helen Sard Hughes identifies the 'friend' as the countess, p. 354.
182. *RGS*, I:192–3.
183. Isaac Watts, *Reliquiae Juveniles*, 2nd edn (1737), xiii.
184. Mee, 5.
185. Ezell, 'Posthumous Publication', 128.
186. Lavoie, 42.
187. Clare Brant, 'Varieties of Women's Writing', 286.
188. For accusations against Grove's account see Theophilus's note in *MW*, xxix, and Ebenezer Turell, *The Life and Character of the Reverend Benjamin Colman, D.D. late Pastor of a church in Boston New-England* (Boston, 1749), 35–42.

189. Bunker Wright found nine letters from Matthew Prior to Elizabeth Singer in the Prior papers at Longleat; however, Elizabeth's letters have never been found.
190. MS 110, Letter 86, f. 213 and Letter 97, f. 234.
191. See Lavoie for an account of the afterlife of Rowe's life in later anthologies, 40–3.
192. Carter, *GM* 7 (April 1737), 247. All subsequent quotations are from the same issue and page number.
193. Carter, *GM* 9 (March 1739), 152. All subsequent quotations are from the same issue and page number.
194. Norma Clarke also singles out this passage in, 'Soft Passions and Darling Themes: from Elizabeth Singer Rowe (1674–1737) to Elizabeth Carter (1717–1806)', *Women's Writing* 7:3 (2000): 353–71.
195. *Memoirs*, 44.
196. Ibid., 44.
197. Claudia Thomas, '"Th' Instructive and Moral, and Important Thought": Elizabeth Carter Reads Pope, Johnson, and Epictetus', *The Age of Johnson* 4 (1991): 137–69, 152.
198. Hester Chapone, *The Posthumous Works of Mrs. Chapone* (1807), 123–4, London, 31 July 1761.
199. *Memoirs*, 44 and Hawley, xxxi.
200. Cheryl Turner estimates Burney's subscription earnings from *Camilla* at between £2,000 and £3,000, *Living By the Pen: Women Writers in the Eighteenth Century* (London: Routledge, 1992), 108–13.
201. Frances Burney, *Camilla, or A Picture of Youth*, eds. Edward A. Bloom and Lillian D. Bloom (Oxford: Oxford University Press, 1972, reissue 1999), x and 7. Subsequent references to this edition are included in the text.
202. Margaret Anne Doody, *Frances Burney: The Life in the Works* (Cambridge: Cambridge University Press, 1988), 206.
203. Ibid., 214.
204. Doody cites a letter from Burney's sister Esther noting the similarities in the names d'Arblay and Arlbery, 250.
205. Frances Burney, *The Early Journals and Letters of Fanny Burney. Volume 1: 1768–1773*, ed. Lars E. Troide (Oxford: Clarendon Press, 1988), 7–8.
206. The pictorial heritage that had, by this time, attached itself to Rowe's works depicts many scenes similar to the ones Burney describes. See the 1786 (London) edition of *Friendship*. In 1796 and 1797 C. Cooke published editions of *Devout* and *Friendship* embellished with engravings.
207. A previous raffle, in Volume I Book II, was a memorable moment for Edgar and Camilla when he refunded her ticket so that she could help a distressed family.
208. William St Clair, *The Reading Nation in the Romantic Period* (Cambridge: Cambridge University Press, 2004), 137.
209. Editions Imprints appeared in 1738 (5th edition from T. Worrall); 1740, 1741, 1743, 1745, 1746, 1750, 1752, 1753, 1756, 1760, 1762, 1763, 1764 (London?), 1768, 1770, 1774, 1775, 1780, 1783, 1784, 1786 (with engravings), 1790 (possibly York), 1793, 1797 (Cooke's edition with engravings), 1804, and 1818.
210. In 1737 (2nd edition with the full ten books), 1738 (a reissue of the 2nd edition), 1741 (3rd edition), 1742 (Dublin), 1744 (4th edition), 1759, 1760,

1767 (Philadelphia), 1778, 1783 (Glasgow), 1784 (Hartford), and 1807 (Boston). As part of collected editions it appeared in 1750, 1756, 1770 (Edinburgh), 1772, 1795, 1796, and 1820.
211. Ebenezer Turrell, *Memoirs of the life and death of the pious and ingenious Mrs. Jane Turell* [sic] (London, 1741), 5.
212. *Ibid.*, ll. 8–12, p.19. A note indicates that the prophetess referred to is Huldah.
213. *Ibid.*, 21.
214. Anna Aikin Barbauld, 'Verse on Mrs. Rowe', *Poems* (1773), 101–3.
215. Stuart Curran, 'Romantic Women Poets: Inscribing the Self', *Women's Poetry in the Enlightenment: The Making of a Canon, 1730–1820*, eds. Isobel Armstrong and Virginia Blain (London: Macmillan Press Ltd, 1999), 145–66.
216. John Duncombe, *The Feminiad. A Poem* (1754), 160, ll. 153–62.
217. Boswell, I: 312.
218. The list of subscribers is dominated by women and clergymen. Elizabeth Harrison, *Miscellanies on moral and religious subjects, in prose and verse* (1756).
219. BL Add. MS 4265, f.48r, entitled, 'Some Imperfect memoirs of Mrs: Cockburn'. The author is unidentified, but Henry Etough, in letters to Thomas Birch, identifies himself as having put together a rough memoir (BL Add. MS 4326. B, ff.27v, 30v, and 33r). Henry Etough (d. 1757 at age 70) was rector of Therfield in Hertfordshire, attended the same dissenting academy as Thomas Secker and Thomas Birch, who remained lifelong friends, but had a mixed reputation amongst contemporaries (see John Nichols, *Literary Anecdotes of the Eighteenth Century* (1812–14), v.viii: 261–4, and v.ix:807).
220. See Chapter 4.
221. See Anne Kelley, *Catharine Trotter*, 1 n. 1; Kelley, 'Corrections to Thomas Birch (Ed.) The Works of Mrs. Catharine Cockburn', *Notes & Queries* 47 (245), no.2 (June 2000): 192–3; and her entry on Cockburn in the *ODNB*. Also *Works*, I:iv. Birch queried her birth date in BL Add. MS 4265, f. 43r, which suggests that it was Cockburn's family and not Birch at fault for the date. The change of birth date means that Cockburn and Rowe were the same age, but there are no contemporary connections between the two except Birch, who once sought Hertford's patronage through Rowe and became Cockburn's editor and biographer.
222. Her father died from the plague in 1683/4, while convoying a fleet to Iskanderun, in southeast Turkey, leaving the family defrauded of his effects, and in severely straightened circumstances for the remainder of their lives. See *Works* I: iii.
223. Kelley, *Catharine Trotter*, 8.
224. *Works* I: ii, iv, and xlvii.
225. Kelley's attention to the manuscript heritage is particularly thorough. She provides facsimile reproductions of a number of Cockburn's and her correspondents' letters, as well as her Last Will and Testament. *Catharine Trotter*, Appendix IV, 262–72.
226. For examples, see BL Add. MS 4265, f.85 and Add. MS 4302, ff. 290–2. See also Kelley, *Catharine Trotter*, 2.
227. In BL Add. MS 4265, ff. 108r-9v, Patrick Cockburn addresses someone responsible for trying to get Cockburn's unpublished works on Locke and Holdsworth printed. No date or name is given but Etough is a probable

candidate. See chapter 4 for an account of the editorial history of the posthumous works. William Warburton was a literary editor and polemicist, later the Bishop of Gloucester; Edmund Keene was the Vice-Chancellor of Cambridge; Thomas Sharp was Archdeacon of Northumberland.
228. Warburton to Henry Etough, 28 September 1749: 'I esteem Mr Birche's kindness in this affair as a favour done to my selfe, both as it eases me, who have indeed at present my hands full, and as I shall have the pleasure of se[e]ing justice done to Mrs Cockbourn's memory, as well in the memoirs of her life as in the selection of her works' (BL Add. MS 4326.B, f. 31r).
229. *A Discourse Concerning A Guide in Controversies, in Two Letters. Written to One of the Church of Rome, By a Person lately Converted from that Communion* (1707), sig. a2.
230. *Remarks upon the Principles and Reasonings of Dr. Rutherforth's Essay on the Nature and Obligations of Virtue* (1747), vi–vii.
231. See Birch, *Works* I:xxxv and xlviii; Kelley, *Catharine Trotter*, 6.
232. There has been some debate over the attribution of this work to Cockburn, but both Kelley and Jeslyn Medoff draw attention to Birch's notation of it in BL Add. MS 4265, f. 43. See Kelley, *Catharine Trotter*, 55, and Medoff, 'The Daughters of Behn and the Problem of Reputation,' in *Women, Writing, History, 1640–1740*, eds. Isobel Grundy and Susan Wiseman (London: B.T. Batsford Ltd., 1992): 33–54, 207n. 41.
233. BL Add. MS 4264, f. 245v.
234. In Manley's, *The Royal Mischief. A Tragedy* (1696).
235. In Mary Pix's, *Queen Catharine, Or The Ruines of Love. A Tragedy* (1698).
236. *The Nine Muses, or, Poems written by Nine Severall Ladies Upon the Death of the late Famous John Dryden, Esq.* (1700), 15–17.
237. It was finally published in *GM* 7 (May 1737), 308. Birch was one of the judges. On the history and popularity of Cave's magazine see Thomas Keymer's introduction to *The Gentleman's Magazine in the Age of Johnson*, 16 vols, *Volume I: 1731*, (London: Pickering and Chatto, 1998).
238. Possibly a daughter or relation of Sir John Reresby of Yorkshire (1634–89), a staunch royalist and Jacobite politician, who may also be the Margaret Tilly (née Reresby) whom Manley mentions in the *New Atalantis*. See Delarivier Manley, *The Selected Works of Delarivier Manley*, gen. eds. Ruth Herman and Rachel Carnell, 5 vols, *Volume 2: The New Atalantis (1709)*, ed. Rachel Carnell (London: Pickering & Chatto, 2005), 115 and 344n. 378. Hereafter cited as *Atalantis*.
239. BL Add. MS 4265, ff. 74-81.
240. 'I was some time after adressed from Ireland by some lovers of poetry, as to a Muse, desiring my inspiration: To which these verses were sent in answer but never publishd' (BL Add. MS 4265, f. 58).
241. *A Defence of the Essay of Human Understanding, written by Mr. Lock, Wherein Its Principles, with reference to Morality, Revealed Religion, and the Immortality of the Soul, are consider'd and justify'd: in answer to some Remarks on that Essay* (1702).
242. See Medoff, 40–1 and Kelley, *Catharine Trotter*, 87, n.58.
243. BL Add. MS 4264, ff. 263–5.
244. Elizabeth Burnett, née Blake, other married name Berkeley (1661–1709), was in Lincoln's Inn from 1696 till her marriage to Gilbert Burnet in 1700.

245. Kelley, *Catharine Trotter*, 87, n.58, and quoting from BL Add. MS 4264, f. 265v.
246. Ibid., 87, n.58. Burnet's letter to Locke is in *The Correspondence of John Locke*, ed. E.S. de Beer, 7: 638, Letter no. 3153, 20 June 1702.
247. Sharp wrote to Cockburn in 1748, asking 'whether the 3 plays found at London are different from those you have?' BL Add. MS 4264, f. 93v. In another projected list of contents for volume two of the *Works* Birch tried to include *The Revolution of Sweden* (BL Add. MS 4264, f. 2r). See John Cockburn's letter, BL Add. MS 4302, f. 292, 29 March 1756; and Thomas Sharp's listed above for further discussion of the printing costs and volume contents, respectively.
248. Backscheider, 'Stretching the Form', 444–5; Kelley, *Catharine Trotter*, 40–2; Jacqueline Pearson, *The Prostituted Muse: Images of Women and Women Dramatists, 1642–1737* (New York: St Martin's Press, 1988), 70, 183–5; Staves, *A Literary History*, 109.
249. Backscheider, 'Stretching the Form', 444.
250. Pearson, 189.
251. MS Rawlinson J 4°6 (105), f.260.
252. John J. Conley, S.J., *The Suspicion of Virtue: Women Philosophers in Neoclassical France* (Ithaca and London: Cornell University Press, 2002), 97.
253. Charlotte Lennox, *Meditations and Penitential Prayers, Written By The celebrated Dutchess De La Valliere* (1774).
254. According to Birch the letters were private until Winch Holdsworth (1679–1761) convinced Cockburn to print her half and he immediately followed with his answer. *Works* I: xxxvi.
255. *Works* II: 314.
256. Ezell's study of the continuation of manuscript culture alongside print technology limits her scope from the 1650s up to a decade after the copyright act (1710); however, evidence suggests this dual culture extends well into the latter half of the eighteenth century (*Social Authorship*, 15–16). On Grub Street, see Paula McDowell, *The Women of Grub Street: Press, Politics, and Gender in the London Literary Marketplace, 1699–1730* (Oxford: Clarendon Press, 1997).
257. Delarivier Manley, *The Selected Works of Delarivier Manley*, gen. eds. Ruth Herman and Rachel Carnell, 5 vols. *Volume 4: The Adventures of Rivella (1714), The Power of Love (1720)*, ed. Rachel Carnell (London: Pickering & Chatto, 2005) and *Atalantis*. See chapter 4 for a discussion of Manley's representations of Cockburn.
258. Lady Betty Gordon is mentioned in Cockburn's letters as a learned lady who 'was a great reader' and one who 'has read Mr. *Locke's Essay*, and the controversies he was engaged in, upon which she speaks very judiciously' (*Works* II: 290–1). Cockburn was asked to send her a fair copy of the poem on the queen's hermitage and, in return, a correspondence was begun. Presumably she is Lady Elizabeth Gordon (c.1720–69), daughter of the second Duke of Gordon, who married the Rev. John Skelly, a vicar at Shilbottle then Stockton-on-Tees. Katharine Gordon, the Duchess of Gordon (1718–79), subscribed to the *Works*.
259. She provided two answers in reply to a question concerning the lawfulness of suicide and death penalties in the face of non-voluntarist views about individual will. Reprinted in *Works* II: 139–42.

260. *GM* 7 (May 1737), 308.
261. See *Works* I: xxxix–xliv, or the unedited version in BL Add. MS 4265, ff. 31–2.
262. *Works* I: xl.
263. Reprinted in *Works* I as, *A Defence of Mr. Locke's Essay of Human Understanding* (1751). References in the text refer to the *Works*.
264. Heather King, '"Be Mistress of Your Self, and Firm to Virtue": Female Friendship in Catharine Trotter's *The Unhappy Penitent* (1701)', *Eighteenth-Century Women: Studies in their Lives, Work, and Culture*, ed. Linda V. Troost, vol. 3 (November 2003): 1–23.
265. Staves, *A Literary History*, 50–2, 100.
266. *The London Stage, 1660–1800*. Part I: *1660–1700*, ed. William Van Lennep, Emmett L. Avery, and Arthur H. Scouten (Carbondale, IL: Southern Illinois University Press, 1965), 449.
267. Delarivier Manley, 'To the Author of Agnes de Castro', *Agnes de Castro* (1696), sig. A2r.
268. Pearson, 23.
269. Catharine Trotter, *The Unhappy Penitent* (1701), sig. A2v.
270. Ibid., sig. A3.
271. Ibid., 13.
272. H. King, 2.
273. Backscheider, 'Stretching the Form,' 444.
274. Peter Nidditch, ed., *An Essay on Human Understanding* by John Locke (Oxford: Oxford University Press, 1975), vii.
275. For accounts of contemporary praise see *Works* II:175; Kelley, 19; and John Yolton, *John Locke and the Way of Ideas* (Oxford: Oxford University Press, 1956), 19n. 5. For example, John Toland praised Cockburn in *Letters to Serena* (1704). He writes, 'you may find a Lady not personally known to me, who is absolute Mistriss of the most abstracted Speculations in the Metaphysics, and who with an easy Turn of Stile and Argument has defended Mr. *Lock's Essay of Human Understanding*, against the Letters of an Eminent Divine' (sig. a6v–a7r).
276. Thomas Burnet, *Remarks upon An essay concerning human understanding in a letter address'd to the author* (1697), *Second Remarks upon An essay concerning humane understanding in a letter address'd to the author, being a vindication of the first remarks against the answer of Mr. Lock, at the end of his reply to the Lord Bishop of Worcester* (1697), and *Third remarks upon An essay concerning humane understanding in a letter address'd to the author* (1699). All published anonymously.
277. Nidditch, ix–x.
278. See Kelley, chapter two.
279. Victor Nuovo, 'Catharine Cockburn's Enlightenment' (Paper presented as part of the panel, 'Women, Metaphysics and Enlightenment', Institute of Philosophy, London, 24 March 2006), 3. I would like to thank Prof. Nuovo for making his paper available to me and for the knowledge which he so generously shared in many enlightening conversations on the subjects of Cockburn and Locke.
280. Felicity Nussbaum, in *The Autobiographical Subject: Gender and Ideology in Eighteenth-Century England* (Baltimore: The Johns Hopkins University Press, 1989), writes that Cockburn 'takes on a male persona throughout her anonymous defense of Locke' (39); however, this persona only appears in

the dedication and no further reference is made to the gender of the text's speaker.
281. Nuovo, 2, n.4.
282. *Remarks upon some writers* was written in defence of Samuel Clarke's 1704 and 1705 Boyle lectures and contested the views of Edmund Law, Isaac Watts, William Warburton, Thomas Johnson, and George Johnston. See Birch, *Works* I: xxxviii.
283. Martha Brandt Bolton, 'Some Aspects of the Philosophical Work of Catharine Trotter', *The Journal of the History of Philosophy* 31:4 (October 1993): 565–78, rpt. in *Hypatia's Daughters: Fifteen Hundred Years of Women Philosophers*, ed. Linda Lopez McAlister (Bloomington and Indianapolis: Indiana University Press, 1996), pp. 139–64, 139–40 and 142.
284. See Bolton, 145 and chapter 4. Stephen wrote: 'Mrs. Cockburn here accepts and defends the ethical theory of Clarke, and it is not much to the credit of her philosophical acuteness that she does not perceive it to be inconsistent with the theories of her old teacher Locke', *DNB* XI, 183.
285. See chapter 4.
286. See BL Add. MS 4264, ff. 333–4.
287. For Sophia, see BL Add. MS 4264, f. 121r; and for Leibniz, see *Works* II: 164 or BL Add. MS 4264, f. 113r.
288. O'Brien, 5. She includes Elizabeth Carter in this group.
289. O'Brien, 5 and B.W. Young, *Religion and Enlightenment in Eighteenth-Century England: Theological Debate from Locke to Burke* (Oxford: Clarendon Press, 1998).
290. See, for example, BL Add. MS 4264, ff. 113, 114 and cf. *Works* II:164. F. 114 appears to be Cockburn's edited version of f. 113.
291. The hand on many of these letters looks very similar to Cockburn's. However, Birch was responsible for trimming down the eventual selection of Burnet letters and, in one instance, reduces four double-sided octavo-sized pages of Burnet's minute hand to one page. See BL Add. MS 4264, ff. 117–19 for the original, f. 120 for Birch's transcription, and *Works* II: 169 for the printed text.
292. BL Add. MS 4264, f. 112.
293. BL Add. MS 4264, f. 113. See also Burnet's letter of 17 July 1704, *Works* II: 171–2.
294. See *Works* II: 169–73 for Burnet's letters. At one point he declares, 'Yet I cannot conceal, that I have the most passionate ardour of mind and soul to cultivate a perpetual friendship with you' (171). He also asks if he might commission a portrait, in miniature, of her.
295. He had just spent months imprisoned in the Bastille.
296. Cf. BL Add. MS 4264, ff. 124–5, which looks like a fair copy in Cockburn's hand.
297. Due to a printing error, the page sequence 177–92 is used twice in succession. The above letter is on the second set of pages designated as 186–7.
298. See *Works* I: xxx.
299. Kelley, *Catharine Trotter*, 151–2.
300. See, for example, *Works* II: 215, 2 June 1707. Cockburn writes to Patrick, 'More particular, I must not be, for you are too much *Arwide*'s friend to be trusted with what she would not impart to him.'
301. See Backscheider, 'Stretching the Form'.

302. *RGS*, I: 24.
303. Ibid., I:53.
304. Conley, 97.
305. Ibid., 97.
306. Ibid., 97–8.
307. Bod. MS Rawlinson J 4° 6 (105) f. 260.
308. *Works* II: 200 and BL Add. MS 4264, f. 146. In his next letter, 29 November 1707, he mentions the Catholic mystic and prophet Antoinette Bourignon, against whom John Cockburn, Patrick's father, had published the work *Bourignianism Detected* in 1698.
309. The letters to Walsham are not dated but are transcribed on paper with David Trotter's address on the reverse. I concur with Kelley in assuming that, based on the address and the childish hand, these were written quite early in Cockburn's career. See Kelley, 211–12 and BL Add. MS 4264, f.244.
310. Hannah More, *Florio: A Tale of Fine Gentlemen and Fine Ladies; and, The Bas Bleu; or, Conversation: Two Poems* (Dublin, 1786).
311. Haywood, of course, also produced non-scandal fiction. See her *The Tea Table* (1725) and *Epistles for the Ladies* (1749–50), in vols 1 and 2 respectively of *Selected Works of Eliza Haywood*, eds. Alexander Pettit and Christine Blouch (London: Pickering & Chatto, 2000).
312. Camilla's letter to Seraphina discusses how a mind not exercised frequently can affect the vigour of the rational soul, and also that, though retirement can aid philosophic contemplation, people are 'Born for Society' and the 'Right use of our Reason teachs us to be Content in all Stations' because it all concurs 'to ye good of ye whole' (BL Add. MS 4264, f. 259r). Serena's letter to the unidentified man deals with the propriety of a single female corresponding on philosophic topics with a single man, and concludes that, as a 'Platonist', she does not care if the world decides to be scandalised by such rational behaviour (BL Add. MS 4264, f. 258).
313. BL Add. MS 4264, f. 256r.
314. BL Add. MS 4264, f. 256v.
315. BL Add. MS 4264, f. 257r, 4 April 1717.
316. BL Add. MS 4264, f. 261r, 29 September 1722.
317. BL Add. MS 4265, ff. 148–184 and BL Add. MS 4264, ff. 218–19, 224–5. Birch's list of them is in BL Add. MS 4265, f. 107.
318. Kelley, *Catharine Trotter*, 197.
319. See, for example, Kelley's account of some excised gossip, 207–8. The gossip concerned Cockburn's daughter Kitty as well as her niece Anne. It is likely that Anne did not want this information printed and it does not materially influence our image of Cockburn one way or another as she dismisses the report in about two sentences herself. Cf. *Works* II: 255–9 and BL Add. MS 4265, ff.110–111.
320. See Bigold, 'Letters and Learning', 179–81, for a discussion of the editorial changes to Cockburn's 'Letter to her Niece upon Moral Virtue.'
321. Ibid., 180.
322. Identifying the transcriber of some of the edited folios is difficult. The hand does not match letters written by Cockburn, though they do bear some similarities with her son's, John Cockburn's, handwriting. Frustratingly, it does appear that Cockburn's hand changed significantly over the years.

There are original letters of the early 1700s (complete with seals intact) in which Cockburn's handwriting is completely different from letters in the 1730s and 1740s (also with seals intact). We cannot definitively attribute the arrangement or editing of these letters and tracts to Cockburn, though perhaps we can infer the selection as her own given the changes in the arrangement of them made after her death.

323. For information on Thomas, see chapter four in Rebecca Mills, '"Thanks for that Elegant *Defense*" Polemical Prose and Poetry by Women in the Early Eighteenth Century', DPhil. Diss. (University of Oxford, 2000).
324. *Works* II: 267–71; 'Miscellaneous Pieces' transcription, BL Add. MS 4264, f. 14; original with seal, BL Add. MS 4264, ff. 193–5.
325. Staves, *A Literary History*, 94.
326. Thomas Sharp, *The Works of Thomas Sharp*, 6 vols, Volume II: *Containing Tracts on Various Subjects* (1763).
327. Richard Price, *A Review of the Principal Questions and Difficulties in Morals* (1758), 153–4 and 407. He quotes Sharp in the first instance, but his arguments are in line with Cockburn's.
328. Price, 407.
329. BL Add. MS. 4264, ff. 279–83.
330. BL Add. MS. 4264, f.281. See chapter 4, O'Brien, and B.W. Young, *Religion and Enlightenment*, for a discussion of the Anglican debates around Locke's and Clarke's theories on the foundation of morality and obligation.
331. BL Add. MS 46690, f. 7r–v.
332. BL Add. MS 46690, f. 7v
333. *Memoirs*, 65.
334. Robert Douglas-Fairhurst, *Victorian Afterlives: The Shaping of Influence in Nineteenth-century Literature* (Oxford: Oxford University Press, 2002), 5–6.
335. Letter to Pope c. 1738 in *Works* I:xxxix–xliv. The unedited version, in BL Add. MS 4265, ff. 31–2, is not substantially different from the printed one.
336. Kelley, *Catharine Trotter*, 40 and 41.
337. On the curricula at Aberdeen and Cambridge see Paul B. Wood (1992) *The Aberdeen Enlightenment: The Arts Curriculum in the Eighteenth Century* (Aberdeen: Aberdeen University Press) and John Gascoigne *Cambridge in the Age of the Enlightenment: Science, Religion and Politics from the Restoration to the French Revolution* (Cambridge: Cambridge University Press, 1989).
338. See Medoff, 40.
339. Ballaster notes that the key identifies Daphne as Mrs Griffith but that the biography provided by Manley clearly signifies that it is Cockburn. Rosalind Ballaster, ed. (1992), *New Atalantis* (London: Penguin Books), xiii. References in the text are to the Pickering & Chatto *Atalantis*.
340. The female cabal, to which the patron Zara (Piers) introduces Daphne (Cockburn), is described as a gynocentric community where women engage in mysteriously passionate friendships that have the power to break the bonds of heterosexual unions.
341. Margarette R. Connor, 'Catharine Trotter: An Unknown Child?', *American Notes and Queries*, 8: 4 (Fall 1995): 11–14, 12. Kelley discounts Connor's arguments based on the impossibility of Cockburn having a son old enough to be married with children in 1707 (39).

Notes 259

342. In an unknown hand in Birch's manuscripts there are a set of queries regarding Cockburn's life. One asks, 'if not better to omit mentioning the Attalantis &c', BL Add. MS. 4265, f. 43.
343. Kelley, *Catharine Trotter*, 2.
344. BL Add. MS 4326.B. f. 29.
345. This may have eventually been printed under the guise of the treatise against Holdsworth; however, a letter from Etough suggests otherwise.
346. *Letters* (1809), II: 49.
347. See BL Add. MS 4264, ff. 93–4r for Sharp and Warburton's proposals; BL Add. MS 4264, f. 2 and 4265, f. 43v, for Birch's (or Etough's) comments on the contents; and BL Add. MS 4265 ff.108–9 for a copy of a letter from Patrick Cockburn regarding the proposed contents and search for the missing plays.
348. Reynolds, 111.
349. Leslie Stephen, *Dictionary of National Biography*, 66 vols (London: Smith, Elder, & Co., 1885–1901), XI, 183, and Edmund Gosse, 'Catharine Trotter, the Precursor of the Bluestockings', *Transactions of the Royal Society of the United Kingdom. Second Series. Vol. XXXIV* (London: Oxford University Press, 1916), pp. 87–118, 114.
350. BL Add. MS 4265, ff. 48–54, 'Some Imperfect memoirs of Mrs: Cockburn'.
351. W. M., *The Female Wits: or, The Triumvirate of Poets at Rehearsal* (1704), 8.
352. *Female Wits*, 5.
353. Medoff, 40.
354. BL Add. MS 4265, f. 52.
355. BL Add. MS 4265, f. 53.
356. Duncombe, 14, ll. 133–8.
357. Cockburn's selection comprises the manuscript pieces added to the *Works*: 'Calliope's Directions how to deserve the muses', which includes a note saying how the poem came about as a result of manuscript exchange; 'The Caution'; 'The Platonic'; 'The Needless Deceit'; 'A Poem, occasioned by the busts set up in the Queen's Hermitage'; and 'The Vain Advice'. *Poems by Eminent Ladies*, 2 vols, eds. George Colman and Bonnell Thornton (1755), 229-38. Rowe and Carter are also featured in these volumes.
358. Anne Fisher, *A new English exercise book. Calculated to render the construction of the English tongue, easy and familiar, independent of any other language* (Newcastle, 1770), 55.
359. Lady (Cecilia) Isabella Finch (1700–71), whose great-aunt was the philosopher Anne Conway, was a courtier and patron of many women writers, including Charlotte Lennox.
360. BL Add. MS 4326.B. f. 27.
361. BL Add. MS 4326.B. f. 29, 7 October 1749.
362. A guinea for a two-volume work was quite high for the period. Sarah Fielding sought a guinea during her subscription appeal for *The Lives of Cleopatra and Octavia* (1757), signalling her attempt to secure 'well-heeled patrons'. For her translation of *Xenophon* she sought six shillings. Betty Schellenberg (2005), 109.
363. BL Add. MS 4326.B. f. 35, 28 September 1751. Etough writes to Birch: 'Your undertaking ye work giveth great satisfaction to […] worthy Persons, & your personal Application to them will be of ye utmost service to ye subscription.

You will learn from ye List at Knaptons how few of ye Bench are yet subscribed. Few or none would refuse was there a proper Application. I hope You are acquainted with Bp Hayter & will ingage his Assistance.'
364. BL Add. MS 4326.B. ff. 37v–38v.
365. BL Add. MS 4326.B. f. 38.
366. Schellenberg (2005), 100.
367. Young, *Religion and Enlightenment*, 2.
368. O'Brien's recent work, *Women and Enlightenment*, devotes considerable space to Cockburn's interventions in Enlightenment debates, and, utilising Young's account, develops similar arguments regarding Cockburn's importance.
369. Emma Jay, 'Caroline, Queen Consort of George II, and British Literary Culture', DPhil. Diss. (Oxford, 2004).
370. Written in 1732, first published in *GM* 7 (May 1737), 308, and included in *Works* II: 572–5. References in the text refer to *Works*.
371. Stephen Taylor, 'Caroline [Princess Caroline of Brandenburg-Ansbach] (1683–1737)', in *ODNB*, http://www.oxforddnb.com/view/article/4720 (accessed 26 April 2012).
372. Shaftesbury added an illustration of the judgement of Hercules in some of the 1714 editions of *Characteristicks*, and included it in all editions thereafter based on his 1713 text, *A Notion of the Historical Draught or Tablature of the Judgement of Hercules*. See *RGS*, II: 102–3. Cockburn read and commented on *Characteristicks* at length in her letters to her niece. See *Works* II, *passim*.
373. BL Add. MS 4264, f. 121, Hanover, 29 July 1704.
374. Sarah Hutton, 'Anne Conway, Margaret Cavendish and Seventeenth-century Scientific Thought', in *Women, Science and Medicine, 1500–1700: Mothers and Sisters of the Royal Society*, eds. Lynette Hunter and Sarah Hutton (Gloucestershire: Sutton Publishing, 1997), 218–34, 219.
375. Young, *Religion and Enlightenment*, 7.
376. Gascoigne, 2.
377. Ibid., 7.
378. *Works* II: 125–7. Date of composition unknown.
379. See Shaftesbury's anti-clerical *Several Letters Written by a Noble Man to a Young Man at the university* (1716), 7. Cockburn comments on this text in *Works* II: 341.
380. Charles Rollin, *The method of teaching and studying the belles lettres* (London, 1734). The title page notes that it is 'Designed more particularly for STUDENTS in the UNIVERSITIES'.
381. BL Add. MS 4265, f. 126*. I have followed Kelley in using an asterisk symbol to distinguish the second of two folios with the same number. She notes that 'This situation usually occurs when a series of leaves of a small folded letter are allocated one folio number', Kelley, *Catharine Trotter*, 64 n. 36.
382. BL Add. MS 4264, f. 306, 27 January 1709.
383. Young, *Religion and Enlightenment*, 3 and 10.
384. Ibid., 10–11.
385. See Bolton, 146 and Cockburn, *Works* I: 59.
386. Bolton, 140 and 143.

387. That is, from a divine law, which would suggest a voluntarist approach to religion, or from human nature, which would maintain Locke's non-voluntarist stance.
388. Bolton, 153.
389. Bolton cites, as evidence of Cockburn's political agenda, a passage about the wrongs enacted by various sects in England and on the Continent in the name of religion, 154. Cockburn's emphasis is clearly not on the political manipulation of religion, but on religionists' wrong-headed interpretations of controversial points in religion. The passage is in *Works* II:268–9.
390. Cited in *RGS*, II, 227–8n. 295.
391. Price, 17.
392. Thomas Sharp, *Tracts on various subjecs [sic]. Formerly printed separately. Now collected into one volume* (1763).
393. See Barbara Taylor, *Mary Wollstonecraft and the Feminist Imagination* (Cambridge: Cambridge University Press, 2003).
394. BL Add. MS 4265, f. 51.
395. See Summit *passim*.
396. From Thomas Birch's review for Carter's anonymous Algarotti translation in *History of the Works of the Learned*, Art. XXXI (1 June 1739), 392.
397. Quoted in Boswell's *Life of Samuel Johnson*, I: 122–3, no date.
398. Subsequent editions in 1742 and 1765.
399. *Letters* (1809), II: 351, Lambeth, 17 September 1760.
400. I am indebted to Ros Ballaster for identifying this idea.
401. *Memoirs*, 5.
402. *GM* (November 1734), 623.
403. E.J. Clery notes the possible monetary impetus behind Nicholas Carter's championing of his daughter in *The Feminization Debate*, 76.
404. Myers, 46.
405. *Memoirs*, 40.
406. Letter from Nicholas Carter to Elizabeth Carter, 27 March 1738, in Gwen Hampshire's private collection. See Gwen I. Hampshire, 'An Edition of Some Unpublished Letters of Elizabeth Carter, 1717–1806, and a Calendar of Her Correspondence', B.Litt. Dissertation (Oxford, 1972), x. Hereafter cited as Hampshire B.Litt. Hampshire has since published an edition of some of the letters, *Elizabeth Carter, 1717–1806: An Edition of Some Unpublished Letters*, ed. Gwen Hampshire (Newark: University of Delaware Press, 2005). The letter from Nicholas Carter is not included in this work. See also Myers, 58 (citing Hampshire Collection, Malton, 12 July 1738).
407. *Letters* (1809), II: 200–1, St Paul's, 7 February 1755. The owl referred to is Carter's 'Ode to Wisdom'. Four of Carter's poems eventually appeared in Dodsley's *Collection*. See Robert Dodsley, *A Collection of Poems by Several Hands*, ed. Michael F. Suarez, S.J. Vols I–VI (London: Routledge/Thoemmes Press, 1997): 'Ode to Wisdom', III: 217; 'To a Gentleman, on his intending to cut down a Grove to enlarge his Prospect', III: 221; 'Ode to a Lady in London', V:330; 'To Miss ****, The midnight moon serenely smiles', VI: 244.
408. *Letters* (1809), II: 203, Deal, 5 March 1755.
409. See *Memoirs*, 69 (c. August 1750).
410. It appears from the date of these letters that Carter had refused to submit anything to the fourth volume, which went to press around January 1755

and was published on 18 March 1755. However, Pennington may have misdated the letter and they could easily refer to the first volumes issued in 1748. The two poems included in volumes V and VI had already appeared in Benjamin Martin's periodical, *Miscellaneous Correspondence*, in August 1755, 131 and September 1755, 149, respectively.
411. Guest, *Small Change*, 16.
412. *Memoirs*, 25.
413. Nicholas to Elizabeth, 27 March 1738, Hampshire B.Litt.
414. Judith Hawley, 'Carter, Elizabeth (1717–1806)', Judith Hawley in *ODNB*, http://www.oxforddnb.com/view/article/4782 (accessed 13 September 2010).
415. Francesco Algarotti, *Sir Isaac Newton's Philosophy Explain'd for the Use of the Lades. In Six Dialogues on Light and Colours. From the Italian*, trans. Elizabeth Carter, 2 vols (1739), and Jean Pierre de Crousaz, *An Examination of Mr. Pope's Essay on Man, From the French of M. Crousaz*, trans. Elizabeth Carter (1739).
416. *GM*, 315–16. It was later revised for *Poems on Several Occasions* and cited in *Memoirs*, 364–6. See also Hawley, 444, n.11.
417. *Memoirs*, 16.
418. Ibid.
419. 'Wright, Thomas (1711–1786)', David Knight in *ODNB*, http://www.oxforddnb.com/view/article/30060 (accessed 13 September 2010). Wright's diary is in the BL Add. MS 15627.
420. *Memoirs*, 16; Hampshire B.Litt., xlvi; and Hampshire (2005), 34.
421. *Letters* (1809), I: 1.
422. *Letters* (1809), I: 3–4, 28 January 1741.
423. See *Letters* (1809), II: 29 for Carter's views on marriage.
424. *Letters* (1809), II: 165, Deal, 18 March 1754. Some proof copies, with corrections, are in the Trinity collection.
425. Trinity College, O.12.57[20], formerly classified as O.12.27[20].
426. Ibid., Deal, 9 May 1752.
427. Trinity College, R.4.57, f. 19r, Deal, 11 October 1752. The third book was never printed.
428. Warburton knew of Carter (see his letters to Birch in BL Add. MS 4320, f. 131v, 27 August 1738; f. 143r, 16 September 1738; and f. 147v, 6 April 1739), but there is no evidence they were acquainted. There is a supportive letter from Herring to Nicholas Carter in the Althorp Papers regarding the Athanasian Creed controversy in Deal. See BL Add. MS 75696, 8 February 1753 (unbound, no folio numbers).
429. On Harris see *Memoirs*, 122, and *Letters* (1809), II:137–8n.
430. Bod. MS Facs. c. 44, f. 10, Deal, 4 June 1750. S. Highmore cites Browne as one of those petitioning Carter for a tribute to Leapor. See Hampshire (2005), 137–8 for a full transcription.
431. Brean Hammond, *Professional Imaginative Writing in England, 1670–1740: 'Hackney for Bread'* (Oxford: Clarendon Press, 1997).
432. *Letters* (1809), I: 315, 20 June 1749. In a backhanded compliment, Carter complains that Richardson does not know evil well enough to portray the true range of human nature.
433. 'Original Letters of Miss E. Carter and Mr Samuel Richardson', *Monthly Magazine* 33 (1812): 533–43, 533–4, Canterbury, 13 December 1747.

434. *Letters* (1809), I: 249, 20 January 1747.
435. 'Original Letters', 534.
436. *Letters* (1809), II: 13, 4 March 1751.
437. She later partially retracts this statement when Talbot argues that he was only directing his comments at vacuous women. For Talbot's arguments, see *Letters* (1809), II: 16, Piccadilly, 16 March 1751, for Carter's reply, II: 18–19, Deal, 24 March 1751.
438. See *Letters* (1809), I: 244. Later, Montagu echoes Richardson and likens Carter to Clarissa. See Leonore Helen Ewert, 'Elizabeth Montagu to Elizabeth Carter: Literary Gossip and Critical Opinions from the Pen of the Queen of the Blues', Ph.D. diss. (Claremont Graduate School, 1968), 56.
439. BL Add MS 4302, f. 104, Cave to Birch, 28 November 1738. Cave writes that Johnson suggested Carter translate Boethius. She went with Birch's suggestion of Algarotti instead.
440. Clery, 76–7.
441. See *An Examination of Mr. Pope's Essay on Man, passim*.
442. See *Sir Isaac Newton's Philosophy Explain'd*, I: 22, 24, and 72.
443. Samuel Johnson, *The Letters of Samuel Johnson*, ed. Bruce Redford, 5 vols (Princeton: Princeton University Press, 1992–4), I: 17, April 1738 to Edward Cave.
444. Roger Lonsdale, *Eighteenth-Century Women Poets*, 167.
445. *Memoirs*, 9.
446. Myers, 157.
447. Robert DeMaria, Jr., *The Life of Samuel Johnson: A Critical Biography* (Oxford: Blackwell Publishers, 1994), and Anthony W. Lee, 'Who's Mentoring Whom? Mentorship, Alliance, and Rivalry in the Carter–Johnson Relationship', *Mentoring in Eighteenth-Century British Literature and Culture* (Farnham: Ashgate, 2010), pp. 191–210.
448. DeMaria, xi.
449. Lee, 194.
450. DeMaria, 46.
451. Ibid., 47.
452. *Memoirs*, 26.
453. Lee, 201–4.
454. See Hawley for possible motivations for her departure, xiv.
455. The appearance of the Philips poem came at the request of a female correspondent, Anticlea, who sent the verses to Cave,12 March 1744, *GM* 14 (July 1744), 389.
456. DeMaria, 79.
457. Ibid., 74.
458. Ibid., 74.
459. Hawley, xxviii.
460. Cave to Nicholas Carter, 20 November 1746, Hampshire, B.Litt., xii.
461. It went through ten collected editions before Johnson's death.
462. Talbot writes, 'I like the Adventurers; we all like them exceedingly; and I fancy they will soon become very generally fashionable... They want nothing but now and then a little of your assistance, for such writers should be assisted, that they may by the help of their correspondents now and then get a holiday. Look over your *considering drawer*, and if you have any

old sketches that were intended for the Rambler, bring them up, I beseech you' (*Letters* (1809), II: 109, St Paul's Deanery, 29 January 1753).
463. *Letters* (1809), II: 79.
464. Ibid., II: 101.
465. 1,018 copies were printed in the first run and 250 more when these proved insufficient for the subscribers, many of whom ordered multiple copies. Richardson printed *Epictetus* and Andrew Millar, the Dodsleys, and John Rivington sold it. *Memoirs*, 140.
466. Montagu tells Carter, 'the manuscript must be printed so my dear Urania away with your lamentation, sit down, revise, correct, augment, print & publish' (Ewert, xvi, quoting from MO 3055, c.1762).
467. Hawley, xvi.
468. *Letters* (1817) title page.
469. Helen Small, 'For the Use of the Ladies: How the First Bluestockings Prized Knowledge and Virtue above Feminism', *TLS* 6 (April 2001):3–4, 4 and 3.
470. See Gary Kelly's introduction in *Bluestocking Feminism*, I: 3.
471. Guest, *Small Change*, 17.
472. Hammond, 9. However, Jennifer Wallace rightly reminds us of the 'ambiguous implications' of these models for the classically trained, exceptional woman in 'Confined and Exposed: Elizabeth Carter's Classical Translations', *Tulsa Studies in Women's Literature* 22:2 (Fall 2003): 315–34, 316–17.
473. *Letters* (1809), II: 23–4, Deal, 12 April 1751.
474. Ibid., I: v.
475. *Memoirs*, 11.
476. *Letters* (1809), II: 186, 26 November 1754.
477. Ibid., III: 90, Clarges Street, 6 February 1764.
478. The portrait (c.1765) is now in Dr Johnson's House, London. Katharine Read (1723–78) was a fashionable portrait painter of the day.
479. *Poems by Eminent Ladies*, I: sig. A2. See Lavoie for an account of its genesis and publication history.
480. Ibid., I: 172.
481. Edward Moore, *The World. By Adam Fitz-Adam*, vol. 3. New edition (1772) No. 131 (Thursday 3 July 1755): 159–65. See also Guest (2000), 40–1.
482. Moore, 163.
483. Ibid., 164. Italics mine.
484. See *Memoirs*, Letter to Talbot, 124, and Letter to Talbot, Deal, 3 May 1756, 145.
485. Guest, *Small Change*, 41.
486. See Ibid., 100, for an account of William Pitt's tutor, Dr Edward Wilson, asking the young Pitt to construct a comparative essay on the subject of Carter and Montagu. The letter appears in *Mrs. Montagu, 'Queen of the Blues', Her Letters and Friendships from 1762 to 1800*, ed. Reginald Blunt, 2 vols (London: Constable, n.d. [1923?]), II: 99–100.
487. James Fordyce, *Sermons for Young Women*, 2 vols (London, 1766), I: 202–3, Sermon V.
488. *Letters* (1809), III: 141, Lambeth, 23 August 1766.
489. Ewert, 123 (MO 3317, Sandleford, 6 August 1773). Joshua Reynolds and James Beattie, two male members of the Bluestocking coterie, were among the 15 men who received honorary doctorates upon the occasion of

Lord North being installed as Chancellor of Oxford, 9 July 1773. Samuel Johnson's honorary doctorate, awarded by Lord North in 1775, is often attributed to his political writings for North.
490. Guest, *Small Change*, 135.
491. The book was *The Ladies New and Polite Pocket Memorandum-Book* (1778), and the print was advertised in the *London Chronicle*, 8–11 November 1777. See Lucy Peltz, 'Living Muses: Constructing and Celebrating the Professional Woman in Literature and the Arts', *Brilliant Women: 18th-Century Bluestockings*, ed. Elizabeth Eger and Lucy Peltz (London: National Portrait Gallery, 2008), 57–93 (90, n.15).
492. A reference to her *Essay on Shakespeare* which targeted Voltaire as one of the 'filthy spiders'. See Leonore Helen Ewert, 'Elizabeth Montagu to Elizabeth Carter: Literary Gossip and Critical Opinions from the Pen of the Queen of the Blues', Ph.D. diss. (Claremont Graduate School, 1968), 146 (quoting MO 3435, Sandleford, 24 November [1777].) Also cited in Guest, *Small Change*, 101.
493. *Letters* (1817), Letter CCVI, Deal, 23 November 1777, III:47.
494. See *Brilliant Women* for reproductions of the Carter portraits.
495. BL Add. MS 32573, f. 21.
496. Ian Michael, *The Teaching of English from the Sixteenth Century to 1870* (Cambridge: Cambridge University Press, 1987). See tables on pp. 196–8. Michael admits the statistics are slightly misleading because he only considers anthologized authors. The most popular work for children was Watts's *Divine Songs* (168), which would have been included in an English curriculum on its own.
497. Michael, 193.
498. Harry M. Solomon, *The Rise of Robert Dodsley: Creating the New Age of Print* (Carbondale and Edwardsville, IL: Southern Illinois University Press, 1996), 115.
499. See Hawley, 1.
500. Carter originally edited and published Talbot's works at her own expense in 1772.
501. Pennington did not approve of Johnson's biographers, however, and stresses the importance of respecting the writer and 'not those conversations *in which he only argued for victory, so imprudently given to the public*' (*Memoirs*, 2n.).
502. *Memoirs*, 34. The Duchess of Somerset is the Countess of Hertford, the one-time patron of Rowe.
503. Elizabeth Montagu, *The Letters of Mrs. Elizabeth Montagu, with some of the letters of her correspondents, published by M. Montagu* (1809–13). Two volumes, up to 1761, were published in 1809 and two more volumes in 1813.
504. Ruth Perry, *Women, Letters, and the Novel*, ix–x.
505. Ibid., 95 and 120.
506. He writes, 'In the lives of many of the good and learned, there are no events from which to choose, no remarkable circumstances to engage the attention, and no adventures to amuse […] their hours passed in the "cool sequestered vale of life"' (*Memoirs*, 1).
507. Armstrong, *Desire and Domestic Fiction*, 4.
508. For example, William Hayley, tongue firmly in cheek, dedicated the first and second editions of *A Philosophical, Historical, and Moral Essay on Old*

Maids. By a Friend to the Sisterhood, 3 vols (1785, 2nd edn 1786), to Carter. The third edition (1793) omitted the dedication.
509. Gosse, 114.
510. Monthly Review LVI (July 1808): 225–40.
511. The 2005 edition does not go into as much detail about Pennington's editorial intrusions.
512. Hampshire B.Litt., xxxv, cf. Memoirs, 70.
513. Ibid., xxxiii.
514. Hampshire B.Litt., xxxvii.
515. Hampshire B.Litt., xviii and Letters (1809), I: 297, 22 October 1748.
516. Hampshire, B.Litt., xxxix. Cf. Memoirs, 90 and 291 with Letters (1809), I: 103; Memoirs, 110 with Letters (1809), I: 206; Memoirs, 116 with Letters (1809), I: 216.
517. Hampshire B.Litt., xl.
518. Ewert, 'Elizabeth Montagu to Elizabeth Carter'.
519. Ibid., lxi–lxii.
520. Ibid., lx–lxi.
521. For criticism of Pennington's editions see Hawley, xi and Hampshire, B.Litt., xlix.
522. Hawley, ix.
523. Letters (1809), IV: 143. To Vesey, Deal, 7 June 1776.
524. Letters (1817), I:37. To Montagu, Bristol, Letter IX, 23 April 1759.
525. On Carter's conservatism see Harriet Guest, 'Bluestocking Feminism,' in Reconsidering the Bluestockings, eds. Nicole Pohl and Betty A. Schellenberg (San Marino: Huntington Library, 2003): 59–80, 59, and Hawley, xv.
526. Taylor, see chapter 3, especially 98–102.
527. Ibid., 102.
528. Guest, Small Change, 17–18.
529. Marshall, 5.
530. See Susan S. Lanser, 'Befriending the Body: Female Intimacies as Class Acts', in Eighteenth-Century Studies 32:2 (1998–9): 179–98.
531. Isabel Rivers, The Poetry of Conservatism, 1600–1745: A Study of Poets and Public Affairs from Jonson to Pope (Cambridge: Rivers Press, 1973), x.
532. Bowerbank, Speaking for Nature: Women and Ecologies of Early Modern England (Baltimore, Maryland: The Johns Hopkins Press, 2004), 20.
533. Ibid., 20, 83, 90.
534. Ibid., 99.
535. Leslie Stephen, History of English Thought in the Eighteenth Century, 2 vols, 3rd edn (London: Smith, Elder, & Co., 1902), II: 74–5.
536. Adam Smith, The Theory of Moral Sentiments, ed. Knud Haakonssen (Cambridge: Cambridge University Press, 2002), viii.
537. Letters (1817), I: xvii.
538. Guest, Small Change, 16.
539. Mrs Underdown was a Kent friend and her letter book is in Hampshire's possession.
540. Hampshire (2005), 53–4, London, 14 September 1738. 'Scrawler' refers both to her messy handwriting and to writing more generally.
541. Hampshire (2005), 130, Canterbury, 17 April 1742.
542. A reference to The London Farthing Post, Hampshire (2005), 55, n.5.

543. Hampshire (2005), 55, London, 14 November 1738.
544. Samuel Johnson, *The Rambler: The Yale Edition of the Works of Samuel Johnson, Volumes III–V*, eds W.J. Bate and Albrecht B. Strauss (London: Yale University Press: 1969). V: 46, No. 152. Hereafter cited as *The Rambler*.
545. *The Rambler*, V: 47, No. 152.
546. *Letters* (1809), I: 56.
547. The poetic excerpt is from John Byrom. It first appeared in *The Spectator*, No. 603, Wednesday 6 October 1714, and reprinted in *GM*, February 1745. Talbot has altered Byrom's lines: 'Does ought of its Sweetness the Blossom beguile,/ That Meadow, those Daisies, why do they not smile?' See *The Spectator*, 5 vols, ed. Donald F. Bond (Oxford: Clarendon Press, 1965, reissued 1987) 61–4 (63, Stanza VIII).
548. Bowerbank, 20.
549. Carter's letters were read to Talbot's mother and to Thomas Secker, Bishop of Oxford. See Carter's mock-terror at the news that Secker reads them in *Letters* (1809), I: 79, 84 and 158.
550. See Bowerbank on the moderate Anglican ideal of uniting Martha (the active sister) and Mary (the contemplative one), 85–6.
551. Tillotson in his preface to John Wilkins's, *Of the Principles and Duties of Natural Religion* (1675). Quoted in *RGS*, I: 25.
552. Talbot often reminds Carter of the worth of her letters: '[I]n this time of idleness I have betaken myself (a very pretty compliment you will say) to read over all the Letters you have wrote me for many a year past. They have edified and humbled me greatly'; 'I have lately been reading over with most sincere gratitude, and with many good resolutions, the kind, the truly kind Letter, you sent me on our last parting' (*Letters* (1809), II: 108, 29 January 1753, and II: 26, 23 December 1762). See also II: 84.
553. 'And by the way the Bishop of Norwich, who very particularly enquired after you, and sent you his compliments, desired me to engage you if possible to enliven those Papers by throwing in something of your own, which he thought you better capable of doing than any body. I did not tell him how good you had been, because I did not know whether you would care I should' (Talbot to Carter, *Letters* (1809), II: 3).
554. Paul J. Korshin, 'Johnson, the essay, and *The Rambler*', in *The Cambridge Companion to Samuel Johnson*, ed. Greg Clingham (Cambridge: Cambridge University Press, 1997), 51.
555. Korshin, 52. *The Rambler* quickly came out in a two-volume folio edition in Edinburgh between 1750 and 1752, a duodecimo edition in six volumes in 1752, and a four-volume octavo in 1756.
556. *The Rambler*, III: xxi n.1.
557. *Letters* (1809), I: 262. No year is provided, but Pennington appears to attribute it to 1748 given its placement in the text.
558. Smith, 11.
559. Ibid., 28. Cf. Carter in *Letters* (1809), II: 23–4, Deal, 12 April 1751.
560. *The Rambler*, III: 256.
561. In his last *Rambler*, No. 208, Johnson wrote, 'The essays professedly serious, if I have been able to execute my own intentions, will be found exactly conformable to the precepts of Christianity, without any accommodation to the licentiousness and levity of the present age' (*The Rambler*, V: 320).

562. Haakonsen, xvi.
563. See, for example, the career of the theologian and natural philosopher William Whiston (1667–1752), who lost his university post because of his anti-trinitarian views. Stephen D. Snobelen in *ODNB*, http://www.oxforddnb.com/view/article/29217 (accessed 26 April 2012).
564. *Letters* (1809), II: 43, Deal, 12 August 1751.
565. Basil Willey, *The Eighteenth Century Background: Studies on the Idea of Nature in the Thought of the Period* (London: Chatto & Windus, 1950), 189.
566. Guest, *Small Change*, 146.
567. *Monthly Review* (November 1752), 339–40.
568. J.N.D. Kelly, *The Athanasian Creed* (London: Adam & Charles Black, 1964), 125.
569. [William Hopkins], *An Appeal to the Common Sense of All Christian People* (1753), iii. There must have been an earlier edition for O'Donnell to have responded to it and for the *Monthly Review* to include it in their November 1752 issue.
570. Thomas McDonnell, *A Sincere Christian's Answer to the Appeal to the Common Sense of all Christian People* (1751), iii–iv.
571. On reading Cockburn see *Letters* (1809), II: 49.
572. BL Add. 75696 (Althorp Papers), f. 1.
573. Ibid., f. 1v.
574. Ibid., f. 2r.
575. Ibid., f. 2r.
576. Ibid., f. 2.
577. Ibid., ff. 2v–3r.
578. Carter, *Letters* (1817), I: 167–9, Letter XLIII, Deal, 2 July 1762.
579. Taylor, 100.
580. Ibid., 102.
581. Woolf, 93, 98.
582. For example, Victor Nuovo states that, 'Immortal bliss and the Law of Nature are themes that are basic to the philosophical project to found morality that was an original motive of Locke's major work, *An Essay concerning Human Understanding*.' See John Locke, *The Reasonableness of Christianity, as delivered in the scriptures*, ed. Victor Nuovo (Bristol: Thoemmes Press, 1997), xvi.
583. Guest, 'Bluestocking Feminism,' 68.
584. See, for example, David McKitterick, *Print, Manuscript and the Search for Order, 1450–1830* (Cambridge: Cambridge University Press, 2003), 4; Adrian Johns, *The Nature of the Book: Print and Knowledge in the Making* (Chicago and London: The University of Chicago Press, 1998), 458–9; and Julie Stone Peters, *The Theatre of the Book, 1480–1880: Print, Text, and Performance* (Oxford: Oxford University Press, 2000), 42–3. Stone Peters notes that even in the world of drama, manuscript copies were 'still an important way of circulating plays, certainly in the early seventeenth century and still (in some places) in the eighteenth', 42.
585. See Guest and Anthony Fletcher, *Gender, Sex and Subordination in England 1500–1800* (New Haven: Yale University Press, 1995), 283–4.

Bibliography

Manuscripts

The Archives of the Duke of Northumberland at Alnwick Castle, Northumberland
DNP: MS 110: Frances Thynne Seymour's letter book.

Bodleian Library, Oxford
MS Facs. c. 44: Letters of Elizabeth Carter to various.
MS Don. D. 137: Letter of Elizabeth Carter to Mrs C. Lutwidge, f. 170.
MS Autogr. d. 24: Letters of Elizabeth Carter to various.
MS Autogr. b. 1.: Letters and mss of George Ballard; print of Elizabeth Carter, f. 39; transcription of Elizabeth Carter's prayer (1758), f. 40.
MS Rawl. J 4° 6(105): Patrick Cockburn subscription proposal, f. 260.

British Library, London
Birch Collection: Add. MS 4254; Add. MS 4264; Add. MS 4265; Add. MS 4266; Add. MS 4267; Add. MS 4291; Add. MS 4297; Add. MS 4302; Add. MS 4320; Add. MS 4321; Add. MS 4326 B.; Add. MS 4371: Catherine Cockburn's *A Vindication of an Essay concerning Human Understanding*, ff. 65–93; Add. MS 4456: 'Poetical Fragments Volume I'; Add. MS 4457: 'Poetical Fragments Volume II'.
Add. MS 15627: Thomas Wright's Diary
Add. MS 32573: J. Mitford Notebooks, Vol. XV.
Add. MS 39311: Berkeley Papers Vol. XIII, includes letters from John Cockburn to Henry Etough; Catherine Talbot to various; Samuel Richardson to Catherine Talbot.
Add. MS 39312: Berkeley Papers Volume IX, includes letters from Catherine Talbot; Elizabeth Montagu; Elizabeth Carter.
Add. MS 46688: Catherine Talbot's Journal, ff. 8–37.
Add. MS 46690: Catherine Talbot's Journal, ff. 1–102r.
Add. MS 75696: Althorp Papers, includes letters from Elizabeth Carter to Countess Spencer; Thomas Herring to Nicholas Carter.
Stowe 748: Dering Correspondence, includes letters from Elizabeth Carter to Edward Cave.

Trinity College, Cambridge
Trinity R.4.57
Trinity O.12.57[20] (Formerly O.12.27[20])

Primary sources

Algarotti, Francesco. *Sir Isaac Newton's Philosophy Explain'd for the Use of the Ladies. In Six Dialogues on Light and Colours. From the Italian*. Trans. Elizabeth Carter. 2 vols. London, 1739.

Anon. *An Useful and Entertaining Collection of Letters upon Various Subjects; Several now first Printed from their Original Manuscripts, By the Most Eminent Hands*. London, 1745.

——. *Five Love-Letters from a Nun to a Cavalier* (1678). Trans. Roger L'Estrange. In *The Novel in Letters: Epistolary Fiction in the Early English Novel 1678–1740*. Ed. Natascha Würzback. London: Routledge and Kegan Paul, 1969, 1–23.

Ballard, George. *Memoirs of Several Ladies of Great Britain who have been celebrated for their writings or skill in the learned languages, arts and sciences*. Ed. Ruth Perry. Detroit: Wayne State University Press, 1988.

Boswell, James. *The Life of Samuel Johnson*. Ed. George Birkbeck Hill, rev. L.F. Powell. 6 vols. Oxford: Clarendon Press, 1934.

Browne, Isaac Hawkins. *De Animi Immortalitate*. London, 1754.

[Burnet, Thomas]. *Remarks upon An essay concerning human understanding in a letter address'd to the author*. London, 1697.

——. *Second Remarks upon An essay concerning humane understanding in a letter address'd to the author, being a vindication of the first remarks against the answer of Mr. Lock, at the end of his reply to the Lord Bishop of Worcester*. London, 1697.

——. *Third remarks upon An essay concerning humane understanding in a letter address'd to the author*. London, 1699.

Burney, Frances. *Camilla or A Picture of Youth*. Eds. Edward A. Bloom and Lillian D. Bloom. Oxford: Oxford University Press, 1972, reissue 1999.

——. *The Early Journals and Letters of Fanny Burney. Volume 1: 1768–1773*. Ed. Lars E. Troide. Oxford: Clarendon Press, 1988.

Bussy, Roger de Rabutin, comte de. *Les Memoires de Messire Roger de Rabutin, Comte de Bussy*. 2 vols. Paris, 1696.

Carter, Elizabeth. *All the Works of Epictetus which are now Extant; Consisting of His Discourses, preserved by Arrian, in Four Books, The Enchiridion, and Fragments*. London, 1758.

——. *Bluestocking Feminism: Writings of the Bluestocking Circle, 1738–1785*. Gen. Ed. Gary Kelly. *Volume II: Elizabeth Carter*. Ed. Judith Hawley. London: Pickering and Chatto, 1999.

——. *Letters from Mrs Elizabeth Carter to Mrs. Montagu, between the Years 1755 and 1800. Chiefly upon Literary and Moral Subjects. Published from the Originals in the Possession of the Rev. Montagu Pennington*. 3 vols. London, 1817.

——. 'On the Death of Mrs Rowe', *Gentleman's Magazine* 7 (April 1737), 247.

——. 'On the Death of Mrs. Rowe', *Gentleman's Magazine* 9 (March 1739), 152.

——. 'On the foregoing verses. Inscrib'd to Miss L–CH of Canterbury', *Gentleman's Magazine* 14 (July 1744), 389.

——. 'Original letters of Miss E. Carter and Mr Samuel Richardson', *Monthly Magazine* 33 (1812), 533–43.

——. *Poems on Several Occasions*. London, 1762.

——. *Remarks on the Athanasian Creed; on a Sermon Preached at the Parish Church of Deal, October 15, 1752; and On a Pamphlet, lately published, with the Title, 'Some short and plain Arguments, from Scripture, evidently proving the Divinity of our Saviour.' In a Letter to the Rev. Mr. Randolph, Rector of Deal. By a Lady.* n.d. [1752/3?].

——. *A Series of Letters between Mrs. Elizabeth Carter and Miss Catherine Talbot, from the Year 1741 to 1770. To which are added, Letters from Mrs. Elizabeth Carter to Mrs. Vesey, between the Years 1763 and 1787; published from the original manuscripts in the possession of the Rev. Montagu Pennington, M.A.*, 4 vols. 2nd edn. London, 1809.

Chapone, Hester. *The Posthumous Works of Mrs. Chapone.* London, 1807.

Cockburn, Catharine Trotter. *The Adventures of a Young Lady.* In *Letters of Love and Gallantry and Several Other Subjects, All Written by Ladies.* 2 vols. London, 1693–4.

——. *Agnes de Castro, A Tragedy. As it is Acted at the Theatre Royal, By His Majesty's Servants, Written by a Young Lady.* London, 1696.

——. 'Calliope: The Heroick Muse', in *The Nine Muses, or, Poems written by Nine Severall Ladies Upon the Death of the Late Famous John Dryden, Esq.* London, 1700, 15–17.

——. *A Defence of the Essay of Human Understanding, written by Mr. Lock, Wherein Its Principles, with reference to Morality, Revealed Religion, and the Immortality of the Soul, are consider'd and justify'd: in answer to some Remarks on that Essay.* London, 1702.

——. *A Discourse Concerning A Guide in Controversies, in Two Letters. Written to One of the Church of Rome, By a Person lately Converted from that Communion.* London, 1707.

——. *Fatal Friendship. A Tragedy. As it is Acted at the New Theatre in Little-Lincolns-Inn-Fields.* London, 1698.

——. *Love at a Loss, or, Most Votes carry it. A Comedy. As it is now Acted at the Theatre Royal in Drury-Lane, by His Majesty's Servants. Written by the Author of Fatal Friendship.* London, 1700.

——. *Olinda's Adventures: Or the Amours of a Young Lady, by Mrs. Trotter.* In *Familiar Letters of Love and Gallantry, and Several Occasions, by the Wits of the Last and Present Age. With the best of Voiture's Letters, Translated by Mr. Dryden and Mr. T. Brown. Also the Remains of the Celebrated Mr. T. Brown; being the Letters, Poems and Dialogues on the Times; not Printed in his Works, vol. 2.* 2 vols. London, 1718.

——. *Remarks upon some Writers in the Controversy concerning the Foundation of Moral Virtue and Moral Obligation; Particularly the Translator of Archbishop King's Origin of Evil and the Author of the Divine Legation of Moses. To which are prefaced some Cursory Thoughts on the Controversies concerning Necessary Existence, the Reality and Infinity of Space, the Extension and Place of Spirits, and on Dr. Watts's Notion of Substance.* In *The History of the Works of the Learned*, August 1743, 79–162.

——. *Remarks upon the Principles and Reasonings of Dr. Rutherforth's Essay on the Nature and Obligations of Virtue: In Vindication of the contrary Principles and Reasonings, inforced in the Writings of the late Dr. Samuel Clarke. Published by Mr. Warburton with a Preface.* London, 1747.

——. *The Revolution of Sweden. A Tragedy. As it is Acted at the Queens Theatre in the Hay-Market.* London, 1706.

——. *The Unhappy Penitent. A Tragedy. As it is Acted, At the Theatre Royal in Drury Lane, by his Majesty's Servants. Written by Mrs. Trotter.* London, 1701.

——. *The Works of Mrs. Catharine Cockburn, Theological, Moral, Dramatic, and Poetical. Several of them now first printed. Revised and published, with an account of the Life of the Author, by Thomas Birch.* 2 vols. London, 1751.

——. 'Verses, occasion'd by the *Busts* in the *Queen's Hermitage*, and Mr. *Duck* being appointed Keeper of the Library in *Merlin's Cave*. By the Authoress of a Treatise (not yet publish'd) in Vindication of Mr. *Lock*, against the injurious Charge of Dr. *Holdsworth*, in his Defence of the Resurrection of the Same Body', *Gentleman's Magazine* 7 (May 1737), 308.

Colman, George and Bonnell Thornton, eds. *Poems by Eminent Ladies. Particularly, Mrs. Barber, Mrs. Behn, Miss Carter, Lady Chudleigh, Mrs. Cockburn, Mrs. Grierson, Mrs. Jones, Mrs. Killigrew, Mrs. Leapor...* 2 vols. London, 1755.

Crousaz, Jean Pierre de. *An Examination of Mr. Pope's Essay on Man, From the French of M. Crousaz.* Trans. Elizabeth Carter. London, 1739.

Dodsley, Robert, ed. *A Collection of Poems by Several Hands.* Ed. Michael F. Suarez, S.J. 6 vols. London: Routledge/Thoemmes Press, 1997.

——. *A Muse in Livery.* London, 1732.

Duncombe, John. *The Feminiad. A Poem.* London, 1754.

Fisher, Anne. *A new English exercise book. Calculated to render the construction of the English tongue, easy and familiar, independent of any other language.* Newcastle, 1770.

Fordyce, James. *Sermons for Young Women.* A facsimile reprint of the third edition (1766) in *Female Education in the Age of Enlightenment, Volume 1.* Intro. Janet Todd. London: Pickering and Chatto, 1996.

The Gentleman's Magazine in the Age of Samuel Johnson, 1731–1745. Intro. Thomas Keymer, 16 vols. London: Pickering and Chatto, 1998.

Gibbons, Thomas. *Memoirs of Eminently Pious Women, who were ornaments to their sex, blessings to their families, and edifying examples to the Church and the World.* 2 vols. London, 1777.

——. *Memoirs of Eminently Pious Women of the British Empire. A New Edition embellished with Eighteen Portraits. Corrected and Enlarged by Samuel Burder.* 3 vols. London, 1815.

Harrison, Elizabeth. *Miscellanies on moral and religious subjects, in prose and verse. By Elizabeth Harrison.* London, 1756.

Hayley, William. *A Philosophical, Historical, and Moral Essay on Old Maids. By a Friend to the Sisterhood.* 3 vols. 2nd edn. London, 1786.

Haywood, Eliza. *Selected Works of Eliza Haywood, Set I, Volume 1: Miscellaneous Writings, 1725–43.* Ed. Alexander Pettit. London: Pickering & Chatto, 2000.

——. *Selected Works of Eliza Haywood, Set I, Volume 2: Epistles for the Ladies.* Eds. Alexander Pettit and Christine Blouch. London: Pickering & Chatto, 2000.

Hertford, Frances Seymour, Countess of. *Correspondence Between Frances, Countess of Hartford, (Afterwards Duchess of Somerset,) and Henrietta Louisa, Countess of Pomfret, Between the Years 1738 and 1741.* 3 vols. London, 1805.

[Hopkins, William]. *An Appeal to the Common Sense of All Christian People.* London: 1753.

Johnson, Samuel. *A Dictionary of the English Language.* 2 vols. London, 1755.

——. *The Letters of Samuel Johnson.* Ed. Bruce Redford. 5 vols. Princeton: Princeton University Press, 1992–4.

——. *The Rambler: The Yale Edition of the Works of Samuel Johnson, Volumes III–V.* Eds. W.J. Bate and Albrecht B. Strauss. London: Yale University Press, 1969.

L, G. *The last houers, of the right reverend Father in God Andrew Rivet, in his life time Dr. and Professour honorable of Divinity, in the Universitie of Leyden, tutor to the late High and Mightie P. William by the grace of God Prince of Orange, in his younger yeares, and curator of the illustrious schoole & college of Orange at Breda. Faithfully collected translated by G. L.* Hague: Samuel Broun, 1652.

Law, William. *A Serious Call to a Devout and Holy Life: Adapted to the State and Condition of All Orders of Christians. By William Law, A.M.* London, 1729.

Lennox, Charlotte. *Mediations and Penitential Prayers, Written By The celebrated Dutchess De La Valliere, Mistress of Lewis the Fourteenth of France. After her Recovery from a dangerous Illness, when she first formed the Resolution of quitting the Court, and devoting herself to a Religious Life. Translated from the French. With some Account of her Life and Character, extraced from Voltaire, Sevigné, and other Writers of that Time. By Mrs. Charlotte Lennox.* London, 1774.

Locke, John. *An Essay on Human Understanding.* Ed. and foreword by Peter H. Nidditch. Oxford: Oxford University Press, 1975.

———. *The Reasonableness of Christianity, as delivered in the scriptures.* Ed. and introduction by Victor Nuovo. Bristol: Thoemmes Press, 1997.

M, W. [unknown]. *The Female Wits: or, The Triumvirate of Poets at Rehearsal. A Comedy. As it was Acted several Days successively with great Applause at the Theatre-Royal in Drury-Lane. Written by Mr. W.M.* London, 1704.

Manley, Delarivier. *New Atalantis.* Ed. Ros Ballaster. London: Penguin Books, 1992.

———. *The Selected Works of Delarivier Manley.* Gen. Eds. Ruth Herman and Rachel Carnell. 5 vols. *Volume 2: The New Atalantis (1709).* Ed. Rachel Carnell. London: Pickering & Chatto, 2005.

———. *The Selected Works of Delarivier Manley.* Gen. Eds. Ruth Herman and Rachel Carnell. 5 vols. *Volume 4: The Adventures of Rivella* and *The Power of Love.* Ed. Rachel Carnell. London: Pickering & Chatto, 2005.

Martin, Benjamin. *Miscellaneous Correspondence, Containing a Variety of Subjects, Relative to Natural and Civil History, Geography, Mathematics, Poetry, Memoirs of monthly Occurences, Catalogues of new Books, &c.* Vol. 1. *For the Year 1755–1756.* London, 1759.

McDonnell, Thomas. *A Sincere Christian's Answer to the Appeal to the Common Sense of all Christian People.* London, n.d. [1751/2?].

Montagu, Elizabeth. *The Letters of Mrs. Elizabeth Montagu, with some of the letters of her correspondents, published by M. Montagu.* 4 vols. London, 1809–13.

The Monthly Review; or, Literary Journal. By Several Hands. Vol. LVI. London, 1808.

Moore, Edward. *The World. By Adam Fitz-Adam.* 4 vols. New edition. London, 1772.

More, Hannah. *Florio: A Tale of Fine Gentlemen and Fine Ladies; and, The Bas Bleu; or, Conversation: Two Poems.* Dublin, 1786.

Nichols, John. *Literary Anecdotes of the Eighteenth Century.* 9 vols. London, 1812–14.

Pascal, Blaise. *Pensées De M. Pascal Sur La Religion et Sur Quelques Autres Sujets, Qui ont esté trouvées après sa mort parmy ses papiers. Nouvelle Edition, Augmentée de plusiers pensées du mesme Autheur.* Paris, 1678.

———. *Thoughts on Religion, and other Curious Subjects. Written Originally in French By Monsieur Pascal. Translated into English by Basil Kennet, D.D.* 2nd edn. London, 1727.

Pennington, Montagu. *Memoirs of the Life of Mrs. Elizabeth Carter with A New Edition of her Poems, some of which have never appeared Before; to which are added, some Miscellaneous Essays in Prose, together with her Notes on the Bible and Answers to objections concerning the Christian religion.* London, 1807.

———. *Redemption; or, A View of the Rise and Progress of the Christian Religion, from the Fall of Adam, to its Complete Establishment Under Constantine the Great.* London, 1811.

Philips, Katherine. *Poems by the Most Deservedly Admired Mrs. Katherine Philips the Matchless Orinda.* London, 1667.

———. *The Collected Works of Katherine Philips, The Matchless Orinda: Volume I – The Poems.* Ed. Patrick Thomas. Stump Cross, Essex: Stump Cross Books, 1990.

———. *The Collected Works of Katherine Philips, The Matchless Orinda. Volume II – The Letters.* Ed. Patrick Thomas. Stump Cross, Essex: Stump Cross Books, 1993.

———. *The Collected Works of Katherine Philips, The Matchless Orinda. Volume III: The Translations.* Eds. Germaine Greer and R. Little. Stump Cross, Essex: Stump Cross Books, 1993.

Pope, Alexander. *Eloisa to Abelard.* 2nd edn. London, 1720.

Richardson, Samuel. *Clarissa, or The History of a Young Lady.* Ed. Angus Ross. London: Penguin Books, 1985.

———. *The History of Sir Charles Grandison, In a Series of Letters, Published from the Originals, by the Editor of Pamela and Clarissa.* Ed. Jocelyn Harris. Oxford: Oxford University Press, 1986.

Rollin, Charles. *The method of teaching and studying the belles lettres, or an introduction to languages, poetry, rhetoric, history, moral philosophy, physicks, &c... Translated from the French.* 4 vols. London, 1734.

Rowe, Elizabeth Singer. *Devout Exercises of the Heart in Meditation and Soliloquy, Prayer and Praise. Review'd and Published at her Request, by I. Watts, D.D.* London, 1738.

———. *Friendship in Death: in Twenty Letters from the Dead to the Living. To which are added, Letters Moral and Entertaining, in Prose and Verse. In Three Parts. By the same Author.* 3rd edn. London, 1733.

———. *The History of Joseph. A Poem. In Eight Books.* London, 1736.

———. *The History of Joseph. A Poem. In Ten Books.* London, 1737.

———. *Letters on Various Occasions, in Prose and Verse. By the Author of Friendship in Death. To which are added Ten Letters By Another Hand.* London, 1729.

———. *The Miscellaneous Works in Prose and Verse of Mrs Elizabeth Rowe. The Greater Part now first Published, by her Order, from her Original Manuscripts, By Theophilus Rowe. To which are added, Poems on Several Occasions, By Mr. Thomas Rowe. And to the whole is prefix'd, An Account of the Lives and Writings of the Authors.* 2 vols. London, 1739.

———. *A New Miscellany of Original Poems on several occasions.* London, 1701.

———. *Poems on Several Occasions by Philomela.* London, 1696.

Scott, Mary. *The female advocate; a poem. Occasioned by reading Mr. Duncombe's Feminead. By Miss Scott.* London, 1774.

Sévigné, Madame De Rabutin Chantal, Marchioness de. *Letters of Madame de Rabutin Chantal, Marchioness de Sevigné*[sic]*, to the Comtes* [sic] *de Grignan, Her Daughter. In Two Volumes. Translated from the French.* London, 1727.

Shaftesbury, Anthony Ashley Cooper, third Earl of. *Characteristicks of men, manners, opinions, times.* 3 vols. 2nd edn rev. London, 1714.

———. *Several Letters written by a Noble Lord to a Young Man at the university*. London, 1716.
Sharp, Thomas. *Tracts on various subjecs [sic]. Formerly printed separately. Now collected into one volume*. London, 1763.
Smith, Adam. *The Theory of Moral Sentiments*. Ed. Knud Haakonssen. Cambridge: Cambridge University Press, 2002.
The Spectator. 5 vols. Ed. Donald F. Bond. Oxford: Clarendon Press, 1965, reissued 1987.
Talbot, Catherine. *The Works of the Late Miss Catherine Talbot. First Published by the Late Mrs Elizabeth Carter*. Ed. Montagu Pennington. 7th edn. London, 1809.
Tickell, Thomas. *A Poem, To His Excellency the Lord Privy-Seal, On the Prospect of Peace*. London, 1713 [1712].
Turnbull, George. *Observations on Liberal Education*. London, 1742.
———. *The Principles of Moral and Christian Philosophy. An Enquiry into the wise and good Government of the Moral World*. 2 vols. London, 1740.
Turrell, Ebenezer. *Memoirs of the life and death of the pious and ingenious Mrs. Jane Turell, ... collected chiefly from her own manuscripts by her consort the Revd. Mr. Ebenezer Turell, ... To which is added, two sermons preached ... by her father Benjamin Colman, D.D*. London, 1741.
Wesley, John. *Collection of Moral and Sacred Poems From the most Celebrated English Authors*. 3 vols. Bristol, 1744.
Wilford, John. *Memorials and Characters, Together with the Lives of Divers Eminent and Worthy Persons*. London, 1741.
Woolf, Virginia. *A Room of One's Own*. London: Hogarth Press, 1929.
Young, Edward. *Conjectures on Original Composition. In a Letter to the Author of Sir Charles Grandison*. London, 1759.

Secondary sources

Achinstein, Sharon. '"Pleasure by Description": Elizabeth Singer Rowe's Enlightened Milton'. *Milton and the Grounds of Contention*. Ed. Mark R. Kelley, Michael Lieb, and John T. Shawcross. Pittsburgh: Duquesne University Press, 2003.
———. 'The Poltics and Aesthetics of Dissent'. *The History of British Women's Writing, 1690–1750*. Ed. Ros Ballaster. Houndmills, Basingstoke: Palgrave Macmillan, 2010, 81–95.
———. 'Romance of the Spirit: Female Sexuality and Religious Desire in Early Modern England'. *English Literary History* 69:2 (Summer 2002): 413–38.
Altman, Janet Gurkin. *Epistolarity: Approaches to a Form*. Columbus: Ohio State University Press, 1982.
Anderson, Howard, Philip B. Daghlian, Irvin Ehrenpreis, eds. *The Familiar Letter in the Eighteenth Century*. Lawrence: University of Kansas Press, 1966.
Armstrong, Nancy. *Desire and Domestic Fiction: A Political History of the Novel*. New York and Oxford: Oxford University Press, 1987.
Backscheider, Paula R. *Eighteenth-Century Women Poets and Their Poetry: Inventing Agency, Inventing Genre*. Baltimore: The Johns Hopkins University Press, 2005.
———. *Spectacular Politics: Theatrical Power and Mass Culture in Early Modern England*. Baltimore and London: The Johns Hopkins University Press, 1993.

——. 'Stretching the Form: Catharine Trotter Cockburn and Other Failures'. *Theatre Journal* 47:4 (December 1995): 443–58.
——. and Timothy Dystal. *The Intersections of the Public and Private Spheres in Early Modern England*. London: Frank Cass, 1996.
Ballaster, Ros. *Seductive Forms: Women's Amatory Fiction from 1684 to 1740*. Oxford: Clarendon Press, 1992.
Bannet, Eve Tavor. *Empire of Letters: Letter Manuals and Transatlantic Correspondence, 1688–1820*. Cambridge: Cambridge University Press, 2005.
Barash, Carol. *English Women's Poetry, 1649–1714: Politics, Community, and Linguistic Authority*. Oxford: Clarendon Press, 1996.
Barker, John. *Strange Contrarieties: Pascal in England during the Age of Reason*. Montreal and London: McGill-Queen's University Press, 1975.
Bigold, Melanie. 'Letters and Learning'. *The History of British Women's Writing, 1690–1750*. Ed. Ros Ballaster. Houndmills, Basingstoke: Palgrave Macmillan, 2010, 173–86.
Blunt, Reginald, ed. *Mrs. Montagu, 'Queen of the Blues', Her Letters and Friendships from 1762 to 1800*. 2 vols. London: Constable, n.d. [1923?].
Bodenheimer, Rosemarie. *The Real Life of Mary Ann Evans: George Eliot, Her Letters and Fiction*. Ithaca and London: Cornell University Press, 1994.
Bolton, Martha Brandt. 'Some Aspects of the Philosophical Work of Catharine Trotter'. *Journal of the History of Philosophy* 31:4 (October 1993): 565–78. Rpt. in *Hypatia's Daughters: Fifteen Hundred Years of Women Philosophers*. Ed. Linda Lopez McAlister. Bloomington and Indianapolis: Indiana University Press, 1996, 139–64.
Bowerbank, Sylvia. *Speaking for Nature: Women and Ecologies of Early Modern England*. Baltimore, Maryland: The Johns Hopkins University Press, 2004.
Brant, Clare. *Eighteenth-Century Letters and British Culture*. Houndmills, Basingstoke: Palgrave Macmillan, 2006.
——. 'Varieties of Women's Writing'. *Women and Literature in Britain: 1700–1800*. Ed. Vivien Jones. Cambridge: Cambridge University Press, 2000, 285–305.
Broad, Jacqueline. *Women Philosophers of the Seventeenth Century*. Cambridge: Cambridge University Press, 2002, rpt. 2004.
Clarke, Norma. *The Rise and Fall of the Woman of Letters*. Pimlico: London, 2004.
——. 'Soft Passions and Darling Themes: from Elizabeth Singer Rowe (1674–1737) to Elizabeth Carter (1717–1806)'. *Women's Writing* 7:3 (2000): 353–371.
Clery, E.J. *The Feminization Debate in Eighteenth-Century England: Literature, Commerce and Luxury*. Houndmills, Basingstoke and New York: Palgrave Macmillan, 2004.
Conley, John J., S.J. *The Suspicion of Virtue: Women Philosophers in Neoclassical France*. Ithaca and London: Cornell University Press, 2002.
Connor, Margarette R. 'Catharine Trotter: An Unknown Child?'. *American Notes and Queries* 8:4 (Fall 1995): 11–14.
Curran, Stuart. 'Romantic Women Poets: Inscribing the Self'. *Women's Poetry in the Enlightenment: The Making of a Canon, 1730–1820*. Eds. Isobel Armstrong and Virginia Blain. London: Macmillan Press Ltd., 1999, 145–66.
Day, Robert Adams. *Told in Letters: Epistolary Fiction Before Richardson*. Ann Arbor: The University of Michigan Press, 1966.
DeMaria, Robert, Jr. *The Life of Samuel Johnson: A Critical Biography*. Oxford: Blackwell Publishers, 1994.

Doody, Margaret Anne. *Frances Burney: The Life in the Works*. Cambridge: Cambridge University Press, 1988.
Douglas-Fairhurst, Robert. *Victorian Afterlives: The Shaping of Influence in Nineteenth-Century Literature*. Oxford: Oxford University Press, 2002.
Ewert, Leonore Helen. 'Elizabeth Montagu to Elizabeth Carter: Literary Gossip and Critical Opinions from the Pen of the Queen of the Blues'. Ph.D. Diss. Claremont Graduate School, 1968.
Ezell, Margaret. '*The Gentleman's Journal* and the Commercialization of Restoration Coterie Literary Practices'. *Modern Philology* 89:3 (1992): 323–40.
——. *The Patriarch's Wife: Literary Evidence and the History of the Family*. Chapel Hill and London: University of North Carolina Press, 1987.
——. 'The Posthumous Publication of Women's Manuscripts and the History of Authorship'. *Women's Writing and the Circulation of Ideas: Manuscript Publication in England, 1550–1800*. Eds. George L. Justice and Nathan Tinker. Cambridge: Cambridge University Press, 2002, 121–36.
——. *Social Authorship and the Advent of Print*. Baltimore and London: The Johns Hopkins University Press, 1999.
——. *Writing Women's Literary History*. Baltimore and London: The Johns Hopkins University Press, 1993.
Fairchild, H. N. *Religious Trends in English Poetry*. 2 vols. *Volume II: 1740–1780, Religious Sentimentalism in the Age of Johnson*. New York: Columbia University Press, 1942.
Ferguson, Moira. *First Feminists: British Women Writers 1578–1799*. Bloomington: Indiana University Press, 1985.
Findlen, Paula. 'Ideas in the Mind: Gender and Knowledge in the Seventeenth Century'. *Hypatia: a Journal of Feminist Philosophy* 17:1 (Winter 2002): 183–196.
Freeman, Lisa A. '"A Dialogue": Elizabeth Carter's Passion for the Female Mind'. *Women's Poetry in the Enlightenment: The Making of a Canon, 1730–1820*. Eds. Isobel Armstrong and Virginia Blain. London: Macmillan Press Ltd., 1999, 50–63.
Gallagher, Catherine. *Nobody's Story: The Vanishing Acts of Women Writers in the Marketplace, 1670–1820*. Oxford: Clarendon Press: 1994.
Gascoigne, John. *Cambridge in the Age of the Enlightenment: Science, Religion and Politics from the Restoration to the French Revolution*. Cambridge: Cambridge University Press, 1989.
Gilbert, Sandra M. and Susan Gubar. *The Madwoman in the Attic: The Woman Writer and the Nineteenth-Century Literary Imagination*. New Haven: Yale University Press, 1979.
Goldgar, Anne. *Impolite Learning: Conduct and Community in the Republic of Letters, 1680–1750*. New Haven and London: Yale University Press, 1995.
Goodman, Dena. 'Letter Writing and the Emergence of Gendered Subjectivity in Eighteenth-Century France'. *Journal of Women's History*, 17.2 (2005): 9–37.
——. *Republic of Letters: A Cultural History of the French Enlightenment*. Ithaca and London: Cornell University Press, 1994.
Gosse, Edmund. 'Catharine Trotter, the Precursor of the Bluestockings'. *Transactions of the Royal Society of the United Kingdom. Second Series. Vol. XXXIV*. London: Oxford University Press, 1916, 87–118.
Guest, Harriet. *Small Change: Women, Learning, Patriotism, 1750–1810*. Chicago and London: The University of Chicago Press, 2000.

———. 'Bluestocking Feminism'. *Reconsidering the Bluestockings*. Eds. Nicole Pohl and Betty A. Schellenberg. San Marino: Huntington Library, 2003, 59–80.

———. and Anthony Fletcher. *Gender, Sex and Subordination in England 1500–1800*. New Haven: Yale University Press, 1995.

Habermas, Jürgen. *The Structural Transformation of the Public Sphere: An Inquiry into a Category of Bourgeois Society*. Trans. Thomas Burger. Cambridge, MA: MIT Press, 1994.

Hammond, Brean. *Professional Imaginative Writing in England, 1670–1740: 'Hackney for Bread'*. Oxford: Clarendon Press, 1997.

Hampshire, Gwen I. 'An Edition of Some Unpublished Letters of Elizabeth Carter, 1717–1806, and a Calendar of Her Correspondence'. B.Litt. Diss. Oxford, 1972.

———. ed. *Elizabeth Carter, 1717–1806: An Edition of Some Unpublished Letters*. Newark: University of Delaware Press, 2005.

Hansen, Marlene R. 'The Pious Mrs. Rowe'. *English Studies* 76:1 (1995): 34–51.

Hawes, Clement. *Mania and Literary Style: The Rhetoric of Enthusiasm, From the Ranters to Christopher Smart*. Cambridge: Cambridge University Press, 1996.

Hawley, Judith, ed. *Bluestocking Feminism: Writings of the Bluestocking Circle, 1738–1785*. Gen. Ed. Gary Kelly. *Volume II: Elizabeth Carter*. Ed. Judith Hawley. London: Pickering and Chatto, 1999.

Hobby, Elaine. *Virtue of Necessity: English Women's Writing, 1649–1688*. London: Virago, 1988.

Hughes, Helen Sard. *The Gentle Hertford: Her Life and Letters*. New York: The Macmillan Company, 1940.

Hunter, J. Paul. *Before Novels: the Cultural Contexts of Eighteenth-Century English Fiction*. New York & London: W.W. Norton, 1990.

Irlam, Shaun. *Elations: The Poetics of Enthusiasm in Eighteenth-Century Britain*. Stanford: Stanford University Press, 1999.

Jay, Emma. 'Caroline, Queen Consort of George II, and British Literary Culture'. DPhil. Diss. Oxford, 2004.

Johns, Adrian. *The Nature of the Book: Print and Knowledge in the Making*. Chicago and London: The University of Chicago Press, 1998.

Jones, Vivien, ed. *Women and Literature in Britain, 1770–1800*. Cambridge: Cambridge University Press, 2000.

Karian, Stephen. *Jonathan Swift in Print and Manuscript*. Cambridge: Cambridge University Press, 2010.

Kelley, Anne. *Catharine Trotter: An Early Modern Writer in the Vanguard of Feminism*. Aldershot, Hampshire: Ashgate, 2002.

———. 'Corrections to Thomas Birch (Ed.) The Works of Mrs. Catharine Cockburn'. *Notes & Queries* 47 (245), No.2 (June 2000):192–3.

———. '"In Search of Truths Sublime": Reason and the Body in the Writings of Catharine Trotter'. *Women's Writing* 8:2 (2001): 235–50.

Kelly, J.N.D. *The Athanasian Creed*. Adam &Charles Black: London, 1964.

King, Heather. '"Be Mistress of Your Self, and Firm to Virtue": Female Friendship in Catharine Trotter's *The Unhappy Penitent* (1701)'. *Eighteenth-Century Women: Studies in their Lives, Work, and Culture*. Ed. Linda V. Troost, vol. 3 (November 2003): 1–23.

King, Kathryn. 'Elizabeth Singer Rowe's Tactical Use of Print and Manuscript'. *Women's Writing and the Circulation of Ideas: Manuscript Publication in England,*

1550–1800. Eds. George L. Justice and Nathan Tinker. Cambridge: Cambridge University Press, 2002, 158–81.

Knott, Sarah and Barbara Taylor, eds. *Women, Gender and Enlightenment*. Houndmills, Basingstoke: Palgrave Macmillan, 2005.

Korshin, Paul J. 'Johnson, the Essay, and *The Rambler*'. *The Cambridge Companion to Samuel Johnson*. Ed. Greg Clingham. Cambridge: Cambridge University Press, 1997.

Lee, Anthony W. 'Who's Mentoring Whom? Mentorship, Alliance, and Rivalry in the Carter–Johnson Relationship'. *Mentoring in Eighteenth-Century British Literature and Culture*. Farnham: Ashgate, 2010, 191–210.

The London Stage, 1660–1800. Part I: *1660–1700*. Ed. William Van Lennep, Emmett L. Avery, and Arthur H. Scouten. Carbondale, Ill.: Southern Illinois University Press, 1965; Part II: *1700–1729*. Ed. Emmett L. Avery, Carbondale, Ill.: Southern Illinois University Press, 1960.

Lonsdale, Roger, ed. *Eighteenth-Century Women Poets: An Oxford Anthology*. Oxford: Oxford University Press, 1990.

Love, Harold. *The Culture and Commerce of Texts: Scribal Publication in Seventeenth-Century England*. Oxford: Clarendon Press, 1993, rpt. Amherst: University of Massachusetts Press, 1998.

Lowe, E.J. *Locke on Human Understanding*. London: Routledge, 1995.

Lowenthal, Cynthia. *Lady Mary Wortley Montagu and the Eighteenth-Century Letter*. Athens, GA: University of Georgia Press, 1994.

Maclear, J.F. 'Isaac Watts and the Idea of Public Religion'. *Journal of the History of Ideas* 53:1 (1992): 25–45.

Madigan, Mary Kathleen. 'Forever Yours: The Subgenre of the Letter from the Dead to the Living with Thematic Analyses of the Works of Elizabeth Singer Rowe and Meta Klopstock'. Ph.D. Diss. The University of North Carolina at Chapel Hill, 1988.

Marotti, A.F. *Manuscript, Print and the English Renaissance Lyric*. Ithaca, NY: Cornell University Press, 1994.

Marshall, David. *The Figure of Theater: Shaftesbury, Defoe, Adam Smith, and George Eliot*. New York: Columbia University Press, 1986.

Marshall, Madeleine Forell. 'Teaching the Uncanonized: The Examples of Watts and Rowe'. *Teaching Eighteenth-Century Poetry*. Ed. Christopher Fox. New York: AMS Press, 1990, 1–24.

——. and Janet Todd. *English Congregational Hymns in the Eighteenth Century*. Lexington: University of Kentucky Press, 1982.

May, Steven. 'Tudor Aristocrats and the Mythical "Stigma of Print"'. *Renaissance Papers*, 10 (1980): 11–18.

McDowell, Paula. 'Consuming Women: The Life of the "Literary Lady" as Popular Culture in Eighteenth-Century England'. *Genre* 26 (1993): 219–52.

——. *The Women of Grub Street: Press, Politics, and Gender in the London Literary Marketplace, 1699–1730*. Oxford: Clarendon Press, 1997.

McKitterick, David. *Print, Manuscript and the Search for Order, 1450–1830*. Cambridge: Cambridge University Press, 2003.

Medoff, Jeslyn. 'The Daughters of Behn and the problem of Reputation'. *Women, Writing, History, 1640–1740*. Eds. Isobel Grundy and Susan Wiseman. London: B.T. Batsford Ltd., 1992, 33–54.

Mee, Jon. *Romanticism, Enthusiasm, and Regulation: Poetics and the Policing of Culture in the Romantic Period*. Oxford: Oxford University Press, 2003.

Michael, Ian. *The Teaching of English from the Sixteenth Century to 1870*. Cambridge: Cambridge University Press, 1987.
Miel, Jan. *Pascal and Theology*. Baltimore and London: The Johns Hopkins University Press, 1969.
Mills, Rebecca May. '"Thanks for that Elegant *Defense*": Polemical Prose and Poetry by Women in the Early Eighteenth Century'. DPhil. Diss. University of Oxford, 2000.
Myers, Sylvia Harcstark. *The Bluestocking Circle: Women, Friendship, and the Life of the Mind in Eighteenth-Century England*. Oxford: Clarendon Press, 1990.
Nuovo, Victor. 'Catharine Cockburn's Enlightenment'. Paper presented as part of a panel on 'Women, Metaphysics and Enlightenment', Institute of Philosophy, London, 24 March 2006.
———. 'Cockburn, Catherine (1679?–1749)'. *The Dictionary of Seventeenth-Century British Philosophers*. Ed. Linda Lopez McAlister. Bloomington and Indianapolis: Indiana University Press, 1996, 68–91, rpt. Bristol: Thoemmes Press, 2000.
———. ed. *The Reasonableness of Christianity, as delivered in the scriptures*. By John Locke. Bristol: Thoemmes Press, 1997.
Nussbaum, Felicity. *The Autobiographical Subject: Gender and Ideology in Eighteenth-Century England*. Baltimore: The Johns Hopkins University Press, 1989.
O'Brien, Karen. *Women and Enlightenment in Eighteenth-Century Britain*. Cambridge: Cambridge University Press, 2009.
O'Donnell, Sherry. 'Mr Locke and the Ladies: The Indelible Words on the Tabula Rasa'. *Studies in Eighteenth Century Culture* 8 (1978): 151–64.
O'Neill, Eileen. 'Disappearing Ink: Early Modern Women Philosophers and their Fate in History'. *Philosophy in a Feminist Voice: Critiques and Reconstructions*. Ed. Janet A. Kourany. Princeton: Princeton University Press, 1998, 17–62.
Pebworth, Ted-Larry. 'John Donne, Coterie Poetry, and the Text as Performance'. *Studies in English Literature, 1500–1900* 29 (1989): 61–75.
Perry, Ruth. 'Radical Doubt and the Liberation of Women'. *Eighteenth-Century Studies* 18:4 (Autumn 1985): 472–93.
———. *Women, Letters and the Novel*. New York: AMS Press, 1980.
Peters, Julie Stone, *The Theatre of the Book, 1480–1880: Print, Text, and Performance*. Oxford: Oxford University Press, 2000.
Pettit, Alexander. 'Terrible Texts, "Marginal" Works, and the Mandate of the Moment: The Case of Eliza Haywood'. *Tulsa Studies in Women's Literature* 22:2 (Fall 2003): 293–314.
Prescott, Sarah. 'The Debt to Pleasure: Eliza Haywood's *Love in Excess* and Women's Fiction of the 1720s'. *Women's Writing* 7:3 (2000): 427–45.
———. 'Provincial Networks, Dissenting Connections, and Noble Friends: Elizabeth Singer Rowe and Female Authorship in Early Eighteenth-Century England'. *Eighteenth-Century Life* 25:1 (Winter 2001): 29–42.
———. *Women, Authorship and Literary Culture, 1690–1740*. Basingstoke, Hampshire and New York: Palgrave Macmillan, 2003.
Rabb, Melinda Alliker. 'The Work of Women in the Age of Electronic Reproduction: The Canon, Early Modern Women Writers and the Postmodern Reader'. *A Companion to Early Modern Women's Writing*. Ed. Anita Pacheco. Oxford: Blackwell Publishing, 2002.

Rambuss, Richard. *Closet Devotions*. Durham and London: Duke University Press, 1998.
Ready, Kathryn J. 'Damaris Cudworth Masham, Catharine Trotter Cockburn, and the Feminist Legacy of Locke's Theory of Personal Identity'. *Eighteenth-Century Studies* 35:4 (2002): 563–76.
Reconsidering the Bluestockings. Eds. Nicole Pohl and Betty A. Schellenberg. San Marino: Huntington Library, 2003. (Also published as vol. 65, nos. 1 and 2 of the *Huntington Library Quarterly*.)
Redford, Bruce. *The Converse of the Pen: Acts of Intimacy in the Eighteenth-Century Familiar Letter*. London: University of Chicago Press, 1986.
Reynolds, Myra. *The Learned Lady in England, 1650–1760*. Boston: Houghton Mifflin Company, 1920.
Richetti, John J. 'Mrs. Elizabeth Rowe: The Novel as Polemic'. *PMLA* 82:7 (December 1967): 522–29.
———. *Popular Fiction Before Richardson: Narrative Patterns, 1700–1739*. Oxford: Clarendon Press, 1969, rpt. 1992.
Rivers, Isabel. *The Poetry of Conservatism, 1600–1745: A Study of Poets and Public Affairs from Jonson to Pope*. Cambridge: Rivers Press, 1973.
———. *Reason, Grace, and Sentiment: A Study of the Language of Religion and Ethics in England, 1660–1780. Volume I Whichcote to Wesley*. Cambridge: Cambridge University Press, 1991.
———. *Reason, Grace, and Sentiment: A Study of the Language of Religion and Ethics in England, 1660–1780. Volume II Shaftesbury to Hume*. Cambridge: Cambridge University Press, 2000.
———. 'Shaftesburian Enthusiasm and the Evangelical Revival'. *Revival and Religion Since 1700: Essays for John Walsh*. Eds. Jane Garnett and Colin Matthew. London and Rio Grande: The Hambledon Press, 1993, 21–39.
Ruhe, Edward. 'Birch, Johnson, and Elizabeth Carter: an episode of 1738–39'. *PMLA* 73 (1958): 491–500.
Salzman, Paul. *Reading Early Modern Women's Writing*. Oxford: Oxford University Press, 2006.
Saunders, J.W. 'The Stigma of Print: A Note on the Social Bases of Tudor Poetry'. *Essays in Criticism*, 1 (1951): 139–64.
Schellenberg, Betty A. *The Professionalization of Women Writers in Eighteenth-Century Britain*. Cambridge: Cambridge University Press, 2005.
Sherman, Nancy. *The Fabric of Character: Aristotle's Theory of Virtue*. Oxford: Clarendon Press, 1989.
Showalter, Elaine. *A Literature of their Own: British Women Novelists from Brontë to Lessing*. Princeton: Princeton University Press, 1977.
Siskin, Clifford. *The Work of Writing: Literature and Social Change in Britain, 1700–1830*. London: The Johns Hopkins University Press, 1998.
Small, Helen. 'For the Use of the Ladies: How the First Bluestockings Prized Knowledge and Virtue above Feminism'. *TLS* 6 (April 2001): 3–4.
Smith, Hilda. *Reason's Disciples: Seventeenth-Century English Feminists*. Urbana, Chicago, and London: University of Illinois Press, 1982.
Solomon, Harry M. *The Rise of Robert Dodsley: Creating the New Age of Print*. Carbondale and Edwardsville: Southern Illinois University Press, 1996.
Southam, Brian. '*Mansfield Park* – What did Jane Austen Really Write? The Texts of 1814 and 1816'. *British Women's Writing in the Long Eighteenth Century:*

282 Bibliography

Authorship, Politics and History. Eds. Jennie Batchelor and Cora Kaplan. London: Palgrave Macmillan, 2005, 88–104.

Spencer, Jane. *Aphra Behn's Afterlife*. Oxford: Oxford University Press, 2000.

——. *The Rise of the Woman Novelist: From Aphra Behn to Jane Austen*. Oxford: Basil Blackwell, 1986.

St Clair, William. *The Reading Nation in the Romantic Period*. Cambridge: Cambridge University Press, 2004.

Staves, Susan. *A Literary History of Women's Writing in Britain, 1660–1789*. Cambridge: Cambridge University Press, 2006.

——. 'Church of England Clergy and Women Writers'. *Reconsidering the Bluestockings*. Ed. by Nicole Pohl and Betty A. Schellenberg. San Marino: Huntington Library, 2003, 81–103.

Stecher, Henry F. *Elizabeth Singer Rowe, the Poetess of Frome: A Study in Eighteenth-Century Pietism*. Frankfurt: Peter Lang, 1973.

Stephen, Leslie. *Dictionary of National Biography*. 66 vols. London: Smith, Elder, & Co., 1885–1901.

——. *History of English Thought in the Eighteenth Century*. 2 vols. 3rd edn. London: Smith, Elder, & Co., 1902.

Stevenson, Jane. 'Still Kissing the Rod? Whither Next?'. *Women's Writing*, 14:2 (August 2007): 290–305.

Stewart, Keith. 'Towards Defining an Aesthetic for the Familiar Letter in the Eighteenth Century'. *Prose Studies* 5 (1982): 179–89.

Sutherland, Kathryn. 'Editing for a New Century: Elizabeth Elstob's Anglo-Saxon Manifesto and Aelfric's St. Gregory Homily'. *The Editing of Old English: Papers from the 1990 Manchester Conference*. Eds. D.G. Scragg and Paul E. Szarmach. Cambridge and Rochester, NY: D.S. Brewer/Boydell and Brewer, 1994, 213–37.

——. *Jane Austen's Textual Lives: from Aeschylus to Bollywood*. Oxford: Oxford University Press, 2005.

——. 'Writings on Education and Conduct: Arguments for Female Improvement'. *Women and Literature in Britain, 1700–1800*. Ed. Vivien Jones. Cambridge: Cambridge University Press, 2000.

Sweet, Rosemary. *Antiquaries: The Discovery of the Past in Eighteenth-Century Britain*. London and New York: Hambledon and London, 2004.

Taylor, Barbara. *Mary Wollstonecraft and the Feminist Imagination*. Cambridge: Cambridge University Press, 2003.

Thomas, Claudia. '"Th' Instructive and Moral, and Important Thought": Elizabeth Carter Reads Pope, Johnson, and Epictetus'. *The Age of Johnson* 4 (1991): 137–69.

Turner, Cheryl. *Living by the Pen: Women Writers in the Eighteenth Century*. London: Routledge, 1992.

Waldron, Jeremy. *God, Locke, and Equality: Christian Foundations of John Locke's Political Thought*. Cambridge: Cambridge University Press, 2002.

Wallace, Jennifer. 'Confined and Exposed: Elizabeth Carter's Classical Translations'. *Tulsa Studies in Women's Literature*, 22:2 (Fall 2003): 315–34.

Walmsley, Peter. 'Whigs in Heaven: Elizabeth Rowe's Friendship in Death'. *Eighteenth-Century Studies* 44:3 (2011 Spring): 315–30.

Warner, William. *Licensing Entertainment: The Elevation of Novel Reading in Britain, 1684–1750*. Berkeley, Los Angeles and London: University of California Press, 1998.

Willey, Basil. *The Eighteenth Century Background: Studies on the Idea of Nature in the Thought of the Period*. London: Chatto & Windus, 1950.

Williamson, Marilyn L. *Raising Their Voices: British Women Writers, 1650–1750*. Detroit: Wayne State University Press, 1990.

Wood, Paul B. *The Aberdeen Enlightenment: The Arts Curriculum in the Eighteenth Century*. Aberdeen: Aberdeen University Press, 1993.

Woudhuysen, H.R. *Sir Philip Sidney and the Circulation of Manuscripts, 1558–1640*. Oxford: Clarendon Press,1996.

Wright, H. Bunker. 'Matthew Prior and Elizabeth Singer'. *Philological Quarterly* 24:4 (October 1945): 71–82.

Yolton, John. *John Locke and the Way of Ideas*. Oxford: Oxford University Press, 1956.

Young, B.W. *Religion and Enlightenment in Eighteenth-Century England: Theological Debate from Locke to Burke*. Oxford: Clarendon Press, 1998.

———. 'Theological Books from *The Naked Gospel* to *Nemesis of Faith*'. *Books and Their Readers in Eighteenth-Century England: New Essays*. Ed. Isabel Rivers. Leicester: Leicester University Press, 2001 (rpt. London: Continuum, 2003), 79–104.

Index

Note: 'n' after a page reference denotes a note number on that page.

Achinstein, Sharon, 18
aesthetics, 3, 35–6; changing values, 3, 5, 12
affection, 12–13, 56, 70–3, 84, 95, 106, 112–30, 133–4 138, 213, 215–17, 228–30, 235–6; *see also* Smith, Adam
afterlife, definition, 143; heaven, 49–50, 54–5, 57–8, 105; literary afterlife, 14–15: Carter, 170–1, 193, 202–12, 214; Cockburn, 94, 142–68; Rowe, 62–91, 251n191
agency, 5, 14, 170, 191, 193–4, 214, 216, 226, 236; moral: Carter,193, 213, 216, 232, 236; Cockburn, 106–7; over authorial image: Rowe, 19, 66; Cockburn, 135; Carter, 211, 213
Algarotti, Francesco, 169, 177, 185, 261n396, 263n439
Anne (queen of England), 10, 31, 35, 101
anthologies, miscellanies, collections, 4, 8, 19, 26, 34, 63–6, 69, 71, 75, 90, 97, 174–5, 183, 195, 201–2, 204, 207–8, 225, 241n27, 251n191, 261n407
apocrypha, 130–5, 143, 166–7
Arbuthnot, Anne, 103, 112, 130, 135–9
Aristotle, 48, 132, 151
Astell, Mary, 2, 5, 35, 101, 106, 136, 149, 161, 183, 216
Athanasian Creed, 190, 229–34, 236, 262n428
Athenian Mercury, 11, 18–19, 28, 76, 245n74; *see also* Dunton, John
Austen, Jane, 82, 212, 241n25

Backscheider, Paula, 101, 107
Balguy, John, 141

Balguy, Thomas, 156
Ballard, George, 2, 69, 212
Ballaster, Ros, 49
Bannet, Eve Tavor, 11, 243n50, 250n178
Barash, Carol, 9
Barbauld, Anna Laetitia, 64, 68, 89, 163, 203, 250n166
Barker, John, 40–5
Baratier, John Phillip, 188–9
Behn, Aphra, 5, 8, 49, 79, 92, 106–7, 195, 241n25
Birch, Thomas, 15–17, 34, 93–9, 101, 104, 113, 115–16, 123, 132, 135–9, 142, 144–54, 156, 173, 177–8, 184–5, 202, 208–9, 211, 252n219, 252n221, 253n228, 253n232, 253n237, 254n247, 254n254, 256n291, 259n342, 259n347, 259n363, 263n439
Bluestocking Circle, 1, 7, 106, 133, 166, 172–3, 191, 194, 202–3, 210, 215–17, 226, 237
Bolton, Martha Brandt, 110–11, 164–6, 261n389
Bowerbank, Sylvia, 216, 221, 267n551
Brant, Clare, 11–12, 75, 243n48
Browne, Isaac Hawkins, 179–80, 189–90, 262n430
Bunker Wright, H., 20, 251n182
Burnet, Elizabeth, 100, 104, 116, 123, 144, 161, 253n244
Burnet, Gilbert (Bishop of Salisbury), 34, 96–7, 104, 123, 253n244
Burnet, Thomas (controversialist), 108–9
Burnet, Thomas (of Kemnay), 100, 104, 106, 108, 115–25, 131, 138, 140, 145, 159, 232, 256n291
Burney, Frances, 63–4, 78, 82–8, 241n25, 251n200

284

Byatt, A.S., *Possession*, 1

Caroline (queen of England), 98, 157–60, 164, 176
CARTER, ELIZABETH, 1, 5–7, 10–16, 61, 64, 66–8, 77–82, 89, 98, 104, 106, 113, 130, 142–3, 148, 153, 156, 163, 169–238, 241n25, 261n403
 affection, 213, 215–17, 228–30, 235–6 (*see also* Smith, Adam); afterlife, 170–1, 193, 202–12, 214; appearance in anthologies, 174–5, 201–2, 259n357, 261n407, 261n410; appearance in Fordyce's *Sermons for Young Women*, 198–9; Athanasian Creed, 190, 229–34, 236, 262n428; authorial identity, 169–70, 173–6, 191–5, 217–9; biography, 172–3; and Birch, 16–17, 156, 173, 177–8, 184–5, 261n396, 263n439; Bluestockings, 7, 106, 172–3, 191, 194, 202–3, 210, 215–7, 226, 237; and Browne, Isaac Hawkins, 179–80, 189–90, 262n430; classical scholarship, 169, 179–80, 185–7, 190, 192, 194–5, 200, 205; conservatism, 170, 174, 202, 206, 211, 214–16, 223, 230, 238; coterie culture, 177–84, 188, 190, 193, 195, 202, 226, 237; domesticity, 170, 183–5, 196–201, 204–6, 214, 218, 224; education, 163, 169, 172, 187, 190, 197, 201, 210; enlightenment, 204, 230, 237; exemplary image, 171, 175, 183–4, 197–9, 201, 204–6, 211–12, 224, 235–8; friendship, 172, 175, 179, 183–5, 189–91, 215–24; happiness, 171, 193, 214–15, 221–3, 227, 229, 235; humanism, 171, 185–6, 189; and Johnson, Samuel, 169, 172–3, 181, 185–92, 203–4, 225–6, 229, 263n439; learned woman, 170, 180, 184, 191, 193, 198–9, 201, 205–6, 211, 214, 231, 237; letters, 190, 202–12: (as biography), 202–12; (as formative writing), 190, 216, 237; (Pennington's editions), 203–12; (performative nature), 206, 216; literary style and themes, 200–1, 211, 220–1, 226–8; manuscripts/manuscript culture, 170–2, 175–88, 192–3, 202, 207–12, 214–15, 217–19, 226, 234, 237–8, 264n466; patronage, 170, 176–9, 184, 237; Pennington as editor, *see* Pennington, Montagu; poetry, 169, 171, 173–8, 180–1, 188, 190, 195; portrait, 195, 199; print culture/publication, 170–7, 181, 184, 186–8, 191–3, 199–202, 219, 225, 237–8, 264n466; professionalism, 170, 173, 175–7, 179–81, 184–5, 187, 191–3, 202, 212, 214, 217–18, 237; religion, 171, 175, 177, 186–7, 190, 197, 211, 214–16, 223–4, 226–37; republic of letters, 169, 172, 185, 187, 191–2, 202, 237; and Richardson, Samuel, 169, 172, 181–4, 188, 204–5, 226; 262n432, 263n437; on Rowe, 78–82, 173, 250n170; translations, 169, 172–3, 177, 179, 184–5, 187, 190, 193–5, 224, 263n439; and Wright, Thomas, 177–9, 189
 Selected works: *Epictetus*, 1, 81, 142, 169, 173, 180, 184–5, 190–1, 193–5, 202–3, 224, 264n465; *Letters* (1809), 203, 205, 207–8, 220–9; *Letters* (1817), 81, 203, 208–9; 'Ode to Wisdom', 169, 181–2, 188, 195, 202, 204, 261n407; *Poems on Several Occasions*, 78, 80, 169, 184, 184, 190–1, 193, 202; *Rambler, No.44* and *100*, 81, 181, 190, 201, 224–6, 263n462
Carter, Nicholas, 172, 176, 188–9, 208, 221, 224, 229, 261n403, 262n428
Cave, Edward, 66, 98–9, 104–5, 156, 172–4, 177, 184, 186–9; *see also Gentleman's Magazine*

Cavendish, Margaret, Duchess of
  Newcastle, 5, 8, 241n25
Chapone, Hester Mulso, 81, 172,
  174–5, 181, 183–4, 190, 196, 204,
  226
Church of England, 2, 41, 63, 100,
  102, 106, 115, 123, 126, 171,
  229–36
Clarke, Norma, 250n169
Clarke, Samuel, 92, 110–12, 123, 138,
  140–1, 143, 158, 160–1, 164–5,
  256n282, 258n330
class, 10, 25, 41, 56, 90, 198, 237–8
clergy, 2, 63, 115, 123, 156, 160, 164,
  230, 232, 252n218
Clery, Emma, 184
COCKBURN, CATHARINE
  TROTTER, 1, 5–7, 10–15, 67,
  92–168
  affection, 95,106, 113–34, 138;
  afterlife (hereafter), 105, (literary),
  94, 142–68; apocrypha, 130–5,
  143, 166–7; biography, 93, 150;
  Birch as editor of, 93–9, 101,
  115–6, 123, 135–9, 142, 144–54,
  202, 208–9, 211, 252n221,
  253n228, 253n232, 254n247,
  254n254, 256n291, 259n342,
  259n347; and Clarke, 110–12,
  123, 138, 140–1, 143, 158, 160–1,
  164–5; coterie culture, 92, 98–9,
  103, 144; critical reception, 92–3,
  97, 102–3, 110, 113–14, 142–68;
  drama, 92, 101–2, 106–8, 148–9;
  education, 93, 106, 117, 139, 144,
  160, 162–3, 169; enlightenment,
  92–3, 114, 118, 138, 145, 156–66,
  230, 260n368; exemplary image,
  92–4, 116, 127–9, 143, 146–8,
  150–3, 166, 168; friendship, 93,
  104–6, 115–16, 119–27, 129,
  134, 138, 142–4; happiness, 105,
  107, 112, 114, 118, 120–1, 125,
  128, 130, 134; letters, 92–106,
  114–30: (as formative writing),
  106, 110–11, 114–15, 148, 163,
  (compositional genetics), 119,
  135–6, (performative nature),
  109, 111, 114, 124–7, (to Anne
  Arbuthnot), 112, 135–9, 160,
  163, (to Burnet of Kemnay), 100,
  115–23, (to Edmund Law), 103,
  139–41, (to Patrick Cockburn),
  100, 115, 123–8, (to Thomas
  Sharp), 139–41, 144–5, 165–6;
  literary style, themes, 97, 106,
  114–15, 119, 121; and Locke,
  108–118, 138, 143, 148, 157–8,
  160–2, 164–6, 183; and Manley,
  100, 144–7, 150–1; manuscripts/
  manuscript culture, 94–106,
  115, 121, 123–4, 135–6, 138–41,
  147, 150, 152, 154, 160, 166–7;
  252n225; miscellaneous genres,
  99, 105, 162–3; patronage, 92–3,
  96–9, 100–4, 142–3, 146–7,
  152–3, 158–9, 164, 167; poetry
  92, 95, 98–9, 148, 157–9; print
  culture/publication, 93–106,
  135–6, 141, 143, 147–8,
  166–8; on reason and rational
  knowledge, 93–4, 106–7,112–3,
  118, 126–9, 137–8, 162–5;
  religion, 93–4, 97, 108–22, 163,
  165; republic of letters, 96,
  109, 117, 141, 142, 157; and
  Shaftesbury, 112, 126, 137–8,
  159–60, 162; subscription for
  the *Works*, 142–3, 148, 153–6,
  161
  Selected works: *Agnes de Castro*,
  101, 106–7; *Defence of the Essay
  of Human Understanding*, 99,
  106, 108–11, 113–18, 120, 165;
  Fatal Friendship, 101, 106; *Guide
  in Controversies*, 96, 100, 102,
  106, 111, 115, 123; *Letter to Dr
  Holdsworth*, 102, 104; 'Letters of
  Aspasia', 98, 102, 132–4, 147,
  166; *Love at a Loss*, 101, 107, 125;
  Remarks upon some Writers (1743),
  102, 110, 137, 140, 165; *Remarks
  upon the Principles* (1747), 96, 103;
  Revolution of Sweden, 101, 107,
  124; *Unhappy Penitent*, 101, 107;
  Works, 94–103, 142–4, 147–9,
  153–6, 161–2, 166
Cockburn, John, 97, 150, 257n322

Cockburn, Patrick, 93, 100, 102, 104, 106, 115, 123–8, 131–2, 147, 252n227, 256n308, 257n308, 259n347
collections *see* anthologies
Colman, Benjamin, 75, 89
Colman, George and Bonnell Thornton, 195–6; *see also Poems by Eminent Ladies*
Congreve, William, 99, 103, 105, 144, 171
Conley, John, J., 131
conservatism, 5, 9, 11, 82; *see also* Carter: conservatism
coterie culture, 9, 13, 199; *see also* entries in Carter, Cockburn, and Rowe
Curll, Edmund, 65, 67
Curran, Stuart, 89

Dacier, Anne, 16, 138, 153, 159, 169
Defoe, Daniel, 2
DeMaria Jr., Robert, 186–9, 192
dissent *see* nonconformity
Dodsley, James, 132
Dodsley, Robert, 173–5, 195, 201–2, 247n104, 261n401
domesticity, 85, 134–5, 137, 170, 183–5, 196–201, 204–6, 214, 218, 224, 246n100
Doody, Margaret Anne, 82
Douglas-Fairhurst, Robert, 143, 149
Duck, Stephen, 98, 104, 158
Duncombe, John, 89, 180; *The Feminiad*, 89, 152
Duncombe, William, 156, 175, 179–80, 195
Dunton, John, 18–19, 22–3, 76

editing, 3, 9, 12, 14–15; *see also* Birch, Etough, Pennington, Rowe: compositional genetics, Warburton
education, female, 2, 41, 82, 91, 93, 106, 117, 139, 144, 160, 163, 169, 172, 190, 210, 239; male, 75, 84, 160, 162–3
Eger, Elizabeth, 172

enlightenment, 13, 15–16, 92–3, 114, 118, 138, 145, 156–66, 204, 230, 237, 260n368
enthusiasm, 20–1, 25, 29, 35, 39–40, 50, 52, 54–5, 59, 61, 63–4, 68, 71–3, 76–8, 80–1, 113, 125, 204, 221; definitions, 21, 54
Epictetus, 1, 81, 142, 169, 173, 180, 184–5, 190–1, 193–5, 202–3, 224, 264n465
Etough, Henry, 95, 97, 145, 147–8, 150, 152–5, 166–7, 177, 211, 252n219, 252n227
Ewert, Leonore Helen, 209–10
exemplarity, 2, 5, 14, 17; *see also* entries in Carter, Cockburn, and Rowe
Ezell, Margaret, 2–11, 18, 67–8, 74; *Patriarch's Wife, The*, 3–4, 7, 10; *Social Authorship and the Advent of Print*, 7, 10, 254n256; *Writing Women's Literary History*, 2–4

Fairchild, H.N., 22
Farquhar, George, 103
Feminiad, The see Duncombe
Fielding, Henry, 34, 156, 181
Fielding, Sarah, 2, 155, 259n362
Finch, Anne, (Countess of Winchelsea), 24, 98, 241n25
Finch, Lady Isabella, 154, 155, 259n359
friendship, 7, 9, 11, 78, 83–7, 250n175; *see also* entries in Carter, Cockburn, and Rowe

Gallagher, Catherine, 167
Gascoigne, John, 160–2
gender, 3, 16, 39, 109, 131, 137, 174–5, 183, 186–7, 192, 216, 231, 237–8
genre, 3, 12, 15, 23, 33, 49, 54, 63, 79, 90, 132, 238; *see also* letters
Gentleman's Magazine, 11, 65–6, 78, 99, 104, 169, 172–4, 176–7, 184, 186, 188, 191, 195
ghosts, 14, 28, 48, 84, 149–50, 206, 220–1
Gilbert, Sandra and Susan Gubar, 4

Index

Gordon, Betty, lady, 104, 254n258
Gosse, Edmund, 149, 206, 237
Grove, Henry, 20, 22, 34, 61, 63, 66, 71, 74–7, 82, 90, 211
Grundy, Isobel, 12
Guest, Harriet, 172, 175, 197, 199, 201, 214, 217, 230, 237

Habermas, Jürgen, 237
Hampshire, Gwen, 178, 207–9
happiness, 13–14; see also entries in Carter, Cockburn, and Rowe
Hawley, Judith, 172, 177, 189–91, 212
Haywood, Eliza, 12, 18, 49, 58, 133
Hertford, Frances Thynne Seymour, Countess of (Duchess of Somerset), 1, 20–5, 28–33, 37, 51–3, 59–60, 65–6, 69–72, 74–5, 77–8, 85, 89, 98, 133, 155–56, 177, 184, 204, 245n79, 247n109
Hughes, Helen Sard, 24
humanism, 11, 13, 171, 185–6, 189

Jackson, John, 141
Jay, Emma, 157
Johnson, Samuel, 12, 48, 54–5, 81, 89, 90, 104–5, 169, 172–3, 181, 185–92, 203–4, 219, 225–26, 229, 263n439, 265n490
Jones, Mary, 2

Keene, Edmund, 95, 156, 253n227
Kelley, Anne, 93–4, 100–1, 123, 135, 144, 147–9
Ken, Thomas (Bishop of Bath and Wells), 22, 33, 41
Kennet, Basil, 41–2
King, Heather, 106
King, Kathryn, 6, 11
Knott, Sarah, 15, 160

La Vallière, Louise-Françoise de la Baume Le Blanc, Mlle de, 102, 130–3, 161, 166
Lavoie, Chantal, 75
Law, Edmund, 103, 114, 139–41
Law, William, 21, 34, 44–5, 52
Leapor, Mary, 2, 180

learned woman, 2, 5, 7, 14, 91, 93, 95, 110, 116, 135, 142, 147, 149–53, 159, 164, 166, 170, 180, 184, 191, 193, 198–9, 201, 205–6, 211, 214, 231, 237, 254n258
Lennox, Charlotte, 102, 132, 259n359
letters, 11–15; see also republic of letters and entries in Carter, Cockburn, and Rowe
Locke, John, 43, 92, 98, 100, 102, 104, 106, 108–18, 138, 140, 143, 148, 157–8, 160–2, 164–6, 183, 229–30
Lonsdale, Roger, 185

Manley, Delarivier, 5, 49, 98, 100–1, 103–4, 107, 133, 144–7, 150–1, 253n238
manuscripts/manuscript culture, 1–13, 16, 150, 201, 240n8, 247n103, 254n256; see also letters and entries in Carter, Cockburn, and Rowe
Marshall, David, 14, 38
Masham, Damaris, 104, 116–18, 161
Mee, Jon, 72
Methodism, 63–4
Michael, Ian, 201
miscellanies see anthologies
Mitford, John, 201
Montagu, Elizabeth, 81, 133, 166, 171–3, 175, 179–80, 190–1, 193, 197–200, 203–4, 208–10, 224–6
Montagu, Lady Mary Wortley, 2, 12, 153
Moore, Edward, 196
More, Hannah, 163, 172, 175
Mulso, Hester see Chapone

Newton, Isaac, 44–5, 141, 157–8, 161–2, 164, 169, 177, 185
Nidditch, Peter, 108
nonconformity, 19–22, 89, 118, 125–6, 160–1, 166
Norris, John, 34, 119, 136, 161, 164, 166, 182–3
novel, rise of, 10, 23, 63, 204
Nuovo, Victor, 109

O'Brien, Karen, 17, 118, 160, 172, 260n368

Pascal, Blaise, 34, 40–7, 56, 170, 235
patronage, 6, 9, 11, 13, 173; *see also* entries in Carter, Cockburn, and Rowe
Pearson, Jacqueline, 101, 107
Pennington, Montagu, 15, 80, 175, 212, 238
Perdita, 12
performance acts *see* letters
periodicals, 11–12, 18, 104–5, 135, 171, 174, 176–7, 184, 186–7, 191–2, 196, 201, 225–6, 262; *see also Athenian Mercury, Gentleman's Magazine, The Rambler*
Philips, Katherine, 2, 5, 8–10, 28, 106, 188, 195, 216
Piers, Lady Sarah, 93, 100–1, 103, 116, 132, 144, 163
piety, 5, 13, 18, 26, 34, 40, 63, 71–2, 78, 82, 87, 204, 214, 221, 235–6
platonic love, 9, 27, 133; poems about, 28, 99
Poems by Eminent Ladies, 152, 195, 201, 264n479; *see also* Colman and Thornton
Pope, Alexander, 12, 19, 26, 34–5, 43, 65, 70, 80, 89, 95, 105, 137–8, 144, 147, 150, 152, 169, 171, 177, 185–6, 195, 201
Prescott, Sarah, 18, 65
Price, Richard, 139, 145, 165–6
print culture/publication, 1–17; *see also* entries in Carter, Cockburn, and Rowe
Prior, Matthew, 19–22, 26, 34, 41, 89
professionalisation, 6, 21, 32, 77, 82, 147, 153, 170, 173, 175–7, 180–1, 184–5, 187, 191–3, 202, 212, 214, 217–8, 237

Rambler, The, 81, 105, 181, 183, 189–90, 209, 219, 224–7, 229, 263n462, 267n556
Read, Katharine, 195, 199, 264n478
Redford, Bruce, 12, 14

religion, 5, 13–14; *see also* entries in Carter and Cockburn
religious language, reinvigoration of, 5, 13–14; *see also* Rowe
republic of letters, 7, 11, 15–17, 23–4, 32, 63, 90, 92, 96, 109, 117, 141–2, 152, 169, 172, 185, 187, 191, 202, 237
Reynolds, Myra, 149
Richardson, Samuel, 12, 26, 70, 169, 172, 181–4, 188, 203–5, 226, 243n582, 262n432, 264n465
Rivers, Isabel, 35–6, 125
ROWE, ELIZABETH SINGER, 1–2, 5–7, 10–15, 18–91
afterlife (hereafter), 26, 32, 44, 47–52, 54–60, (literary), 62–91, 251n191; Alnwick MS, 20, 23–30, 33, 44, 52–3; amatory style, 18, 49, 54–9, 81; biography, 19–20, 63–4, 68, 75, 81; Burney on Rowe, 63, 82–8; Carter on Rowe, 77–82; coterie culture, 20–6, 32, 47, 50, 53, 60, 65, 67–8, 74–5; critical reception/legacy, 18, 62–91; education, 41, 64, 91; enthusiasm, 20–1, 26, 28–30, 36, 39–40, 52, 54–6, 59, 61, 63–5, 68, 71–83; exemplary image, 18–19, 22–5, 47–8, 62–91 *passim*; friendship, 21, 24, 26–8, 33, 35, 60, 66, 70; happiness, 37, 42, 44–7, 55, 60, 70; Johnson on Rowe, 54–5, 90; letters, 22–33, 90: (as biography), 20–4, (as formative writing), 19, 22–6, 30, 48, 60, 63, (compositional genetics), 23–32, 48, 50, 53, (performative nature of), 23–4, 26, 28, 38, 47–50, 53–4, 60, (republic of letters), 24, 33, 63, 90; literary style, themes, 26–30, 32–3, 35, 46–50; manuscripts/manuscript culture, 19–32, 44, 49, 60–1, 67–8, 72, 74–6, 78, 89; moral philosophy, 33, 35–6, 55–7; nonconformity, 20–1, 63–4, 89; patronage, 33, 89; poetry, 23, 28, 35 (political), 18, 35–6;

ROWE, ELIZABETH
SINGER – *continued*
print culture/publication, 19–20, 22, 25, 30–2, 49, 60, 62–4, 67–8, 72, 74, 88; reading, 33–5, (of Pascal), 40–7, (of Shaftesbury), 34–40; reinvigoration of religious language, 19–22, 26, 28, 30, 32–3, 40–57, 59–61, 63, 69, 72–3, 77, 84, 88, 90; retirement, 25, 30–3, 37, 45–6, 52, 57, 59; rise of novel, 23, 63; Watts on Rowe, 71–4
Selected works: 19, 'Upon the Death of Thomas Rowe', 26; *Friendship in Death*, 30, 47–60, 66, 69, 75, 88–90; *Letters* (1729), 30, 37–40, 43–4, 52, 62, 88; *LME*, 30, 48, 62, 66, 69, 76, 88; *Devout Exercises*, 62, 64, 66–9, 71–4, 77, 88; *History of Joseph*, 64, 67, 88; *MW*, 33, 42–3, 66, 68–71, 74–6, 88–9
Rowe, Theophilus, 15, 20, 28, 34, 61, 63, 67, 69, 71, 74–8, 82, 156, 211
Rowe, Thomas, 19, 26, 33, 75

Saunders, J.W., 9–10
Savage, Richard, 173, 186, 188
Schellenberg, Betty, 172
scholarship (latin, classical), 179, 189, 194
scribal culture *see* manuscripts/manuscript culture
Secker, Thomas (Bishop of Oxford; Archbishop of Canterbury), 97, 148, 156, 195
Seymour, Frances *see* Hertford
Sévigné, Marie de Rabutin-Chantal, marquise de, 2, 26, 114, 130, 247n103
Shaftesbury, Anthony Ashley Cooper, third earl of, 21, 34–40, 46–7, 55–6, 112–13, 126, 135, 137–8, 159–60, 162, 170, 230
Sharp, Thomas, 95, 103, 114, 139, 141, 144–5, 147–8, 154, 156, 165–6
Sherman, Nancy, 48
Showalter, Elaine, 4

Singer, Elizabeth *see* Rowe
Siskin, Clifford, 16
Smith, Adam, 216–17, 228–9
social networks *see* coterie culture
Somerset, Duchess of *see* Hertford
Staves, Susan, 2–3, 5, 12, 21, 106, 137
Stecher, Henry F., 20, 22
Stephen, Leslie, 110, 149, 216
Stevenson, Jane, 15, 17, 131
subscription, 95, 102, 131, 143, 148, 154–5, 161, 173, 180, 251, 259
sympathy, 55, 216–17, 228; *see also* Smith, Adam

Talbot, Catherine, 1–2, 25, 64, 77–8, 98, 113, 142, 153–4, 156, 170, 172–5, 178–9, 183–4, 188–91, 194–6, 198, 203–4, 207, 209, 219–22, 224–30
Taylor, Barbara, 15, 160, 214, 236–7
theology, 15, 22, 31, 33, 87, 118, 141, 147, 160, 164, 209, 232
Thomas, Claudia, 80
Thomson, James, 21, 34–5, 84, 201
Thynne, Frances *see* Hertford
Thynne, Grace, 22, 24–6, 28, 48, 50, 89
Tickell, Thomas, 31, 34
Toland, John, 136, 255n275
tradition, 1–6
translation, 4, 31, 34, 41–2, 75, 89, 102, 132, 138, 140, 142, 151, 166, 169–70, 172–3, 177, 179, 184–5, 187, 190, 193–5, 202, 224
Trotter, Catharine *see* Cockburn
Turrell, Jane, 89

Underdown, Mrs, 156, 218, 266n540
universities: Carter's association with, 169–70, 195, 199; education, 84, 163, 169; enlightenment controversy within, 155, 161–2, 230; support for Cockburn, 156, 162, 176

Vallière, Louise-Françoise de la Baume Le Blanche, Mlle de la, 102, 130–3, 161, 166
Vesey, Elizabeth, 203–4, 207, 222

Warburton, William, 95–7, 103, 105, 114, 147–8, 150, 154, 156, 179
Waterland, Daniel, 141
Watts, Isaac, 13, 21–2, 26, 34, 69, 102, 201; as editor of *Devout Exercises*, 66, 69, 71–7; on Rowe's enthusiasm, 21, 61, 63, 82, 83
Wesley, John, 63, 250n163

Wilford, John, 63
Woolf, Virgina, 6, 167, 236, 240n25
Woudhuysen, H.R., 9–10
Wright, Thomas, 177–9, 189, 220

Young, B.W., 118, 156–7, 160–1, 164–5
Young, Edward, 34, 48–52, 201

The manufacturer's authorised representative in the EU is Springer Nature Customer Service Centre GmbH, Europaplatz 3, 69115 Heidelberg, Germany. If you have any concerns regarding our products, please contact ProductSafety@springernature.com

Printed and bound by CPI Group (UK) Ltd, Croydon, CR0 4YY
23/03/2026
02076662-0016